ADVANCED READERS

We prayerfully selected a diverse cross-sect
review our book—across age, gender, culture,

CW01500022

"In the complicated and deeply private adventure of marriage, couples regularly locate themselves at crossroads, confronted with choices that may both refine and fortify their bond or cause irreparable damage. This book—*Trilogy Refining Decisions*—a miraculous love story of renewal, reconciliation, and restoration—serves as a guiding framework for navigating the demanding situations of a damaged and subsequently reunited marriage and shows that God indeed can make good of every situation in life.

I would like to sincerely congratulate Olufunké and Olúségun Adeniji for the time, effort, and vulnerability it took to document the events that unfolded in their marriage, and the sincere life lessons that everyone can benefit from. Realistic, well researched, and well written, it is a difficult-to-put-down book."

—**Pastor Ituah Ighodalo**, *Senior Pastor of the Trinity House Church, Lagos, Nigeria*

"*Trilogy Refining Decisions* is a powerful testament to the resilience of love and the redeeming power of faith. Funké and Ségun Adeniji have written with raw honesty and grace, taking the reader through the valleys of separation, the wrestle of identity, and the hope of reconciliation. As a Relationship and Divorce Coach, I know how rare it is for couples to speak so vulnerably about the messiness of marriage and the miraculous possibility of restoration. This book doesn't offer easy platitudes; it offers truth, lived experience, and a faith-centered roadmap that will resonate with anyone navigating the complexities of love, family, and spiritual growth. It is more than a story; it is a beacon of hope for those who may believe all is lost."

—**Natasha Mahtani**, *Relationship & Divorce Coach*

"*Trilogy Refining Decisions* shimmers like rain-washed dusk, where love fractures into shards, only to gather itself in radiant return. Chapter Ten stands as a haunted mirror, reflecting Nigerian women's lives: prejudice etched into culture; silent, yet muffling the law's voice. Yet Scripture flickers like fireflies in the dark, urging confrontation with cultural "giants" and reclaiming divine identity. 'Ignorance—whether of our spiritual authority or of God's willingness to act' constructs invisible chains, but faith-filled prayer sparks breakthrough. Pain, courage, and revelation entwine in a narrative that resonates long after the last page. A must-read."

—**Prof. Konyin Ajayi** *SAN (Senior Advocate of Nigeria)*

"*Trilogy Refining Decisions* is a powerful testimony of God's redemptive grace. It shows how He can heal hurts, restore families, and bring new life to unions. This book is so open and honest about love, mistakes, and the hard parts of starting over. Nothing felt sugar-coated, which made the story even more powerful. What stayed with me the most was the hope running through it—the sense that even after deep hurt, things can be rebuilt. I finished feeling inspired and reminded that restoration is possible and that nothing is too broken for God to restore."

—**Dr. Blossom Maduafokwa**

A Love Story Like No Other—Bold, Honest, and Divinely Guided

"When Ségun first shared the story of his six-and-a-half-year separation from Funké and the astonishing redemption that followed, I was moved. But *Trilogy Refining Decisions* goes far beyond a single testimony. It is a masterfully crafted account of love lost, faith found, and hearts reforged in the furnace of time, distance, and divine grace.

This is not your typical "boy meets girl, boy marries girl, boy deserts girl" tale. Nor is it merely about reconciliation. *Trilogy Refining Decisions* is a spiritual reckoning—a tender yet unflinching look at the real cost and miraculous reward of choosing and trusting love again.

At its core, the book offers a profound revelation: It takes three to build and sustain a marriage—he, she, and that noiseless, all-knowing, ever-present Third Voice. God is not just a figure in the margins here; He is central—guiding, correcting, healing, and ultimately restoring.

With *Trilogy Refining Decisions*, Funké and Ségun Adeniji give us more than their story. They offer a manual. A mirror. A searchlight. A roadmap to the deep wells of patience, sacrifice, forgiveness, and the kind of enduring love that today's world often discards. Their honesty is bracing. Their vulnerability, disarming. Their storytelling, utterly compelling.

I had the rare privilege of reviewing early drafts of this remarkable book. Yet nothing prepared me for the power of its final form—the pace, the depth, the divine choreography. *Trilogy Refining Decisions* will enthrall you with its big steps, wild turns, quiet moments, and the real, raw humanity of two people who dare to let love lead.

If you've ever loved, lost, or longed to begin again, this book is for you. Read it. Reflect on it. Share it.

And let it remind you: Love doesn't just return. It is reborn."

—**Remi Okunlola**, *Lagos, Nigeria*

"Redemption will always be an all-time favorite of mine, so imagine having to write a snippet on this compelling evolution (interpersonal, emotional, spiritual, and financial) between Funké and Ségun. 'Numerous books and opinions exist on topics such as faith, forgiveness, prayer, and others. I'm simply adding my voice—not as an authority but as a fellow traveler, someone who has wrestled with doubt, waited in silence, and learned to rely on God's Word amid real-life trials.' The efficacy of God's Word is beyond palpable, and the originality of their experiences and the "Rear-view Mirror Lesson" positions make flipping these pages easy. I could not wait to see what was next, and I highly recommend this read to anyone on this journey of life—a beautiful story of strength, cooperation, and absolute dependency on God."

—**Adenike Oyetunde-Lawal**, *Lawyer, Author, and Disability/Inclusion Advocate*

"I love the fact that this is an authentic and hope-filled book, and the authors have been able to strike a balance between vulnerability, testimony, and encouragement for others.

I have been strengthened through their raw honesty about pain, separation, and near-divorce. This, for me, is a very relatable book that highlights courage. I also love the fact that they don't just dwell on their pain and rough years, but they consistently point toward healing, reconciliation, and God's grace.

Both of them acknowledge that marriage struggles are never one-sided. This transparency is really highly commendable. The highlighting of God's role, His faithfulness, and His intervention is priceless. The book speaks directly to couples at different stages of marriage, and this widens the book's relevance."

—**Ayodeji Megbope**, *Founder, No Left Overs Nigeria Limited*

"*Trilogy Refining Decisions—A Miraculous Love Story of Renewal, Reconciliation, and Restoration*" is not just a story about marriage; it is a testimony of surrender, restoration, and God's transforming love. As I read, I was moved by the raw honesty and vulnerability that stirred deep emotions within me. Funké and Ségun resist the temptation to present themselves as perfect; instead, they invite us to see what God can do with two imperfect people fully yielded to Him. This book points beyond itself to Christ, the ultimate restorer, and will leave every reader both challenged and inspired."

—**Kaltume Mshelia**

"This book takes you on a journey. A deep and honest reflective account of what happens when love in marriage goes south, the pain of loss, and the possibility of restoration.

It touches on salient issues in marriage and relationships, starting with the importance of getting the foundation of courtship right, as well as navigating external relationships and influences. Very importantly, it details the significant role that God and personal faith play in the restoration of self and identity, recovering from a broken marriage, and sustaining a lasting and fulfilling union. The Adenijis' story is a powerful one of love, faith, and hope."

—**Ayo Mairo-Ese**, *Broadcast Journalist*

Foreword by **DR. CHRIS E. STOUT**

A MIRACULOUS LOVE STORY OF RENEWAL,
RECONCILIATION, AND RESTORATION

Trilogy
Refining
Decisions

ERNESTINA OLUFUNKE ADENIJI
and VICTOR OLUSEGUN ADENIJI

Cover design by Jennifer Federico Stimson

Cover image by Kristina Houser Wikle | visualmusestudio.com

Photo from Lasting Love event courtesy of Funmi Adeyi, founder of Lasting-Love International

Interior design/formatting by KUHN Design Group | kuhndesigngroup.com

Edited by Lezli Urlacher

Website: tryhardglobal.com
Email: admin@tryhardglobal.com

Look, Mom, we made it! God did it!

I dedicate this book to my beloved mother—my first teacher, fiercest defender, and most loyal friend. Your unwavering faith and quiet strength were my light in the darkest season of my life. You stood firm beside me through every storm, showing me what true love is—and how to live it out with grace, wisdom, and courage, even in battle. Thank you, Mom, for every prayer, sacrifice, and sleepless night that helped shape the woman I've become. Your legacy of faith and resilience continues to guide me every day. You were right, Mom—God can be trusted. He heard your prayers, and your dreams for me have come true.

"Great faith is a product of great fights.
Great testimonies are the outcome of great tests.
Great triumphs can only come out of great trials."

SMITH WIGGLESWORTH

Contents

PART 3: THE RELIABLE ROADMAP

Foreword

Life is an intricate mosaic of experiences, challenges, and triumphs, and this book masterfully captures the essence of navigating through it all. With profound insights, remarkable transparency, and honesty, Olufunké and Oluségun's book, *Trilogy Refining Decisions: A Miraculous Love Story of Renewal, Reconciliation, and Restoration*, becomes not just a guide but a trusted tome of practical wisdom on the journey of self-discovery, personal growth, and love. Their ability to weave together their experiences with biblical grounding and heartfelt storytelling makes this work a compelling read for anyone seeking to transform, augment, or enhance their loving relationships. A must-read for those dedicated to understanding the deeper aspects of human existence and striving for transcendence.

Dr. Chris E. Stout
Licensed Clinical Psychologist
Founding Director, The Center for Global Initiatives

Introduction

The year 2024 marked three significant milestones for us—our 50th and 60th birthdays, along with our 26th wedding anniversary. During that season of thanksgiving and deep reflection, we began to notice a recurring pattern of "threes" woven into our journey. We called it our "trilogy." Traditionally, a trilogy is seen as a series of three related works that form a unified whole. However, for us, it has become a lens through which we see God's hand at work in our story.

In Scripture, the number three carries profound significance—it symbolizes resurrection and new life, divine completeness and perfection, as well as confirmation and validation of testimony. For us, it became more than a coincidence; it was a reminder that God Himself had scripted our story. Different threads of three—whether in moments of joy, seasons of trial, or times of pivotal decision making—were intricately woven together to shape our path and bring us to where we are now. It wasn't just one defining moment; it was a succession of events, choices, and divine interventions that carried us into our *New Beginning*.

THREE KEY DECISION-MAKING RESPONSES

We all make critical choices throughout our lives that are extremely consequential. These are sometimes referred to as "destiny-defining decisions," which aptly describe the potential life trajectory-altering and shaping effect they often have on an individual, those connected to them, and generations to come. During our journeys, we make many decisions that are not just pivotal but also transformative—influencing and refining us through the circumstances we face.

The three key decision-making responses—"Yes," "No," and "Maybe"—represent fundamental choices that determine a particular course of action. These responses are simple yet significant in acting as a framework for how we navigate and react to various situations every day. They provide a structure for evaluating options, help us quickly sort our choices, and guide our next steps based on our goals and circumstances. Most importantly, they are building blocks that shape the outcomes of weightier decisions.

Throughout much of the early years of our relationship, Ségun and I were not sufficiently adept at using these response patterns in navigating the crucial decisions of marriage, separation, or divorce. Thankfully, based on fresh perspectives that followed the discovery of reasons to try again, we've been able to say "yes" to reconciliation.

THREE KEY OPTIONS—STAY MARRIED, SEPARATE OR DIVORCE, OR RECONCILE

As a married couple, we underwent a forced process of improvement and maturation when choosing between these three options, resulting in self-discovery, God-rediscovery, and growth. This book is a layered narrative that tells how each decision we made played a distilling role in revealing the essence of character and our understanding of relationships as we sought greater clarity, strength, wisdom, and purpose. One important takeaway from our experience is the value of introspection and the wisdom of avoiding permanent decisions based on temporary situations or fleeting emotions.

"Trilogy" in the context of this book implies a series of three interconnected parts, each representing a significant choice or turning point that affects the overall story. It is a winding road paved with the three defining phases of our marriage—falling in love, our separation, and the eventual reaffirmation of our lifelong commitment to each other—and our spiritual journey's critical role in determining the growth and outcome that unfolds.

THE THREE-IN-ONE: DIVINE INTERVENTION

This is the story of two individuals who got married, drifted from God's path, and, by His grace, found their way back—ultimately aligning their lives with Him. At the heart of our journey is the unwavering presence of the Trinity—the Father, the Son, and the Holy Spirit—who sustained us through every challenge (Matt. 28:19; John 10:30; 2 Cor. 13:14; 1 Pet. 1:2; Ps. 18:13). God remained faithful to His promise to never leave nor forsake us, mercifully pulling us back from the brink. As Scripture reminds us, *"…a threefold cord is not quickly broken"* (Eccles. 4:12b)—a truth we've personally experienced through God's perfect love and the wholeness we have in Christ (Col. 2:10; Phil. 1:6).

Trilogy Refining Decisions takes a deep dive into our choices—how we make them, the outcomes they set in motion, and the impact they have on our personal and relational development across all areas of life. It depicts a multilayered exploration of our relationship over time and the external influences we encountered along the way. The reader is presented with two distinct narratives of our challenges—Funké's version and Ségun's version ("Through Ségun's Lenses")—and their evolution juxtaposed against God's truth.

So, get ready to embark on a journey filled with flashbacks and a whirlwind of emotions, as it reveals the defining moments that changed us. Along the way, we'll revisit the should-haves, could-haves, and would-haves that lingered in the shadows and the whispers of roads not taken.

> *"Blessed [gratefully praised and adored] be the God and Father of our Lord Jesus Christ, the Father of mercies and the God of all comfort, who comforts and encourages us in every trouble so that we will be able to comfort and encourage those who are in any kind of trouble, with the comfort with which we ourselves are comforted by God."* (2 Cor. 1:3-4 AMP)

Author's Note

(ERNESTINA OLUFUNKÉ ADENIJI)

There was a time when our marriage seemed lost, when hope felt distant, and separation seemed like the only option. My husband, Ségun, and I found ourselves on opposite sides of a ravine with no clear path to bridge the divide. For six and a half years, we lived that reality—apart, disconnected, and wrestling with each other and the pain that comes when a love story begins to unravel.

This book is not just about the heartache of separation. It is about the almost unbelievable restoration that followed—the healing I had prayed and longed for but my husband never imagined possible. In the weeks leading up to what was supposed to be the finalization of our divorce, something shifted. We were given a second chance—undeserved and incredibly beautiful.

Through this journey, I've learned that vulnerability can become a source of strength, and reconciliation may not always be the outcome we receive—nor does it always come in the form we expect. It's easy to hide behind pride, fear, anger, and bitterness, but true healing begins when we dare to be open—naked and unashamed. And that is what this book is: my attempt to strip away the layers, to share the raw moments, the missteps, and the lessons learned.

I felt compelled to write this book because many couples quietly struggle in their relationships. I know the pain of pretending everything is okay when, in reality, things are falling apart. I know what it feels like to walk the fine line between giving up and holding on, unsure of which direction to go. And I know the frustration of not finding relatable examples to connect with or glean from while going through difficulties in marriage.

The more Ségun and I narrate our story and see lives touched, the more we realize that it isn't ours to keep but to share. Our journey is a constant reminder that the comfort one receives in times of great sorrow or distress is intended to make one "comfort-able"—equipping one to assist and strengthen others facing similar difficulties. It gives us so much joy to receive affirming feedback and to hear how our account of God's intervention and spectacular eleventh-hour interruption of our divorce plans has positively impacted the lives of individuals and couples as they go through rough patches or crises in their relationships.

The response we have received makes it obvious to us that tried-and-tested solutions shouldn't be restricted to just a few when so many people stand to benefit immensely from them. Hence, I decided to write this book to widen our reach, and I am thrilled that Ségun has agreed to join me in this project by including his version of events. As you know, there are always two sides to a story and, sometimes, differing eye-witness accounts depending on perspective. However, there is always the ever-reliable truth (God's version), which was a crucial part of our reconciliation and continues to be our meeting point … our Anchor.

Some people believe we have cracked a code and should hide the secret formula in a vault, while we've heard a couple of remarks that attribute our marital turnaround to a fluke or sheer luck! It was not luck but grace! We consider ourselves very fortunate to have weathered many raging storms and are now thriving through deliberate, thoughtful actions and partnership with God. I pray you'll find your own flicker of hope through our story. You'll see that reconciliation and healing are possible even when things seem to be at their darkest. It's not easy and may not be quick, but it is possible. I want you to know that you are not alone if you're in the midst of a marital storm.

While some aspects of our story reflect cultural nuances embedded in the marital journey of an African couple living within African societal constructs, the truth remains that the challenges married couples face are universal—they simply manifest in different ways. This book is for anyone whose relationship has gone sour, for those navigating the heartbreak of separation, wondering whether there is a way back from the edge, and longing for healing, restoration, or even a second, third, or fourth chance at love. As unique as our journey may be, we readily admit that we are still a work in progress. Yet, we believe this book can serve as a beacon of hope for others walking through similar struggles, or those who wish to be anchored before the storm arrives.

If you're in a good place in your relationship and all is well, this resource can still be valuable in helping you build resilience for those unexpected moments. Challenges are a part of life, and being prepared can make all the difference when they arise. Life can sometimes surprise us with missteps, misunderstandings, disappointments, unfulfilled expectations, doubts, fears, setbacks, illness, or difficult times. Equipping ourselves with the right tools can help us navigate these moments with strength and hope.

As you turn these pages, I pray that you will be encouraged, inspired, and reminded that love, no matter how broken it may seem, can be healed.

Author's Note

(VICTOR OLUSÉGUN ADENIJI)

Any man who has experienced an extreme marital crisis when divorce is in the cards knows just how disruptive and destabilizing it can be. The addition of children to the mix increases the degree of complexity. Things become even more convoluted when members of one's extended family and friends get involved and almost invariably close ranks behind their kin.

As someone who has been down this pothole-laden road during a lengthy and acrimonious separation, with two young children caught in the middle, I learned firsthand that the level of discord and breakdown in communication between husband and wife increases exponentially as the level of ambient noise from third-party "advisers" increases. There was no shortage of family members, friends, and even strangers willing to throw in their two cents. In one case, this included an individual who had never met me yet and decided to start circulating a baseless rumor about me simply because it made the narrative more appealing. The individual in question simply wanted to appear to be in the know about what was going on between Funké and me.

With the benefit of hindsight, it is easy to see how a spouse can compound an unsteady marital relationship by stubbornly clinging to a narrative that is little more than a biased perspective a person has embraced and on which one decides to dig in one's heels. The longer a person refuses to move beyond such narratives, the more difficult it is to allow objectivity to interrogate the validity of one's opinion and justify modification when necessary.

This is compounded by the natural instinct to shirk responsibility in situations where one anticipates the apportionment of blame by society, which is often quick to do so in the case of failing or failed relationships. Nature truly abhors a vacuum, and nowhere is this more evident than in a relationship that is falling apart at the seams with the court of public opinion baying for blood and actively searching for where to pin premade labels of "aggressor" and "victim."

When Funké asked me to share my perspective in this book, I was initially hesitant. I felt that revisiting the past might reopen old wounds, lead to a bumping of heads over differences in recollection, or create an unlevel playing field where third parties mentioned are denied a right of reply. From a personal standpoint, there was the added risk of allowing myself to be examined under a giant microscope by total strangers.

However, I then realized that, apart from possibly being cathartic for Funké and me, chronicling our journey honestly and openly—from our respective viewpoints—might provide help and hope for desperate couples, particularly husbands, struggling to stay afloat in their marriages. The fact that so many men all over the world—from different backgrounds—continue to inflict unimaginable and, sometimes, irreparable damage on themselves and their families when caught in relational nightmares means the solution to such problems remains elusive.

Perhaps men who have saved difficult marriages—unions that seemed destined to fail at one time or another—are not sharing their experiences with other men, or at least not on a sufficiently large scale. There is, clearly, a lack of "debriefs" for husbands from their "fellow combatants" who have walked in, suffered in, and made missteps in their shoes—leaving the latter to work things out on their own or rely on advice or prescriptions that are too abstract to have any real meaning for them.

As men typically internalize their feelings, often to their disadvantage, I felt that reading a man's warts and all accounts of how—and why—I gave up on my marriage before Funké and I were miraculously pulled back from the brink, might pave the way toward true and lasting reconciliation for other men facing similar trials. Although the focus is usually concentrated on women, it is undeniable that, if not addressed, marital turbulence can result in men feeling lonely, exasperated, and afraid. From my general observations and discussions with men of different nationalities and cultures over the years, even the toughest of us can be pushed to the limit, with suicide being a serious consideration when our lives, and those of our family members, are completely upended. I vividly recall times when I felt like I was floundering in the dark and on the verge of drowning. The lack of a reference point to cling to—someone who truly understood what I was going through—made it infinitely more difficult to stay afloat.

I pray that I succeed in filling a similar gap for someone through my contribution to this book. At the end of each chapter, you'll find a section entitled "Through Ségun's Lenses" which includes a "Rearview Mirror Lesson." My hope is that a marriage—or even a life—will be saved, and love restored.

It took me a while, but I eventually learned vital life lessons after a long period of meandering, mistakes, and pain. By remaining still and accepting my helplessness and limitations, something shifted, and I could see things with greater clarity, almost like after visiting an optometrist. There are some voids in our lives that only God can fill, and although it took a lot of kicking and screaming, He finally got my attention before it was too late.

PART 1

A Bumpy Start

Building Love, Frame by Frame

Rising financial sector executive.

Bright college student.

Our love for each other was evident to all.

Dating was fun!

Finally! 18 April 1998.

Honeymoon...Funké was completely smitten!

Proud Dad with his boys.

Honeymoon in Paris.

November 1993 - "The First Encounter"

It seems like only yesterday - on that cool November night,
when our eyes met and my heart felt that warm refreshing light.
I couldn't help but notice her extraordinary smile,
that brief moment some four years ago made my whole life worthwhile.

We met again and then I knew that ours was going to be,
the kind of love that's true and pure and lasts eternally.
Just when I think I've seen it all from the one who I adore,
she reaches into her heart of hearts and gives me so much more.

- Segun

July 1997 - "The Proposal"

What struck me was his tenderness - the way he made me feel,
he was there for me both night and day and showed his love was real.
If I was down, he'd come around and fill me with good cheer,
and comfort me with these four words, "sweetheart, I'm always near."

The day he asked if I'd be his wife, perhaps my expression showed,
the answer to that question was made some four years ago.
As we exchange our marriage vows, we'd like you all to pray,
that our love grows in leaps and bounds with every passing day.

- Funke

Excerpt from our wedding keepsake booklet.

1

In the Beginning

"But why do you call Me 'Lord, Lord,' and not do the things which I say? Whoever comes to Me, and hears My sayings and does them, I will show you whom he is like: He is like a man building a house, who dug deep and laid the foundation on the rock. And when the flood arose, the stream beat vehemently against that house, and could not shake it, for it was founded on the rock. But he who heard and did nothing is like a man who built a house on the earth without a foundation, against which the stream beat vehemently; and immediately it fell. And the ruin of that house was great."

LUKE 6:46-49

THE "APPLE" DILEMMA!

Like Eve, who had wandered off independently in the Garden of Eden, I felt like a rebellious child who had tasted the forbidden fruit and wanted to hide from my Father. After a few months in university, I had *"…become so well-adjusted to (my) culture that (I) fit into it without even thinking.…dragging (me) down to its level of immaturity."* [1] I felt I had let my Heavenly Father down, but rather than dealing with feelings of shame and guilt from my poor decision and running back into His waiting arms, I chose the path of the "prodigal." "Everyone is having pre-marital sex, and after all, I am doing so with the person I am going to marry" was my justification for giving in to Ségun's pressure to ditch my decision to be chaste

---

1. Rom. 12:1-2 (MSG and TPT)

29

until we got married. But my excuse still didn't make it right! "Everyone" did not live by the same set of guiding principles I had committed to and standards I was bound by, which served as a foundation for decision-making, behavior, and life in general. I had been a born-again Christian since the age of eleven and had recently renewed my devotion to Christ through a powerful campus fellowship—then this wonderful man, Ségun showed up!

I had inadvertently gotten into the habit of excluding God and living life on my terms, not His. I overstepped God's boundaries,[2] which weren't meant to cage me in or cramp my style but to protect me and keep me from harm or straying into danger. I decided to chart a different course by compromising because I was afraid to lose this "rare find" represented by Ségun. "Find" is the operative word here, as I erroneously believed it took *my* effort to be discovered by this exceptional man and, therefore, it would take *my* effort to keep him. I wanted this "good thing" to be added before seeking God's Kingdom and His righteousness[3]—*His way of doing and being right.*

It wasn't about fitting in with my peers; besides, I didn't discuss intimate details about my personal life with anyone. So, if it wasn't peer pressure driving me, why was my identity in Christ and the love I professed for Him not enough to keep me from falling? I clearly understood what was expected of me and knew some scriptures—enough to know there's no correct way of doing the wrong thing. Yet, I found a way to dress up a mistake to make it right. A part of me had always felt "less than"—a sense that I was not measuring up, but I hid it well behind my quiet demeanor.

I had read in the Bible that God placed a premium on me and that I am a woman of high value to Him, but I hadn't fully grasped or understood what that meant other than He gave His precious Son to die for me. The depth of a father's love felt somewhat abstract to me … a gap that took years to understand and embrace fully. With Ségun, I found some of those missing pieces, and I craved more. He was dependable and doted on me consistently. He made me feel that I was enough and I was everything he needed. There was no way I could let that go at that time … sadly, not even for God.

In James 1:13-18, the Bible teaches that temptation does not originate from God but from our own flaws when we are dragged away, enticed, and baited to commit sin by our own worldly desire (lust, passion).[4]

> *"Let no one say when he is tempted, 'I am being tempted by God,' for God cannot be tempted with evil, and he himself tempts no one. But each person is tempted when he is lured and enticed by his own desire. Then desire when it has conceived gives birth to sin, and sin when it is fully grown brings forth death. Do not be deceived,*

---

2. Acts 17:26-30
3. Matt. 6:33
4. James 1:13-14 (AMP)

my beloved brothers. Every good gift and every perfect gift is from above, coming down from the Father of lights, with whom there is no variation or shadow due to change. Of his own will he brought us forth by the word of truth, that we should be a kind of firstfruits of his creatures." (James 1:13-18)

In Christianity, chastity is emphasized during dating and before marriage because it reflects biblical principles of purity, respects God's design for relationships, and upholds the sanctity of marriage. The call to live in purity and holiness before the Lord is central to the Christian life. These aren't old-fashioned virtues reserved for religious zealots or an impossible set of requirements for hot-blooded youths. This lifestyle is attained through Christ's redemptive work, sustained by the grace of God rather than personal effort. Holiness and purity are core expressions of Christian life, along with faith, love, humility, righteousness, peace, and joy.

Just as Christ cannot be removed from CHRISTianity, these two virtues cannot be separated from a genuine relationship with God. Many people try to airbrush them from their walk with Jesus, but God wants us to be set apart for Him, embodying moral purity[5] and striving (through His all-sufficient grace) to align our lives with His character. Jesus tells us to come as we are but not to stay as we are! *"… You must be holy because I am holy."*[6] Purity emphasizes the absence of sin or defilement, inner cleanliness, and moral uprightness—particularly in specific areas such as sexuality, speech, and thought life. Holiness reflects a life filled with God's Spirit and guided by His will. A pure heart and mind are essential for living a holy life. Both holiness and purity are part of sanctification, the process by which believers grow closer to God and reflect His image. Here are some key reasons for the emphasis Christianity places on chastity before marriage:

1. Spiritual alignment with God's plan:

- Chastity reflects obedience to God's Word, particularly teachings about sexual purity (e.g., 1 Cor. 6:18-20, Heb. 13:4). It encourages individuals to view their bodies as temples of the Holy Spirit, reserved for the sacred covenant of marriage.

- It helps couples focus on spiritual and emotional connection rather than physical intimacy, fostering a stronger foundation for their relationship.

2. Cultivation of self-control and patience:

- Practicing chastity teaches discipline, self-control, and patience, which are essential qualities for a healthy marriage.

---

5. 1 Tim. 4:12
6. 1 Pet. 1:16

- These traits can help couples navigate challenges and temptations in their marriage, building trust with God-honoring regard for each other.

3. Mutual respect and appreciation:

- By abstaining from sexual intimacy before marriage, couples demonstrate respect for each other's dignity and value themselves beyond physical attraction. This fosters a deeper emotional connection that can strengthen and enrich a future marriage.

4. Prevention of guilt and regret:

- Chastity helps avoid emotional or spiritual baggage that can stem from engaging in sexual activity outside of marriage. This can lead to a clearer conscience and a more positive start to the marital relationship.

5. Setting clear boundaries and fostering effective communication:

- Couples who practice chastity often develop strong communication skills and establish healthy boundaries. These practices can contribute to better conflict resolution and understanding within marriage.

The potential benefits of chastity on marriages include:

- **Deeper trust:** Couples may have more confidence in each other's commitment, knowing they respected boundaries before marriage.

- **Stronger emotional intimacy:** A relationship built on emotional and spiritual foundations rather than physical attraction alone is often more resilient.

- **Faith-centered bond:** Aligning with biblical principles creates a shared spiritual foundation that strengthens the couple's connection and purpose.

- **Reduced comparisons or insecurities:** Chastity can minimize the potential for emotional baggage or comparisons to past experiences, allowing couples to focus solely on their unique relationship.

Scriptures like 1 Thessalonians 4:3-5 emphasize that God's will is for His followers to abstain from sexual immorality, which includes saving sexual intimacy for marriage. Adhering to these principles is seen as honoring God, oneself, and one's future spouse.

God loves us, but He hates sin, and the longer we remain in willful sin (rebellion), the further it drives us away from Him. Sin damages our relationship with God by causing us to reject Him in favor of someone or something else. I should have trusted God more—and embraced

His promise that His plans are to prosper me and not to harm me, plans to give me hope and a future.[7] The acceptable response to God's will is obedience. Selective obedience or delayed obedience still amounts to disobedience. My impatience made me disobedient and believe the lie that I was undeserving of the extravagant love of my Heavenly Father and His wisdom and strength, moreso at a very crucial phase of my life.

MY BELOVED IS MINE

Ségun and I met on a cool November night in 1993 when I was nineteen. Despite all the hiccups we experienced in the early years of our marriage, we both agree and know fully well that we didn't meet serendipitously and that our paths converged through divine orchestration. I was home for a short break from university and decided to return some movies to a video rental within walking distance of my mother's house. My best friend, who accompanied me on the walk, suggested that we buy some cakes on our way home. Ségun was driving by, spotted us, and decided to follow us into the "Big Treat" bakery. The actual "treat" that night was our encounter! Being the irresistibly charming guy that he is, Ségun struck up a conversation with me in the bakery. We literally spoke for hours on the phone later that night and began dating soon afterward, only to discover that our mothers had attended the same primary school and even had the same first name. That practically sealed it. Well, so I thought!

We became husband and wife after an intense five-year courtship. Following our unforgettable honeymoon, we settled down to build what we thought would be a perfect "happily ever after" life. After all, we were head over heels in love, and that was all that mattered. I had married a good man—a loving and doting Prince Charming who was more mature than I was (being nine years and four months older). He was (and still is) a brilliant and perfect gentleman, my very own knight in shining armor who racked up countless air miles for years, traveling between two cities just to see me until he finally won the prize!

We got married for all the right reasons, and our differences (age gap, concepts of faith, etc.) didn't matter at the time. At least they didn't appear to be anything worth worrying about. We both had high expectations for the family we were eager to start and, as far as we were concerned, our union possessed the right ingredients for a near-perfect relationship. However, we took for granted the critical elements that sustain marriages year after year.

Things were great at first, which lulled me into a false sense of security and made me oblivious to the stealth with which the enemy crept into our home through the cracks in our foundation. Isolation from God not only breeds pride but also makes a person an easy prey.[8] The

---

7. Jer. 29:11
8. Prov. 18:1

sense I had in my mind of a fissure between God and me grew bigger and bigger while Ségun and I were dating and well into our marriage. We worked hard to build our home and life together during those early years and soon got caught up in everyday living, working, traveling together, and making babies. We had our first son about a year and a half into our marriage, and our second son came along three years later.

I unwittingly continued to reject God's guidance due to inexplicable defiance as I grew accustomed to living according to my standards and moral codes. I had fully backslidden while Ségun and I were dating and ignored the path to repentance after we got married. That was all I needed to do ... to have genuine remorse for my past wrongs, ask for forgiveness, and put God back at the center of my life, where He should be.

Making a U-turn while we were dating seemed difficult as it probably would have ended the relationship—maybe for a season if Ségun was indeed mine, or maybe forever if he wasn't. However, I wasn't prepared to take that risk then and felt my way was foolproof. So, I kept deceiving myself that it was okay to continue sharing physical intimacy with Ségun.

The truth is that decisions become easier when our will to please God outweighs our will to please ourselves, and in order to please God, we may have to disappoint some people, even if only temporarily. God hasn't left us on our own to make what may sometimes appear to be tough decisions,[9] and His grace is sufficient for us, just as His strength is made perfect in weakness.[10] If we (really) love God, we will keep and obey His commandments.[11] Loving God empowers us to follow His Word—not just some of it, but all.

> *"Whoever says 'I know him' but does not keep his commandments is a liar, and the truth is not in him, but whoever keeps his word, in him truly the love of God is perfected. By this we may know that we are in him: whoever says he abides in him ought to walk in the same way in which he walked."* (1 John 2:4-6)

Perhaps if I had taken a stand from the beginning and walked the talk that I professed, I would have been better prepared for our marriage. I could have been "salt" and "light" in our marriage—sparing both of us the complications and consequences of indirectly shutting God out of our lives. I am not implying that our marriage would have been perfect, but we definitely wouldn't have crashed and burned within five years with the same fire and intensity that characterized the early part of our relationship. God understands our frailties and failings.[12]

---

9. Rom. 8:26-27
10. 2 Cor. 12:9
11. John 14:15
12. Eccles. 7:20; Rom. 3:23

Therefore, He isn't asking for human perfection. What He requires is our heart,[13] and He has freed us from the penalty for our failings through our faith in Jesus.[14]

So, I had the man and marriage I wanted and a beautiful home as a bonus. God is merciful, but He cannot be mocked! Ségun had become the object of ALL my affection and, in essence, my idol. An idol is anything or anyone elevated to a position of intense devotion, admiration, or love, often beyond question or critique. In retrospect, after deep reflection and honesty, my relationship with Ségun fits this definition perfectly regarding what I adored and loved most at the time. However, he didn't mount a pedestal and ask to be worshiped; instead, I created that position in my heart for him, and I guess he enjoyed it ... at first, until it became stifling!

Scripture tells us that God is a jealous God—not in a possessive or insecure way, but with a holy zeal that desires our undivided love and loyalty.[15] He will not share His glory with another because He alone is worthy of it. His jealousy is rooted in His deep love and covenant commitment to us, much like a faithful spouse who longs to protect a sacred bond. Unlike human jealousy, which can stem from fear, insecurity, or selfishness, God's jealousy is pure, protective, and always for our good.

God is deliberate in not wanting us to worship other gods or idols; as Psalm 24:4-5 says, we will end up losing our way as idol worship will lead us outside God's love and guidance. This highlights God's steadfast devotion to us and His call for us to uphold our commitment to Him in return. You and I were made for Him. We are His own, set apart for His glory. When anything—our spouses, children, careers, money, or friends—claims more of our affection, time, thoughts, or desires than He does, it stirs His protectiveness. His love for us is unmatched, and He knows that nothing can truly satisfy us and bring the fulfillment we find when we follow His ways. We must learn to put everyone and everything in the correct place and in the right order of importance.

DRUNK ON LOVE!

I was head over heels in love with Ségun, which in and of itself can be problematic in a relationship—because the "love hormone" or "bonding hormone" (oxytocin) surges in early romance, sometimes producing effects loosely similar to the intoxication of being "drunk on love." Researchers have found that oxytocin can boost pro-social behaviors such as altruism, generosity, and empathy. However, contextual and individual factors can influence these reactions.

On the downside, in negative or stressful social experiences, the hormone may amplify memories and heighten fear and anxiety. Elevated oxytocin levels may sometimes impair

---

13. Matt. 22:37

14. Rom. 3:22-24

15. Deut. 4:24

judgment—raising our trust and lowering our caution—so that we might overlook red flags or may contribute to overly optimistic assessments of people or situations. It's therefore wise not to underestimate the role of hormones and brain chemistry in social behavior and emotional responses—especially in partner selection, bonding, and the journey of relationship growth.[16]

I've always been reserved, so in the early days of our marriage, apart from going to work, I rarely left the house. I didn't hang out with friends, our social outings as a couple became less frequent, and church attendance was irregular. So, I lived and breathed Ségun as I finally had someone and something I could call "my own." He was my world; my life revolved around him, and I was certain nothing or no one would get between us.

Troubles started to brew—the typical ones that plague even the best relationships and marriages. The reality that true love is much more than a mixture of emotions, feelings, urges, and impulses quickly set in. We managed to stay afloat for a few years thanks to the combination of our affection for each other, our desire to be together, and the bits of advice and pre-marriage counseling we had taken on board amid the excitement of planning our wedding. Things deteriorated rapidly when seemingly minor issues kept resurfacing and escalating, and our once peaceful home became a battlefield of unending discord. Our love had waned from the constant arguments, fights, distrust, resentment, and frequent episodes of giving each other the silent treatment. The layers of masking tape eventually gave way as they could no longer withstand the constant tension, and what began as hairline fractures in our relationship became gaping holes.

With problems mounting and things spiraling out of control, the will to put out the fire was lacking, and even the desire to pray or be together rapidly diminished. When instability on the home front eventually turned into a crisis, we lacked proper support, and all attempts at self-help[17] were ineffective. We were ill-equipped and too proud to admit we didn't know what to do. We took wrong turns and strayed deeper into unfamiliar territory before completely losing our way. Ironically, my first instinct was to turn to Ségun to steady our ship, clinging to him tightly as if my life depended on it, but it proved to be an exercise in futility.

Over time, all we could see in each other were our inadequacies and faults (which were magnified by interfering third parties who had been given unfettered access to our relationship). This preoccupied our time and thoughts, and our civil conversations were limited. We constantly tried to change each other and failed to consider God (our Creator, Maker,

16. Association for Psychological Science, "Oxytocin Makes People Trusting, but Not Gullible, Study Suggests," *ScienceDaily*, August 25, 2010, https://www.sciencedaily.com/releases/2010/08/100824103535.htm;

Universität Bonn, "Oxytocin Increases Social Altruism," *ScienceDaily*, November 26, 2015, https://www.sciencedaily.com/releases/2015/11/151126104203.htm;

University of Haifa, "'Love Hormone' Oxytocin: Difference in Social Perception Between Men and Women," *ScienceDaily*, July 31, 2013, https://www.sciencedaily.com/releases/2013/07/130731093257.htm;

Miranda Olff, "The Role of Oxytocin in Social Bonding, Stress Regulation and Mental Health: An Integrative Review," *European Journal of Neuroscience* 32, no. 3 (August 2010): 347–72, https://www.sciencedirect.com/science/article/pii/S0306453013002369.

17. Prov. 14:12

Manufacturer, Owner, Source, and Author of all things good)[18] as our first resort. Rather than wait until things got out of hand, we should have taken God's product (marriage) and ourselves back to Him (the Authorized Service Center) to fix or at least get instructions on proper usage. From the onset of our relationship, we unwittingly relegated God to the background, and as the years rolled by, we figured things out on our own, trusting that they would somehow work out instead of following His guidance. We foolishly ended up trying to put our spin on the product (marriage) He designed, bent on doing it our way and expecting it to function correctly and for us to get the best out of it.[19]

Unlike the prodigal son who came to his senses and returned to his father's house for reconciliation, I got even more comfortable and complacent, leaving most things to chance. Looking back now, I realize that I just went with the flow. I'm profoundly grateful that "Goodness" and "Mercy" have truly been our constant companions,[20] as so much more could have gone wrong. I continued to believe that I was too far gone on the "Lone Ranger Trail" and even avoided certain sections of the Word of God as I didn't want to be called out on my shortcomings. I believe I got stuck in this rut because I focused more on the "fire and brimstone" side of God than on His love and mercy. I didn't have to work for or earn His love and forgiveness; all I had to do was accept His gift of being made right through Christ.[21]

There was an unrelenting tug at my heart and a longing to reconnect more deeply with my Heavenly Father. I knew what that relationship was like because I had tasted and seen that the Lord is consistently good. I tried to fill the void with Ségun, my children, and the small circle of friends I just about managed to maintain, but something was missing. This resulted in me pining for even more attention from my husband and pouring myself into motherhood. It was an uncomfortable place, but it ultimately got my focus back to God.[22]

Sometimes, God allows certain experiences to gently redirect our hearts and bring us back into alignment with Him through repentance. Grace often works in unexpected ways. For some of us, life's hard lessons—whether prompted by rebellion, pride, selfishness, youthful exuberance, or simply poor choices—have become classrooms at the "School of Hard Knocks" where God's love, patience, and mercy are most powerfully revealed.[23] We graduated *summa cum laude* by the mercy of God with degrees in "Reckless Optimism," "Overconfident Studies," "Finding Out the Hard Way," "Creative Chaos Management," and "The Fine Art of Bouncing Back!"

Marriage is not a man-made institution but a divine design created by God to honor Him

---

18. Gen. 1:4-31; James 1:17; Ps. 107:8-9; 119:68; 1 Tim. 4:4-5; 1 Sam. 12:16; 2 Chron. 20:17

19. Ps. 127:1

20. Ps. 23:6

21. Rom. 10:10; 1 Cor. 1:30; 2 Cor. 5:19-21

22. Prov.18:12 (MSG and TPT)

23. Titus 3:3-8 (AMP and MSG)

through love, unity, holiness, and faithfulness. It is also meant to nurture godly children who reflect His nature. God intended marriage to be beautiful, and we are called to *enjoy* it as a by-product of glorifying Him, rather than to merely *endure* it as a duty, obligation, or pastime.[24] People make marriage ugly when the Creator's instruction manual is distorted or discarded.[25] Marriage enables mature individuals to flourish through learning, friendship, and trust. It's a sacred union between a man and woman—two imperfect people who choose perseverance over giving up, even as they are tested, refined, shaped, and sharpened for the Master's purpose.

Great marriages don't happen by sheer luck or accident; they result from a consistent invest-ment of prayer, time, thoughtfulness, forgiveness, affection, compassion, mutual respect, and a rock-solid commitment between a husband and wife. Marriage is not just a two-way part-nership but a **three-way covenant** that includes God. "*...the Lord is the witness between you and the wife of your youth...she is your partner, the wife of your marriage covenant*" (Malachi 2:14, NIV). No one finds or stumbles on a happy home. We all set out to build one, and our choices from the onset determine the outcome.

THROUGH SÉGUN'S LENSES

I had a good idea of the sort of person I wanted to marry and spend the rest of my life with. Nine-and-a-half years younger than me, Funké embodied all those qualities—intellect, beauty, a good sense of humor, a deep-rooted sense of loyalty, and most impor-tantly, a love for God. I was relieved that the search was over, although I had to wait for her to graduate from university before we married.

In the meantime, I ensured we spent as much time together as possible, especially after she returned from university. I did a lot of traveling at the time, and she accompa-nied me whenever possible. We got engaged before her finals, and after asking her par-ents for her hand in marriage in early 1998, we finally walked down the aisle together on April 18, 1998.

To my mind, our age difference and the fact that I had experienced more of life was a justifiable basis for me to take the lead in setting the agenda for our marriage. As far as I was concerned, I was eminently qualified and well-intentioned to make key deci-sions in the interest of both of us and, later on, that of our children. Nigerian husbands have long been held, and indeed encouraged to be, the (much) greater of two equals

---

24. Gen. 1:27-28; 2:24; Mal. 2:15; 1 Cor. 7:2-3; Eph. 4:32; 5:33; Col. 3:18-19; 1 Pet. 4:8
25. Prov. 10:17; 30:5-6; Hosea 4:6

in a marriage. This remains a widely held view, especially if the man is a provider for his nuclear and extended family.

I was a partner in a financial advisory firm and worked hard to ensure that my family wanted for nothing, and the future certainly looked bright. We had a nice apartment about twenty minutes from my office, and I could not have been happier, given how things were evolving on the home and business fronts. I showered Funké with attention and spoke about how we saw our lives evolving over the coming years, including her plans to pursue further education.

A few months into our marriage, disagreements turned into arguments, which became more frequent and intense. Funké became pregnant about nine months after we got married. Although this marked a period of excitement, it was preceded by a phase during which we were constantly bickering, often over nothing of significance. When Funké lost her temper, she became an entirely different person. I didn't like it and made my feelings known, which exacerbated things to the point where, on several occasions, we had to involve our respective family members.

I then took it upon myself to help mold her into the best version of herself. I didn't see any other way and considered that part of my responsibilities as her husband. Knowing that her parents had split up when she and her brother were young, I took Funké's explosive temperament to be due to transferred aggression. When I told her as much, although I didn't mean it in a spiteful way, it was not well received, which resulted in a more unstable environment in our home. I became increasingly convinced I was right and that my sense of the need to help her course-correct was justifiable and necessary.

The fact that our relationship had begun to suffer in the build-up to her pregnancy made the prospect of an addition to our family bittersweet, as seeds of discord had already been sown in our home. Funké gave birth to our first child in October 1999.

With the benefit of hindsight, I realize the fact that Funké stopped working after she became pregnant was not healthy for either of us, particularly given her plan to continue with her education and the need for her to discover her own identity. This is arguably a blind spot that many African men of my generation easily miss when it comes to looking out for their wives' interests and recognizing and supporting the attainment of their dreams.

Rearview Mirror Lesson

In retrospect, I now know with absolute certainty that only God can bring about change in human beings, especially change of a fundamental nature. Anything that even remotely resembles a straitjacket has no place in a marriage. What one partner considers to be guardrails in a marriage can be viewed as prison bars by the other. Without the proper training or tools, in a bid to establish a solid base on which to build a relationship, one can unknowingly end up building a house on the shakiest of foundations that even the most inconsequential of storms can reduce to rubble.

The Word of God trumps human wisdom and sifts through our emotions and fleeting feelings to produce a unique essence based on His truth. Furthermore, while it may seem obvious, self-actualization is vital for both partners in a marriage. Feelings of underachievement or underappreciation can result in frustration and resentment. In the African context, it is very easy for men to bury their heads in the sand, thinking that all is well in their homes, whereas their wives' voices are either not being heard or their message is lost in translation.

2

Catching the Little Foxes

*"Catch the foxes for us, the little foxes that spoil
the vineyards, for our vineyards are in blossom."*

SONG OF SOLOMON 2:15

THE WILY THINGS

The Bible tells us in Song of Solomon 2:15 to watch out for the "little foxes" which have been described as:

> "the first risings of sinful thoughts and desires, the beginnings of trifling pursuits which waste the time, trifling visits, small departures from truth, whatever would admit some conformity to the world; all these, and many more, are little foxes which must be removed. This is a charge to *believers to mortify their sinful appetites and passions, which are as little foxes, that destroy their graces and comforts, and crush good beginnings. Whatever we find a hindrance to us in that which is good, we must put away.*" [1]

When we choose to carry these seemingly "little foxes" as excess baggage or treat them as pets—feeding and nurturing them—they often multiply and grow. This ultimately wreaks havoc on our vineyard, whether it be our relationships, marriage, spiritual life, or personal growth. These "little foxes" could represent various issues that harm relationships and spiritual growth.

---

1. Matthew Henry, *Commentary on the Whole Bible*, on Song of Solomon 2:14, *Christianity.com*. https://www.christianity.com/bible/nlt/song-of-solomon/2-14

41

They include unforgiveness that develops into bitterness and resentment, feelings of neglect and loneliness, pride, jealousy, anger, minor misunderstandings that escalate due to miscommunication, stonewalling, selfishness, unrealistic expectations, lack of trust, and unresolved conflicts. Furthermore, moral failings such as dishonesty, cheating, lying, stealing, greed, selfishness, or betrayal, along with negative influences that encourage poor choices, can jeopardize our relationship with God, weaken the foundations of love, erode trust, and compromise our moral integrity.

At first, Ségun and I did everything together. We went everywhere as a couple, such as dinners, parties, family functions, Oxbridge Balls, concerts, and even lounges... until one night when he was schooled in the rudiments of the "married men's code" in the Nigerian social scene—particularly in Lagos, where we lived at the time. In certain circles, the practice is that after marriage, wives don't accompany their husbands everywhere, particularly to a boys' night out. Ségun did not make that distinction, so he, clearly, had not received the memo! We were two peas in a pod, and he shared everything with me—at least until that incident.

He called from work one evening to tell me to get ready for a night out to celebrate a business deal he had brokered and closed. I was notoriously late for everything, so we had agreed that he would give me ultra-early notice and extra time to prepare for events. I wouldn't say I don't like impromptu plans or surprises, but I'm just not a spur-of-the-moment type of person. I'm a stickler for planning, structure, scheduling, and organization. I needed to know details such as the time and location of events, the type of occasion, who would be attending or visiting and when they would arrive, and preferences for food if we were hosting. I'm sure you get the picture! But Ségun was the complete opposite. He did not need much lead time to prepare for anything and ensured he had a fabulous, stylish wardrobe for every occasion. I loved stepping out with him, and I believe he enjoyed showing me off in our early days too! We understood each other in that sense and did not let our differences get in the way. Oh, and by the way, I'm still working on my timekeeping!

Regarding that night, I had been cooped up in the house for a few days and was looking forward to getting out for what sounded like a fun evening, especially having recently attended some events where I felt like a fish out of water! It was still early in our marriage, but the implications of the age difference between Ségun and me became increasingly apparent. Settling in with his peers felt awkward initially since I had never dated a much older man, and we didn't socialize with the same crowds or move in the same circles. Navigating those waters wasn't easy, and some people weren't exactly kind or welcoming—especially the women!

I had to take a more active interest in the financial sector where Ségun worked and quickly get up to speed on financial jargon—which, to be honest, sounded like gibberish to me! At the time, the ink on my psychology degree certificate had barely dried, so it was refreshing and rewarding to step out of my comfort zone, expand my knowledge, and occasionally engage in thoughtful and enlightening discussions with some of the older folks.

Now, back to how that night unfolded. We went to a popular lounge near our home where Ségun and his associates had planned to meet for a celebratory night out. What caught my immediate attention was the startled look in the eyes of one of the men as we approached their table. He was the only person I knew in the group, so introductions were made, and we settled down to have dinner and conversation. I noticed that the gentleman appeared uneasy throughout dinner. It then occurred to me that it might have been because Ségun was the only one who came with his wife, while the other women had been introduced as "friends."

The plan was to move straight to the lounge proper after dinner, but the gentleman quickly called Ségun aside for a brief chat. The next thing I heard was Ségun apologizing to everyone on my behalf that I had suddenly taken ill and had to go home!!! Who?! Me?! How?! What?! When?! Oh no, he didn't! …certainly not after taking me away from what would have been a quiet and relaxing evening—watching TV or tidying up or reading a book or whatever else I did to unwind back then after making dinner.

I was livid, but I complied. I wasn't stupid and told Ségun precisely what I figured he had been "advised" to do … Plus I'm a pretty good lip reader, so he couldn't deny it. To rub salt in the wound, when we got home, Ségun passed me the house keys and said he'd be back soon. I had erroneously thought that the "excuse" provided was made for both of us. My imagination ran wild as I waited for Ségun's return. All I could do was check the time while trying to remember how many female "friends" were at the table and their profiles to ascertain which one may have been assigned to my husband! Fortunately, he kept his word and returned early to look after his "sick" wife.

I threw a fit about how I was mistreated and embarrassed in front of strangers, and he was profoundly apologetic. I knew it wasn't his fault and that he had been forced to make an on-the-spot decision on how to salvage the situation so as not to ruin the entire evening for the rest of the associates visiting from another country. He understood how I felt and promised to always read the "fine print" on future invitations. I'm sure Ségun was subsequently teased for being a novice and reprimanded for breaking the "code" that night. Conversely, I discovered an unspoken rule that married women in Nigerian society adhere to for the sake of peace in their homes. At that time, some popular ones were: "See no evil, hear no evil," "What you don't know won't hurt or kill you," "Let him be and have your peace," "Focus on your children and live your life," "Live and let live," "Choose peace" …

PINING DAY AFTER DAY …

So lounges were now off-limits, but Ségun and I still found fun ways to spend time together and enjoy each other's company. We loved traveling too, so his business meetings and conferences abroad were perfect opportunities to accompany him on those trips. The birth of our first child did not slow us down; we simply packed the stroller, and off we went! Well, until a cutting remark was made, highlighting that we had started growing our family, and it was expected that I would now settle down to building my home instead of "gallivanting all over the place with my husband!" … So our trips together became less frequent, and opportunities to continue bonding gradually disappeared.

I didn't play any sports, but Ségun was an ardent tennis enthusiast, and he often played matches on the court at our home. I occasionally came out with our son to watch him when I could stand the heat, but even that time together began to wane. His business meetings took him out of town more frequently at a certain period, so we started to spend even more time apart. They say absence makes the heart grow fonder, but I'll add that too much distance can make it grow colder.

CONDONING BREEDS PREVALENCE

Over the years in Nigeria, because wives typically didn't want to deal with the stress of going against the grain, many accepted such situations as the norm. By so doing, in effect they enabled, excused, and endorsed their husbands' excesses until things reached breaking point. On the other hand, some took everything in their stride and quietly endured their struggles, focusing on gaining financial independence or waiting until their children were grown. Only then did they start to explore legitimate but subtle escape routes or ways to move on with their lives. This could include spending long periods away from their husbands under the guise of looking after their grandchildren. This dreadful combination of "married men's codes" and "wives' compliance" with society's sexist tendencies created an environment that has been churning out recruits on both sides, from one generation to the next.[2] This was certainly not what I had signed up for!

It was a rude awakening for me and marked my introduction to this side of married life in our environment—one that makes it difficult for good people and marriages to survive, let alone thrive, amid such vices and unacceptable behavior. What I had witnessed at dinner that night and the many tales I subsequently began to hear had a profound impact on me. It started to erode the unequivocal trust I had in Ségun after seeing first-hand how easy it was to get sucked into the proverbial "Sodom and Gomorrah" lifestyle found in many societies. As all of this occurred over two decades ago, one can only imagine how the "married men's code" has evolved since then and how many more "codes" have emerged for different groups of people, including those who hide under the cloak of religion. Maybe that explains part of the additional burden that has been placed on marriages these days, worsened by technological

---

2. Gal. 5:9

advancement and a myriad of readily available opportunities for a warped sense of camaraderie to be shrouded in greater secrecy as the boundaries of bad behavior are expanded.

Loyalty within these groups often takes precedence over honesty and faithfulness in relationships and any sense of moral obligation to religious teachings. Similarly, as I experienced when Ségun and I were dating, people sometimes neglect or selectively avoid God's truth because of the fear of being confronted with their own brokenness, inadequacies, or sinfulness. Such avoidance often arises from discomfort with confronting difficult truths about oneself, the burden of accountability, or the effort needed for genuine repentance and transformation.

There might also be apprehension about the process and potential "cost" of allowing one's life to be overhauled and restored to its intended design—since this may require releasing deeply ingrained habits, relationships, or lifestyles that are misaligned with God's purpose.[3] Addressing this problem at its core often demands courage, honesty, humility, and reliance on God's grace. While there's no cost to receive this gift of salvation[4]—since Jesus already paid the price to redeem us from sin and eternal separation from God—embracing the gift involves repentance, faith, and a willingness to let God transform our lives.

It's crucial to address potential risks before they become issues that could harm one's marriage. This means putting safeguards in place, such as establishing clear expectations and boundaries for relationships outside the marriage. Surely, there should be no pressure, shame, or guilt in choosing not to conform to situations or behaviors that conflict with one's values. In certain scenarios, being a passive observer is harder than being an active participant. Sometimes, leaving a gathering early or removing oneself entirely from uncomfortable situations might feel awkward, but it's a sign of strength and integrity, not weakness—even if it means being the "odd one out" or the person who is famous for saying "no" consistently. It is perfectly fine to be the "killjoy" or the "party pooper" when it's required. Be bold—be the *Frequent Flee-er*![5]

These choices are easier when we see them as essential to protecting what matters most—our loved ones and our lives. Staying true to our commitment is worth the effort. We mustn't allow the "little foxes" to linger and evolve into destructive forces capable of bringing down even the strongest foundations. After all, bad company—or evil companions—ultimately corrupts good morals and character.[6]

These are practical precautions we can all take; there's no need to overspiritualize simple, logical steps that can effectively safeguard ourselves and our marriages. However, lasting behavioral change must begin with a renewal of the mind and a steadfast and consistent reliance on God's strength rather than our own. It requires discernment, mutual accountability, and/or

3. John 3:16; Eph. 1:7-12

4. Rom. 6:23

5. Ps. 37:27-29; 1 Cor. 6:18-20; 1 Tim. 6:11; 2 Tim. 2:22

6. 1 Cor. 15:33 (TPT)

seeking out an accountability partner—not someone encouraging irresponsibility or indulgence.[7] The Bible warns that judgment is coming for *"… those who call evil good and good evil, who put darkness for light and light for darkness, who put bitter for sweet and sweet for bitter."*[8]—a notice to those who normalize or condone what is wrong,[9] as doing so can lead to moral confusion and widespread acceptance of corrupt influences.

It's interesting how, through poor choices or indecisions, we sometimes allow the negative influences of society and people around us to dictate, direct, or shape our lives. More and more people are resigning to the belief that the rise of moral decadence is inevitable, adopting a passive stance—either as sitting ducks, merely waiting for the consequences to unfold, or as lame ducks, rendered ineffective in addressing the problem. This often translates into people embracing an "if you can't beat them, join them" mindset, ignoring the issue, wishing it away, or simply bracing for the worst—until it shows up uninvited, perhaps even threatening their own families or marriages.

I compare this collective societal acceptance to a wife who knowingly turns a blind eye to her husband's pilfering from the office coffers, raising no objections as long as the spoils benefit her. Yet, the moment her share dwindles and she discovers the surplus is being spent on a mistress, all hell breaks loose! Stealing or cheating is tolerable until the untamed "little fox" takes on a different form or threatens her comfort, pride, and stability. Watch out for the "little foxes"—those sins, attitudes, and habits we often overlook, excuse, or defend.

THROUGH SÉGUN'S LENSES

Ominous storm clouds began to hover overhead within a few months of our return from a blissful honeymoon in Paris. Arguments over the most seemingly insignificant things became increasingly frequent, and frustration began to boil over on both sides. Although we could express our feelings, we seemed incapable of explaining the basis for those feelings or our right to feel a particular way to one another. We often made hurtful assumptions while trying to fill in the blanks vis-à-vis the latter. Those assumptions were frequently voiced uncharitably, compounding the problem and sowing seeds of marital discord.

One of my earliest recollections of sensing that trouble was brewing was when my mother decided to personally help Funké and me sew a set of curtains for our new

---

7. Ps. 1:1; Prov. 13:20; 27:6

8. Isa. 5:20-25

9. Eph. 5:11

apartment. A whiz with a sewing machine, my mother has been sewing all manner of clothing and household décor for as long as I can remember. She was trying to be helpful by offering her services to save us time and money by not having to farm out the task to a third party. However, following an incident, the details of which I could never unravel, my mother ended the exercise prematurely. I took this as a failure on my part, having heard so much about the much-parodied dynamic between daughters-in-law and mothers-in-law. It was particularly confusing and painful, having resolved that I would ensure that the two most important women in my life got along famously from the get-go. Of course, I was conflicted after learning something happened between my wife and mother. Playing the honest broker was not an option because I was at fault for not having given them cover in both women's eyes. That seemingly insignificant incident was a stark reminder of the vast difference between human wisdom and God's wisdom, which husbands must actively seek through prayer when managing such issues. As the saying goes, "The best time to address a crisis is before it starts."

On another occasion, Funké felt I was paying more attention to members of my university's alumni association, whose meetings I occasionally hosted at home as the club secretary, than her. Once again, I was at a loss as to what could have triggered such feelings. Her outbursts after my guests left made no sense to me because after listening to her accusations, I knew nothing could have been further from the truth. I could not help but lay the blame squarely at Funké's feet because, as far as I was concerned, up until that point, as a husband, I had been doing everything humanly possible to ensure that she felt loved and appreciated.

I was not a night crawler or a womanizer and believed that this fact alone would give Funké tremendous peace of mind. My outings without her were few and far between, and I went out of my way to ensure that she would accompany me on as many of my international business trips as possible. I believed that spending a lot of time together would strengthen our bond.

However, rifts began to emerge due to what I considered unjustifiable suspicions, which I disliked. At times, I would think Funké was joking when she aired her concerns, and I would make light of it only for a full-blown argument to ensue. We would patch things up, but as the patching became more frequent, the underlying problem became more prominent.

I began to shut out her criticisms, and after a while, I no longer cared what she had to say because I could not reach her. Many of the choices I later made and the decisions I took were due to my inability to fix things between us. They became convenient justifications, even when my behavior was indefensible, and I could blame her for having pushed me onto the wrong path.

Rearview Mirror Lesson

Although it is helpful for couples to spend quality time together, what was glaringly missing in our relationship was time spent in God's presence. We neither prayed together when the going was good nor when things became rough. The consequence was over-reliance on one another, a recipe for disaster as reliance on God's wisdom and faithfulness was replaced by reliance on our knowledge and understanding of what marriage should entail.

Even though I admitted my mistakes to myself, I did not own them because, in my mind, if Funké had not behaved in a certain way, I would not have reacted in the way that I did when we were not seeing eye to eye. This made it impossible for me to focus on becoming a better person—and husband—by working on my shortcomings.

3

Help Meet vs. Help Meat

*"He who finds a wife finds a good thing
and obtains favor from the LORD."*

PROVERBS 18:22

TUMBLEWEED ON A PRAIRIE

We continued settling into marriage and parenthood, working to merge our individual lives into a cohesive unit. While Ségun and I tried to nurture the love that had brought us together, we became increasingly disconnected as our lives and marriage evolved. Everything started to feel superficial to me, lacking the depth our relationship once had. It seemed like we were going through the motions or coasting along. I began to notice that I experienced the best of Ségun, especially when I was agreeable and went along with things. However, whenever I objected to something or offered suggestions, I was met with resistance. I believed that continuous honest communication was crucial to weaving our lives together and maintaining intimacy and emotional closeness. However, deep discussions usually ended up in misunderstandings and disagreements.

Since I was home most of the time, my daily routine usually ended with me eagerly listening to a recap of my husband's activities during the day after his return from the office—his wins, his struggles, his big ideas for the company he was managing at the time, his upcoming trips, his concerns, his investments, and updates on people he was helping to build and turn their dreams into reality… Everything seemed to be about his career, growth, development,

49

needs, etc. I soon began to wonder where I featured in the overall scheme of things, and feelings of being left behind gnawed at me after his daily "downloads."

I understood Ségun was doing his best to provide for our family. I was fully aware of the pressure that emanated from the nature of his work, so I tried my best to give him all the support I could in taking care of his needs and those of our son while ensuring a happy environment in which we could all live and thrive. I knew Ségun had good intentions for our family and me, but I wanted us to map out concrete, long-term plans beyond decisions about the schools our children would attend or the vacation destinations we would visit. I didn't want us to rely solely on his sincere efforts, well-meaning promises, positive aspirations, and hopeful outlook. Having honest discussions with me about well-defined plans for the present and future, our personal goals, and how best to support each other in achieving them would have allayed my real or imagined concerns.

Rather than provide the clarity, comfort, understanding, encouragement, support, and perhaps the validation I desperately needed then, Ségun often deflected the issues and turned them back on me for "criticizing and judging" him. What followed were the most hurtful words and a few unprintable ones, for good measure, that took years to overcome. Sometimes, we forget that once those missiles (words) leave our launch pads (mouths), we no longer control the damage they may cause or how the recipient will respond. To top it all off, I was expected to move on after an apology and even enthusiastically fulfill my conjugal duties with joy and excitement.

Ségun believed his age, experience, and wisdom were enough to lead our home effectively, and he knew what he was doing. The problem was I didn't know what he was doing! It was a clear case of *"If I'm fine, then you and our son will or should be in good shape."* Most attempts at having meaningful conversations usually ended with him saying he didn't need my opinion on how he decided to run his life and, by extension, ours. Overlooking these issues or pretending they did not exist amounted to kicking the can down the road, but I was ready to be patient, hoping that he would get more comfortable with me as our journey progressed. After all, trust is developed and earned, not demanded or taken by force.

Ségun's repeated use of specific hurtful words during our disagreements and his attitude in certain areas led me to believe he had trust issues. I had never knowingly given him any reason to doubt my love, loyalty, or sincerity in any way. I did not have any ulterior motives behind my questions or suggestions. My entire life was an open book to my husband; he knew everything about me. I disliked uncertainty and preferred clear, transparent situations. I struggled to function in environments where people were not straightforward and important matters were shrouded in secrecy or treated as privileged information. I was a meticulous planner, and Ségun knew this about me. I had lists, spreadsheets, schedules, and timetables all over the house. I meant well and was convinced I was looking out for his (our) interest and wanted to help simplify our lives in any way I could.

TREASURE OR THORN

Unfortunately, my patience ran out when I didn't see the desired changes, and I repeatedly broached those sensitive topics without making any headway. This was very frustrating as I had tried to be everything (and more) I thought Ségun wanted … But what did Ségun really want? A wife or a beef patty that he could press (oppress), ground down, flatten, chop up, and reduce or reshape to fit into whatever role (mold) needed—with no space to breathe or grow? Was I a valuable partner to my husband or just a nice-looking filler in the middle of everything? This wasn't what I understood as a help meet! I thought it meant I was my husband's right-hand companion and lifelong partner, who supported, completed, and complemented him—not just a cheerleader who complimented him! A partner who walked and worked alongside her husband in unity and purpose—contributing to the direction and success of their family—and not tucked away somewhere behind him.

I love being a homemaker; it is a gift I cherish and do not take for granted. There's no greater joy for a mother or wife than seeing her family flourish—thriving in love, harmony, and purpose, knowing her dedication has contributed to their well-being and growth. But frustration began to set in when there was a mounting disregard for my own needs or desires, constantly leaving me with a lack of fulfillment in our relationship. No matter how much I gave, it was never enough to be seen or appreciated. It looked like someone had hit the "pause" button on my life, and I got even more restless in what appeared to be an endless wait on the back burner. I just wanted a clear direction of where we were headed and a plan that accommodated my dreams and aspirations. I was cautious about going ahead with some of my personal development goals as things were already complicated enough. I didn't want to be accused of going against my husband's wishes or not working in tandem with him and, in turn, contributing to the growing list of my flaws.

I couldn't reconcile the views and attitudes of the man I had dated for five years with those of the person I was married to after less than two years. In the not-too-distant past, while I was preparing for my finals and project at the university, this same Ségun became my chief research analyst. He did this with such zeal and care that the only thing he didn't do was study for me and write my papers! He couriered bundles of materials to me every week—books, printouts of tons of journals, citations, and other resources. Ségun went above and beyond to ensure my success. Maybe it was his last-minute attempt to redeem himself for being such a delightful distraction—but his effort was both sincere and deeply appreciated.

Ségun also took swift action to ensure my National Youth Service Corps (NYSC) deployment was in Lagos, even securing some job interviews and a position for me at a major oil and gas company. This was a significant achievement, as we got married just a few months after my graduation, and the mandatory post-university NYSC scheme could have taken me hundreds of miles away from home for one year. The NYSC scheme, established by the Nigerian government after the Civil War to "reconstruct, reconcile and rebuild the country,"[1] was strictly enforced at that time. Graduates under the age of thirty were ineligible for employment in most government and private establishments without completing the program.

So, his sudden reluctance to discuss my career aspirations or support my professional growth as time went on was disheartening and left me confused, especially given the enthusiasm and effort he had initially shown in helping me secure such promising job opportunities. It took me some time—being young and naïve—but I eventually learned a profound lesson from that season: Never seek validation from anyone to the extent that it compromises your sense of identity, self-worth, or alignment with God's purpose for your life.

Young women especially need to know they are already worthy in the eyes of their Heavenly Father. They are so valuable and precious that He seeks them out and calls them His own. God's approval outweighs any human opinion, and His Word provides the ultimate benchmark to aspire to. Falling short of His standards, no matter how often or deeply, does not result in disqualification or being cast aside. Every woman thrives on genuine empowerment, which is cultivated through pursuing passions, hobbies, careers, or work that brings fulfillment. This, in turn, allows for meaningful contributions to personal growth, family, and the broader community.

Another sore point in our marriage at the time was how Ségun ignored or dismissed my concerns whenever I expressed my reservations about his interactions with other women. Sometimes, I felt Ségun deliberately stayed out late attending "business meetings" to provoke and get me riled up. Whatever he was doing and why he did it was blatantly disrespectful and completely disregarded my feelings. His usual response to my complaints was incredibly condescending—he claimed he couldn't help with my insecurities or my tendency to panic whenever he was around his friends, particularly women.

It seemed to me that my husband was being blindsided by pride, arrogance, and success in his career in a way that made him unable to recognize the setups and pitfalls around him. I was worried that the path he had chosen to "run his life" had the potential to ruin everyone else's as well, but talking wasn't working, and I had no desire to pray for him because his words and actions deeply wounded me. It's hard to admit, but I just wanted him to slip on a banana peel and have a brain reset from hitting his head (slightly) on concrete as he made his way to one of his "business meetings"! I replayed that scene many times in my head, alternating the site of the fall with smelly, grimy gutters and potholes—so he'd come home muddy and remorseful instead of brazenly reeking of that intense mix of smoke, sweat, perfume, and cologne! Thankfully, my thoughts never took effect, or I might have permanently turned my handsome "Prince Charming" into an ugly frog in a fit of anger!

---

1. "About the Scheme," National Youth Service Corps (NYSC), https://www.nysc.gov.ng/aboutscheme.html.

I felt emotionally drained and believed Ségun was taking both me and our marriage for granted. I began to think that perhaps he had a hidden agenda all along—to marry a much younger woman he could presumably control with ease, not only keeping her barefoot and pregnant but stripped to the bare bones! Trust had become a battleground for both of us, with the enemy watching gleefully from the sidelines while we turned against each other, trading accusations instead of building each other up. Each grievance from our fights left us vulnerable to division and despair.

A TIME TO EMBRACE … OR NOT?!

Despite our constant quarrels, we still had some beautiful moments, which resulted in our second pregnancy. But even that, too, was threatened by mindless games! Ségun soon resumed his new habit of staying out late after our misunderstandings, and sometimes, he only returned in the morning for a change of clothes and left for work—only to repeat the cycle the next day. When this pattern of behavior began, I would stay up for him because I was worried sick. I pretended to be asleep when he finally got home and crawled into bed. I got fed up with this routine and couldn't stand that he felt it was ok to come and go as he pleased and not let me know where he was or how late he might be. So, anytime he returned, I ensured no one got any sleep! He subsequently moved to the guest room and now had the desired freedom.

I spent many nights alone, thinking about ways to break this reckless pattern of behavior. At one point, I even resorted to unconventional methods—like cutting off buttons from my husband's work shirts and pants—but that plan backfired spectacularly! I ended up spending hours painstakingly sewing every button back on, torn between guilt and amusement at how easily emotion can outsmart reason.

One day, I decided I'd had enough and locked him out of the house! I'm his wife, not his housekeeper—and most definitely not a *help meat* whose sole purpose is to meet his physical needs whenever he wishes! My emotions had gone wild on account of how insensitive he was to leave his pregnant wife and toddler all day and most nights. He thought he would stroll back into the house as usual but was shocked that I had bolted the front door. He rang the doorbell, knocked on the doors, and called my phone incessantly, but I refused to let him in. I got up early the following day to drop off our son at his daycare, and Ségun was home by the time I returned. He was packing some items of clothing and didn't speak to me until he left, but I wasn't bothered.

I was used to his late nights and disappearing acts, but I became a bit concerned this time when he didn't call after two days to check on our son, whom he was very fond of. Ségun was (and still is) an excellent father. He doted on our son, just like he did with me before all the madness started. I called his office pretending to be someone else, and they confirmed he was at work. So, I had established he was safe. His mom called that evening and asked if I knew where her son was and when I had last seen him. I told her honestly that I didn't know. She then asked if I thought my response was befitting of a good wife. She mentioned it was strange that I could stay at home seemingly unbothered, eating and sleeping, instead of actively search-ing for Ségun, starting with a call to her. Her words made it clear that she knew what hap-pened between us and where he was. I had nothing more to say and chose to let the situation unfold. And so began the waiting game!

Marriage, especially within the Christian faith, can be profoundly tested by hurt, pain, offense, anger, and a range of overwhelming emotions that can overshadow biblical principles, making it easy to forget the commitments made before God and each other. In difficult situ-ations, the natural tendency is for the core tenets of faith—meant to guide every action—to be set aside. Vulnerability often peaks in these times, leaving individuals feeling weak, suscep-tible, fearful, confused, exposed, or uncertain, yet this is also when the presence and support of a spouse is most critical. When difficulties arise, it is important to lean on God through faith rather than allow adversity and the adversary (satan) to drive a wedge between spouses.

All too often, this is where some husbands or wives give in, give up on each other, fight the hardest, or abandon ship entirely. Complexities and complications may emerge during these challenges, which understate the crucial role of a husband or helpmeet, especially when try-ing to understand the deeper needs within the relationship and how best to address the root causes of conflict. Through it all, God remains a loving and faithful Father. No trial or temp-tation is entirely unique; others have walked similar paths. God's presence is unwavering, offer-ing strength and guidance to navigate tests and hardships[2]—whether they arise as trials of faith, mistreatment by others, or spiritual challenges. He will never abandon His children or allow them to face more than His grace can sustain. Even when temptations feel overwhelm-ing, they are never insurmountable.[3] As Scripture assures, "... *but with the temptation he will also provide the way of escape, that you may be able to endure it*" (1 Cor. 10:13).

There has been a cultural shift in the way many Christians generally approach challenges, spiritual growth, and relationships, highlighting the need for a deeper reflection on how mod-ern Christianity may fail to recognize the importance of character development through real-life trials. Patience, resilience, endurance, and perseverance (P.R.E.P.) are virtues referenced throughout the Bible and emphasized in James 1:2-4, Galatians 5:22-23, and Deuteronomy 8:2-14. Yet, many believers seem to shy away from cultivating these qualities today. The con-cept of *P.R.E.P.* as God's prescribed tools for preparation and guidance through life's journeys has nearly disappeared from the awareness, understanding, and language of a growing num-ber of Christians, and it seems that some churches rarely teach or preach about them anymore.

---

2. 1 Cor. 10:13 (MSG)

3. Jer. 29:11-13; 2 Pet. 2:9; James 1:2-4

This underscores the disconnect between the biblical call to persevere through hardship and the current pop culture mindset that prioritizes immediate gratification or avoidance of difficulty, particularly in relationships and marriages.

These essential building blocks of Christian character, cultivated by the Holy Spirit and serving as evidence of God's work in our lives, are now viewed by many as outdated or even as signs of weakness. They are now being replaced with rigid "dealbreakers" and non-negotiable conditions that can be judgmental, subjective, unforgiving, and often rooted in pride and a vengeful spirit. As believers, we should encourage one another to embrace and emulate the qualities of Jesus Christ, who is both the Lion[4] and the Lamb,[5] rather than reject or shy away from these vital virtues. Jesus embodies the perfect balance of strength and humility, and we are called to reflect this in our own lives.

Furthermore, we must not delay in promptly returning the "product" to the "Manufacturer." While signing in one's spouse (through prayer) and listing all their faults or challenges encountered in the marriage, it may be worth asking for a self-evaluation form. You might just discover that you, too, could benefit from some fine-tuning or an upgrade! God designed or allowed trials and testing to prove our faith,[6] prune our character,[7] and perfect us into the image of Christ.[8]

Scripture tells us that Jesus does not give up on people just because they are weak; He loves and strengthens us when we are most undeserving.[9] We are called to love as Jesus loves[10] and forgive as He forgives[11]—embodying gentleness rather than harshness, unkindness, criticism, condemnation, or unforgiveness. Jesus' approach is to gently send the Gospel into hearts, accompanied by His mighty power. His light and comfort transform lives by enlightening understanding, softening wills, influencing decisions, and uplifting and redirecting affections from self-absorption to God and others. His Spirit and grace work powerfully from within us until completion—reflecting Christ's character and fulfilling His purposes in our lives. Partnering with God through faith, patience, obedience, and total reliance on Him—with absolute trust in His power—creates the right conditions in our hearts and fosters an atmosphere in our homes that can lead to the desired changes or outcomes in our marriages.[12]

---

4. Rev. 5:5-6

5. John 1:29

6. 1 Pet. 1:6-7

7. John 15:2

8. Deut. 8:2-14; James 1:2-4

9. Matt. 12:20

10. John 13:34-35; 1 John 4:16-19

11. Colossians 3:13

12. Heb. 6:10-12 (AMP)

HELPING WITHOUT HINDERING

I honestly believed that I was "helping" Ségun recognize what I perceived were potential risks looming around us. However, this had the opposite effect. He accused me of pontificating, constantly badgering him, being overbearing, and acting as an unsolicited "general overseer" or his spiritual monitor. He saw me as trying to dictate or interfere with his relationships and spiritual journey. The more I brought up unresolved issues for discussion, the more I was perceived as being overly controlling, intrusive, and judgmental. So, I left him to his devices, and he left me to mine.

Although I felt Ségun's excessive mistrust and suspicion of my motives were unfounded, I now understand that part of his resistance and distrust toward me might have stemmed from the fact that, up to that point, I had displayed a form of outward godliness (religion), that lacked the transformative power to change me and those around me.[13] Perhaps in his mind, he wondered what moral integrity I had to criticize or condemn someone else if I didn't have the reverential fear of God that could restrain me from acting out or compel me to at least do right despite his behavior and our quarrels, particularly in showing him respect. Behind closed doors, there wasn't any tangible perennial fruit or proof of who I claimed to be since I had continued to resist and defy the same truth I was preaching to him. Sadly, my conduct (so far) nullified my claim of faith![14]

If Ségun had reservations about my being a faithful Christian while we were dating because of some of the choices I made with him, perhaps he ruled it out completely soon after we got married![15] Submitting to and partnering with my husband became dependent on our circumstances and my emotions. I couldn't adhere fully to biblical standards because I didn't trust God enough to defer to my husband or adapt myself fully to him.[16] There were moments I didn't believe that God would fulfill His promises, and in some cases, I felt His timing was slow.[17] There was also little chance that biblical principles would win over my husband, since I became discouraged and stopped applying them when I didn't see immediate rewards or results. My behavior became more disrespectful,[18] and I definitely wasn't using many pleasant, gracious, salt-seasoned, soft, gentle, honeycombed words in all my conversations![19] During that period, all Ségun saw and heard was Funké and very little Christ. He often told me it wasn't what I said that really bothered him but the manner in which I said it. Maybe, just maybe, he

---

13. 2 Tim. 3:5
14. 2 Tim. 3:5 (AMP)
15. 1 John 2:4-6 (MSG)
16. 1 Peter 3:5b (NLT)
17. Col. 4:6
18. 1 Pet. 3:1-6 (AMP and MSG)
19. Col. 4:6

would have been more receptive to what I had to say, and I might have had more influence, if everything I did had been done in love.[20] But *full-time love* had become difficult … I had been madly in love with him, but now, I was just mad at him most of the time!

My love for God and Ségun was tested repeatedly. My choices, especially under pressure or impulsivity, became the real litmus test of my faith and commitment. They revealed far more about me than they did about Ségun or the challenges we faced—most notably, my level of submission and dependence on God. During this complex period, my primary assignment was to extend grace, as exemplified in John 8:3-11. Instead, I chose not to and justified my constant talking (correcting, nagging, complaining, and directing), ultimately missing the opportunity to reflect God's steadfast love, which has the power to guide us away from the wrong path, prevent poor choices, and lead us toward growth.[21]

Love should be expressed in ways that genuinely meet a partner's needs, not by projecting personal assumptions, interpretations, or catering to subjective desires and misconceptions. Meaningful love involves listening, observing, and responding to a partner's concerns. Open and consistent communication helps us understand our partner's emotional, mental, spiritual, and relational well-being, fostering deeper connection and understanding. The most effective way to achieve this is by seeking God's guidance—for He alone is omniscient and knows each of His creation perfectly. God's model of love emphasizes empathy, intentionality, and responsiveness, and is grounded in *agape* love—a love that transcends human logic and nurtures maturity and selflessness.

No human can love unreservedly and consistently this way without seeking God's wisdom, discernment, and strength through prayer—for it is only through Christ, who strengthens us, that we can do all things.[22] *"With man it is impossible, but not with God. For all things are possible with God."* (Mark 10:27) With God helping us, we have His ability to do His will—what His Word says we should do—even if it seems taxing, inconvenient, inconceivable, or too restrictive.

Of course, many wonderful marriages exist among couples who may not identify as Christians. Some people even follow God's principles unknowingly—living selflessly, lovingly, joyfully, and respectfully—treating one another with the same honor they desire for themselves (Eccles. 9:9 MSG). These principles are found in various cultures as moral guidelines. However, they lack the transformational power that only a genuine relationship with God through Jesus Christ can provide and sustain. While good morals can promote a happy relationship, true fulfillment comes when we surrender to the One who owns the principles and embodies perfect wisdom. Only then can we experience marriage as He designed it—vibrant, purposeful, and overflowing with grace.

---

20. 1 Cor. 16:14
21. James 5:19-20
22. Phil. 4:13

There's a deeper dimension available to those who go directly to the Designer of marriage Himself, seeking His thoughts and plans for lasting success. You haven't truly lived until you've experienced what He has prepared for you (John 10:10-11). God desires that we live life to the fullest—including in our marriages—not just the way we think we should, but the way He intended from the beginning.

Merely practicing Christian principles in isolation from God can lead to frustration and burnout when faced with trials—hence the "giving up" phase husbands and wives experience in their marriages. Simply following moral guidelines to the best of one's ability has many limitations in terms of wholeness,[23] depth,[24] vision,[25] and truth[26] and is devoid of the power[27] which only their Source—God through the Holy Spirit—can provide, sustain, and amplify. The Bible consistently calls believers to embrace the entirety of the Gospel without compromise, which includes the complete message of salvation, sanctification, and God's eternal plan. Only God can effectively transform the inner person, aligning actions with a renewed mind and heart that consistently seek to please Him, even in challenging situations.[28] True Christianity is not about following rules but being connected to God, who provides the power to live fully and faithfully in every area of our lives—even our marriages.[29]

When I eventually decided to pray, I realized my prayers were futile because my motives were wrong, and my heart wasn't in the right place.[30] Through timely and effective prayer, I could have, at least, minimized the influence of the tempter and played an active role in de-escalating our conflicts, quickly diffusing the tension in our home, and closing the growing rift between us. Instead, I was driven by anxiety and fear—of the unknown, impending doom and gloom, feeling unprepared, rejection, or being trapped in a failed marriage. I even feared facing consequences or punishment for having "eating the forbidden fruit"—a case, I, not God, kept open.[31] The Bible teaches that there's no room for fear in love, and well-developed love drives out fear.[32] It felt as though fear had paralyzed me, leaving me unable to operate in faith, peace, and trust, or to express "agape love"—the unconditional love God first showed us.

I believed that acting or reacting any other way than I did meant that I was endorsing, condoning, or approving the things Ségun was doing at the time. The last thing I wanted was a

---

23. Ezek. 36:26-27

24. Acts 17:28

25. Prov. 3:5-7

26. John 14:6

27. Acts 1:8; Eph. 1:19-20; John 14:26

28. Ps. 51:10; Phil. 2:13

29. Matt. 28:19; Acts 20:27; Gal. 1:8-9; Col. 1:25-27; 1 Cor. 15:1-4; 2 Tim. 3:16-17

30. James 4:3-4

31. Rom. 8:1

32. 1 John 4:18-19

marriage of convenience like the ones rapidly growing in our society. My whole being rejected that idea, and it showed. I didn't realize that loving my husband despite his shortcomings was far more powerful than any strategy I could have devised.[33]

> *"So, as God's own chosen people, who are holy [set apart, sanctified for His purpose] and well-beloved [by God Himself], put on a heart of compassion, kindness, humility, gentleness, and patience [which has the power to endure whatever injustice or unpleasantness comes, with good temper]; bearing graciously with one another, and willingly forgiving each other if one has a cause for complaint against another; just as the Lord has forgiven you, so should you forgive. Beyond all these things put on and wrap yourselves in [unselfish] love, which is the perfect bond of unity [for everything is bound together in agreement when each one seeks the best for others]. Let the peace of Christ [the inner calm of one who walks daily with Him] be the controlling factor in your hearts [deciding and settling questions that arise]. To this peace indeed you were called as members in one body [of believers]. And be thankful [to God always]."* (Col. 3:12-15 AMP)

Extending grace in strained relationships is a true mark of maturity. It does not mean one is excusing, encouraging, or enabling wrongdoing or mistakes. It's not giving permission to be hurt or mistreated by others. Grace can transform by offering love and support even amid flaws, gently guiding individuals toward repentance and a renewed way of life.[34] While grace doesn't guarantee reconciliation in marriage—since free will is exercised in responding to grace—it gives access to God's intervention. Grace enables divine action to preserve and protect as one aligns with His will. It fosters an environment where prayers can be effective[35] and God's Word can grow and transform the situation. Trusting in God's power and timing allows grace to support both parties through the storm, even when complete reconciliation between the husband and wife might not occur or might be delayed. It helps one discover, obey, and trust God's greater plan rather than relying solely on human effort for restoration and healing in relationships or life situations.

Like prayer, the effectiveness of the Word of God in a person's life is influenced by their faith,[36] as well as how its teachings are applied and practiced,[37] in alignment with God's purpose.[37] Have you ever paused to reflect on whether you truly believe God's Word is real and

---

33. Ps. 114:1-2; Eph. 2:8-9; Titus 2:11-12

34. Rom. 2:4; 2 Pet. 3:9

35. Mal. 2:13-17

36. Heb. 4:2

37. James 4:3

trustworthy—not just a collection of inspiring stories but a living truth that works in our lives?[38] Following Abraham's example, are we fully convinced of God's promises, or do we find it easier to accept modern-day voices—such as relationship experts, influencers, love gurus, horoscopes, psychics, or even reality TV shows—for guidance? What settled truths from God's Word do we carry with us to keep ourselves and our families steady when life feels chaotic?[39] What principles do we rely on to sustain and guide us when our faith is tested?

I've had to wrestle with these questions, especially during storms when I felt tempted to seek stability elsewhere. Taking time to reflect on foundational beliefs can help prepare for life's uncertainties. It's not a matter of *if* challenges will arise, but *when*. Anchoring in the Word equips us to face those moments with faith, clarity, and resilience rather than being caught off guard or swept away by inevitable storms.

THROUGH SÉGUN'S LENSES

We almost did not need a reason to start raising our voices, but the arguments began coming thick and fast at some point. We had to involve our parents at different times when we could not make headway in resolving things by ourselves. Their interventions did not help as their advice, no matter how sensible or well-intentioned, barely scratched the surface of the problem. The tension in our home did not dissipate but was buried under words of encouragement or anecdotes from parents until they resurfaced, sometimes with even greater fury.

After a while, I began staying out late, hoping that Funké would be in bed by the time I returned home. This went on for a while, during which communications between us were minimal and, at best, superficial. The mere fact that I was staying out late inevitably compounded an already tense situation on the home front, but by that stage I wanted to spend as little time as possible in Funké's company. It was clear that while unhealed wounds were festering, with each passing day, each of us was digging our heels even deeper into the ground, believing—indeed, convinced—that we were the wronged party. Nature truly abhors a vacuum, and with each lost opportunity to sit down together to speak frankly about what was going on, we were making it even more inevitable that something eventually had to give.

On returning home one night, I discovered that Funké had cut off the top buttons

---

38. Luke 6:46-49 (MSG)
39. Ps. 119:9-12 (TPT)

of the dress shirts I wore to work. Anyone who has watched the film *Waiting to Exhale* will probably be thinking of the iconic scene where Bernadine Harris, played by the legendary Angela Bassett, after learning about the infidelity of her husband of 32 years, empties the entirety of his possessions in their walk-in wardrobe into one of his cars and sets it ablaze. I should consider myself fortunate that my belongings did not meet a similar fate!

When things got to a head, I moved out of the house, convinced that was the best course of action to allow things to simmer down. Although the thought of being away from our young son made it a particularly agonizing decision, I felt that I had no choice under the circumstances. The problem with my decision is that leaving my marital home had set the precedent as an option for conflict resolution.

Hearing Funké accuse me of treating her like a piece of property and relegating her to the background of our marriage was particularly hard to swallow. Although I did my best to take it in my stride, it got to me after a while as I saw it as a staggering indictment of everything I stood for and my qualities as a husband. No matter how often I tried to see things from her perspective, it seemed as if nothing I could do or say would satisfy her. Her reactions were usually so extreme when trying to talk things through with her that it looked like she had erected a mental barrier I could not penetrate. That was the excuse I needed to withdraw into my shell, whereas I should have spent more time trying to see things from Funké's perspective and making any necessary adjustments.

Rearview Mirror Lesson

Men will always find reasons to justify unjustifiable behavior, but no such reasons exist. Admittedly, Funké's behavior and utterances in the build-up to our separation often left me dumbfounded and hurt. Still, it is clear to me that God (instead of family members, friends, counselors, etc.) should have been our first port of call when things started to get out of hand. However, prayer was the last thing on my mind because we had relegated it to the background and were both operating from a place of frustration, pain, and anger. Getting into the habit of praying regularly with Funké would have been the surest way of avoiding a situation where prayer was not even an option when difficulties arose.

Who knows whether inviting God into our marital crisis would have helped us avoid a separation or one that lasted so long? But I don't see how it could have worsened the situation. My wedding vows presupposed a willingness to go over and beyond in ensuring that I did not fan any flames of discord—but instead to do everything possible to extinguish them.

4

And the Two Became Two

"So they are no longer two but one flesh.
What therefore God has joined together, let not man separate."

MATTHEW 19:6

JOY AND PAIN

A few months before the birth of our second son, Ségun returned home after moving out for about three months. He had imposed this extreme measure following the incident where I locked him out of the house due to his late nights and my uncertainty about where he was or whom he was with. I later discovered from receipts that he was camped in a nearby hotel. This was, by far, the most heartless thing Ségun had ever done—not just to me, but to our son and the baby we were expecting. The man who returned that day was unrecognizable; his eyes, devoid of emotion, looked straight through me when our gazes accidentally met. I tried to get him to talk to me, but he seemed intent on quickly gathering more clothes and whatever else he needed, as though he couldn't leave fast enough.

In a desperate, on-the-spot attempt to make him stay, I told him I had attempted suicide while he was away and threatened to do so if he ever deserted the three of us or left us stranded again. It was a warped attempt at emotional blackmail, hoping to rekindle the love he once had for me. But I was met with cold indifference instead of the expected empathy. Ségun drove me straight to my mother's house, leaving me there overnight so she could "talk some sense into me and straighten me out." It was yet another glaring sign that he no longer saw me as his responsibility—or his problem.

My mother knew me well enough to understand that it was a childish attempt at attention-seeking. Still, a twisted version of the story was relayed to other parties, and blame was swiftly apportioned to me for making Ségun disengage from me emotionally and physically. They concluded that I deserved everything I was going through and what I got in return. Even if I was indeed on the verge of depression, was his treatment the cure? The signs of where my marriage was heading were already clear, but I was reluctant to acknowledge them. I felt helpless, unsure of how to undo or change the negative trajectory that had been set. At least the threat of me harming myself got him to move back home for a while. Perhaps he did it so his conscience would not have to bear the guilt of having caused injury or death to someone. Soon enough, he resumed his late nights, which I reckoned was to get back at me for putting a dampener on his plans.

I still don't know how I survived that period due to the misery and strain I endured physically and mentally. I was hospitalized for exhaustion and severe weight loss for a few days, and after I was discharged from the hospital, I didn't get much support. Although my mother lived just twenty minutes away, she had to help me recuperate remotely to the best of her ability so she wouldn't be accused of "invading" our home. She arranged for a chef who had been with her family for decades to help with meal prep. There were noticeable disparities, such as some family members feeling more welcome and at ease than others in our marital home.

I was encouraged to focus on the baby and told to try to be happy in order not to give birth to a colicky newborn because babies sense their mother's moods. Although that's largely regarded as an old wives' tale, it's worth noting that expectant mothers should be mindful of stress, as scientific research suggests a connection between high levels of prolonged maternal stress or anxiety during pregnancy and infant temperament or physiological development due to stress hormones like cortisol crossing the placenta.[1] So, putting the welfare of our baby first, I tried my best to embrace joy by immersing myself in uplifting activities like listening to inspirational music and journaling with a focus on gratitude. These practices helped me maintain an optimistic outlook and emotional balance.

Things gradually started to improve between Ségun and me as he began to stay home more and soften toward me. I later learned that he wanted me to travel abroad for a comprehensive medical checkup given the difficulties that accompanied my pregnancy, resulting in hospitalization, and to give birth to our second son before returning to Nigeria. We had done this for our first child, and to be honest, it was the best decision because both pregnancies were

---

1. Anna-Lean Zietlow et al., "Emotional Stress During Pregnancy – Associations With Maternal Anxiety Disorders, Infant Cortisol Reactivity, and Mother–Child Interaction at Pre-school Age," *Frontiers in Psychology* (2019): https://www.frontiersin.org/articles/10.3389/fpsyg.2019.02179/full;

Nicole R. Bush et al., "Effects of Pre- and Postnatal Maternal Stress on Infant Temperament and Autonomic Nervous System Reactivity and Regulation in a Diverse, Low-Income Population," *Development and Psychopathology* 29, no. 5 (2017): 1553-71, https://doi.org/10.1017/S0954579417001237.

classified as "high-risk." I vehemently refused his plan this time. I felt it was a cunning plot to get me out of the way so he could get on with his other life without his conscience weighing on him…basically, to have more freedom to do as he pleased.

I strongly resisted as he made plans and sought the help of my friends and family to persuade me to travel. Eventually, I agreed, but only on the condition that our son would accompany me. I wasn't comfortable leaving him in the care of others, particularly those who had caused me pain and whose feelings toward me had been less than kind. After a lot of to-ing and fro-ing, Ségun finally agreed at the last minute, and I secretly hoped the airline would turn me back for not being fit to travel. But God had other plans. We arrived safely and were looked after by wonderful family-friends and a community of "angels" God had prepared for me. It was a time of proper rest, rejuvenation, and deep thinking, which I desperately needed. I was homesick and felt an intense longing for my husband, but the time apart helped me reconnect with God and take my mind off some of our problems.

Ségun came to visit us but was distant and distracted throughout his stay. We put up a convincing united-and-happy-family front before our hosts and everyone around us. He appeared to be merely fulfilling obligations and was in a hurry to leave. I understood he had work to get back to, but I didn't believe he could only get a week off on leave to be with his family, especially as he now had a more senior role and competent colleagues who could step in while he was away. I asked him to extend his stay by a few days so I could get some sleep while he helped with our older son, but he only offered to take him back to Nigeria. That was completely out of the question!

After his departure for Lagos, I would cry myself to sleep almost every night and struggle to take care of an energetic toddler and an infant who was eating practically 24/7. The baby weighed 8 lb., which is significant in relation to my small frame, and after cleaning out every morsel of food in my womb, he still came out eating like he had been starved for nine months! The resilient Nigerian in me wouldn't admit that I was going through postpartum depression (PPD), which was compounded by all the unresolved issues between Ségun and me. There were moments when I literally thought I was losing my mind, but I knew I had to be strong for myself and our children…and prepare for the battles I anticipated were awaiting me on my return home. I had started praying more consistently and felt God's overwhelming peace around me. I found strength through the prayers of the wonderful family and friends who stood in the gap for me.

I am eternally grateful to my host family for their love and support. Although they had no clue about what was happening on my home front, as medical professionals, they had the presence of mind and generosity of spirit to recognize that an urgent intervention was required. Despite their busy schedules, the entire family went above and beyond to ensure I got the rest I needed by babysitting my sons, constantly checking up on me, and catering to our every need. I was able to shorten my recovery time, schedule my post-delivery checkup for Lagos, and convince Ségun that I was ready to come home early once it was safe for our baby to travel.

FEELING ENCIRCLED

When I returned home to Nigeria, it seemed like Ségun was playing out a particular script. His actions appeared calculated—some felt like setups, provocations, and subtle tests designed to get a reaction from me. Unfortunately, I played into his hands many times. My emotions would get the better of me, and instead of holding my peace as the Bible encourages in Exodus 14:14, I reacted predictably. All Ségun had to do was press the right buttons, and I would explode—releasing a barrage of hurtful words. Anger became my default defense, but instead of resolving issues, it only deepened the rift between us.

> *"The wise woman builds her house [on a foundation of godly precepts, and her household thrives], But the foolish one [who lacks spiritual insight] tears it down with her own hands [by ignoring godly principles]."* (Prov. 14:1 AMP)

I kept falling into the trap of the "enemy," and Ségun didn't show much restraint either in the face of provocation. He, too, could be scathing with his words, so we both used our "swords" to cut each other down instead of building and lifting each other up.[2] The more we spoke negatively to and about each other, the more those things manifested in our lives and home because of the authority our words wield. We unwittingly agreed to uproot, tear down, and destroy rather than plant and build.[3] *"Fools have short fuses and explode all too quickly; the prudent quietly shrug off insults."* (Prov. 12:16 MSG)

Ségun appeared to be ticking off my misdemeanors on his checklist until he had enough to justify getting me to leave our home of my own volition. He began making this demand more frequently after a particular intervention by our fathers to diffuse the situation following a blowout at our home, after which Ségun decided he would move out. During a private discussion they had with Ségun that day, which I overheard, his father advised against his leaving and suggested that I should go to my mother's house temporarily for the sake of peace. My father approached it from a "men will be men" angle and, in a nutshell, told Ségun to do what he wanted to do without hurting his daughter or jeopardizing our marriage. Neither of us left the house that night as our fathers eventually got us to sheath our swords.

While our respective fathers had good intentions, their proposed solutions seemed more focused on prioritizing and protecting their own child. They echoed the deep-rooted beliefs

---

2. Prov. 18:20-21
3. Jer. 1:10; Eph. 6:10

and age-old practices in our profoundly patriarchal society, where giving the upper hand to husbands takes precedence over fairness for both parties. This vicious cycle continues to this day! Male camaraderie was on full display in our home on that occasion, and it definitely felt like a gang-up against me! Condoning and excusing bad behavior among men in such an unfair manner is prevalent in certain cultures. However, it doesn't make it right or easier for wives, marriages, or even the men themselves.

I wasn't prepared to leave our home, and no one or nothing would force me out! So Ségun returned to the guest room and stopped eating the food I painstakingly prepared while looking after a baby and a toddler. He casually displayed ready-made meals, which he stored in our freezer. I had a strong feeling about where they had come from, but I chose not to make a big fuss about it. Perhaps you're reading this and wondering if I'm a good cook. (For the record, Ségun and my growing food fan club still shower me with compliments!) You might also question why I would be bothered by my husband shunning my cooking—it should have been a welcome relief amidst all the stress I was experiencing. So, what's the big deal if he suddenly preferred eating out, buying takeaways, or having someone else cook for him?

In Nigerian culture, a husband's refusal to eat his wife's food is often viewed as an insult or as a subtle way to express mistrust, dissatisfaction, anger, or displeasure—whether about unresolved issues or the overall state of their relationship. This refusal might sometimes arise from fear of perceived harm or danger in extreme cases. The act is deeply rooted in cultural norms, societal values, and expectations, as food is not just a necessity but also carries emotional, social, and relational significance in most Nigerian homes. It symbolizes love, nurturing, care, respect, tradition, and a wife's dedication to her role as a homemaker. Such actions are rarely taken lightly and may lead to serious discussions, interventions, or mediation by family elders and clergy to address underlying problems. We had already exhausted all these avenues of conflict resolution without achieving positive outcomes. I believe this was Ségun's way of creating emotional and physical distance, as he appeared determined to pursue the separation he desired.

I'm not sure this kind of "boycott" still works or holds the same weight in Nigerian households these days. From what I hear, the new-generation wife doesn't tolerate that anymore. *You're either hungry, or you're not! Enough with the innuendos and petty theatrics; let's have an honest conversation*—that's the response I imagine a modern wife would give. It was an extremely painful situation back then, especially considering who I believed was behind the cooked meals Ségun brought into our home and ate in front of me. I felt humiliated and deeply betrayed, like everyone had let me down. It seemed like everything was stacked against me, and my mind started racing with all kinds of worst-case scenarios. How did I end up in this situation? I couldn't understand how anyone—especially my beloved husband—could turn against me like that. What did I do to deserve such disregard, disrespect, and rejection? It felt like a concerted effort to get rid of me. Honestly, it was one of the most challenging times in my life because I felt completely unprotected, having never witnessed or experienced anything like that before.

SPROUTING TREE

I began taking my relationship with God and my prayer life more seriously while paying closer attention to what was going on around me; after all, as Proverbs 27:12 (NLT) states, *"A prudent person foresees danger and takes precautions. The simpleton goes blindly on and suffers the consequences."* I no longer took Ségun's threats of separation lightly and decided to hope for the best but prepare for the worst. Instead of merely drifting along and waiting for Ségun's designated "judgment day," I viewed this period as the wake-up call I needed and an opportunity to set the stage for positive and lasting changes.

During our second pregnancy, I realized that my eagerness to return to work was unrealistic and decided it would be better to wait until our second son started daycare at eighteen months, as his older brother had done. He was still under one year old, and I considered resuming my computer programming course and French classes, but no one needed to tell me it was time to begin searching for a job. Thankfully, within a few weeks, I found the perfect job with great hours that would allow me time for my children . . . and husband.

Getting a job without Ségun's knowledge or assistance made me feel independent. It boosted my confidence that I could handle a lot on my own through God's grace. Ségun had many reasons to say it wasn't a good idea, that the timing was wrong, and that I hadn't thought things through—especially about our children. But I had. We would have had to adjust our schedules, but nothing major, and I would have been the main person affected. My work hours were perfect, so I'd always be home on time. I made a temporary arrangement with my mother, who lived nearby. She was happy for me to drop off our eight-month-old baby before I went to work, and she also agreed to do the afternoon school runs for our older son. Both children would be fed and bathed by the time I picked them up at 4 p.m., making bedtime prep much easier.

It was no longer enough to be just Ségun's wife and a mother of two, which was a blessing, but there was so much more to me. I was tired of having every day of my life determined by the whims and caprices of my husband. After all, I have a purpose and a destiny to fulfill, just like him. Why should my life be put on hold to support or pave the way for his dreams and vision when we could both work toward our goals simultaneously? We could grow side by side while each of us contributed to building our home. We were meant to complement each other, but this wasn't the case back then.

Although Ségun wasn't pleased to find out about the job after the fact, I had made my decision. The circumstances at the time didn't allow for regular or normal communication, and there were now more glaring signs of our disconnect. I didn't know where this new path would lead me, but I knew I could trust God. He is not a God of confusion but of peace, clarity, and order, so I believed He would guide me through the uncertainty ahead. It was an unusual kind of courage I had this time—it wasn't defiance, but a sense of urgency and a belief that I need not worry or fear. I knew my Heavenly Father cared about even the smallest details of my life.[4] I threw myself into work, our children, church, and spending more time with my mother. I had made up my mind and now braced myself with bated breath, anticipating Ségun's next move. In the meantime, I was going to enjoy the fresh air!

THROUGH SÉGUN'S LENSES

By the time I moved out of our home for the second time, I had concluded that my marriage was over even though Funké was pregnant with our second child. I could not see how we could resolve our differences and had dug in my heels. Apart from the fact that I felt a physical separation was in both our interests at that time, given how unstable our relationship had become, I also wanted to send a clear message to Funké, who did not want to contemplate the possibility of divorce whenever I raised the subject.

On this occasion, I was away for about three months, during which I stayed at a hotel relatively close to our home. Although I returned periodically to visit our son and went to the office from the hotel, I ensured that Funké did not know where I was.

One afternoon, I stumbled on a group of beauty pageant contestants staying at the hotel for a camp ahead of a competition. I struck up a conversation with one of them. We met up for dinner at the end of the competition, which resulted in me being unfaithful to Funké, something that just a few weeks earlier I could never have imagined, despite my marital problems. I felt a deep sense of guilt and shame but justified my actions to myself by heaping the blame on Funké, having been told that my professed love for her was a counterfeit. As far as I was concerned, she had pushed me and disrespected me to a point where my only options were to walk away from the marriage or to stay as things went from bad to worse and hope for the best. I made the wrong decision on that night at the hotel, although it was only much later that the harmful domino effect of my infidelity on my family and me—which many husbands either ignore or trivialize—became more obvious.

I ended the relationship with the person in question soon afterward, but the damage was done. I had broken a vow I had made with Funké and God on my wedding

---

4. Matt. 10:30-31

day. 1 Corinthians 6:19-20 asks, *"Do you not know that your bodies are temples of the Holy Spirit, who is in you, whom you have received from God? You are not your own; you were bought at a price. Therefore honor God with your bodies."*

When I returned home, I felt even more disconnected from Funké. I was angry about my infidelity, which I kept to myself. However, I was angrier toward her as she did not appear to know or care about the toll our differences had begun to take on me. It became difficult for me to bear as when we aired our grievances, the focus was almost always on her feelings and how I could not dictate how she should feel, regardless of my intentions.

In truth, I was neither oblivious of nor indifferent toward significant factors such as her pregnancy at the time that perhaps should have changed my decision to move out of the house or at least made me consider delaying it. However, our relationship had deteriorated to such an extent that that was not an option when I considered possible outcomes if things continued to go downhill. More importantly, I saw her behavior as a continuation of worrisome traits that I had pointed out to her early into our marriage and described as a bee in her bonnet that she couldn't shake off. My inability to reach her, particularly given what I was getting back from her in return, slowly but surely eroded my willingness to keep trying. It was at that point that I should have sought God's guidance, but instead I stubbornly kept allowing myself to be led by what I considered to be appropriate behavior.

Even when third parties tried to mediate, I felt that not even those I confided in could fully understand what it was like living with someone who was telling me that my best was not good enough. Although the birth of our second son in September 2002 ushered in an improvement in our relationship, it did not last for long. The wall between Funké and me kept getting higher, given the ineffectiveness of the tools we used to try to dismantle it.

Rearview Mirror Lesson

I knew I was making a huge decision when I left my home and moved to the hotel. However, I didn't realize just how slippery a slope I was climbing. By stating publicly that my marriage was on the rocks, I gave the enemy an entry point into our marriage through the power of the tongue and my negative confessions.

Although it felt liberating being away from Funké and the unbearable atmosphere at home, I ended up putting myself in a spiritual straitjacket through a combination of my actions and inactions. This undoubtedly contributed enormously to our subsequent six-and-a-half-year separation and set the stage for a longer extra-marital relationship I entered a few years into that separation.

Once the door to infidelity is cracked open just a touch, there is the danger of it being flung wide open. Of course, this comes with a myriad of attendant consequences and risks, hence the importance of resisting temptation and not succumbing to the urge to normalize infidelity on an individual or societal level.

By not using prayer to fortify my home, I allowed my loose words to replace God's Word, and words carry enormous weight. James 3:4-6 (NIV) says, *"Or take ships as an example. Although they are so large and are driven by strong winds, they are steered by a very small rudder wherever the pilot wants to go. Likewise, the tongue is a small part of the body, but it makes great boasts. Consider what a great forest is set on fire by a small spark."*

Each negative declaration I made over my marriage in exasperation as I responded to the outward signs that Funké and I had serious problems in our relationship was tantamount to starting and pouring accelerant on a forest fire. Instead of focusing on signs of wear and tear, I should have taken a close look at the foundation of my marriage from the first signs of conflict. After all, Psalm 127:1 clearly states that *"Unless the Lord builds the house, the builders labor in vain,"* highlighting the importance of relying on God to fortify the foundation of relationships such as marriage.

5

Carnal Weapons of Fiery Prophylactics

"For though we walk in the flesh, we do not war according to the flesh. For the weapons of our warfare are not carnal but mighty in God for pulling down strongholds, casting down arguments and every high thing that exalts itself against the knowledge of God, bringing every thought into captivity to the obedience of Christ."

2 CORINTHIANS 10:3-5

RAGE LEADS TO HARM

We've all probably heard the saying, "Hell hath no fury like a woman scorned!" While this may hold some truth, not every scorned woman reacts in the same way. Various factors influence how people respond to emotional pain, and many do so in unconventional ways. If you've never experienced the anguish of a broken heart, it's wise to withhold judgment on how others cope with such pain. Many people assume that crimes of passion happen in moments of uncontrollable rage, but the reality is often a gradual buildup of emotions that lead to the event. The deeper the love, the greater the pain when trust is broken or feelings are betrayed.

One particular week during our first five years of marriage still stands out as the "breaking point." Our constant arguments, fights, and suspicions—whether justified or not—led me to assume the fictional roles of Inspector Clouseau and prospector Yosemite Sam. I was determined to uncover the truth behind the unusual developments in our marriage and the furtive actions of my husband. The more I searched, the more "evidence" I uncovered. I used every available opportunity to work with my "tools" (codes, passwords, phone recorders, and even a long umbrella to pry open locked suitcases) to confirm my suspicions. However, I hadn't anticipated the deep pain the whole "investigation" would trigger. Then, one day, I struck "gold": boxes of condoms hidden in a locked suitcase! I couldn't believe my luck! Fueled by blind rage and already fragile emotions, I impulsively grabbed hot sauce from the refrigerator and a syringe we used as a medicine dispenser for our younger son. I planned to discreetly inject every sachet of condoms in that suitcase with some spicy "flavor"!

Thankfully, as I devised my plan, I had the presence of mind to call my mother and tell her what I was about to do. She tried to talk me out of executing my so-called masterstroke, but I could barely hear her words through my uncontrollable wailing. I was sprawled on the kitchen floor, like the lead actress in a classic "heartbreak" or "jilted lover" scene from a Nollywood (Nigeria's equivalent of Hollywood) movie. Tired of being told that my mind was playing tricks on me and feeling utterly foolish, I resolved that now was the time to claim my pound of flesh—literally!

My mother tried to reason with me, offering absurd and downright funny explanations for my husband's hidden stash of condoms: "Maybe he wanted to give them away at a friend's stag party!" or "He might have planted them there because he knows you snoop!" She blamed negative influences around Ségun but ultimately tried to comfort me, saying, "At least he's protecting you too." We both knew there was no way to put a positive spin on this discovery, but my mother did her best to get me out of the dark hole I was spiraling into. Known for her no-nonsense yet gracious nature, she began to pray for me and reminded me of Ségun's positive traits before our quarrels began. "This just isn't his character. . . . Something is amiss," she insisted.

I had a few "scorned women" in my circle at the time—some well-meaning but ready to support my "mission," even sourcing and dropping off Carolina reaper peppers (one of the world's hottest peppers) at my home that morning. Fortunately, I called my mother first! The importance of having the right people in your corner—especially in desperate moments—cannot be overemphasized. So, choose your inner circle wisely. While we often instinctively seek human advice before turning to God, developing intimacy with Him ensures He's our first resort.

I yielded to frantic pleas to stand down that day, averting a potential major incident. I didn't want to break my mother's heart or make her worry over what could have transpired between Ségun and me when he returned home. I'm sure I must have scared her with my pre-fight trash-talk as I painted a vivid picture of what I was preparing to do to him! But what quelled the fire was the deployment of the correct "weapons," and I couldn't resist God's superior power (grace), which constrained me and repelled the real enemy of my home.[1] My revenge formula that day was a *condom-hot-sauce-combo knockout punch,* but there were other occasions on which I felt like grabbing items around the house to use as projectiles in a bid to "warn" my husband when he suddenly started returning home in the wee hours of the morning, uncharacteristically reeking of the typical "club smell" or that fresh *straight-out-of-a-shower-he-did-not-take-at-home* fragrance! That's a perfect setup for an "accident" or disaster waiting to happen!

The problems in our marriage did not begin with infidelity, but it later became a corrosive component of it. I didn't realize it then, but bit by bit, I was feeding fat on deep hurt, anger, rejection, betrayal, discontentment, resentment, and frustration—inadvertently allowing other people's actions to bring out the worst in me. The "evidence" was mounting—real and imagined! I had secretly gathered phone records, audio recordings, transcripts from phone conversations, receipts, text messages, etc. I didn't let Ségun know about these things, but I kept feeding my negative emotions, and my appetite for revenge grew daily. These revelations brought to the fore already emotionally charged issues that we frequently suppressed or ignored during our temporary ceasefires. I became increasingly confrontational and combat-ready—everything seemed to set me off, driving us further apart.

Untamed emotions can have devastating consequences if left unchecked. There are heartbreaking cases of people using everyday items like boiling water, piping hot food, or even chemicals as weapons against their partners, leaving behind not only physical scars but also irreversible harm or even loss of life. Some incidents escalate even further, tragically spilling over into violence against entire families, all stemming from a "love gone wrong." It's sobering to think that many of these tragedies could be prevented if people approached relationships and breakups with more kindness and empathy and sought timely and targeted interventions, and if communities—including families, churches, coworkers, and schools—paid closer attention to those showing signs of emotional distress. Some investigations reveal that many acts of violence are not spur-of-the-moment decisions but carefully thought-out plans, rationalized by the perpetrator long before they're carried out. Such actions may grow from toxic emotions that fester and spiral into uncontrollable rage, which eventually leads to devastating outcomes.

Self-preservation often plays a significant role in these situations. This instinct can fuel constructive or harmful responses, depending on the circumstances and triggers. In some situations, these reactions are reflexive, especially when individuals seek to protect themselves from real or imagined harm, danger, or emotional distress. These responses include fight, flight, freeze, appease, and avoidance, depending on the perceived threat or stress.

---

1. John 10:10-11

When self-preservation instincts take a harmful turn, they can be interpreted in different ways. Some people might view these behaviors as signs of inherent evil, while others dismiss them as character flaws such as selfishness, vindictiveness, or cruelty. Others might see them as deeper issues rooted in past trauma or underlying mental health conditions, especially when examined through a psychological lens. Negative responses or threats that pose a danger to oneself or others should not be trivialized or ignored, as they can be complex and may require professional help or intervention.

Beyond the factors mentioned, people sometimes resort to extreme acts of violence against a spouse or partner due to a lack of effective conflict resolution skills. Intense emotional impulses or outbursts—triggered by loss, pain, fear, feelings of betrayal, rejection, abandonment, humiliation, injustice, or a perceived need to reclaim respect, establish self-worth, or assert control—can show up in harmful ways, especially when someone feels profoundly hurt or betrayed. Even passive self-preservation responses, like detachment, can cause as much damage as more aggressive behaviors. They shut down communication, weaken intimacy, and create a gap for emotional disconnection to take root and grow unchecked. Healthy relationships thrive on trust, intimacy, honest communication through active listening, and a willingness to confront uncomfortable emotions rather than avoiding or passively expressing them.

COOL YOUR PIPES!

"Understand this, my beloved brothers and sisters. Let everyone be quick to hear [be a careful, thoughtful listener], slow to speak [a speaker of carefully chosen words and], slow to anger [patient, reflective, forgiving]; for the [resentful, deep-seated] anger of man does not produce the righteousness of God [that standard of behavior which He requires from us]." (James 1:19-20 AMP)

Hurting others out of personal pain is counterproductive. Life can get better even if a marriage or relationship doesn't work out. Night always makes way for a new day. Avoid self-sabotage before the sun rises. One should focus on maintaining and promoting overall well-being through mindful intentions and actions. This can be supported by prayers and grace, which provide guidance through difficult or unpleasant situations. Giving in or partnering with dark thoughts or pent-up negative emotions for revenge may lead to long-term regret and leave a trail of destruction.

Anyone experiencing deep emotional hurt of any kind should seek support at the first signs of anger, bitterness, or resentment toward others—it's a sign of strength, not weakness. Walking away from clear and present danger during a marital crisis is better than causing harm or being harmed while trying to "make things work." Sometimes, mutually agreed, planned, and purposeful time apart may be necessary temporarily while seeking effective interventions. Having the proper resources, the right people, and access to timely, practical guidance is crucial when facing dire situations and deep hurts.

On the day of my great testing, I turned to the right person—my beloved mother—who helped me see reason by speaking wisdom and clarity into my life. I can't imagine the repercussions if I had carried out those "stinking thinking" plans that day. Perhaps the least harmful outcome would have been my "victims" dancing the *electric boogaloo* for a few hours, which they'd probably never forget! But, in the worst-case scenario, the whole episode could have led to my arrest and charges brought against me for causing grievous bodily harm. This is in no way justifying, trivializing, condoning, or making excuses for acts of violence and infidelity in any shape or form, but unfortunately, such things happen more often than one would imagine. It's no laughing matter as the consequences of impulsive reactions can be costly— jail time, a criminal record, loss of child custody, significant changes in family dynamics and friendships, or even the death of a spouse. Moreover, God's plan for "new beginnings" could be unknowingly hindered.

It was only several years into our separation that, with the benefit of hindsight, I began to see beyond those boxes of condoms and everything they represented. I understood that the dangerous combination of our vulnerabilities—especially when facing constant temptations, our need for validation, and any strain in the marriage—and the sideling of God to the background could potentially ruin lives and relationships. All it takes is a door or window left ajar or even a tiny crack in the protective spiritual hedge around the home. In Ephesians 4:26-27 (TPT), we are admonished not to let *"the passion of (our) emotions lead (us) to sin"* and not to let *"anger control (us) or be fuel for revenge, not for even a day."* We are further cautioned, *"Don't give the slanderous accuser, the devil, an opportunity to manipulate (us)!"*

The Bible instructs us to guard our hearts and to focus our minds on what is true, noble, pure, lovely, admirable, and praiseworthy (Phil. 4:8). This passage urges us to protect our inner thoughts and concentrate on God's truth. Guarding our hearts means being intentional about what influences our actions and decisions. Fixing our minds on positive, godly things helps us grow spiritually, align with God's will, and find peace amid life's challenges. Rather than use this as a "filtration system," I spent many lonely days and nights while my husband was away, imagining negative scenarios, nurturing and amplifying unhealthy emotions, and writing horror movie scripts about my marriage. An idle mind, lacking the mindset of Jesus Christ, can become the devil's workshop. *"In your relationships with one another, have the same mindset as Christ Jesus."* (Phil. 2:5 NIV)

Having the right support system or relationships can profoundly influence decisions, especially during tough times. I've personally experienced this over the years through family, a small circle of friends, connections within my church community, and more recently through regular, deep-dive conversations over tea, coffee, meals, follow-up phone calls, and intentional prayers of agreement. I've also prioritized connections with trusted girlfriends who share my faith, values, and beliefs. It's truly a blessing to share mutual support, encouragement, and accountability as we navigate life together. Experiencing a marital crisis can create a void within and around a person. God never intended for us to do life alone; He sets the lonely in families.[2]

We should encourage more open conversations and understanding within our communities to create safe spaces where people can freely share their experiences or stresses—especially in more conservative or closed cultures. It's also important to strike a healthy balance between seeking support and relying excessively on therapy, which seems to have become prevalent in some Western societies. This trend appears to hurriedly label issues as mental health challenges, sometimes overlooking other factors that may contribute to an individual's struggles. In some instances, this approach can exacerbate problems, particularly when it leads to the prescribing of unnecessary, sometimes life-altering medication without fully exploring alternative solutions that target the root causes. When seeking help, interventions, or solutions, we should thoughtfully do so through prayer and independent research. And remember, "Quick fixes won't stick; they're just a trick—they patch up the cracks but never fix the brick™"!

There are many proven and reliable methods, acceptable to God, for resolving conflicts and marital challenges, each with His guarantee of success when applied correctly. Ecclesiastes 3:1-7 reminds us that *"There's an opportune time to do things, a right time for everything on the earth."* The Bible is rich with depictions of various times and seasons...a time to plant, harvest, speak up,[3] be silent, engage, confront,[4] wage war, make peace, intervene,[5] forgive,[6] embrace, mend, weep, laugh, heal, love, walk away,[7] and be still and wait on the Lord's guidance.[8] The key is discerning what is needed in each moment through humility, earnest prayer,[9] skillful and godly wisdom,[10] direction from the Word of God,[11] leading of the Holy Spirit,[12] and good counsel.[13] The outcome may not always align with our expectations or occur within our preferred timelines, but God can be trusted to always come through. His wisdom is infallible, and His ways are always for our good, even if we don't immediately see the results we desire.

---

2. Ps. 68:6
3. Eph. 4:29
4. Matt. 18:15
5. Prov. 31:8-9
6. Matt. 6:14-15
7. Prov. 22:24-25 (TPT)
8. Ps. 46:10
9. James 5:16
10. Prov. 2:3-6
11. Ps. 119:105
12. John 14:26; Rom. 8:14
13. Prov. 24:6

I learned many lessons the hard way through my own missteps and found myself on the receiving end of the same "seeds"—love, grace, mercy, compassion, patience, and forgiveness—that I had sown sparingly in my marriage. In my case, I hadn't consistently nurtured those "seeds" or protected them enough to let them take root, grow steadily, and eventually produce the desired harvest. In hindsight, I admit that there were times I uprooted budding shoots prematurely and even crushed the fragile fruits that had barely begun to ripen. My impatience and lack of trust in the process often sabotaged the very outcomes I longed for, leaving me with regret, although I learned many valuable lessons along the way. Ségun and I did our best, but each person's efforts were put into doing it "my" way, not God's, which led us through very challenging circumstances and trying times. But for God's amazing grace and mercy, there wouldn't have been a "comeback story" to tell!

My experiences have taught me to dig deeper and look beyond myself, isolated events, or temporary circumstances to understand the bigger picture. God sometimes reveals the "secret things" to us—such as extra-marital affairs, addictions, debts, fears, vulnerabilities, temptations, and more—so we can pray and take the right steps in helping each other, not use them as weapons to hurt, mock, or whip our spouse into shape! God brings certain things to light to draw our attention to issues that could have grave consequences for all concerned parties if left unchecked. Trust God to lead and direct you into all truth (His truth), and when He does, *"Don't jump to conclusions—there may be a perfectly good explanation for what you just saw"* (Prov. 25:8 MSG).

The Scripture provides perspective, wisdom, direction, and much more to live joyfully, successfully, and with fulfillment in every area—including marriage. It is heartbreaking to see married couples endure unnecessary detours and setbacks despite their hopes and efforts, often delaying or even preventing the fulfillment of their deepest desires. This happens when we take our eyes off God's standards and focus on the changing demands or expectations of the people and the world around us. Unrealistic portrayals of marriage can distract us and tempt us to seek validation or solutions outside of God's will. A Christ-centered marriage is built on the eternal truths of Scripture, which is a living guide for growth, healing, and purpose in the union.

THE HEART OF THE MATTER
MAY BE A MATTER OF THE HEART

Proverbs 4:23 (NLT)—*"Guard your heart above all else, for it determines the course of your life"*—gives us insight into how the condition of the heart (such as personal motivations, desires, love, peace, pride, forgiveness, and bitterness) can influence the way we navigate life, including challenges and experiences. A heart consumed by frustration, unforgiveness, or hatred can lead to a path marked by resentment or conflict. Imagine the toll on a person's life when these destructive emotions dictate their actions and relationships. The Bible encourages Christians to forgive as it is integral to living out faith and reflecting Christlikeness.

Forgiveness is not merely a suggestion or advice but a clear expectation for believers. Jesus explicitly teaches this in passages like Matthew 6:14-15 and Ephesians 4:32. It's a deeply personal act of obedience to God that frees us emotionally and spiritually, allowing God to work on our behalf. While forgiveness doesn't guarantee repentance from the offender, it aligns individuals with God's grace, which offers salvation to everyone.[14] Fundamentally, the work of God's grace takes place within our hearts, and whenever grace is allowed to flourish, visible spiritual evidence eventually appears.

Forgiveness is a decision, not a drawn-out process. This is where grace intervenes, accomplishing what the wounded heart resists and the mind deems impossible. For grace to work, it's vital to let go of self-righteousness and approach situations with humility and compassion, particularly when provoked, offended, or faced with adversity. Brothers and sisters, let's step down from our sanctimonious high horses! Romans 3:23 reminds us of our shared imperfection: *"All have sinned and fall short of God's glorious standard."* Mercy, therefore, is not just a duty but a gift that benefits both the giver and receiver—a pure reflection of God's grace. God is merciful and delights in extending mercy to all. No one is beyond His reach or redemption. Our actions in difficult times reveal whether our hearts align with God's.

Matthew 5:43-48 emphasizes the importance of loving others, even those who oppose or mistreat us, just as God loves everyone impartially. Believers are called to live out their God-identity[15] by being generous and gracious, reflecting His boundless love. Beauty can arise from the ashes of life through love, grace, and forgiveness.[16] Embodying God's mercy enables individuals to become vessels of His redemptive power in relationships, marriages, and communities. According to biblical principles, seeking forgiveness requires extending forgiveness to others. Similarly, to experience love, one must demonstrate love to others.

The principle of reaping what is sown applies across all beliefs, whether rooted in faith in God, the universe, karma, or the concept of nemesis. What goes around comes around. Sowing sparingly (casually, carelessly, flippantly, heedlessly, indifferently, selfishly, thoughtlessly), rather than intentionally, results in a meager harvest.[17] Conversely, sowing generously into a spouse and marriage yields an abundant harvest, and the grass is indeed greener where it is watered. Although, sometimes, the full harvest or reward may be laid up in Heaven!

People often wonder why the burden of forgiveness seems to fall on the wronged party, and I frequently hear this from women. In marriage, the responsibility for initiating forgiveness

---

14. Titus 2:6-11
15. 2 Pet. 1:3-4
16. Isa. 61:3
17. 2 Cor. 9:6-11

or reconciliation isn't solely on the wife or the husband but on the individual whose heart is yielded toward God or whose attention He captures. God partners with the willing—the person attuned to His voice and committed to pleasing Him above "self," emotions, and the offense. Interestingly, women are more often in this position, showing a greater willingness to forgive and seek reconciliation than men in similar scenarios of marital conflict. This trend can be partly explained by cultural, social, spiritual, and psychological factors, as well as by inherent differences in how women and men approach faith, relationships, and community. This observation—supported by research and studies, including the Pew Research Center (2016), the World Values Survey, and Oxford Studies on Gender and Spirituality—shows that women make up a higher percentage of worshipers across most religions and tend to adhere to godly principles, faith-based practices such as regular prayer, and participating in spiritual activities. These patterns suggest that women are often more inclined toward self-reflection, emotional resilience, and seeking resolution through faith.

Historically, many cultures have assigned women the roles of caregivers, nurturers, and peacemakers in the family. This continuous conditioning of women and interpretations of biblical concepts such as the *"wise woman builds her home or family"* (Prov. 14:1) probably explain why some societies tend to view wives as the "marriage fixers" when marital conflict arises. While these factors highlight the influence women can have within their families as the "emotional backbone," they can also be used to further entrench this widely held belief that women hold the primary responsibility for the success or failure of a household—especially when it comes to maintaining and repairing relationships.

This expectation to "make the marriage work" often falls disproportionately on women across many cultures, placing them under immense and unfair pressure, especially in societies where divorce or marital failure carries significant stigma. Consequently, women may begin to prioritize the family's stability over their own well-being, enduring hardship or neglect to "save" the marriage. Frustration, resentment, emotional exhaustion, and a sense of helplessness can develop when wives feel solely responsible for outcomes beyond their control. These feelings may intensify when husbands refuse to seek joint solutions or interventions for their problems, causing many wives to resort to self-help or dispense with help entirely.

It isn't God's plan for women to shoulder the weight of marital crises alone[18] or feel boxed in by societal demands and expectations. So, our starting point in addressing such a crisis is to return to His original design. Marriage is a partnership with shared responsibility. It isn't just an agreement between a husband and a wife but also a spiritual bond with God, who is an active witness and participant in the relationship.[19] He is not just an overseer but central to

---

18. Ps. 55:22
19. Mal. 2:14-15

the covenant of marriage, which is two becoming one with the Father.[20] In Ephesians 5:31-32, Apostle Paul compares marriage to the relationship between Christ and His Church. He highlights mutual submission out of reverence for Christ, God's love, and unity with His people. Ecclesiastes 4:12—*"a cord of three strands is not quickly broken"*—is often interpreted to highlight the strength of a marriage when God is included as the third strand, which reinforces the relationship between husband and wife.

Rediscovering Ecclesiastes 4:9-12 in this season of my marriage was liberating as it reminded me about the power of partnering with God. If one strand unravels itself from the cord, at least the remaining two strands are still much stronger—*"But he who is joined to the Lord becomes one spirit with him"* (1 Cor. 6:17). In my view, the broader war against the unfair burdens often placed on wives begins with victories in smaller, more personal battles within their immediate sphere of influence. Just like my experience during our marital crisis, some people lose focus by becoming fixated on fighting against the tide, ultimately losing the battle right on their own turf. Victory is achieved by focusing on God, who provides the strategy for winning the war, rather than being overwhelmed by the magnitude of the problem.

Some battles require riding the tide and weathering the storm, anchoring firmly in wisdom and faith in Jesus—our firm foundation—until the tide turns. At other times, the solution may be speaking directly to the storm: *"Peace, be still."* Seeking God's plan in every situation is important. As a loving Father, He has equipped His children to live godly lives and face life's challenges.[21] Numerous biblical examples highlight how listening to and following God's instructions leads to success. In various situations, God directs His people to wait, stand still, stand firm, hold their position, or reflect on His works and commands. (See Numbers 9:8; 1 Samuel 12:16; Exodus 14:13; 2 Chronicles 20:17.)

Ephesians 6:10-18 emphasizes the reality of spiritual warfare, revealing the true nature of the battles we face and identifying the real enemy—evil forces, not human adversaries or physical opponents. It explains the need for spiritual preparedness by putting on God's full armor, equipping us to stand firm against the enemy's schemes with truth (the Word of God), righteousness, faith, salvation, peace, and prayer—all while relying on Him for the victory He has already ordained.

God has assured us of overwhelming victory through Christ, who loves us.[22] He has also provided endless grace to strengthen us in every situation, enabling us to persevere and triumph. This doesn't mean we simply accept or settle for everything life throws at us. Instead, we are empowered to overcome and thrive in our unique circumstances by clearly understanding the Word of God and skillfully using it as a roadmap to navigate life effectively.

---

20. Gen. 2:24

21. Phil. 4:13; 2 Pet. 1:2-4

22. Rom. 8:37

Throughout our journey, I discovered that some of the most unfair, unpleasant, and seemingly nightmarish situations became my greatest seasons of growth and transformation. These experiences shape us as we are properly postured *(in heart, attitude, and approach exemplified by faith, humility, obedience, and openness)* and positioned *(spiritually, mentally, and physically in alignment or preparedness demonstrated by focus, clarity, and resilience)* to fulfill God's purpose. *"Consider it a sheer gift, friends, when tests and challenges come at you from all sides. You know that under pressure, your faith-life is forced into the open and shows its true colors. So don't try to get out of anything prematurely. Let it do its work so you become mature and well-developed, not deficient in any way."* (James 1:2-4 MSG)

KNOWING GOD ... ARMED TO DO EXPLOITS

"... but the people who know their God shall be strong, and carry out great exploits."
(Dan. 11:32b)

While Jesus walked the earth, His strength also manifested through meekness—a quality that seemed unassuming to many. Meekness is not weakness; it is strength under control, a defining trait of Jesus Christ that both men and women are called to embody. It reflects power, humility, and reliance on God rather than self. The Bible describes a woman's strength as multifaceted,[23] deeply rooted in her faith in God. She is wise, humble, patient, kind, resilient, courageous, protective, and nurturing. She leads with love, firmly anchored in confidence in God's promises. A woman's meekness reflects Christ's gentle and humble heart[24]—a quiet yet powerful testimony of her faith and dependence on God.

Beyond mere influence or persuasion, many Christian women, especially those shaped by societal limitations, remain unaware of their spiritual power and authority through their identity in Christ and the transformative power of the Holy Spirit.[25] This divine empowerment enables women to confront challenges boldly, speak life into situations, and stand firm in faith, not by their strength, but through God's grace and provision. A woman's most authentic self (identity), effective authority, and strength are found in God. It is essential to remain consistently rooted and grounded in God's truth rather than second-hand interpretations, cultural dictates, or ever-changing societal expectations.

On the other hand, women in less traditional settings or restrictive environments who embrace more egalitarian principles may tend to grapple with finding the right balance between embodying the Lion (strength, boldness, and authority) and the Lamb (meekness, gentleness,

---

23. Prov. 31:10-31

24. 1 Pet. 3:4-6

25. Luke 10:19; Eph. 1:18-19; 2 Tim. 1:7

humility, and sacrificial love), qualities that Christ exemplifies in perfect harmony.[26] Maintaining this delicate balance is essential for all God's people as they navigate life's challenges and relationships while striving to reflect Christ's character.

The first step in achieving this is answering the same question Jesus asked the disciples about their understanding of His identity. This underscores the importance of personal revelation and faith in recognizing who Jesus Christ is. The full context is found in Matthew 16:13-20 where Jesus asks, *"Who do people say that the Son of Man is?"* and then directs the question more personally to His disciple: *"But who do you say that I am?"* Peter then responds with the famous declaration: *"You are the Christ, the Son of the living God."* And Jesus answered him, *"Blessed are you, Simon Bar-Jonah! For flesh and blood has not revealed this to you, but my Father who is in heaven."* So, who do you say He is? Savior, Lord, Master, Deliverer, Confidant, Friend, Helper, Healer, Provider, Miracle Worker, Way Maker, Good Shepherd...?

Next is to get (re-)acquainted with Jesus—*"... learn from me, for I am gentle and lowly in heart, and you will find rest for your souls"* (Matt. 11:29). God wants believers to grow in the grace and knowledge of the Lord and Savior, Jesus Christ (2 Pet. 3:18). This knowledge fortifies faith, ensuring its effectiveness and fruitfulness. It cultivates strength, progress, and impactful actions while preventing misinterpretations or misapplications of God's Word which can lead to missteps. In Hosea 4:6, God rebukes the Israelites for their lack of knowledge and rejection of His law. The priests, who were responsible for teaching the people, had failed in their duty, leading to widespread ignorance and disobedience. True faith in Jesus requires knowing Him and understanding God's will. Without faith, it is impossible to please God.

Human knowledge—whether gained through intellect, experience, education, or observation is inherently limited. In contrast, revelational knowledge, revealed through the Holy Spirit, is powerful, transformative, and life-giving. It enlightens our understanding, disciplines our desires, and equips us to respond with wisdom rather than impulse. Knowing who we are in Christ and what He requires of us keeps our flesh in check—especially when we're tempted to reach for physical or carnal solutions to fight spiritual battles. True victory begins not with what we can reason or resist in our own strength, but with what we receive through divine revelation and surrender.

As Scripture reminds us, *"His divine power has granted to us all things that pertain to life and godliness, through the knowledge of him who called us to his own glory and excellence, by which he has granted to us his precious and very great promises, so that through them you may become partakers of the divine nature, having escaped from the corruption that is in the world because of sinful desire."* (2 Pet. 1:3-4)

---

26. Rev. 5:5-12

THROUGH SÉGUN'S LENSES

Contrary to what Funké thought then, my intention on the occasions I moved out of our home was not to punish her or exact revenge. Instead, it was primarily to ensure that things did not escalate out of control when our discussions became heated. Some might argue that it would have been easier to seek help or go our separate ways. We had done the former to various degrees without much success, but the fact that we still loved each other, despite our differences, prevented the latter.

At various times in the build-up to our lengthy separation, there were temporary improvements in our attempts at communicating with one another. This included what I believe were sincere apologies from both of us and a commitment to turn a new leaf. However, it was clear that the lines of communication had become badly frayed, and we would quickly return to our default settings, taking up position behind the battle lines we had drawn. The consequences of this reared their heads in different ways. For example, we would withdraw into our shells, making meaningful communication impossible. Also, opportunities for intimacy were often rebuffed by Funké saying that because women are more emotional than men, they are slower at re-engaging sexually after significant disagreements. This exacerbated feelings of rejection and detachment.

Although in my quiet moments, I gave considerable thought to Funké's criticisms regarding the primary role she attributed to me in our seemingly unending turmoil, the deck was stacked against me. It was as if she was pursuing a vendetta against me for offenses I had not committed. While I could have handled situations differently, she appeared incapable of recognizing and admitting the part she was playing in creating dysfunctionality in our home. In her eyes, everything was my fault and I did not appreciate her. Listening to her constantly and scathingly mislabel and mischaracterize me was painful, resulting in exasperation and despair.

For years, I felt like I was banging my head against a brick wall with Funké, trying to show her that I loved her deeply and proving that her misconceptions and incorrect assumptions resulted in wrong conclusions. Having a strong personality does not make one a tyrant. Wanting to protect a woman one loves does not make one a manipulator or a control freak. Responding to verbal attacks does not make one an aggressor. Not breaking down in tears during disagreements on sensitive topics does not make one stony-hearted.

It was as if Funké couldn't or wouldn't see beyond what she wanted to believe and that she had totally absolved herself of any blame for our problems. This alienated me to the point where I did not think it was healthy for us to stay together. Instead of drawing her closer, I convinced myself that she was the problem and distanced myself even further from her, thereby making the situation even worse.

Rearview Mirror Lesson

We did the most significant damage to our relationship when we saw each other as the aggrieved party and responded accordingly. As we let our pride take over, we erected stockades around our respective positions and narratives, removing any hope for conflict resolution. Proverbs 11:2 (NIV) says, *"When pride comes, then comes disgrace, but with humility comes wisdom,"* while Proverbs 15:33 says, *"The fear of the LORD is the instruction of wisdom, and before honor is humility."* My refusal to humble myself before God was one of the biggest impediments to peace in our home. The constant pursuit of my own agenda and doing things my way simply exposed the extent of my limited understanding, thereby replacing godly wisdom.

6

A House Divided Against Itself

"But Jesus knew their thoughts, and said to them:
'Every kingdom divided against itself is brought to desolation,
and every city or house divided against itself will not stand.'"

MATTHEW 12:25

SPLINTERED BY FEUDING

There's no mystery or magic about marriage; it's an age-old institution, and indeed, there's nothing new under the sun.[1] You don't need a spiritual awakening to recognize the common issues that plague relationships or marriages. A weak link in a chain will eventually cause it to break, and a single crack in a building's foundation can bring down the entire structure. Likewise, what affects one partner in a marriage inevitably impacts the other and the relationship as a whole.

The real challenge usually lies in recognizing the common enemy and determining whether both parties are willing and able to address the root cause of their marital problems rather than blaming or turning on each other. The fight isn't one individual versus a spouse but a battle against harmful influences and intrusions—such as negative mindsets, external pressures, distractions, and temptations—that both have allowed to infiltrate their marriage.

The challenges that arise in marriages often reflect the choices couples make and reveal the foundations on which they build their family. A house devoid of solid pillars, such as guiding

---

1. Eccles. 1:9

principles, a clear roadmap, and the foundation of God's Word, is destined to collapse. As Christians, we are called to a higher standard or building code, and our mark of distinction is God's love, which transcends human love. This love shapes our way of life, and it motivates us to live in constant readiness, not choosing who deserves it or when to reflect Christ's character. Lest we forget, we're enlisted for active duty—full-time ambassadors of God's love and grace, committed to faithfully representing Him, whether it's convenient or not.

The situation in our home continued to deteriorate, and Ségun's interactions with me grew more volatile. It seemed like a morphed extension of his role as an investment banker was now spilling over into our marriage. Ségun has always been determined, goal-oriented, and confident when pursuing specific objectives, but during this period, his approach became increasingly forceful and overbearing. While his strategies might have achieved the desired results at work, I was determined they would not be tested or tolerated on the home front. I was naturally headstrong at the time, and I felt his behavior was an attempt to dominate or control me, so I put up strong resistance.

In no time, my husband switched from the affectionate man I had been enamored with to a stranger actively striving to "manage" me as decisively as he would his clients' investments. He did this with the same careful planning, logic, and decision-making processes he used at work. Consequently, out went my Ségun, and in came this unrecognizable, controlling, calculating, and transactional boardroom executive who barely demonstrated warmth or emotional flexibility.

Although Ségun was awarded a "Cambridge Blue"—a prestigious award for representing his university in boxing—he was not violent by nature. So, he appeared to have resorted to playing hardball instead by attempting to break my strong will and force me back to the negotiating table to accept his "deal" on his terms, which is often misrepresented and conflated as "biblical submission,"[2] particularly in African marriages.

The situation worsened when he adopted other tactics such as withholding critical support and restricting access to information—which was now only on a need-to-know basis. Yet, he was sharing details about me and our marriage with his family. This created room for scrutiny and fault-finding, allowing third parties to critique or undermine my decisions, making me feel vulnerable, insecure, and inadequate. Those I perceived as potential strong influences on him or differing voices were brought into my emotional and physical space, creating an environment of interactions that made me feel uneasy and less valued in my role and our relationship.

Other hostile takeover strategies that emerged further down this rabbit hole included imposing deadlines (creating pressure to force me to make quick decisions or concessions about moving out of our home), walking away from negotiations (implementing a temporary break that

---

2. Eph. 5:22-25

generated uncertainty and confusion, possibly aiming to force me into a "brain reset"), and finally, resorting to legal threats (pursuing the termination of our marriage contract and other legal maneuvers such as seeking sole custody of our children).

I had overlooked some warning signs when Ségun and I were dating, which were now unfolding in our marriage. He generally had a gentle demeanor and kept his cool 99.8 percent of the time. However, when provoked, wronged, or mistreated, Ségun's response could be fierce, hardline, relentless, and almost impossible to stop … like a pit bull! He would cling to his position, fighting back with unwavering determination, and wouldn't let go until he had asserted his point or achieved retribution. I witnessed this behavior only twice during our five years of dating.

Although I can't recall details of the first incident because it's been over twenty years, I remember being attracted to the intensity and passion Ségun showed while defending his stance, especially on matters of principle. Even now, my husband's doggedness, unwavering nature, and tenacity in pursuit of what he believes is right remain strong qualities. These traits can be admirable when used positively, but in our marriage, they sometimes turned into a battle of wills that left little room for compromise. It became clear that these same qualities, when left unchecked, could either strengthen or strain our relationship, depending on how they were expressed.

The second time I experienced this, I was on the receiving end. Ségun insisted that I take my wedding outfit to show his mother, a request I found unnecessary and a bit odd, so I refused. I had already shared photos from the boutique's brochure, which I believed was sufficient to ensure my wedding dress met her approval. I also wanted to keep the element of surprise, following wedding tradition where the groom or his family doesn't see the dress until the big day. What started as a minor disagreement quickly escalated into a major argument, and he stopped speaking to me for a while. He even went so far as to threaten to call off the wedding unless I gave in. Up to that point, we'd never had a real argument, so his intense reaction shook me. It seemed like an overreaction to something that should have been a non-issue.

Another concern I had early in our relationship was the sense of "conditional love" he expressed, which he presented as an all-or-nothing offer with no middle ground—for example, *"Dating without sex would be pointless."* I brushed it off as his expression of passion and devotion to me and accepted it, not expecting such ultimatums to come up again later in our marriage. Romans 5:8-11 reminds us of God's beautiful, holy love, which isn't based on impossible standards. We are blessed with this love simply because of who God is and what He has done for us, not because of who we are or anything we could ever do for Him.

Worldly love can often be conditional, self-serving, or limited by emotions and circumstances. In contrast, as described in 1 Corinthians 13:4-7, God's love (agape love) is sacrificial, enduring, and even offered to the undeserving. His love can never be earned or fully deserved—it is truly unconditional. Jesus commands us to love one another with this same divine love. As 1 Corinthians 16:13-14 (MSG) urges, *"Keep your eyes open, hold tight to your convictions, give it all you've got, be resolute, and love without stopping."*

Instead of succumbing to the mounting pressure, I started to give as good as I got. It didn't take long before our relationship turned into a game of tit-for-tat, where rights, privileges, and even core Christian virtues like mutual respect, kindness, patience, and gentleness were withheld or limited to punish or gain an advantage over each other. Looking back—and I'm not proud of it—my husband couldn't always count on a home-cooked meal; the menu usually reflected the severity of his "offense," which, on a bad day, meant nothing was prepared. This was my passive-aggressive way of making a point! Plus, it didn't help that he had found a way to spite me by bringing prepared meals for himself into our home, which further "justified" and reinforced my actions.

From then on, our young marriage resembled scenes from *Mr. and Mrs. Smith,* Doug Liman's action-comedy. I watched the movie later in 2005 and couldn't believe how eerily similar the dynamics between the lead characters were to ours! In the film, Brad Pitt and Angelina Jolie play a married couple stuck in a love-hate relationship, and while secretly working as assassins, they are hired to kill each other. The key difference was that Ségun and I were inadvertently working for the same adversary,[3] but thankfully, we could impose boundaries on our actions—to a certain extent. Instead of building our love and nurturing our bond, we unfortunately poured our energy into attacking each other, leaving little room for growth or healing. We were so caught up with tearing down our marriage that it never had a chance to get off the ground. Instead of protecting and supporting each other, we weaponized our knowledge of each other's weaknesses—exploiting fears and emotions in ways that only deepened the divide.

Here is an inexhaustible list of ineffective methods we adopted in trying to "resolve" our marital issues:

1. Missile mouth

My biggest struggle at the time was my habit of expressing my "freedom of speech" in harsh, unfiltered, and unapologetic ways. I made sarcastic comments, snide remarks, and cutting retorts at the slightest provocation. Once triggered, my words turned into heat-seeking missiles, and sadly, my husband was often the primary target of my verbal warfare.

Growing up, I was encouraged to speak up for myself, and I naturally became the self-appointed spokesperson and liaison officer in "Dad-relations" after my parents' separation. Most of the time, I got away with being vocal about frustrations, perceived injustices, or unfairness that I or others close to me experienced. However, my outspokenness was kept in check

---

3. John 10:10

by stern warnings and my grandmother's "old-fashioned," yet effective, disciplinary methods of that era! Looking back, I can admit that it was borderline rudeness, and to Ségun, this behavior was completely unacceptable—honestly, he wasn't wrong! Though often rooted in fearlessness, irritation, conviction, passion, discontent, or a sense of urgency, outspokenness can be valuable when used constructively to address complex or taboo topics people ordinarily shy away from.

Impact: Unfortunately, my boldness didn't always land well. Early in our marriage, my unfiltered way of communicating caused tension and, on many occasions, unnecessarily escalated arguments as words have power. The wrong choice of words can kill a conversation before it starts. Some can extinguish the promise of God over their spouse or marriage with utterances like, *"Oh…he or she can never change; this marriage is doomed!"*

- *"A soft and gentle and thoughtful answer turns away wrath, But harsh and painful and careless words stir up anger."* (Prov. 15:1 AMP)

- *"Whoever guards his mouth preserves his life; he who opens wide his lips comes to ruin."* (Prov. 13:3)

- *"Gracious words are like a honeycomb, sweetness to the soul and health to the body."* (Prov. 16:24)

- *"Death and life are in the power of the tongue, and those who love it will eat its fruits."* (Prov. 18:21)

- *"So also the tongue is a small member, yet it boasts of great things. How great a forest is set ablaze by such a small fire! And the tongue is a fire, a world of unrighteousness. The tongue is set among our members, staining the whole body, setting on fire the entire course of life, and set on fire by hell."* (James 3:5-6)

2. Stonewalling (emotional withdrawal, avoidance, or detachment)

This became our go-to strategy for avoiding confrontation. Instead of engaging in conversation, one of us (the aggrieved party) would withdraw emotionally (usually me) or physically leave (Ségun)—refusing to express feelings or show emotional sensitivity and vulnerability. Remaining silent, changing the subject, or walking out during heated discussions were some of the methods we employed as a defense mechanism to de-escalate tense situations. I felt my husband used it more to exert control and avoid accountability.

Impact: Stonewalling created distance between us and often left unresolved issues simmering beneath the surface, preventing any chance of resolution. This led to a breakdown in communication and trust in our relationship. The effects were far-reaching, evoking feelings of abandonment, neglect, resentment, and emotional disconnection.

- *"Be angry and do not sin; do not let the sun go down on your anger, and give no opportunity to the devil."* (Eph. 4:26-27)

3. Silent treatment

Another favorite "weapon" was the silent treatment. It was deliberate, manipulative, and punitive. We could go on for long periods without speaking to each other, and if one of us needed to bring something to the other's attention, we would text or leave Post-it notes. It sounds ridiculous, but we really did it! I would sulk for days, withholding affection or attention as a passive way to punish or control my husband after feeling hurt or betrayed.

Impact: This passive-aggressive behavior led to feelings of frustration and emotional disconnection, weakening the bond between Ségun and me. This response to conflicts in our marriage created a cold, hostile atmosphere—which sometimes left Ségun confused and frustrated because he couldn't predict my triggers or mood. It deepened emotional wounds for both of us.

- *"If a fellow believer hurts you, go and tell him—work it out between the two of you."* (Matt. 18:15 MSG; see vs. 15-20 for context)

4. Revenge-seeking or retaliation

We acted in ways meant to "get even" with each other, trying to inflict the same pain we felt the other person had caused. Ségun and I failed to defend or protect each other, often airing our grievances to third parties to justify our actions or present ourselves in a more favorable light.

Impact: This reaction can escalate conflicts, deepen resentment, and cause irreparable harm to any relationship. The cycle of retaliation gradually erodes mutual respect, trust, and loyalty, creating a toxic environment. Ségun and I frequently heard exaggerated and fabricated stories about each other from family and friends—accounts that originated from personal details we had shared but had subsequently been twisted into something unrecognizable, similar to the Chinese whispers effect. As I learned, words are powerful and potentially dangerous; they tear down much faster than they build up. One of my husband's main grievances was that I was deliberately vilifying him. I felt the same way, too, about him. Perhaps while that was never our intention, once our words were spoken, we could no longer control how they were perceived or where they might lead.

In the heat of seeking revenge, some people go as far as spreading rumors or engaging in extramarital affairs as a way of numbing their emotional pain or causing similar hurt to their spouse. Even after forgiveness and reconciliation, these actions can leave scars that might last a lifetime. A single "slip-up"—a moment of weakness leading to a one-night stand or repeated acts of indiscretion fueled by anger, lust, loneliness, unmet needs, or desire for payback—can trigger a chain reaction with far-reaching effects. Marital turmoil often exposes or accentuates vulnerabilities, leaving people tempted to seek comfort or happiness elsewhere—in the arms of a substitute.

Some may excuse these actions as accidents, acts of desperation, or set-ups by the enemy during moments of profound weakness, but the consequences remain deeply painful for the spouse on the receiving end. These choices can lead to a variety of complications: unplanned or unwanted pregnancies, children knowingly or unknowingly passed off to the wrong fathers, dealing with baby mama or baby daddy dramas, STDs, scandals, blackmail, and lifelong entanglements that no one anticipates when acting out of hurt, frustration, or other untamed emotions.

- *"You shall not take vengeance or bear a grudge against the sons of your own people, but you shall love your neighbor as yourself: I am the Lord."* (Lev. 19:18)

- *"Do not repay evil with evil or insult with insult. On the contrary, repay evil with blessing, because to this you were called so that you may inherit a blessing."* (1 Pet. 3:9 NIV)

- *"Run away from sexual immorality [in any form, whether thought or behavior, whether visual or written]. Every other sin that a man commits is outside the body, but the one who is sexually immoral sins against his own body. Do you not know that your body is a temple of the Holy Spirit who is within you, whom you have [received as a gift] from God, and that you are not your own [property]? You were bought with a price [you were actually purchased with the precious blood of Jesus and made His own]. So then, honor and glorify God with your body."* (1 Cor. 6:18-20 AMP)

5. Deliberate or unintentional financial manipulation or control

From the early stages of our marriage, my inability to work due to difficult pregnancies meant I couldn't contribute financially to our household. This left me in the dark concerning our finances, as open discussions, suggestions, or questions about money often led to disagreements. My husband's reactions during these conversations made me hesitant to pursue them further. I resorted to maintaining the status quo to avoid being perceived as materialistic, a spendthrift, or unqualified to dispense financial advice. At the time, I didn't realize this could be a potential sticking point in the future, nor did I see how it might contribute to a growing disconnect in our partnership, particularly in trust, communication, and shared decision-making.

Impact: I left my job about a year after we got married due to a difficult pregnancy with our first child. Ségun was doing well in his career, which enabled us to maintain a stable, comfortable standard of living. I didn't return to paid employment until 2003 when our second child was eight months old, during the fifth year of our marriage. By then, the atmosphere in our home had become tense and difficult. Returning to work became necessary as I faced a precarious financial situation. The more conflicts we had, the clearer it became that I had left myself financially vulnerable. Without my own income, I felt stripped of independence, unable to make money-related decisions or access resources without permission from my husband.

I felt helpless, embarrassed, and frustrated as my self-worth diminished over time. I couldn't manage our home, get my hair done, or buy anything for myself without informing my husband. This arrangement was far from ideal and nothing like what I envisioned for our marriage. Growing up, I had taken pride in being a good steward of money. From the age of eleven, I learned to manage my allowances wisely while at boarding school.

During my college years, I consistently demonstrated strong money management skills, often being the only one among my friends with savings or who didn't need to call home for extra cash—or even airfare back home at the end of the semester. Of course, those savings didn't last forever. I eventually "ate" them, along with anything I made from holiday jobs, relied entirely on my folks for support, and didn't consider clever ways to hustle or make a little extra on the side—lesson learned the hard (and laughably humbling) way! I went into marriage practically broke, and by the time my NYSC stipend came through, it was next to nothing.

I hadn't given my husband any reason to distrust me with money, so I consoled myself by concluding that his behavior must come from his own issues rather than anything I had done. However, this created an unhealthy dependency that left me feeling emotionally insecure and anxious about my future. I often worried about how I would cope if he were stranded abroad, decided to leave me, or followed through on his escalating threats to force me out of our home. Over time, this situation eroded my self-confidence and trust in Ségun and heightened my resentment and distress. I felt undervalued and disconnected from my husband, more so because intimacy was now nonexistent.

I married relatively young—just after finishing my first degree from university, while many of my contemporaries pursued advanced studies. When I shared the news of Ségun's marriage proposal with my father, he expressed concern, because it seemed at odds with the goals and aspirations I often discussed with him. He was particularly worried about Ségun's push to marry immediately after I completed my degree. We had been dating for five years, and I felt it would be unfair to make him wait even a moment longer; we were also both eager to make it official. In hindsight, I believe my father foresaw some of the challenges that might arise, but I was too caught up in the excitement of "love" to pay attention to his concerns.

In the years that followed, I often felt dejected, humiliated, exposed, and like a liability because I didn't have my own independent income. Relying solely on my husband for money intensified my feelings of anger and regret, as I felt stripped of the autonomy I once valued. I constantly questioned my choices and often felt shortchanged in ways I hadn't expected when I first said "yes" to marriage.

All of this wouldn't have mattered if we had been operating in *agape* love—a love free from fear and insecurity, where each person covers and carries the other, bearing all things. It would simply have been a case of "what's mine is ours." But as life unfolded and the tables turned for a season, it became interesting to see how I handled things when the roles were reversed—and whether I truly extended the same grace I once expected. God used that reversal to expose what was really in my heart.

- *"And out of your reverence for Christ be supportive of each other in love. . . . So every married man should be gracious to his wife just as he is gracious to himself. And every wife should be tenderly devoted to her husband."* (Eph. 5:21, 33 TPT)

- *". . . rather, serve one another humbly in love. For the entire law is fulfilled in keeping this one command: 'Love your neighbor as yourself.'"* (Gal. 5:13-14 NIV)

- *"Do to others whatever you would like them to do to you. This is the essence of all that is taught in the law and the prophets."* (Matt. 7:12 NLT)

- Excerpts from Proverbs 31: *"Who can find a virtuous and capable wife? She is more precious than rubies. . . . She finds wool and flax and busily spins it. She is like a merchant's ship, bringing her food from afar. . . . She goes to inspect a field and buys it; with her earnings she plants a vineyard. She is energetic and strong, a hard worker. She makes sure her dealings are profitable; her lamp burns late into the night. Her hands are busy spinning thread, her fingers twisting fiber. . . . She has no fear of winter for her household, for everyone has warm clothes. . . . She makes belted linen garments and sashes to sell to the merchants. She is clothed with strength and dignity, and she laughs without fear of the future. . . . She carefully watches everything in her household and suffers nothing from laziness."* (Prov. 31:10, 13-14, 16-19, 21, 24-25, 27 NLT)

6. Sabotaging the relationship

Looking back, I think we both exhibited this behavior, albeit unintentionally, at various points in the first five years of our marriage. It might have been a way to rationalize our actions or mentally prepare for the breakup we feared was inevitable. Instead of addressing our insecurities or fears of rejection, we ruined the relationship by picking fights, escalating conflicts, and pushing each other away.

Impact: This destructive cycle turned our fears into a self-fulfilling prophecy. Our worries about abandonment or betrayal influenced our actions, which in turn led to the very outcomes we dreaded—confirming our worst fears and causing unnecessary pain.

- *"If you bite and devour each other, watch out or you will be destroyed by each other."* (Gal. 5:15 NIV)

7. Suspicion and control

Constant monitoring, accusations, and overbearing influence dominated our actions because we feared being let down or left out. What felt like attempts to secure the relationship only pulled us further apart.

Impact: These actions eroded the foundation of trust, leading to resentment and a sense of being caged or stifled. This fear-driven behavior created destructive patterns, making our relationship feel more like a battle than a partnership.

- *"Trust in the Lord with all your heart and lean not on your own understanding; in all your ways submit to him, and he will make your paths straight."* (Prov. 3:5-6 NIV)

- *"Love never gives up, never loses faith, is always hopeful, and endures through every circumstance."* (1 Cor. 13:7 NLT)

- *"It is better to take refuge in the LORD than to trust in man."* (Ps. 118:8)

- *"Now to Him who is able to keep you from stumbling, And to present you faultless Before the presence of His glory with exceeding joy…"* (Jude 1:24)

8. Passive-aggression

This is an indirect and deliberate expression of anger or frustration manifested in subtle behaviors such as sarcasm, withholding praise or support, procrastination, intentional lateness, criticism, or backhanded compliments instead of addressing issues head-on.

Impact: Such actions left much room for misunderstandings, latent hostility, and confusion. They created a toxic environment in which we often second-guessed each other's intentions, allowing conflicts to fester rather than addressing and resolving them openly and promptly.

- *"But I say, walk habitually in the [Holy] Spirit [seek Him and be responsive to His guidance], and then you will certainly not carry out the desire of the sinful nature [which responds impulsively without regard for God and His precepts]."* (Gal. 5:16 AMP)

- *"In these you too once walked, when you were living in them. But now you must put them all away: anger, wrath, malice, slander, and obscene talk from your mouth."* (Col. 3:7-8)

9. Emotional numbing or emotional anesthesia

Suppressing our feelings or building emotional walls became a habitual defense mechanism to shield ourselves from more pain. Over time, this significantly increased our emotional distance and created a growing sense of apathy on both sides. Some of our actions ranged from petty to downright absurd—like deliberately refusing to laugh at a joke or funny scene from a movie we were both watching because of unresolved issues. We would intentionally avoid shared activities we once enjoyed as a silent way of expressing our dissatisfaction. Communication became minimal and dismissive, with curt "yes" or "no" answers dominating our interactions. Affection was weaponized by withholding simple gestures like hugs and kisses, sitting close to each other, or even calling one another by our usual terms of endearment. Ironically, this felt like self-inflicted punishment since I'm naturally expressive and affectionate.

Impact: Intimacy in our relationship was eroded entirely, leaving our children as our only remaining connection. For me, this was devastating. I felt profoundly rejected, neglected, unloved, and unsupported, amplifying the sense of isolation in what should have been a beautiful partnership.

- *"And I will give you a new heart, and a new spirit I will put within you. And I will remove the heart of stone from your flesh and give you a heart of flesh. And I will put my Spirit within you, and cause you to walk in my statutes and be careful to obey my rules."* (Ezek. 36:26-27)

- *"Create in me a clean heart, O God, And renew a right and steadfast spirit within me."* (Ps. 51:10 AMP)

10. Bottling up emotions:

At the time, we often suppressed our frustration, sadness, worry, or anger in an effort to keep the peace, instead of honestly expressing what we felt.

Impact: Bottled-up emotions led to eventual outbursts or emotional shutdowns. This created an unhealthy cycle where problems weren't addressed until they became overwhelming, which caused us to detach more and more from any feelings we may still have had for each other.

- *"For when I kept silent, my bones wasted away through my groaning all day long."* (Ps. 32:3)

- *"Come to me, all who labor and are heavy laden, and I will give you rest."* (Matt. 11:28)

- *"Trust in Him at all times, you people; Pour out your heart before Him; God is a refuge for us."* (Ps. 62:8)

11. Giving in (Emotional submission)

Ségun and I sometimes yielded to each other's demands to avoid conflict or maintain peace, even when it went against our own preferences, feelings, or needs. However, due to the expectation that a wife should submit, I often gave in to his wishes, demands, or perspective—sometimes under pressure, out of fear of rejection, or to avoid stirring up trouble.

Impact: While this may have temporarily kept the peace, it ultimately resulted in feelings of powerlessness, dissatisfaction, and bitterness. Over time, I felt unheard—unless my voice was raised or accompanied by tears. My true emotions remained suppressed, and my needs went unnoticed and unmet. We increasingly acted out of obligation toward each other rather than from genuine care, affection, or a desire to nurture our relationship.

- *"Be devoted to one another in love. Honor one another above yourselves."* (Rom. 12:10 NIV)

12. Feigning indifference (Deflecting or minimizing concerns)

There were periods when we pretended not to care about each other or the issues bothering the other person. We would downplay or dismiss each other's feelings or concerns to avoid acknowledging faults and confronting difficult emotions or situations, often by changing the subject, making excuses, or shifting blame.

Impact: We deliberately acted indifferently to make each other feel undervalued and unimportant. This passive approach reflected a lack of empathy, as its primary purpose was to stifle communication and prevent genuine emotional connection, making it difficult to resolve issues or bond on a deeper level. We often ignored efforts to reconnect and acted as though milestones (birthdays, wedding anniversaries, etc.), accomplishments, challenges, and even illnesses were insignificant.

- *"Do nothing out of selfish ambition or vain conceit. Rather, in humility value others above yourselves, not looking to your own interests but each of you to the interests of the others. In your relationships with one another, have the same mindset as Christ Jesus."* (Phil. 2:3-5 NIV)

13. Emotional manipulation

Ségun and I resorted to guilt, blame, and even emotional blackmail—sometimes involving our children—to control or manipulate each other's actions and responses. This was often a defense mechanism to avoid feeling vulnerable or powerless.

Impact: Manipulation undermines trust and breeds insecurity in a relationship. It can leave the other person feeling trapped, coerced, and undervalued, which erodes mutual respect.

- *"Do not withhold good from those to whom it is due, when it is in your power to do it."* (Prov. 3:27)

Eventually, Ségun and I both ran out of ineffective "weapons" to hurl at each other, and our arguments devolved further. I regret to admit there was an unforgettable, ugly incident where I escalated a particular situation by literally throwing objects at my husband! It looked like our home had become a scene from a sci-fi movie, with a barrage of UFOs (unidentified flying objects) suspended in midair! Unfortunately, on a few occasions when things spiraled out of control, we tussled over phones, house keys, or car keys—usually as I tried to stop Ségun from leaving the house, and he attempted to pry his belongings from my hands. Living together in such a volatile environment, especially when boundaries like these are crossed, isn't just unhealthy—it can be downright dangerous. When my soft approach didn't yield the desired results, I became more confrontational and combative instead of conciliatory. Truth be told, I wouldn't have wanted to live with me either![4]

Here's a firm reprimand to my twenty-nine-year-old willful self, delivered in a tone and language that might have provided clarity, insight, and a much-needed reminder of the timeless biblical truths I kept ignoring—while letting my emotions take over!

> *"Post this at all the intersections, dear friends: Lead with your ears, follow up with your tongue, and let anger straggle along in the rear. God's righteousness doesn't grow from human anger. So throw all spoiled virtue and cancerous evil in the garbage. In simple humility, let our gardener, God, landscape you with the Word, making a salvation-garden of your life."* (James 1:19-21 MSG)

THROUGH SÉGUN'S LENSES

The implications of detaching ourselves emotionally while living under the same roof were far-reaching. From my perspective, an unending barrage of inexplicable criticism

---

4. Prov. 27:15-16 (NLT)

where I was essentially being told that my version of love was not fit for purpose took its toll on our relationship and my view of Funké. This gradually eroded my willingness to keep my marriage alive.

I could not pretend things were fine between us when nothing could have been further from the truth. With each external intervention we had to seek, I felt that my privacy was being violated and became exasperated as Funké's criticisms became increasingly unrestrained. She read meaning into my innocent actions and inactions and portrayed herself as an onlooker without any input in our marriage. Because our attempts at talking things through were short-lived, as tempers flared, I frequently found myself prematurely ending conversations to prevent the situation from escalating further.

For me, when arguments broke out in our home, the choice was either to stay and deal with the consequences or leave the room or the house, depending on the level of tension. I increasingly began to opt for the latter, and I sensed that things could quickly escalate out of control, which convinced me that we were standing on thin ice and would eventually have to go our separate ways. Funké felt that I was being vindictive on the occasions when I moved out of the house, whereas the truth was that I did so in the interest of peace and peace of mind—no matter how temporary. I could breathe when I was away without having to confront daily reminders of just how fragile our marriage had become.

However, I should have adopted a different approach as the vacuum that my departure created was inevitably going to be occupied by something or someone else, which is what eventually happened. My playbook for restoring my relationship with Funké—and our marriage—simply required more chapters instead of being discarded entirely.

Rearview Mirror Lesson

Due to the amount of vitriol in our home, we were communicating at different frequencies, so there was no way we could expect a resolution. Third-party involvement, whether in the form of family, friends, or trained professionals, was futile because none of their advice could reach our respective positions around which we had erected impregnable barricades.

Spending time alone, away from distracting and confusing ambient noise would have been a better option for me. It would have allowed me an opportunity to decompress and rid myself of anger and pride by surrounding myself with God's presence and seeking peace, understanding, and encouragement through His Word. Matthew 5:6 tells us, "*Blessed are those who hunger and thirst for righteousness, for they shall be satisfied,"* while Psalm 119:99 says, *"I have more understanding than all my teachers, for your testimonies are my meditation."*

Continuing to engage in confrontation with Funké simply allowed the enemy to continue residing in my marital home, occupying a void that should have been filled with God's presence.

PART 2

Crossroads and Roundabouts

7

Your People Are NOT My People

"For where you go I will go, and where you lodge I will lodge. Your people shall be my people, and your God my God."

RUTH 1:16

SWEET UNITY: ALL OF ME, ALL OF YOU

Marriages in the African culture, particularly in Nigeria, extend beyond the union of two individuals to encompass the coming together of families. While this fosters a sense of unity and support, it can also introduce challenges for the couple if roles and boundaries are not clearly defined. If you haven't experienced a traditional Nigerian wedding, you're missing out on what could easily be considered the eighth wonder of the world!

The celebration is filled with camaraderie, support, and cultural richness, showcased through music, dance, food, vibrant *aṣọ ẹbí* (traditional matching attire symbolizing unity), unique party souvenirs, and much more. Yet, despite all the joyful displays of unity between the two families, that sense of togetherness often fades after the wedding, leaving the inexperienced newlyweds to grapple with the complexities of blending new family relationships into their own.

People dedicate considerable effort to planning their wedding, yet often overlook proper preparation for a lasting marriage beyond the pomp and pageantry of the event. A strong marriage requires wisdom and intentional teamwork between husband and wife to successfully navigate the process of "leaving and cleaving." Without a clear vision, people struggle,[1] so it's essential to have open and honest discussions about everyone's expectations—including those of relevant family members—rather than making assumptions or simply hoping for a seamless integration. The onus is on the husband and wife to set realistic expectations within their respective families from the outset (while dating) and to jointly manage and direct relationships within clear, mutually agreed-upon, and healthy boundaries. We all do our best with the knowledge we have, but even with our best efforts or intentions, there's always room to learn, unlearn, and adjust when necessary. This is especially important for decisions that affect spouses and their future.

I entered marriage unprepared and naïve regarding certain nuances, relationships, and family dynamics. While dating, I had limited interactions with my husband's family because I was away at college in another city. It wasn't until Ségun and I were engaged that I truly began to connect with my in-laws. I wholeheartedly embraced his family, believing that marriage meant not only becoming a wife to my husband, but also a daughter, sister, and part of a new family.

I was raised in a close-knit, loving family, where everyone shared their joys and challenges while embracing and supporting one another—no matter what. After my parents went their separate ways when I was a toddler, my older brother and I were raised by my mother in an overprotective environment. Although our father remained involved in our lives, my mother received tremendous support from her family, especially her mother and siblings. In essence, I was blessed to be raised by a "village," which meant that my brother and I were, to a large extent, overpampered. My middle name, Olufunké, from the Yorùbá tribe of southwestern Nigeria, perfectly reflects my upbringing. The literal translation is *God gave me this child to pamper, love, dote on, nurture, and cherish*—and I like to add: *by providing comfort or special privileges!* I lived this "cocooned life" until I was sent off to boarding school at age eleven, but that's a story for another chapter . . . or book!

So, Ségun came along, caring for me with the same attention and affection I was accustomed to. Apart from the nearly ten-year age difference between us, I assumed that marrying my husband would be a natural fit—or an easy transition—for both of us into our respective extended families since we shared the same religion, tribe, language, and values. I was eager to work with Ségun to recreate the closeness I experienced growing up and to blend our lives together. The saying *"love me, love my dog"* means that if you truly care for someone, you must also be willing to accept and embrace everything that comes with them, including their flaws, habits, and even the things or people they care about. Real love involves accepting a whole person rather than selectively choosing only the parts that are easy to love.[2]

I saw no reason not to extend my love for Ségun to his family, trusting that he would

---

1. Prov. 16:3; 19:21; 21:5; 29:18; Hab. 2:2-3; Luke 14:28
2. John 13:34-35; Eph. 5:1; Phil. 2:3-4; 1 John 4:7-12

reciprocate the same affection to mine—who adored him! In fact, it was my mother who encouraged me to date him even though I had reservations about our age difference. Being the son of one of her old schoolmates gave her considerable comfort. Ségun also won the hearts of both my mother and grandmother. He was respectful, responsible, soft-spoken, pleasant, caring, and a true gentleman. It was obvious to my family that he loved me, and that was the final nudge!

Despite my reserved nature, I was willing to step out of my comfort zone and join my husband's family. Although I was initially apprehensive, I was confident that Ségun had my back. With his support, I felt assured that I had nothing to worry about—he would guide me through the different relationships I was eager to build. In the Yorùbá traditional marriage ceremony, the bride is handed over to the groom's family—specifically his parents or their representatives, which is a deeply symbolic act. I thought this public display of acceptance and unity was a beautiful sign of things to come … but what transpired in our marriage proved otherwise.

FAITHFUL BONDS: THE LEGACY OF NAOMI AND RUTH

Naomi and Ruth's story in the Book of Ruth has always fascinated me. It provides a great example of how relationships that go beyond blood ties can be powerful, showing that true bonds are not only about family by birth but also about the choices we make to love, support, protect, stand by, and generally treat the people God brings into our lives. The different decisions made by Ruth and Orpah to stay with or leave Naomi reveal their individual character, priorities, and their relationships with their mother-in-law. These decisions also highlight broader themes of loyalty, faith, and commitment.

Why did one of Naomi's widowed daughters-in-law insist on accompanying her into an uncertain future in Bethlehem, Judah? What caused the other, Orpah, to decide to return to her own people in Moab after the death of her husband? Naomi tried to persuade the two women, saying: *"Go, return each to her mother's house,"*[3] but Ruth refused. Culturally and maritally, Ruth and Orpah had no further obligations toward Naomi as their bonds were no longer legally binding. Ruth came into Naomi's family as a Moabite woman who didn't worship their God, Yahweh. Yet she was welcomed and allowed to thrive and build connections, which included her relationship with Naomi. Despite their differences in culture and religion, Ruth was accepted and integrated into the family. She embraced Naomi as her mother, and they shared a bond of loyalty, devotion, and faithfulness. Ruth saw her husband's people as her own because she had been treated like one of them, not as an intruder or an outsider.[4]

Naomi clearly had a loving relationship with Ruth and Orpah, as they both initially resisted her emotional plea for them to return to Moab, which was based in her concern for their

---

3. Ruth 1:8
4. Ruth 1:16-18

well-being. The Bible describes a very emotional discussion among the three of them, in which Naomi kissed her daughters-in-law, and they all wept. Orpah decided to leave, but something made Ruth stay with the vulnerable widow. It was apparent that Ruth and Naomi had built mutual trust through a genuine faith conversion—a process that usually occurs through careful observation of good character, especially when the discipler's professed faith aligns with their actions—for instance, when love and forgiveness are not just spoken but actively demonstrated.

I believe Naomi had lived out her faith before her daughter-in-law, providing a deeper layer of relational connection beyond her son. This may have convinced Ruth that Naomi could be trusted, prompting her to take the risk of staying with her mother-in-law, who represented love, faith, friendship, security, and loyalty. Ruth's declaration in Ruth 1:16 reveals that her commitment to Naomi went beyond familial ties—she had embraced Naomi's God, Yahweh. The way Ruth was treated by her husband and his family most likely influenced her decision to prioritize Naomi's well-being over her own comfort and prospects in Moab.

I've often heard this story with the focus on Ruth's extraordinary devotion, steadfast love, compassion, and kindness, which set her apart from Orpah. However, love in any relationship cannot exist in a vacuum; it requires reciprocity. Yes, God's love is unconditional, yet Scripture also teaches a reciprocal expression of love (John 15:12; Peter 1:22). Reciprocity isn't about conditions—it reflects the Spirit-enabled mutuality that sustains covenant relationships. For any relationship to flourish, love must ultimately flow both ways, and to have any meaningful impact, it must be communicated in a way that's understood. It appears Naomi loved Ruth in a way that was consistent and clear, making it easy for Ruth to believe her love was genuine. This was evident in how Naomi continued caring for her daughter-in-law even after they left Moab and arrived in her hometown, Bethlehem. There, Naomi coached Ruth on how to attract Boaz, who was Naomi's relative.

Orpah, on the other hand, made the practical and socially expected decision to return to her family in Moab. While Orpah initially hesitated to leave Naomi, she ultimately chose to return to her homeland, which was probably a more logical choice for her than an emotional one. Staying with Naomi would have meant facing a life of uncertainty and potential poverty in a foreign land. Unlike Ruth, there is no indication that Orpah had embraced Naomi's faith, and perhaps her experience in Naomi's household wasn't as fulfilling as Ruth's. Returning to Moab allowed her to remain within her cultural and religious comfort zone. Although Orpah's change of heart is not portrayed as wrong or selfish in the passage, it provides valuable insight into the interpersonal dynamics that can influence responses. These dynamics may steer decisions toward or away from God's greater plan for our lives.

Ruth and Orpah married into the same family, but their respective relationships with their mother-in-law and the decisions they made charted different paths for each of them and for Naomi. Ruth's unique qualities, combined with Naomi's faith and foresight, highlight the redemptive power of selfless love in their lives. God, who knows the end from the beginning, doesn't act randomly or haphazardly. Unbeknownst to them, He brought Ruth into Naomi's life to fulfill a predestined purpose. They both nurtured and preserved this relationship to their own advantage and the benefit of mankind, leading Ruth to become part of God's redemptive plan as she later married Boaz and became the great-grandmother of King David and, ultimately, was part of the lineage of Jesus Christ. What a testimony!

Building intentional bonds and healthy relationships emanates from love, understanding, mutual respect, fairness, and an alignment of values and purpose. Ruth and Naomi loved the same man—each in her own God-ordained role—yet they chose to complement rather than compete with each other. This bond continued even after the shared connection between them—Ruth's husband and Naomi's son—was gone.

Many relationships formed through marriage thrive on shared faith, business interests, food, shopping, entertainment, school or church activities, grandchildren, family gatherings, festive seasons, and vacations. More than just "chemistry" or leaving things to chance, strong relationships require consistent and deliberate acts of kindness, along with a willingness to be warm, open-minded, hospitable, supportive, compassionate, empathetic, patient, and truthful—all rooted in the love of God and nurtured by the fruit of the Spirit.[5]

1 Corinthians 9:22-23 states: *"I have become all things to all people, that by all means I might save some. I do it all for the sake of the gospel, that I may share with them in its blessings."* In this passage, Apostle Paul describes how he adapted his approach to different groups—whether religious, non-religious, or those who were weak, etc.—so he could effectively share the Gospel. His goal was not to compromise his faith or adopt their way of life but to be accommodating and meet people where they were, in order to lead them to Christ. He sought to understand their perspectives by being empathetic and compassionate.

This Christ-centered approach, empowered by the Holy Spirit, convinced and transformed nations despite Paul's weaknesses or shortcomings. Paul wasn't perfect, but he lived a life that consistently reflected the message he preached—one of love, peace, kindness, faithfulness, and devotion to the Gospel. This was demonstrated not only in his actions but also in his letters, even when he had to be firm. Confident in God's sustaining grace, he encouraged the Corinthians to follow his example, as he followed Christ's example.[6] When we learn about Jesus and imitate Him through His complete and wholesome teaching,[7] our perspective becomes less subjective. Both Paul and Naomi exemplified this by making God—not themselves—the central focus of their lives and interactions. By doing so, they created opportunities for conversion, influence, and discipleship.

---

5. Gal. 5:22-23

6. 1 Cor. 11:1

7. 1 Tim. 5:2; Titus 2:1-8

This is the true calling of every Christian in any relationship—to sharpen, encourage, and build one another up in faith.[8] No spouse's family will be perfect, and not every in-law will be the ideal recipient of your love and goodwill, but God calls us to love unconditionally, regardless of the circumstances.[9] Sometimes, it might simply require a bit of time to learn and adapt to a new "love language" to communicate motives and intentions more clearly. A God-investment is never in vain[10] it's always worth the effort. There may be times when a spouse finds themselves among "outlaws," where the message of love is rejected. That's okay! True Christian living involves embodying the Gospel of Christ in both character and speech in every relationship and in our everyday ordinary life, including evangelism, discipleship, and sharpening others in faith. Success in these areas is not measured by forcing acceptance but by obedience and faithfulness to God's calling. Our role is to plant seeds of love, but it is God who makes them grow.[11] The outcome is in God's hands. Trust His timing, release any bitterness, rejection, or offense, and shake the dust off your feet.[12] Sometimes, moving forward with grace and choosing to love from a distance is also part of the journey. Prayerfully seek God's guidance for the correct route to take.

"CAN ANYTHING GOOD COME OUT OF NAZARETH?" (JOHN 1:46)

Before and after our wedding, I often had a nagging suspicion that Ségun had certain preconceived notions about me based on my background. It wasn't because he said anything in particular to me about my family, but he frequently referenced my parents' breakup whenever we had misunderstandings. He believed I brought unresolved issues—"baggage," as he called it—into our relationship. Whether or not this was true, having that label constantly hanging over me felt like a millstone. It became his default explanation for any shortcoming on my part, as if he expected certain flaws because of my background—and he felt he just had to put up with it. To me, Ségun was echoing flawed assumptions, possibly influenced by cultural stereotypes ingrained in him as a Nigerian.

Nigerian society can be harsh in its perception of people. Instead of understanding and empathizing with the struggles of an individual or group, it often labels them with awful, negative words. For example, widows without family support can be branded as witches, divorced women and single mothers can be seen as promiscuous, and those from polygamous households

---

8. Prov. 27:17; 1 Thess. 5:11

9. Matt. 5:44; Luke 6:27; Rom. 13:8; Gal. 5:14

10. Rom. 12:17-18

11. 1 Cor. 3:5-7

12. Matt. 10:11-20

can be assumed to lead chaotic lives. Children from so-called "broken homes"—whether due to divorce, separation, or single parenthood—are not spared either. They are sometimes given derogatory names and unfairly assumed to be troubled, disadvantaged, delinquent, or prone to vices.

At one time, the prevailing misconception was that children from such backgrounds lacked good role models, making them less likely to succeed. As adults, they were often considered unfit for marriage and believed to lack the foundation and qualities needed to be good spouses—especially women. Unfortunately, some of these stereotypes persist in Nigeria and many other societies, reinforcing harmful cycles of prejudice. The irony is that a stable two-parent household does not always guarantee a healthy upbringing, as such homes also face challenges that can negatively affect children.

A person's background does not determine their destiny or destination. The phrase *"Can anything good come out of Nazareth?"* was spoken by Nathanael in John 1:46 when Philip told him about Jesus. Nathanael was skeptical because Nazareth was a small town with no great reputation at the time. However, Jesus, the Son of God, came from this humble place, proving that great things and great people can emerge from the most unexpected or underestimated backgrounds. Many children from so-called "broken homes" can rise above societal expectations and achieve greatness through determination, faith, support, and most importantly, God.[13] Human prejudices do not limit God's plans, even though they exist everywhere—including the body of Christ. We can do better than judging, making wrong assumptions, or treating others based on preconceived ideas. God is the true judge of human worth. That person you are tempted to exclude, dismiss, sideline, or look down on is valuable enough for Christ to have died for!

Growing up in my mother's house made me deeply aware of societal prejudices. My older brother and I were often reminded to "never forget whose child you are." We were encouraged not to let our parents' separation define us or allow others to attribute our mistakes or shortcomings to it. My brother and I were fiercely protective of our mother who sacrificed everything for us. In turn, we committed ourselves to succeeding against all odds. She always called us her "pride and joy," and one of our greatest goals was to live up to that honor and protect her from any disrepute. By God's grace, she often received praise for the way she raised us, but there were skeptics and naysayers. My secret desire was to silence them by proving that good things can emerge from unexpected or abandoned places. This desire fueled my perfectionist tendencies, and I always went the extra mile in everything I set my heart on, including my marriage.

This quest proved challenging during the early years of my marriage. Despite my best efforts, I just couldn't seem to break through the barriers or overcome the preconceived notions some

---

13. Phil. 4:12-13

people held about me. At times I felt unfairly judged or treated based on those fixed views. It wasn't yet the era of the many Nollywood (the Nigerian version of Hollywood) movies that we now have, which often focus on wicked in-laws and voodoo, especially at its inception. So, I had no *Nollywood -inspired mentor* to teach me about the dark side of marriage management. I had no negative influences or preconceived notions to fuel any bias or plans to fight against my husband or his family... but I did have a fiery temper that could have easily earned me another lead role in a Nollywood drama—full of intrigue, emotional twists and turns, tension, romance, and the occasional cliffhanger to keep viewers coming back for more! Well, except for Ségun, who didn't care much for drama!

I tried my best to demonstrate the good manners and values instilled in me by my "village." I've always been somewhat reserved, which some people misinterpret as being unsociable or even snobbish. In Yorùbá culture, showing respect to elders is a core value expressed in various ways. Females often curtsy or kneel, while men prostrate or bow low when greeting. Speech likewise reflects honor through the use of titles, terms of endearment, or *relational honorifics* that acknowledge age, status, and connection—for example, *Daddy Lagos, Mama London, Baba Ségun (Ségun's dad), or Mummy Funké (Funké's mom).* Gratitude is also emphasized, with expressions of appreciation continuing for days or even months after receiving a gift or an act of kindness.

I may not have ticked every box on the *original Yorùbá traditional hardcore code of conduct for wives (YTHCCW)*, but I certainly gave my all in being a loving, respectful, modest, warm, polite, generous, considerate, accommodating, and dutiful wife, embracing everyone as part of our extended family. There were times I would clean the family home while my parents-in-law were away and cook special meals to welcome them back from their trips. I'd give myself a solid five-star gold award for my efforts to meet the standards of the modern-day version of the *YTHCCW*—if I do say so myself!...well, maybe a four-star rating, as some might take issue with my calling my husband by his name! Given our age gap, that's considered a no-no, but it's never been an issue for Ségun, and I always tried to remember not to do it when we were around older people who'd see it as "sacrilege"!

Going into marriage, I had a fairy-tale view and wasn't fully aware of some of the subtle yet deeply ingrained cultural nuances of our society. In more traditional households, many of these expectations are unspoken customs that, I believe, women themselves developed as survival strategies in toxic environments. Some of these practices include "eye-service" *(playing to the gallery, people-pleasing, showmanship)*, being a "family doormat" *(a pushover, overly compliant, easily controlled)*, and enduring constant pressure to earn the approval of one's in-laws. I don't have the personality to engage in such pretense, but my motives and intentions have always been consistent and genuine—though they haven't always been expressed perfectly, my heart's desire has always been to please God and seek His approval above all else.

FRACTURED BONDS: THE BURDEN
OF STRAINED RELATIONSHIPS

After Ségun proposed, he moved into our first home alone while I focused on my exams in another city. He wanted to surprise me with the move and didn't want me to be distracted, but when I arrived, everything was already in place—nothing matched what I'd envisioned for our home. I appreciated the gesture and accepted it, choosing not to sweat the small stuff and even extending my gratitude to Ségun's mother, who graciously undertook the task of shopping for some household items and helping Ségun set up the house. However, I let Ségun know I wasn't happy about being excluded from the process, but I was willing to live with the way things were until we had enough money to make the changes that would reflect our tastes and preferences. Unfortunately, some interactions between Ségun's mother and me in the early days of our marriage created friction largely stemming from information relayed to her by Ségun about our marital problems. This shaped our relationship, resulting in misinterpretations of situations, words, and actions on several occasions.

For example, one Sunday morning, Ségun and I were resting after a sleepless night with our infant son. I let our new housekeeper in for a quick tidy-up and went back to bed. When the doorbell rang a few times, Ségun told me not to check, but I quickly got out of bed and did so anyway. My mother-in-law had been at the door, but the housekeeper who saw her through the peephole didn't know her and hadn't let her in. I rushed downstairs to catch her just as she was leaving, explained the situation, and asked her to return, but she said she had just wanted to stop by briefly after church. When this story was retold, it became a misunderstanding where I was accused of refusing to let her into our home. Ségun, who had been right beside me the whole time and knew the truth should have played a better role in resolving things. I felt unsupported, with no ally in my own home. The events of that day seemed to have colored my relationship with my mother-in-law, and the tension deepened with each interaction.

I couldn't understand why Ségun didn't correct the narrative about that incident or misconceptions about me. His actions and inactions fueled the flames of discord between his mother and me. Although Ségun ostensibly adopted the stance of a neutral party in trying to smooth things over, in my eyes he seemed to want to appease his mother at my expense. There were times I suggested that he accompany me to have a heart-to-heart talk with her so we could start afresh, but he said I should resolve things on my own. There was always something to sort out, and, in my opinion, I didn't have any cover from my husband!

My interactions with my mother-in-law became increasingly difficult, and I would receive secondhand reports from Ségun about something I said, didn't say, did, or didn't do. It felt like the more strained the relationship between my mother-in-law and me, the colder Ségun was toward me—almost as if there was a remote thermostat regulating the "temperature" in our home from a distance. Disagreements between Ségun and me regarding our respective mothers extended to who would stay to help after the birth of our first child and, later, who would babysit when we had to travel out of town for an event. I saw these as straightforward decisions based on practicality and fairness rather than matters of someone else's preference or politics, but they often became more complicated than I expected.

Ségun knew how close my mother and I were from the start. They had developed a cordial relationship, but over time, he became distant with her—perhaps due to the issues I was having with his mother. He never initiated our visits to my mom, yet we were at his parents' house frequently. Initially, it didn't bother me, but it began to feel unbalanced.

One incident that deeply hurt me was when my mother came to spend a few weeks with me at our relatives' home where I had been staying prior to the birth of our first child. Given my difficult pregnancy, I needed her help, and she flew thousands of miles at her own expense to be there for me and her first grandchild.

Nigeria is home to over 250 ethnic groups, each with its own unique language, culture, and traditions. In the Igbo tribe, the postpartum practice known as *Omugwo* provides new mothers with physical and emotional support, as well as assistance with childcare. Typically, a maternal figure such as the new mother's mother or an aunt moves in temporarily or hosts the mother in their home to ensure she gets adequate rest, heals properly, and transitions smoothly into motherhood. In our culture (Yorùbá), a similar practice called *Olojojo Omo* exists, with one key distinction: The primary caregiver is traditionally the mother-in-law, as the new mother is considered to have been "handed over" to her husband's family during the traditional engagement rites.

This practice has been valued for generations and is believed to help reduce the risk of postpartum depression (PDD), though its effectiveness depends on the type of support provided and the relationship between the individuals involved. While Omugwo and Olojojo Omo remain cherished traditions, they are not mandatory. In modern times, their practice varies based on individual needs, convenience, personal preference, and, most importantly, the comfort of the new mother.

The delivery went smoothly, but right there in the maternity suite, while we were still basking in the joy of our newborn, Ségun suddenly asked me to tell my mother to leave the room. I understood he wanted those first moments with me and our baby, but the timing and manner in which it was done felt harsh, especially since I didn't think he would have done the same thing with his own mother.

Shortly after, I started shaking and shivering uncontrollably, and I felt extremely cold. The medical team was concerned and had to quickly ascertain if my body had gone into shock, postpartum bleeding, or other complications. It was a frightening moment for all of us. One of the nurses called my mother back into the room and asked her to hold my hand to help soothe me while they placed blankets over me. Ségun stood close by me, carrying our baby, while my mother prayed over me, allaying my fears. Thankfully, everything calmed down and it turned out to be postpartum chills.

What stung most about this incident was that Ségun never apologized for how he treated my mother that day. When I brought it up, he insisted he had done nothing wrong, only admitting years later that he could have handled it differently, but the harm had already been done. That moment stayed with me for years.

The consequences of unhealed emotional wounds and unresolved issues in relationships involving in-laws are often deep, complex, and very painful. They can have devastating effects—especially if they have a lasting negative impact on a couple's lives and marriage. When trust is broken or love is repeatedly tested, the bond between people grows fragile and may eventually shatter, leaving behind deep wounds and disconnection. If these issues aren't addressed and relationships aren't repaired, they not only affect those directly involved but also create uncomfortable situations, emotional stress, and tensions that influence family interactions and decisions—eventually dividing people into team "A" versus team "B."

Ségun could and should have managed things better between his mother and me. Even if he truly believed I created the mess, he was the bridge between us—the one who could have encouraged better understanding, diffused tensions, and treated both of us fairly, instead of just watching as the divide deepened. If I knew back then half of what I know now, I would have kept my feelings in check instead of venting—at least until the "bonding glue" between Ségun and me was completely dry! Wisdom often means knowing when and how to address issues to prevent unnecessary conflicts. While being wise doesn't mean avoiding disagreements altogether, it usually involves finding ways to defuse rather than escalate tension. This includes addressing matters calmly, with empathy, considering different perspectives, and striving for solutions that uphold everyone's dignity and worth. True wisdom seeks resolution, not confrontation for its own sake, to prove a point, or to show dominance.

The foregoing accounts aren't intended to blame anyone or expose faults but rather to illustrate some of the difficult situations that kept us apart instead of drawing us closer in love. As there's a fine line between love and hate, it's easily crossed when anger, pride, bitterness, or resentment take hold. The only true "villain" in the breakdown of our relationship was the enemy, who used circumstances, people—including us—and emotions to sow discord. But when the real enemy is identified, the focus turns to solving the problem, not attacking people. The most important thing is that God turned what was meant to harm us into good, for His glory, and for the saving of many lives (Gen. 50:20).

THE ONE NECESSARY THING

Looking back, I realize I was preoccupied with many things, overwhelmed by trivial matters, and distracted in my quest to prove my worth, capabilities, and role. In the process, I overlooked important warnings and ignored wise counsel, particularly those related to interpersonal relationships. Instead of approaching challenges with caution and wisdom, relying on the Holy Spirit for guidance through unfamiliar territory, I often reacted emotionally. In Luke 10:41-42, Jesus gently reminds Martha that while she was busy with many tasks, Mary has chosen the "one thing" that truly matters—sitting at His feet and listening to His teaching. As we grow in our knowledge of Jesus, we begin to understand ourselves through who He is and what He has done.[14] In Him, we are transformed into who we are truly meant to be.[15]

A good-natured, well-mannered, book-smart, and God-fearing wife is admirable, but it's equally important to apply discernment—knowing when to speak, when to stay silent, when to stand firm, and when to let go. This balance fosters peace, nurtures healthy relationships, helps navigate challenges with grace and wisdom, and ultimately builds a home filled with love, respect, and lasting harmony.

> *"Get wisdom! Get understanding!*
> *Do not forget, nor turn away from the words of my mouth.*
> *Do not forsake her, and she will preserve you;*
> *Love her, and she will keep you.*
> *Wisdom is the principal thing;*
> *Therefore get wisdom.*
> *And in all your getting, get understanding.*
> *Exalt her, and she will promote you;*
> *She will bring you honor, when you embrace her."* (Prov. 4:5-8)

THROUGH SÉGUN'S LENSES

By the time Funké and I got married in 1998, I had attended a fair number of Nigerian traditional wedding ceremonies. For Christians, these are typically grand and colorful events preceding the church wedding, when the groom publicly presents his wife with an engagement ring and prayers are said for the couple by the heads of both families.

The advice given to the intended couple during the traditional wedding echoes that given during the obligatory pre-marriage counseling sessions, particularly regarding disagreements. Here, the central message has long been to avoid outside interference and for husband and wife to resolve their differences by themselves, in good faith and in a spirit of love.

---

14. John 14:6; Col. 3:3-4
15. 2 Cor. 3:18; Eph. 2:10

Although this has been the template for decades, and the expert guidance seems straightforward enough, I do not think enough emphasis is placed on the intricacies of conflict resolution in marriage for newlyweds. In my opinion, practical and "actionable" information on the dynamics of successfully integrating a couple's respective families, a key component of Yorùbá culture, is singularly lacking.

When general information is being dispensed to the couple, the elephant in the room is, arguably, the relationship between wives and mothers-in-law—and to a lesser degree, that between husbands and mothers-in-law—which has the potential to cause serious and lasting damage in a marriage if not properly managed. Nigerian fathers typically play a secondary role when it comes to engaging with their sons- and daughters-in-law and grandchildren, preferring to cede the role of "primary contact" to their wives.

Of our respective parents, Funké's mother and my mother were, understandably, the most actively involved in our married lives. Watching their offspring suffer in a marriage that was causing them so much pain and suffering must have been unbearable and activated their maternal instincts. The greater the erosion of trust between Funké and me, the deeper the wedges we drove between ourselves and our respective mothers-in-law and, by extension, our respective fathers-in-law who were guilty by association. She became increasingly convinced that my mother did not have her best interest at heart and that, at various times, my mother and I worked in tandem to unsettle her. Sadly, this shut windows of communication that may eventually have, directly or indirectly, resulted in useful counsel for Funké and me. Looking back, I missed out on opportunities to reassure Funké that she was not being passed over in favor of my mother.

Rearview Mirror Lesson

Although seemingly justifiable at the time, my decision to give Funké and her parents a wide berth as our marriage crumbled was patently wrong. This simply reinforced her belief that I had chosen my parents, particularly my mother, over her and that she was trapped in a "me versus them" extended family relationship. No matter how uncomfortable, like a first responder, I should have headed for where my attention was most needed—my home—to reassure Funké of the pride of place that she occupies in my life. However, I opted for the more convenient path of giving short shrift to those I believed were directly or indirectly responsible for the problems in my marriage. I wrongly appointed myself the arbiter of whether Funké was justified in feeling otherwise. Instead, I should have remained resolute in allaying her concerns until they disappeared altogether.

8

Leaving and Cleaving

"Have you not read that He who made them at the beginning 'made them male and female,' and said, 'For this reason a man shall leave his father and mother and be joined to his wife, and the two shall become one flesh'? So then, they are no longer two but one flesh. Therefore what God has joined together, let not man separate."

MATTHEW 19:4-6

ROOTS AND WINGS[1]

I frequently reference culture in this book because everyone is shaped by it, and every society has cultural norms—whether formal or informal. There is no culture-free society. Culture influences our behaviors, beliefs, values, and how we perceive the world regardless of education, social status, religion, wealth, location, or technological advancements. Even the highly educated and affluent often hold onto cultural traditions from their upbringing, which influences many aspects of their lives, including marriage. While many cultural practices are beautiful and contribute to the uniqueness and cohesiveness of individual societies, problems arise—especially for Christians—when cultural norms conflict with biblical principles such as "leaving and cleaving." Too often, in such cases, culture takes precedence over God's Word.

"Leaving and cleaving" isn't just a decision on the wedding day or the day after. It results

---

1. I refer to Yorùbá culture in this book because that is the tribe Ségun and I belong to. I'm not an expert in all the traditions and practices of our culture, but I'm sufficiently familiar with the topics I've referred to in this book.

from years of intentional preparation, equipping children to become independent, productive members of society and, for some, future husbands and wives. Everyone is socialized from birth within a cultural framework that forms one's identity, moral compass, preferences, and worldview, often subconsciously guiding one's decisions and beliefs. For Christians, the foundation is the life of Jesus Christ—His way of thinking, being, and doing things.[2] Proverbs 22:6 emphasizes the importance of training children in the right path from an early age so they carry those values into adulthood. Training a child (ages 0-12), raising or nurturing an adolescent/young adult (ages 13-25), and guiding an adult (ages 26 and above) all require different approaches, as each phase comes with unique developmental needs and challenges. Each stage also requires adaptability, patience, and wisdom, ensuring children grow into well-rounded, responsible adults who can pass on the same values to the next generation.

Parents run into problems when they fall short during any of these phases or fail to recognize or distinguish between them. This affects, to varying degrees, their ability to provide their children with adequate discipline, protection, reinforcement, mentorship, support, advice, guidance, or counseling at the right time. Parent-child relationships often face challenges when parents attempt to step in during adulthood to correct or compensate for earlier gaps. These late-stage interventions may stem from fear of the "big bad wolves out there" or a lack of confidence in their own parenting, leading to feelings of inadequacy. Some parents may also struggle with doubts about their children's ability to navigate life on their own.

God hasn't called any parent to be perfect or to raise perfect children—His command is to raise godly offspring.[3] Our trust should rest in God, not in our own abilities or perceived shortcomings. Faith in Him gives us the wisdom to know when to hold on and when to let go, allowing our children to thrive and soar. Our role is to plant the incorruptible seed of God's Word in their hearts and teach them His way of life with love, patience, and consistency—He takes care of the rest.[4]

Being a mother to two young adult sons and a teenage daughter who thinks she's the family CEO has taught me invaluable lessons and given me a fresh perspective on parenting. It's true that you never truly know how you'll respond to certain situations until you experience them. I've realized that a mother's raw instinct for protection and survival is not easily regulated, especially for the one who deeply loves her children, regardless of their age. I've witnessed mothers—some battling mental illness or addiction—fight fiercely to keep their children or put themselves in harm's way just to provide for them. The love of a devoted mother knows no bounds!

I was tested a couple of times in this area when my older son "officially" started dating. It was difficult to simply sit back and watch him make mistakes in some of his choices. I found myself constantly in "momma to the rescue" mode, always ready to unleash my inner lioness—like

---

2. John 14:6; 2 Cor. 5:17; Phil. 2:5; 1 John 2:6

3. Mal. 2:15

4. Deut. 6:6-7; Isa. 54:13-15; Ps. 78:5-7; Prov. 1:8; Matt. 19:4; Eph. 6:4; Col. 3:16

a character from *Voltron,* the 1980s animated series—to defend and protect him! Over time, I learned (and I'm still learning) to surrender my children into God's most capable hands. Our role as parents is not to control every outcome but to seek His grace and guidance in training, raising, and equipping them through each phase of their lives.

Once children reach adulthood, parenting transitions from authority to mentorship and friendship. Parents no longer dictate decisions but serve as wise counselors or trusted advisers. A lighthouse doesn't steer the ship; it simply provides guidance to help it navigate safely. Likewise, parents should offer wisdom without imposing control or overstepping boundaries by trying to orchestrate their children's lives or by dominating and managing their decisions. The line between care or concern and control can easily become blurred, especially in areas that haven't been fully surrendered to God.

Acting in faith rather than being driven by fear, uncertainty, control, or manipulation helps us avoid doing things we might later regret and prevents us from hurting others—especially our children. It preserves our relationships with those connected to them, such as their spouses. Asking God for the grace to pray the right prayers[5] and to maintain our faith is one of the most effective ways to guide our adult children along the right path. A powerful example of trusting God and releasing an adult child is seen in the story of the prodigal son's father (Luke 15:11-32). He allowed his son to make his own choices and mistakes but welcomed him back with grace. As parents, we must trust the values we've instilled in our children and, most importantly, trust God, who can keep them and all of us from falling.[6]

Certain behaviors transcend cultural boundaries; one common example is parents who live vicariously through their children. Some mothers and fathers—whether consciously or unconsciously—derive their sense of identity, self-worth, recognition, fulfillment, purpose, or personal validation from their children's achievements, choices, and successes. In many African cultures, this is especially evident among fathers who, unable to fulfill their own aspirations, attempt to realize them through their children. For instance, they may push their sons or daughters into careers they once desired for themselves—such as medicine, law, or engineering—regardless of the child's personal interests or abilities. Some parents even compel their children to join the family business, pressuring them to fulfill expectations that are not their own. This makes it difficult for adult children to develop autonomy, as they remain tethered to their parents' influence, relying on them for direction and sustenance instead of forging their own path.

In the United States, a notable example is seen among "pageant moms"—mothers who are heavily invested in their children's participation in beauty pageants. Some of these moms may have aspired to become beauty queens but never had the opportunity, so they project their unfulfilled dreams onto their daughters. As a result, their focus and decisions are often

5. James 4:3
6. Jude 1:24

based on their own desires and expectations rather than what is truly best for the child. A balanced approach involves nurturing and guiding children while respecting their individuality and encouraging them to seek God's wisdom in making their own choices.

Children raised in environments where their parents' dreams and desires take center stage can be significantly stunted in their growth, maturity, and independence. In the aforementioned examples, the child's sense of self is often shaped by markers received from their parents rather than their own personal identity, interests, or calling. As a result, such children may never develop a strong foundation for self-discovery or autonomy, as their lives are governed by their parents' ambitions, standards, and expectations.

This lack of independence can be particularly problematic when the children transition into adulthood. As they begin new stages in life, especially relationships outside the home, they may struggle to assert their own identity or make decisions that align with their values and desires. Instead of confidently making choices that reflect their own path, they may continue to seek emotional support, validation, and direction from their parents.[7] This ongoing dependency can hinder the ability to fully "leave and cleave" as they become adults.

When they get married, these individuals may take with them an unresolved pattern of parental attachment, which affects their ability to develop an equal, mutually respectful, and interdependent relationship with their spouse. Their focus may still be on seeking approval from their parents rather than cleaving to their spouse as one flesh, which is the biblical mandate for marriage. The emotional and psychological pull of their parents' wishes can hinder them from creating the healthy boundaries necessary for a successful marriage.

This dynamic—where a child's identity and life choices are continuously tied to their parents—can be incredibly damaging in the long run. It prevents the natural progression of the "leave and cleave" principle, where a person is meant to leave the influence of their parental home and form a new, unified partnership with their spouse. The lack of autonomy may create tension, confusion, and difficulty navigating the complex dynamic between a spouse and the spouse's parent. Consequently, both individuals in the marriage may struggle to embrace their adult roles and responsibilities fully, making it harder to thrive as a couple.

BALANCING LOVE AND BOUNDARIES

Jesus and His mother, Mary, exemplified a relationship rooted in love, respect, and a deep understanding of divine purpose. Their interactions in Scripture beautifully illustrate the delicate

---

7. John Bowlby, *Attachment and Loss: Volume 1: Attachment* (London: Hogarth Press, 1969);

John Bowlby, *A Secure Base: Parent-Child Attachment and Healthy Human Development* (New York: Basic Books, 1988).

balance of love and boundaries in a parent-adult child relationship. On multiple occasions, Jesus honored His mother, while Mary, in turn, respected His divine mission.

In Mark 3:31-35, we see an instance where Jesus' mother and brothers came looking for Him while He was teaching. They stood outside and sent word for Him to come out and talk with them. Before this time, at age twelve (Luke 2:41-52), while Jesus was engaging with the teachers in the temple, rather than pulling Him away or imposing her will, Mary recognized His divine calling—one that would culminate in His sacrificial love for His bride, the Church.[8] She gave Him the space to follow His path, not restricting Him but supporting Him with faith and understanding.

Though Mary was His earthly mother, she did not interfere with His ministry once it began—well, except for that one time at the wedding in Cana when she may have gently nudged destiny a bit earlier than scheduled, perhaps by giving Jesus the look that every son knows means, "you can, and you will!" One of the most memorable examples of this delicate dynamic occurs at that very wedding in Cana. When the wine ran out, Mary turned to Jesus, who responded respectfully but firmly, *"Woman, what does this have to do with me? My hour has not yet come"* (John 2:3-4). But out of respect for His mother's concern, He performed His first miracle by turning water into wine, and the celebration continued (John 2:7-11). Here, Jesus honored Mary's request, while Mary trusted His timing and didn't push Him beyond that initial nudge. Her example shows parents the wisdom of knowing when to step back, even when every instinct says to step in.

Again, in John 19:25-27, as Jesus was being crucified, He saw His mother standing by the cross. Despite His suffering, He ensured that she was cared for by entrusting her to His beloved disciple, John, saying, *"Woman, here is your son,"* and to John, *"Here is your mother."* At this moment, He honored Mary by ensuring her well-being even as He fulfilled His greater purpose.

Mary understood and fulfilled her assignment with grace, preparing Jesus for His divine purpose. She knew when to step aside, never holding Him back or seeking to be first in His life. She didn't compete for attention, assert dominance, or manipulate situations to remain relevant or get recognition. She didn't allow her fears of being sidelined or of her precious Son being taken advantage of to overpower her faith. Instead, she entrusted her adult child to the most capable hands of His Heavenly Father, even as He was crucified. Mary recognized that His suffering was for a greater purpose—the salvation of the world[9]—and surrendered to God's will. There's a place of deep understanding that we must all reach in every relationship—one that comes from the wisdom of God and leads us to complete reliance on Him.

---

8. Eph. 5:25-27

9. John 3:16

THE WEAVING OF ROLES AND THE CULTURE TRAP

In some cultures, a woman's success is often measured by her children's accomplishments, leading to intense involvement in their lives. Some mothers see their children as extensions of themselves rather than as individuals with their own paths. Where these mothers lack their own interests, goals, or strong relationships, they may overly invest in their children's lives, sometimes at the expense of the children's independence.

A case in point can be found in Yorùbá culture, where it is common for mothers to affectionately refer to their sons as *oko mi* (my husband). Although this phrase translates to *my husband,* it is not meant romantically or inappropriately. Instead, it reflects deep love, pride, respect, and a cultural view of sons as important male figures in their mothers' lives. It's supposed to be a term of endearment and affection, similar to how English speakers might say "my dear" or "my love." However, this seemingly harmless expression subtly acknowledges and embeds expectations about the future role of the son, potentially shaping his identity and relationships. In some cases, this practice can program societal views of the son's place in the family, possibly creating challenges when it comes time to "leave and cleave" to his spouse.

Due to misogyny and the general mistreatment of women in Nigerian society, I believe this became one way that mothers overcompensated for unhappiness or unfulfillment in their own marriages. Over generations, they began to rely increasingly on their sons to serve as future protectors and providers—much like a husband is expected to care for his wife. It may seem reasonable to raise sons to take care of their mothers, but it becomes problematic when it encroaches on biblical principles. In such cases, a mother-son relationship can potentially fracture the distinct roles of mothers and wives. A mother who views or treats her son as a *husband* may struggle to accept his wife's role in his life. She might expect him to continue prioritizing her needs over those of his wife (or children), which can lead to significant conflict in their relationship.

This type of relationship can blur emotional boundaries and create emotional enmeshment—as described by Murray Bowen's "Family Systems Theory"[10]—and overdependence, where the son feels responsible for his mother's emotional well-being. This can create divided loyalties when he marries, making it difficult for him to truly "leave and cleave" to his wife. Competition and resentment can arise in the absence of grace and discernment, placing the husband in the challenging position of being caught between two women he loves—sometimes to the point where he feels forced to choose.

I'm not a great proponent of certain aspects of our culture, but I embrace and practice the many good things it offers. Some of these include respect for elders and honoring parents—especially mothers—which acknowledges their sacrifice, wisdom, and irreplaceable role in

---

10. Murray Bowen, *Family Therapy in Clinical Practice* (New York: Jason Aronson, 1978).

families. Honoring our parents is a biblical command.[11] However, people often use culture to exert influence or control out of fear or insecurity. As Christians, the Bible tells us there's no fear in love.[12]

One way our culture is used to reinforce deference to elders is by discouraging adult children from openly challenging them. For example, it is considered inappropriate or disrespectful to directly state that a parent or elder has told a lie. Contradicting or disagreeing with them—even when they are wrong—is often viewed in the same light. Instead, euphemistic or diplomatic language is used to navigate such situations, or one may choose to remain silent rather than dispute or refute an elder's words. The Yorùbá saying *Àgbà kii sẹ̀ké* (An elder does not lie) reflects the belief that elders are inherently wise and truthful, although they are not always right. Similarly, *Ohun tí àgbà bá wí, ó dì 'fá* (What an elder says is like an oracle's declaration) suggests that the words of an elder carry unquestionable authority. Thankfully, as society evolves, younger generations are finding ways to respectfully express differing opinions in their dealings with elders while maintaining cultural decorum.

Yorùbás also believe that *ìyá ni wúrà* (a mother is gold). Since mothers bring life into the world and nurture their children, they are regarded with deep reverence. Sometimes, they are even described in Yorùbá praise poetry as *orìsà aiyé* (an earthly deity or divine being). This is not to imply that mothers are literally considered gods, but rather, it is a metaphor reflecting their invaluable role. Ironically, the same society that subjugates and mistreats women later celebrates mothers when they're old and gray! It's as if their worth and respect are only recognized after years of enduring hardship and "paying their dues."

These beliefs have been passed down through generations via folklore, songs, and intentional upbringing, shaping modern consciousness where mothers hold a sacred and authoritative position—akin to a spiritual guardian in some families. Some believe a mother's blessing can significantly influence a child's success, while her curse carries feared spiritual consequences. As a result, many children are raised with a profound sense of reverence toward their mothers, often discouraged from questioning, contradicting, or upsetting them, as doing so is thought to bring grave repercussions. Unfortunately, some mothers misuse this honor—using it as a badge of superiority or a license to perpetuate the very cycles that once oppressed them.

While the African context adds unique cultural layers that can amplify these relationship dynamics, similar sensitivities exist globally. Across societies, it is widely acknowledged that marriages and relationships connected to them can be complex, requiring love, grace, empathy, patience, and clear communication to navigate successfully.

---

11. Exod. 20:12

12. 1 John 4:18

DIVIDED LOYALTIES

So there I was, navigating the struggles in my marriage while also trying to make sense of related cultural nuances. At the time, it seemed logical to expect that, given women's nurturing and empathetic nature, these dynamics would naturally resolve smoothly. However, I soon realized that the very qualities women bring—such as deep emotional investments, protective instincts, and loyalty to loved ones—often made certain situations more delicate, not easier, to address.

What began as an offer of "help" or an effort to "make things easier for me" gradually evolved into a situation where decisions were made on my behalf. There were certain things Ségun did or allowed—perhaps unintentionally—such as frequently seeking advice on matters we could have handled together, which sometimes left me feeling overlooked or excluded in what was meant to be a partnership. By not establishing clear boundaries, he unintentionally blurred the roles within our marriage, making it feel as if external influences held more weight than they should. In his effort to make others feel valued and included, I often felt as though my own role and voice within our relationship were diminished.

I wasn't given much time to settle into my home and new roles at my own pace. Instead, I often felt closely observed, as if every decision I made was being assessed. While guidance can be helpful, I longed for the space to navigate things in my own way and seek advice when needed. At times, it felt like nothing I did was quite right—one baby was supposedly underfed, while the next was considered overfed. Apparently, I couldn't win! Yet their pediatricians insisted they were both perfectly healthy and hitting all their milestones!

Adjusting to an extended family setting can be challenging for a new wife, especially when subtle comparisons arise in areas like caregiving, cooking, and attentiveness—sometimes against deeply ingrained family expectations. When I shared my feelings with Ségun, our conversations often became more emotional than constructive, making it harder to find mutual understanding and resolution.

Ségun and his mother shared a deep bond of loyalty, standing by each other with unwavering support and devotion. While this is natural and admirable, challenges arise in any relationship when honest conversations become difficult and defensiveness takes precedence over open dialogue. Ségun often confided in his mother about our marriage when problems arose, which gradually eroded the feeling of privacy and trust between us. Over time, this contributed to a growing sense of distance and misunderstanding, making it harder to navigate our challenges together.

Anytime my mother-in-law intervened, I felt my concerns about Ségun were often perceived as criticisms of his upbringing rather than issues to be addressed. It seemed as though he could do no wrong because he had been raised well. Any conflicts were seen as my responsibility, and I was even made to think that I had driven him away and pushed him into the arms of another woman—though my feelings on that matter were dismissed as mere imagination.

Instead of a balanced discussion, the focus was skewed toward what I needed to change—how I should take care of my husband and build my home. As time passed, I felt her approach was neither entirely neutral nor supportive in resolving our disputes, making it difficult for me to trust the process. As I withdrew, I sensed growing anger, distrust, and misinterpretation of my words and intentions. Even simple questions or attempts at clarity were sometimes misread, adding to the tension between us.

I struggled to understand their approach to resolving issues or what appeared to be their unwavering allegiance—even when presented with what I considered clear evidence or different perspectives. Coming from a close-knit family myself, I was accustomed to open conversations where we could call each other out on our shortcomings without it being seen as an attack or betrayal. My grandmother and mother, known for their directness, always spoke the truth—but with grace and tact, embodying the principle of *"speaking the truth in love."*[13] But that was a balance I'd clearly yet to master! Maintaining appearances at family functions and other social events became exhausting as time passed, especially when Ségun had key roles or responsibilities. My absence at these gatherings often raised questions, but at that point, I was more focused on my own well-being than how it might reflect on him.

I was done with the charade! At that time, it seemed like many couples around us were just putting on a façade and hiding their marital struggles. While they were celebrated publicly, there was often a different reality behind closed doors—a reality that wasn't acknowledged but was common knowledge. I didn't want to be part of that pattern or lifestyle, and if Ségun wasn't ready to face our challenges together and work toward healing, I couldn't continue pretending while living a lie and calling it love or loyalty!

We had now reached the fifth year of our marriage, having been together for ten years in total. My husband increasingly sought emotional support from outside sources rather than addressing our issues together. This continued to widen the gap and deepen the division between us, with the focus drawn away from our relationship. I, too, began to avoid bringing up our marital issues, feeling that it only led to further conflict. I poured my energy into our children and work and spent more time with my mother, attempting to divert my attention from growing tensions at home. Unfortunately, our individual choices and inactions over time shifted our attention away from each other.

This period marked a complete lack of emotional and physical connection between Ségun and me. We had become little more than housemates. With fewer interactions amidst his comings and goings, our altercations became less frequent. I felt an overwhelming sense of misery, as though life was slowly draining from me. There were moments when the weight of it

---

13. Eph. 4:15

all and the loneliness felt unbearable, and I even thought about ending my life, but my boys and my mother kept me holding on.

JOY BREAKS THROUGH

But joy came in the morning! One day, a beloved friend of mine reached out to check on me, as we hadn't spoken or seen each other in a while. We had been friends since primary school, and our bond had grown to feel more like family. She and her husband were the lead pastors of a church they had recently started, and she invited me to join their Sunday service. I also knew her husband since we all attended the same university, so I accepted the invitation, thinking it would be a welcome break from the tension at home and a chance to reconnect with old friends.

The warmth and joy I felt at the church were undeniable! I was completely drawn in. Every Sunday thereafter, I would put my two boys in their car seats and drive over to join their service. By this point, I'd opened up to my friend and her husband about the struggles I was facing with Ségun, and they became a steady source of support. Alongside my mother, they helped anchor me in love. I was at my breaking point, desperate for answers on what steps to take next, where to go, and what to do. But I found renewed hope, comfort, peace, and a sense of worth through God's truth. I mattered. The boys and I started spending most of our Sundays after church with my friend and her family, and we cherished every moment. They had two boys around the same age as mine, and their extended families were very welcoming—it was precisely what we needed. Indeed, God places the lonely in families (Ps. 68:6 NLT).

Our second son turned one, and we did our best to create a sense of normalcy for his birthday—cake, photos, presents, and special treats. The two boys were happy that day, and I was too. Even Ségun managed to laugh, and we had some enjoyable moments together as a family. I hoped our children would have good memories of that day since I didn't know if we'd ever get to celebrate their birthdays together again as a family. They were just four and one and probably wouldn't remember much from that period, but I wanted our boys to see the photos one day and know that there was a time when Mom and Dad were together and showered them with love. I saw it as an opportunity to talk to Ségun about trying to work things out between us, and I even invited him to join us at church the following Sunday. However, he wasn't interested and made it clear that things had changed between us. He repeated that he still felt we were better apart and insisted that I find alternative accommodation, which he would help pay for.

I was surprised he was still bringing up this matter, especially since we hadn't had any arguments for a month or two. I had also been praying and fasting, hoping for a divine turnaround. Strangely, all of this seemed to spark skepticism and baseless suspicion of my motives, which were often misunderstood or turned against me. The truth is, I was exhausted from fighting!

Going to church, focusing on other things, and spending more time with loved ones reignited my hope and gave me a new sense of purpose. Yet, my husband couldn't see that—or if he did, it didn't seem to matter anymore. During that conversation, he was distant and cold. His eyes were dark, and he looked right through me…no longer at me. He told me our marriage was over and that I should accept it. He said he still loved me but wasn't in love with me…what did that even mean?!

I didn't know what to make of his statement and wondered why my prayers and fasting didn't seem to have the desired effect. For the next couple of days, I had an uneasy feeling that something was about to happen. Despite the promise I'd made to myself not to go through Ségun's things for the sake of my peace, I couldn't shake the feeling that I needed to find out more. I started searching for clues—anything—that might shed light on his plans. It was on his phone that I uncovered the truth, and what rattled me (but also confirmed my suspicions) was the person he was exchanging messages with regarding his plans. I was devastated and confused. My hands trembled as I read the messages, and I realized what was about to happen, but I didn't know how to stop it.

I shared the information I had gathered with my mother as well as my friend and her husband, who were now my pastors. They were all concerned about my safety and suggested that I let Ségun know I was aware of his plans and agree to his request to leave to avoid a potential eviction from my home that could lead to violence or public humiliation. They believed this would buy me some time and allow me to move my belongings out properly. I refused to listen to them and asked for prayers. No one was going to scare me or force me out of my home! What troubled me a bit was that there was no mention of our children in the conversations I saw on his phone—the part I could view within the brief window of opportunity I had. Was the plan to force me out and take them from me? Each morning after that, I woke up not in fear, but with uncertainty about when the plan would be set in motion.

I don't know where I found the strength—perhaps that was why I felt prompted to be especially prayerful during that period—but I managed to keep my discovery from Ségun. I remained calm and stuck to my daily routine: dropping off our boys at my mother's house since they were on vacation, going to work, picking them up, and heading straight home. My mother pleaded with me daily to, at the very least, move some important things to her house, but I refused. For me, it wasn't just about still loving my husband and wanting our marriage to work—it was also more of a mental or spiritual matter. I didn't want anything to suggest I was the one who gave up on our marriage or moved out of our home. Part of me also wanted to see the full extent of this "coup d'état" unfold.

The only things I decided to take from the house for safekeeping were my old passports, which turned out to be a wise decision given what happened next. I strongly felt D-Day was fast approaching, as I could sense Ségun's growing unease. He was making more phone calls in hushed tones from the guest room, where he had been sleeping—something I had long grown accustomed to. And he barely spoke to me ...

I found it difficult to even look at my husband anymore. Each time I thought about or glanced at the photos I had taken of the conversations on his phone, all I could see was a man who appeared to be heavily influenced by others and was caught in the grip of external pressures. Yet, beneath my anger and frustration, I also felt a deep sadness for him. He was considering only one solution: to crush the so-called insurrection! It was all there in black and white, and this time, no one could deny it or tell me I had imagined this, too!

Large boxes had already been arranged to remove my belongings from my home, standing by and ready for pick up. That's what I had been reduced to in their eyes—an inconvenience, something to be disposed of like trash! There were countless messages, each revealing more than I'd ever imagined about the man I loved with my whole being. But at least now, I had the answers I needed—for my own clarity and for posterity.

Truly, there's a thin line between love and hate that can be crossed in an instant. Yet, we must never forget that while destruction can happen in a moment, rebuilding what is broken or healing from what others have shattered can take a lifetime! But no matter how long the journey of healing takes, remember: *God heals the brokenhearted and binds up their wounds* (Ps. 147:3).

THROUGH SÉGUN'S LENSES

The birth of our second son was a welcome reminder about the sheer joy of parenthood, and Funké and I could not have been more proud or thankful. As the months went by, we were intentional in our attempt to mend our relationship, putting our children front and center of those efforts.

Watching two bright, energetic, and curious little boys grow was a blessing for us. We tried to make the atmosphere in our home as conducive as possible for them. However, after a while it was impossible to hide the fact that Funké and I were struggling once again. As attention shifted back to us and our inability to reconnect from a place of love, understanding, and genuine trust, embers from our previous conflicts that had disappeared began to reignite and spread.

I would say that we were relatively successful in shielding our children from the direct effect of the disarray behind the scenes, but even young children can sense when things are not okay between their parents. For me, the hardest part of going through that period was not knowing just how much their young minds were picking up and, more importantly, how they would respond when faced with what I knew was an inevitable separation.

Funké's longstanding conviction that I was leading a conspiracy against her, with external influence, was unfounded. I was particularly disturbed by her repeated assertion that I was constantly on the lookout for ways to trip her up and that throwing her under the bus had become a virtual pastime for me. The vitriol and scathing criticism that accompanied her outbursts led me to repeatedly question how she thought we could be happy living together under such inauspicious conditions. Having looked back at my response mechanism at the time, it was based on a perceived assault on my manhood and my abilities as a problem-solver, thus hurting my pride. Responses based on pride are at total variance with what God expects of us, as it shuts Him out of the process and ignores His expectations of us.

Rearview Mirror Lesson

There is no denying the fact that from early on in our marriage, I was severely tested by Funké's pointed accusations about where my loyalty lay vis-à-vis my extended family and friends. I was at times dumbfounded by the totality of some of the things I heard.

The bottom line is that I could have dug deeper and accepted the reality that, wittingly or unwittingly, I was not giving Funké the assurance and protection that she sought. This process could have involved playing a more deliberate role in respectfully— and thoughtfully—establishing boundaries to regulate my different relationships to remove any doubt in her mind about the pride of place that she occupied in my life. That would have been in keeping with God's Word that expects husbands to ensure that married life, in its totality, represents a safe harbor for their wives.

9

What I Feared the Most

"For the thing which I greatly feared is come upon me,
And that which I was afraid of is come unto me."

JOB 3:25 KJV

FRIGHT, FLIGHT, OR FIGHT

Everything came to a grinding halt just weeks after our second son's first birthday. Battle lines were drawn, and we each dug in our heels while family on both sides rallied behind their own contender. It was game, set, and match for our marriage! I must have read those messages from Ségun's phone a hundred times, replaying our son's birthday over and over in my mind. Wasn't this the same person who had just played with our children, eaten the cake, taken photos, and carried on as if nothing was about to change? I wanted someone to wake me from the nightmare!

Still in this dreamlike state, I got up each day and went to work, but my mind was elsewhere—consumed by my fate and that of my children. I had just passed the four-month mark of a six-month probationary period at my office, so I couldn't take time off to pull myself together. Yet, even in the midst of the turmoil, God was still at work—He always is![1] Just when I needed it most, I was offered a permanent managerial position—an unexpected blessing at the perfect time. My mother and I called each other on the hour over the next few days, ensuring I was okay and that nothing had happened with the children in case there was an attempt to take them from her home while I was at work. I got through each day on a prayer!

---

1. Ps. 121:4

Going home felt very different now—like stepping into an enemy's camp. In the rare moments we interacted, Ségun would scowl at me and speak with utter disdain. It was as if he was putting in so much effort to convince himself that he hated me or that he no longer had any feelings for me—perhaps to justify his plans. Or maybe I was in denial, and he had never truly loved me.

The day finally came. One afternoon at work, I received a frantic call from my mother. She asked if my husband had called me, and when I said, "No," she hesitated before asking if I could leave work early and come to her house. My heart pounded—I feared something had happened to my children, but she quickly reassured me, urging me to stay calm. She explained that her security guard had just informed her that some delivery men had shown up at her house, claiming my husband had instructed them to deliver two large boxes for me. Concerned, she suggested I call him and advised against going home straight from the office. She had already tried reaching Ségun, but he wasn't answering her calls. Not wanting to disrupt my workday unnecessarily, she had waited, hoping first to assess the situation—unsure of how I would react.

But first things first—what was in the boxes? I asked my mother to open them while I stayed on the line. She confirmed that they contained some of my and my sons' belongings—clothes and shoes shoved into two large cardboard boxes. I immediately tried calling Ségun, but he didn't answer. A flood of emotions hit me all at once—panic, anger, fear, helplessness, embarrassment, shame, rejection, sadness.... *Why Ségun? Why?* I couldn't hold back the tears; they spilled freely down my cheeks. I called my mother again, asking her to get some help to bring the boxes inside and lock herself and the children in the house. Thankfully, it was the end of the workday by the time I hung up. I wasted no time and jumped in my car, driving home as fast as possible.

My first instinct was to try to see Ségun in person since he wasn't taking my calls. I needed answers. But more than that, I had to make sure the boys and I had what we needed—at least enough clothes for work and daily essentials for the next couple of weeks or until Ségun and I figured things out—I was hopeful for a quick resolution. My mind raced through everything I had left behind—items in drawers, suitcases, closets. *Who packed our things? Who decided what I could have and what I couldn't? How could he?* Halfway through the drive, another thought crossed my mind—I could use my connections at work to arrange for armed police officers to escort me into the house. That way, I could retrieve the rest of my belongings and show Ségun that he wasn't the only one who could play dirty. But reality hit. That move could easily spiral out of control. If things escalated, I'd be painted as the aggressor. And I wasn't about to give him that advantage.

The security guards stepped forward, positioning themselves between my car and the gate. Their expressions were firm, almost unreadable. Then came the blow: *Oga* (the boss, Ségun) had given strict orders that morning—under no circumstances was I allowed back on the premises. I stared at them in disbelief. The home I had shared with my husband for five years. The place where we had raised our two boys together. These guards had smiled and greeted me just hours earlier as I left for work. The same men I had frequently tipped—a gesture of appreciation common in Nigeria, especially for blue-collar workers and those in the protective service industry—had turned against me.

After spending about forty-five minutes arguing with the guards, insisting they let me in to at least speak with my husband since I couldn't reach him on the phone, one of them approached my car, seeing how upset I was. He pleaded with me to leave to avoid further embarrassment. My phone had been ringing nonstop during the whole ordeal, and I knew my mother would be worried, so I finally answered to reassure her. She was concerned that something might have happened between Ségun and me.

I thought about so many things I could do to force my way into the house, but I kept hearing that "still small voice" whispering: *Be still, I will fight for you; go to your children.* Two scriptures also came to mind, but I didn't pay any attention to them at the time. I wish I had! Although I'd been praying, I'd been doing all the talking and hadn't really been mindful of God's instructions for this situation. I later noted those scriptures in my journal, but it wasn't until months after the incident that I revisited them to seek clarity. That was when I realized God had been with me all along, right there in the "valley"—even before the separation. In the last few weeks in my home, I sought Him out of fear and desperation, God showed that He is omnipresent and His unrelenting love pursues us no matter where we are.

"Where can I go from Your Spirit?
Or where can I flee from Your presence?
If I ascend into heaven, You are there;
If I make my bed in hell, behold, You are there.
If I take the wings of the morning,
And dwell in the uttermost parts of the sea,
Even there Your hand shall lead me,
And Your right hand shall hold me.
If I say, "Surely the darkness shall fall on me,"
Even the night shall be light about me."
(Ps. 139:7-11)

Despite my fluctuating spiritual life over the years, God never gave up on me, and His mercy was ever-present. An earthly father might have abandoned me at the gate that day, saying, "I told you so," or "You brought this on yourself—deal with it." And even though my husband gave up on me, God didn't. He was right there beside me.[2] Like the parable of the lost sheep in Luke 15:4-7 and the analogy of the wandering sheep in 1 Peter 2:25, who returned to the Shepherd and Guardian of their soul—God seeks us out. He knew exactly how to reach and reassure me. The two scriptures that He impressed again upon my heart that day as I sat in my car—feeling defeated and deflated outside the gate of my own home—marked the beginning of the "signposts" God placed along my personal journey with Him.

While at the gate of my home, I didn't realize that those Bible verses I thought had randomly popped up in my head were road signs and guideposts. Yes, in that moment, they were promptings from the Holy Spirit specifically for me—set up as markers, timely instructions, encouragement, guidance, direction, and prophecies to help me find my way back home— both spiritually to Him and physically from "exile."[3] I finally gave God the rightful place in my life, and in doing so, became attuned to His voice, able to hear Him clearly. I had already kept a journal—a kind of "black book" where I recorded Ségun's "wrongdoings"—but I turned it into a roadmap that guided me through the pain, reaffirmed God's promises, and helped me navigate the path to healing and restoration. Each entry became a step forward, a reminder that I wasn't alone on this journey.

The first scripture: *"Truly, truly, I say to you, unless a grain of wheat falls into the earth and dies, it remains alone; but if it dies, it bears much fruit. Whoever loves his life loses it, and whoever hates his life in this world will keep it for eternal life. If anyone serves me, he must follow me; and where I am, there will my servant be also. If anyone serves me, the Father will honor him."* (John 12:24-26)

This is a parable Jesus shared with His disciples, referring to His own impending death. As a signpost to me at the start of my solo journey, it foretold a path of spiritual growth I would experience through surrender. My flesh would have to die to self-sabotaging choices—"self" being the operative word here—with anger and rage topping the list. It wasn't going to be a pain-free, one-time exercise but a transformation process. It meant taking up my cross and following Jesus—no longer just a scripture verse, a cliché, or a song, but a tangible reality in my life.[4]

The second scripture: *"For we will surely die and become like water spilled on the ground, which cannot be gathered up again. Yet God does not take away a life; but He devises means, so that His banished ones are not expelled from Him."* (2 Sam. 14:14)

I was already familiar with this verse, having used the latter portion to pray for my husband. However, it took a much deeper meaning than I initially realized. This verse was spoken by the wise woman of Tekoa, whom Joab sent to persuade King David to reconcile with his estranged son, Absalom. She used a metaphor comparing life to water spilled on the ground, emphasizing that everyone will face death and that life is fleeting. Yet, she also highlighted God's mercy

---

2. Deut. 31:6, 8; Isa. 41:10; Jer. 23:23-24; Rom. 8:38-39; Heb. 13:5b

3. Jer. 31:21

4. Luke 9:23

and redemptive nature, explaining that while death is inevitable, God does not desire permanent separation. Instead, He provides ways of restoration and reconciliation for those who are estranged, distant, or exiled. The woman urged David to forgive Absalom, reflecting God's own nature—He makes a way for the lost to return through Jesus Christ.

2 Samuel 14:14 became a constant reminder of the brevity of life and the importance of doing what we ought to do—seeking God's forgiveness,[5] embracing peace and reconciliation,[6] and accepting God's mercy and salvation through Christ[7]—while we are alive and still have the opportunity. David and Absalom's story serves as a tragic example of unresolved conflict. While David loved his son Absalom, his inability to fully forgive and restore their relationship fueled lingering resentment, ultimately ending in loss.[8]

As I drove away from my home, uncertain of what the coming days, weeks, and even the next few hours would bring, I couldn't help but wonder what could drive someone to do this to another human being—someone they claimed to love—the mother of their two children. I couldn't fathom what was happening to my boys and me. All I wanted was to get to my mother's house quickly and hold them close, to soothe a heart that felt shattered into pieces. What would I tell them when they asked why we weren't in our home anymore and where their daddy was?

Upon arrival at my mother's house, I sat in the car briefly, gathering what little strength I could before facing my children. Ségun still wasn't answering my calls, so I took a deep breath and entered the house. There they were … our lives, suddenly packed up, stuffed into two recycled cardboard boxes, and left on my mother's porch. I just stood there, staring in disbelief. My sons were distracted, watching cartoons on TV, while my mom hugged me tight, whispering that everything would be all right. She kept telling me not to break down in front of my children and that I had to be strong for them and myself. I couldn't eat; I was numb, stunned! But in a strange way, I felt relieved. At least the suspense was over. I had God, my children, a family and friends that loved me, a job … things could have been worse!

I'm so grateful for the mother God blessed me with. She saw that I was confused and immediately took charge, insisting I quickly inventory what had been sent to me to ensure that I had everything I needed for work the following day. I wanted to call in sick, but she encouraged me to stay busy and keep moving forward with my life. "The end of a marriage doesn't have to mean the end of you," she assured me. "Besides, it's not over until God says so."

She was determined not to let me fall into depression—not that night, not ever! She wouldn't even let me cry in peace until the boys were tucked in and asleep. I couldn't hold it

---

5. Isa. 55:6-7; 1 John 1:9

6. Luke 6:37

7. Isa. 55:7; Lam. 3:22; Acts 4:12; Rom. 10:9-10; Rev. 3:20

8. 2 Sam. 15-18

together any longer, so I let the floodgates open as soon as she took them in to get ready for bed. I wailed and cried out to God, asking, "Why?" The events of the day were too hard to process, and not hearing from Ségun only worsened it. I can't remember if it was that night or the next day when he sent a curt text message saying he had no choice and had to do what he did in everyone's best interest. I thought: *Truly, man's heart is deceitful above all things and desperately wicked; who can know it?*[9]

Some clothes, shoes, and bags had been hastily thrown into the boxes, so I had to sift through them to find something appropriate for work. So many items were missing. While there had been hurtful moments between us before, the events of that day and everything leading up to it carried a weight that was difficult to ignore and took a very long time to fully release.

Many of my belongings remained at the house, and some I never recovered. Among them were my school certificates and important documents, many of which I have yet to replace. When Ségun eventually brought more of our things to my mother's home, those documents were not included. Later on, when I finally had access to them, I found the bag containing them had been exposed to moisture. The contents were damp, moldy, and stuck together—the print had faded, and pages tore with every attempt to separate them. Ségun said he hadn't realized they were in that condition or even aware they had been stored in the house.

This underscores the lasting impact of a painful separation—emotionally and practically. It highlights how the aftermath of a broken relationship can extend far beyond the initial heartbreak, affecting essential aspects of life such as personal records, identity documents, and the ability to move forward with stability. The loss and damage of important documents symbolize a deeper theme: the disruption and erasure of a past life. These papers were not just pieces of paper to me; they represented years of education, achievements, and personal history—elements of identity that became collateral damage in the separation. The time it took to retrieve them and the eventual discovery of their ruined state mirrors the broader emotional journey of trying to reclaim what was lost, only to realize that some things may never be restored to their original form.

Separation or divorce is not always about two people going their separate ways; it can have long-term, unintended consequences. It also raises questions about intent versus neglect—whether these losses were deliberate or merely an unfortunate oversight—illustrating how ripples of impact unfold over time, even after the initial act of splitting up.

I struggled to understand if his plan was meant to teach me a lesson—what about our children? What had they done to deserve this, and what were they supposed to take away from it? What could their mother have done that was so unforgivable that the consequences also extended to them? Did they not matter in all this, or were they simply caught in the crossfire—unintended casualties of a larger conflict? What if I had nowhere to go for refuge that evening?

---

9. Jer. 17:9

The man I had trusted, committed to, and built a life with had chosen to discard not just me but the family we had built together. I wasn't worth fighting for. I wasn't worth the patience, understanding, or time. And rather than taking a careful, measured approach, a forceful, drastic decision was made.

That night, sleep eluded me. I felt raw, duped, and stripped bare, as though the foundation of life I had known had been pulled from under me. Lying next to my children, muffling my sobs into a pillow, I whispered the only prayer my heart could form:

> *Oh God, You see and hear all; nothing is hidden from You … please, vindicate me … let the truth be known!*

> *"You have kept count of my tossings; put my tears in your bottle. Are they not in your book?"* (Ps. 56:8)

> *"In God have I put my trust and confident reliance; I will not be afraid. What can man do to me?"* (Ps. 56:11 AMP)

The next day, I had to put on the proverbial stiff upper lip at work. I wanted nothing more than to disappear into a quiet, hidden space where no one could see me. But my colleagues' concern and repeated questions about my red, swollen eyes made that impossible. I was a complete mess! By midday, my boss pulled me aside, gently suggesting that I go home and rest, as it was clear I wasn't myself. For the next week, I moved through my days on autopilot, barely able to think straight or stomach a proper meal. Sleep became a distant memory—each night was spent lost in thought, tears, or prayer, searching for some semblance of peace.

Ségun finally called about a week later to speak with our boys. The following weeks were spent negotiating the return of our remaining belongings. My parents took the initiative to arrange family interventions and reach out to his parents in hopes of reconciliation, though their efforts were not met with openness.

Yet, life had to move forward. Every attempt to reach Ségun was met with coldness and detachment I had never encountered before. It was difficult to reconcile this version of him with the man I had known since I was nineteen—the one who once promised me the world. I couldn't help but recall his wedding speech, where he declared that I was his wife and his life. Looking back, I wondered if those words had been him waxing lyrical rather than a reflection of what was to come. The change in him hadn't happened overnight, but in my longing to hold on, I failed to see how much we had drifted apart. Now, the reality was undeniably clear for all to see!

I finally woke up from the nightmare into a stark reality I wasn't ready to face—one I had refused to prepare for. I had no strategy, no backup plan; separation or divorce hadn't even been on my radar when I got married. My parents separated when I was about eighteen months old and my brother was only three. It hit me hard that this painful cycle of marital strife and separation had resurfaced in my own life, just as my children were at the same tender age—four and one. It felt as though history was repeating itself, attempting to take root in my own family.

I didn't want dysfunction and all its complexities to affect my children or be passed down to the next generation. I had heard a few sermons about "negative patterns and cycles," and it struck me that, just as destructive habits and sinful cycles can be perpetuated, there's a responsibility on our part to claim freedom through the Word of God and stand firm on the finished work of Christ on the cross. Through repentance, obedience, and embracing God's grace in Christ, these harmful "hand-me-downs" can be stopped. Though they may have been passed down through generations, by my God, they will not pass through me! I realized that destiny-defining decisions had to be made. I was determined to break the cycle and set a positive standard for my lineage. So, I decided to do all I could to seek God's perfect will, not just for me but for my children.

However, I didn't feel ready or equipped to embark on this fight. All I wanted to do was retreat into myself, consumed by anger. Loving the way God instructs us isn't easy, especially when one has been deeply hurt. It's impossible in our human strength, but only through His divine power. At the start of the separation, I couldn't imagine continuing to love Ségun. My bruised ego cried out for revenge! I even wished for the sky to fall on him and anyone who supported him!

I regretted having listened to my mother when she talked me out of using my "carnal weapon" … At least I would've felt like I had a point on the scoreboard! But God's Word always came to the rescue and reined those thoughts in, reminding me to turn the other cheek and choose peace over vengeance. *"Do not be overcome by evil, but overcome evil with good."* (Rom. 12:21) Every time I voiced those thoughts or feelings, my mom would remind me: "That's not Christ-like."[10] She'd say, "You can't hate your husband, the father of your children," followed by her usual mantra: "When you know better, you do better"—her way of calling people to higher standards, no matter the offense.

I wasn't as grace-filled as my mother back then. I believe that knowing the right thing isn't always enough, as it doesn't guarantee that the right actions will follow. It takes character and wisdom to do what's truly right. It requires a renewed mind, a clean heart, and a transformed perspective. Our decisions are often deeply influenced by our habits, values, upbringing, and character—who we truly are. So, instead of focusing solely on making good decisions, we would be better served by developing good character. Some say that cultivating virtue and goodness will naturally lead to good decisions. But according to the Bible, true wisdom comes

---

10. Col. 3:12-17

from seeking God's guidance, trusting in Him, and aligning our choices with His will.[11] Our decisions (even the seemingly mundane ones we make daily) are meant to honor God and reflect His character.

Unknown to me, God had been preparing me long before the separation...even before I was born![12] Nothing surprises Him. He knows the end from the beginning and paves the way for us.[13] Even my background in psychology was part of His design, helping me navigate the journey with a sense of clarity and wholeness. It allowed me to process situations and actions (especially responses)—including mine—with fresh perspective, finding the right balance between heart-driven (emotion-based) and head-driven (logic-based) decisions, and ultimately moving toward making God-centered choices. These God-refined decisions are grounded in His truth, focused on His purposes, and lead us closer to Him while transforming us into the people He has called us to be.

Even from rehashing my raw emotions of grief and anger in the paragraphs above, it's clear that, like many women, I was often driven by feelings, sentiments, desires, intuition, and personal values in weighing the emotional consequences of my husband's actions. In contrast, like many men, Ségun's decisions seemed more logic-driven—analytical, calculated, and solution-focused ("How do I fix this?"). He based his choices on facts, reasoning, and intellect, often focusing on the immediate and short-term impact after considering his version of pros and cons. These decision-making approaches aren't absolute, of course, as numerous other factors, such as personality, environment (settings and situations), biological influences (brain structure and hormones), social conditioning, upbringing, and life experiences, all contribute to how we make decisions or approach problem-solving.[14]

Another strong "driver" during that time was fear. What I faced seemed like insurmountable giants. To move toward victory, I had to choose each day between two responses: flight or fight. Just as Elijah fled in fear in 1 Kings 19:3-4, and David stood his ground against Goliath in 1 Samuel 17:45-50, I was confronted with two offshoots of F.E.A.R.—Forget Everything And Run or Face Everything And Rise.[15] I needed to rely on F.A.I.T.H.: Focus on Allowing

11. Prov. 2:6; 3:5-7; James 1:5

12. Ps. 139:13-17; Isa. 49:1; Eph. 2:10

13. Isa. 45:2; 46:9-10

14. L. Eliot, A. Ahmed, H. Khan, and J. Patel, *How Men's and Women's Brains Are Different* (Stanford Medicine, 2021), https://stanmed.stanford.edu/how-mens-and-womens-brains-are-different;

L. M. Wierenga et al., "Greater within-Sex Variability in Brain Structure and Function in Males than Females: A Multi-Sample Study," *Frontiers in Human Neuroscience* 14 (2020): 244, https://www.frontiersin.org/articles/10.3389/fnhum.2020.00244/full;

"The Impact of Social Conditioning on Women's Leadership," *Cogent Info*, 2023, https://www.cogentinfo.com/resources/the-impact-of-social-conditioning-on-womens-leadership;

K. B. Coffman, C. L. Exley, and M. Niederle, "When Gender Matters in Decision-Making: The Role of Perceived Social Preferences," *The Quarterly Journal of Economics* 140, no. 1 (2025): 40356, https://academic.oup.com/qje/article/140/1/403/7926978.

15. Deut. 31:6; Josh. 1:9; Isa. 41:10

Infinite Trust in Him—trusting in God's protection, guidance, and provision. *"For God has not given us a spirit of fear, but of power and of love and of a sound mind."* (2 Tim. 1:7)

THROUGH SÉGUN'S LENSES

When it became obvious to me that something was about to give, and Funké continued to refuse to consider a separation, let alone a divorce, I knew I had to take drastic action. Although on the surface, it appeared as if our marriage was holding up, dangerous undercurrents were still chipping away at its foundation.

I could not ignore clear signs that she was on an emotional rollercoaster and struggling to cope with the various issues we were dealing with. Previous efforts at drawing her mother's and aunt's attention to worrisome behavior that I felt could result in her hurting herself or me were not treated with the seriousness they deserved. They were explained away by her age and wanting to draw attention to herself. This left me feeling even more concerned as I believed that trivializing serious issues, or completely sweeping them under the carpet, could result in unpleasant outcomes.

At different times and in different ways, such behavior came fully into view, making it impossible for me to pretend that everything was okay. One morning after she left for work, I gathered together as many of her and our two sons' belongings as I could and accompanied a delivery van to her mother's home where they were dropped off after I confirmed that she was there.

Upon returning home, I instructed the guards not to let Funké back onto the premises. I knew Funké would take this badly, but my mind was made up. Until we were able to reach an agreement about the custody of our children, it made sense for them to be with her. I knew that being away from my children would be painful, but it was necessary. Funké and I would have to find a way to cushion the effect of our boys being separated from their parents.

Funké subsequently spoke about the humiliation she felt due to my actions on that day. She was convinced they were part of an orchestrated plan to punish her and teach her a lesson. However, the decision was entirely mine, and my mind was made up after long and careful reflection on the severity of the situation we were dealing with.

Inasmuch as my decision was underpinned by a deliberate thought process, I did not fully appreciate the effect it would have on everyone concerned. This is where I think many parents underestimate the repercussions of separation and divorce, only to have to pick up the pieces later. Being the instigator of the separation, I realize that a better appreciation of the risks involved would have made me more circumspect regarding my actions.

Rearview Mirror Lesson

Marital differences that are not promptly and fully thrashed out can harbor mistrust and resentment between husband and wife. It then becomes easy to find an excuse for actions one has already concluded are necessary or unavoidable. This sums up where I was—mentally and emotionally—which allowed my beliefs to become self-fulfilling prophecies. For these reasons, in the build-up to our separation, I left little space for anything beyond skimming the surface of thorny issues that divided us, as the atmosphere in our home was unconducive. Any remnants of love, mutual trust, and respect soon evaporated as my actions were tantamount to lighting a fuse and awaiting an explosion.

10

The Cost of Ignorance

"The potential of women is often overlooked, underestimated, or even outrightly dismissed—hence the urgent call for us to arise. This is not a call to oppose men, but instead to rise into our God-ordained purpose, break free from ignorance, and confidently walk in the truth of our identity. This isn't a battle that women are meant to face alone, but a shared mission to challenge unjust systems, cultural mindsets, and spiritual strongholds that hinder our collective growth. Men are not our adversaries in this endeavor, but vital partners called to stand alongside women in championing a future where both can thrive in their God-given callings."

FUNKÉ ADENIJI

TRAPPED IN THE FAMILIAR

No one should have to endure what I experienced when Ségun decided to end our marriage. However, such situations are commonplace around the world—especially in Africa—where women, regardless of their education or social status, often face systemic and destabilizing obstacles in marriage, justice, and personal security. Deep-rooted traditions and societal norms continue to influence these realities, leaving many women vulnerable and unable to handle separation or divorce with dignity or fair recourse.

The level of humiliation I went through should never be inflicted on anyone. No individual or group should have unchecked power to control another person's life—whether in marriage, parenting, or property. Yet, more than two decades later, countless women are still being unceremoniously removed from their matrimonial homes and often denied access to their children or possessions. Through our platform, T.R.Y. H.A.R.D.—*Trust and Revere Yahweh; He Always Rewards Diligence*, Ségun and I have encountered instances of women facing similar struggles. Their touching and, oftentimes, heartbreaking stories continue to emphasize the urgent need for structural and cultural reforms.

The environment in which a couple lives can significantly influence how they relate to each other. I've seen how relationships either improve or deteriorate, depending on cultural expectations, legal protections, stereotyping, and faith or religion. If the environment were less tolerant of maltreatment—through the enactment of stronger laws, consistent law enforcement, and appropriate consequences for wrongdoing—such excesses could potentially be curtailed, resulting in more respectful relationships.

Education and empowerment are essential, but if entrenched systems and biases, policies, and cultural frameworks continue to reinforce inequality or afford unconscionable protections to misogynistic offenders, meaningful change will be difficult to achieve. We also need to reconsider how we raise boys today. It's not enough to educate girls and empower women if we're still raising boys with unchecked entitlement mentalities and a predisposition to exhibit domineering attitudes toward women or perpetuate erroneous patriarchal beliefs. These boys become the men who build and lead the very systems that determine the pace and nature of progress, making justice, equity, and true liberation for women difficult, whether slowly or incrementally.

Some of the most painful forms of discrimination and prejudices women face aren't written into law—they're embedded in culture as unspoken rules. I experienced this firsthand while searching for an apartment after our separation. Although I had temporarily stayed with my mother, it became necessary to find a place of my own for the children and me. But time and again, agents and landlords refused to rent their properties to me simply because I was a "single mother." In Nigeria, twenty years ago, divorced or separated women were often viewed with suspicion and contempt—they were believed to be irresponsible, promiscuous, or financially unstable. Instead of receiving empathy, many women were subjected to rejection and disrespect.

Despite my eligibility, and even after my super-supportive childhood friend and her pastor husband stood as guarantors for a prospective property, the landlord—also a clergyman—still declined. I eventually had to settle for a less-than-ideal option—one that met our immediate needs but fell short of what I really wanted. The whole experience revealed how deeply ingrained these societal biases were—and how they had become strongholds, allowing prejudice to masquerade as policy and making vulnerable women feel powerless and helpless. Patriarchy —embedded in culture—isn't a respecter of education, class, money, status, or religion.

Even with these patriarchal structures, some women have managed to break through. Their hard work and resilience have paved the way for others, proving that success is possible even in the face of adversity and limitations. However, many more remain stuck—trapped by cultural beliefs, systemic inequality, and environments that have long silenced and stifled their potential. The consequences aren't just personal; they're generational. When oppressive systems are left unchallenged, they not only replicate but often become deeply entrenched, causing harmful consequences for those who follow.

This is similar to what the Israelites faced in the Promised Land. When Joshua led Israel to conquer Canaan, he drove out most of the giants—the *Anakim*—but some survived and were left behind in the Philistine cities of Gaza, Gath, and Ashdod (Josh. 11:21-22). Those remnants later reemerged as threats. The very giant that David defeated—Goliath of Gath—was likely a descendant of those same giants Israel encountered in the Promised Land, whom they had failed to eliminate.[1] Their presence represented unfinished battles, unvanquished strongholds, and ignored instructions from God. And just as ignorance led to fear and paralysis among the spies in Numbers 13:32-33, it continues to do the same today when we allow misguided cultural norms or spiritual apathy to shape our boundaries.

Because the Anakim remained in Philistine territory, Israel's failure to fully conquer them led to their resurgence as future threats. David's victory over Goliath[2] became a decisive full-circle moment. What one generation feared and left unfinished, a later generation—armed with faith—confronted and overcame. Likewise, what we refuse to challenge today—out of convenience, fear, and cultural familiarity or blind acceptance of the status quo—may grow into stronger systems of oppression for the next generation. When left unchecked, ignorance becomes a tool of the enemy to keep people bound in straitjackets. But once known, truth demands action—and it starts with refusing to remain trapped in established norms that do not serve the good of all people.

Women aren't as helpless, weak, or inferior as culture, tradition, or even religious misinterpretations have led many to believe—especially not by God's standards. Galatians 3:28 teaches that faith in Christ brings equality and unity, not necessarily in roles and responsibilities—but in value, honor, and equal standing before God. It breaks down the walls that society builds, showing that in God's family, no one is second class. Everyone who belongs to Christ is equally accepted, loved, and included in His Kingdom. Scripture consistently reveals that God sees women as strong, wise, and capable of making great impact.[3] Yet, many suffer under the weight of deception, ignorance, and oppressive systems, often unaware of their identity or authority in Christ.[4]

---

1. Num. 13:33; Josh. 11:22; 1 Sam. 17:4
2. 1 Sam. 17
3. Judg. 4:4-9; Prov. 31:25
4. Hosea 4:6

Women have the power to rise above societal expectations and walk boldly in God's truth—just like those who came before us. Take Deborah and Esther, for example. Despite the cultural barriers of their time, they achieved great exploits for God. Deborah was a prophetess, judge, and military leader—roles uncommon for women in ancient Israel—yet she led an entire nation to victory.[5] Esther was a young Jewish woman in the Persian Empire who risked her life to save her people, strategically using her position and influence as queen for God's purpose.[6] These women didn't conform to what was expected of them—they obeyed God, and history was changed. This aligns with Daniel 11:32b: *"… but the people who know their God shall be strong, and carry out great exploits."*

Other women in the Bible who showed remarkable courage, influence, and leadership despite the cultural limitations of their time include:

- **Jael**—A woman who secured victory for Israel by defeating the enemy commander, Sisera. (Judg. 4:17-22)

- **Shiphrah and Puah**—The Hebrew midwives who defied Pharaoh's orders and saved many Israelite babies. (Exod. 1:17, 20-21)

- **The daughters of Zelophehad**—These women boldly challenged unjust inheritance laws and won the right to their father's property, establishing a legal precedent for women. (Num. 27:1-7)

- **Huldah**—A prophetess who confirmed God's word to King Josiah, which led to national repentance. (2 Kings 22:14-20)

- **Abigail**—A wise woman who averted disaster and influenced King David through her diplomacy. (1 Sam. 25:18-35)

- **The woman of Thebez**—Played a decisive role in the downfall of the tyrant, Abimelech, bringing his reign to an end with one act of courage. (Judg. 9:50-53)

- **Mary, the mother of Jesus**—Played a crucial role in God's redemption plan by humbly submitting to His will. (Luke 1:38)

These accounts remind us that God empowers women to walk in authority, fulfill His purpose, and leave a lasting impact. Through faith, wisdom, and courage, these women shaped history, changed laws, led nations, and saved many lives. Their courage and reverence for God brought about His blessing and protection over them.

---

5. Judg. 4:4-9; 5:7
6. Esther 4:14; 8:5-8

Societal, cultural, or systemic structures have long shaped how women are expected to think, act, and live—often confining them to traditional roles rooted in unhealthy patriarchy. These patterns are subtly reinforced through family expectations, economic and educational limitations, media portrayals, and religious influences. Over generations, such conditioning has affected how women see themselves, their worth, and their place in society, relationships, and even in God's Kingdom.

In John 10:10, Jesus says: *"The thief does not come except to steal, and to kill, and to destroy. I have come that they may have life, and that they may have it more abundantly."* One of satan's key strategies is to try to rob people of God's truth. For unbelievers, he blinds them from seeing the light of the Gospel.[7] For believers, he distorts their understanding of their identity and authority in Christ through lies, deception,[8] distraction, and spiritual blindness—keeping many from walking in the fullness of the life Christ offers.

The "abundant life" Jesus speaks of in this passage isn't about status, worldly success, or material wealth. It's a deep, rich, and fulfilling life found in a relationship with Him—one of inner peace,[9] eternal life,[10] freedom from sin and death,[11] divine purpose,[12] true joy and contentment,[13] healing and wholeness,[14] and authentic love expressed in meaningful relationships.[15]

Sadly, while many women yearn for the freedom and fullness Jesus offers, they're still bound by frustrations rooted in patriarchal norms and generational cycles of inequality and oppression. Sometimes, the missed opportunities for change aren't just external—they stem from gaps left by previous generations of women who either couldn't or wouldn't challenge the status quo. In response, some women are redefining institutions like marriage and womanhood through a lens shaped more by cultural pain and personal experience than by God's truth—placing God on the sidelines, if at all.

Family structures and traditional values have undergone major changes. Today, girls are increasingly being raised to be strong, resilient women and encouraged to strive for success—by any means necessary. They are taught to have zero tolerance for minor discomforts and to leave at the first signs of challenging relationship dynamics. Many are also urged to side-step unfavorable societal systems—finding creative ways to thrive despite unfair or discriminatory

---

7. 2 Cor. 4:4
8. John 8:44
9. John 14:27
10. John 3:16
11. Rom. 6:22-23
12. Eph. 2:10
13. Phil. 4:11-13
14. Isa. 53:5; Matt. 8:16-17
15. John 15:12-13

practices. This often means choosing alternative paths in careers, lifestyles, or opportunities that allow them to succeed without waiting for traditional structures to change.

In contrast, many boys are also being shaped to embrace their more compassionate and expressive sides—most often by mothers carrying the heavy responsibility of raising them alone while still bearing the scars of hurt or disappointment. This generation of men is more nurturing, empathetic, and willing to take on household tasks, such as cooking and cleaning. They show greater emotional depth compared to the typical "alpha males" of previous generations. While these traits can be positive, some of these young men seem to lack the drive, resilience, and leadership required to fulfill their God-given roles. Finding a healthy balance is crucial to ensuring that both men and women succeed in their divinely ordained purpose.

Scripture provides clear examples of women who fully embraced God's purpose—some while balancing marriage, motherhood, and meaningful impact—even within deeply patriarchal societies. The Proverbs 31 woman managed her home and enterprise with excellence, while Deborah—prophetess, judge, wife, mother figure, military leader, and devoted follower of God —guided Israel to victory with divine wisdom.[16] These women thrived and influenced society within a male-dominated structure, proving that God's calling and empowerment are never constrained by culture or societal barriers.

Deborah and Esther were women of faith and prayer. Esther, facing a royal decree that threatened her people, called for a three-day corporate fast and prayer to seek God's guidance before stepping into her assignment.[17] Both women understood that their challenges were beyond human strength and wisdom, requiring divine intervention. Their stories remind modern women that true authority and lasting influence come from humility, dependence on God, and alignment with His will. Scripture reinforces this spiritual truth: Believers are called to exercise divine authority against opposition (2 Cor. 10:4; Eph. 6:11-18), walk in God's dominion and purpose (Gen. 1:26-28; Matt. 28:18-20; Luke 10:19), and live out the abundant life Christ promised (John 10:10).

"… men always ought to pray and not lose heart." (Luke 18:1) The Parable of the Persistent Widow in Luke 18:1-8 teaches a powerful lesson on perseverance and prevailing in prayer. Jesus tells the story of a widow who repeatedly pleads with an unjust judge for justice against her adversary. Initially, the judge ignores her, but because of her persistence, he eventually grants her request—if only to stop her from bothering him. Jesus then contrasts this judge with God, who is just and compassionate. If even a corrupt judge can be moved by persistence, how much more will God answer the prayers of His chosen ones who cry out to Him day and night?

This parable teaches us about faith, persistence, and trusting in God's perfect timing. Unlike

---

16. Judg. 4:4; 5:7
17. Esther 4:15-17

the unjust judge, God is righteous[18] and attentive to the cries of His children.[19] The story encourages believers to pray continuously and not lose heart, knowing that God hears and will answer in His perfect way and in His own time. It's also interesting that Jesus uses the analogy of a judge in this teaching. The principle of "pleading a case" before God is reflected in several scriptures where God invites His people to present their petitions, arguments, and concerns or requests—as seen in Isaiah 43:26; Job 23:4; Micah 6:1-2—also highlighting the use of legal language in Scripture when addressing justice and righteousness. These verses emphasize that believers can boldly seek justice, mercy, and divine intervention.

Praying with understanding and persistence is essential to receiving God's answers and outcomes.[20] Ignorance—whether of our spiritual authority or of God's willingness to act—can keep us trapped in cycles of delay and defeat. But faith-filled, consistent prayer opens the way for us to receive from God and provides strategies for breakthrough.

THE PRICE OF PASSIVITY

So, why have these oppressive "giants"—repressive laws, unfavorable systems, and restrictive policies—remained? As women, what pertinent petitions have we brought before the Judge of all the earth[21] over the years? Have we, at some point, quietly resigned ourselves to the status quo, settling into a rhythm of perfunctory prayers born of duty, ignorance, or frustration—simply praying to survive while coexisting with these "giants"? Or have our prayers lacked the faith and authority that move mountains[22] and compel every knee to bow to the name of Jesus?[23]

In many female faith communities, prayer often focuses on husbands, marriages, and children. While these are important and biblical,[24] we sometimes neglect the deeper, systemic challenges shaping these struggles—societal oppression, cultural barriers, and spiritual strongholds that ensnare generations. God calls us to do more than just survive; He has equipped us to confront and dismantle the roots of injustice. One reason He urges us to pray for our leaders and nations is that their decisions directly affect our peace, progress, and the freedom to live out our faith.[25]

---

18. Ps. 11:7 (ICB); 89:14 (NIV); Jer. 9:24 (NIV)
19. Ps. 34:15; 1 John 5:14-15
20. Isa. 59:1-2; James 1:6-7; 4:3; 1 John 5:14-15
21. Gen. 18:25
22. Mark 11:23
23. Phil. 2:10
24. Ps. 127:3; Phil. 4:6
25. Prov. 21:1; Jer. 29:7; 1 Tim. 2:1-2

Even with faith as small as a mustard seed, we have the power to move "mountains"[26]—overcoming challenges both personally and collectively. Through God's strength, we can tear down strongholds,[27] leap over walls, and break through barriers[28] that would otherwise hold us back. In doing so, we not only walk in our full God-given potential for ourselves, our families, and our communities, but also leave a legacy of freedom and faith for future generations.

Our focus shouldn't be on the constraints or limitations we sometimes contend with. Instead, our attention should be on who our God is. Remember, empowered by his faith in God, David used just one of his *pebbles* to bring down Goliath. Then he used Goliath's sword (his tool of oppression) to finish the job, causing the Philistines to retreat![29] We, too, are called to confront the giants of systemic oppression and cultural bondage. It is not enough for a few women to break free while others remain in chains. God has called us to proclaim liberty, dismantle cycles of oppression, and challenge the systems that masquerade as tradition or religion.[30] Jesus died to bring complete freedom, not partial relief.[31]

God has not forgotten women.[32] Through Christ, He has given His daughters the same spiritual blessings as His sons: everything we need for life and godliness and the privilege of being partakers of His divine nature.[33] He has promised us all very great and precious promises.[34] We, too, are co-heirs with Christ, recipients of His promises and Kingdom inheritance.[35]

Women, like men, are created in God's image and hold equal worth and value in His sight—though our roles or responsibilities differ.[36] We are fearfully and wonderfully made, designed with purpose and intentionality.[37] Throughout Scripture, God shows special care and protection for vulnerable women[38] and calls them to leadership and influence—like Deborah and Esther, who fulfilled their divine assignments.[39] Jesus Himself consistently demonstrated the value of women, welcoming them into His ministry, defending their dignity, and showing mercy even when society condemned them.[40]

---

26. Matt. 17:20

27. 2 Cor. 10:4-5

28. Ps. 18:29

29. 1 Sam. 17:40-54

30. Isa. 61:1-3; Gal. 5:1

31. Luke 4:18–19; John 8:36

32. Deut. 4:31; Ps. 9:18; Isa. 44:21; 49:15-16; Heb. 13:5

33. 2 Pet. 1:3

34. 2 Pet. 1:4

35. Rom. 8:17; Gal. 3:28; 4:7; 1 Pet. 3:7

36. Gen. 1:27

37. Ps. 139:14

38. Ps. 68:5; Isa. 46:4

39. Judg. 4:4; Esther 4:14

40. Mark 5:34; Luke 8:1-3; John 4:7-29; 8:10-11

Women of faith, especially those in communities with dominant male authority, must embrace and actively share these truths[41] because identity shapes destiny. Many struggles persist because of a lack of knowledge. Scripture reminds us that satan seeks to steal, kill, and destroy,[42] but the knowledge of God's Word produces faith and wisdom that overcome his schemes.[43] Ignorance keeps believers bound, but truth sets us free.[44]

If we see ourselves as weak or powerless—like "grasshoppers" before "giants"—the enemy will easily intimidate and oppress us. But when we align with God's perspective and see ourselves as His beloved, Spirit-filled daughters (and sons), carrying His authority, the enemy loses ground.[45] The more we are filled with God's Word and the Holy Spirit, the more we walk as the spiritual giants we are in Christ—unshaken, victorious, and influential for generations to come.

None of God's children have been shortchanged, yet many fail to receive what they need simply because they do not ask Him—or they ask with the wrong motives. Scripture warns: *"You want what you don't have ... Yet you don't have what you want because you don't ask God for it. And even when you ask, you don't get it because your motives are all wrong—you want only what will give you pleasure"* (James 4:2-3 NLT). Unanswered prayers are often the result of self-centered motives rather than alignment with God's will. Effective prayer seeks His heart first, not just personal gain.

This truth became a turning point in my own journey. After years of praying and waiting without visible results, everything changed when I began praying according to God's Word—seeking His will above my own. Scripture encourages us to keep praying and not give up,[46] trusting that God hears and answers in His perfect timing.

If you are going through a season of hardship—whether dealing with injustice, betrayal, or personal loss—take courage: God has not abandoned you. He uses the trials that come our way to strengthen, refine, and prepare us for greater purpose.[47] Our pain and discomfort can become platforms for comforting and strengthening others,[48] transforming what the enemy meant for harm into a testimony that brings hope and deliverance.

Joseph, despite being betrayed and mistreated by his brothers, looked at the bigger picture and chose forgiveness over revenge. He expressed this profoundly important lesson in one of my favorite "signposts" for life: *"You intended to harm me, but God intended it for good to accomplish what is now being done, the saving of many lives"* (Gen. 50:20 NIV).

---

41. Deut. 6:6-9
42. John 10:10
43. Hosea 4:6; James 4:7
44. John 8:32
45. Luke 10:19; 1 John 4:4
46. Matt. 7:7; Luke 18:1
47. Rom. 5:3-5; James 1:2-4
48. 2 Cor. 1:3-4

Joseph's trials were not just about his eventual freedom, success, or restoration; they were divinely orchestrated to prepare and position him to save his family and an entire generation from famine. Like Joseph, when we trust God through life's adversities, He uses what was meant for harm to fulfill His greater purpose.[49] In Genesis 45:7-8, he acknowledges that every event in his life—including the hardships and the injustices—was part of God's larger redemptive plan and sovereignty even amid adversity.

We are also called to walk this journey in community. Scripture reminds us that when one part of Christ's body suffers, every part suffers with it.[50] Believers should carry each other's burdens,[51] encourage one another, and demonstrate Christ's love in practical ways.[52] Choosing isolation or passivity in the face of trials robs both us and the body of Christ of the strength that comes through shared faith and mutual support.

LIVING BEYOND THE LIMITS AND LIES

Philippians 2:3-4 instructs us: *"Do nothing from selfish ambition or conceit, but in humility count others more significant than yourselves. Let each of you look not only to his own interests, but also to the interests of others."* It's encouraging to see more women supporting each other today through initiatives that promote career growth, financial literacy, mental health, and empowerment. These platforms are helping women excel in ways that were once out of reach.

Even faith-based communities are adopting aspects of these movements. However, our efforts must remain grounded in God's Word. Secular empowerment often ends in self-reliance or societal validation, but true freedom comes only through Christ. His truth transforms our thinking, breaks strongholds, and frees us from limiting patterns and lies.[53]

Unfortunately, unity among women is not always common. Division and strife often arise when love, humility, and compassion are missing.[54] Sadly, some of the injustices women face are carried out by other women. In certain African cultures, women themselves enforce harmful practices like female genital mutilation (FGM) or support degrading widowhood rites. Women in positions of authority sometimes fail to advocate for their peers, and within families, some mothers-in-law or female relatives promote the mistreatment of daughters-in-law.

Even in professional settings, women can unknowingly perpetuate cycles of pain. A female healthcare worker who ignores a fellow woman's cries during labor pains or a policewoman

---

49. Rom. 8:28
50. 1 Cor. 12:25–26
51. Gal. 6:2
52. John 13:34
53. John 8:32; Rom. 12:2
54. James 3:16–18

who shows little empathy toward a survivor of assault, only deepens that woman's trauma. These actions reveal the cost of internalized lies and ignorance—where personal hurt, cultural conditioning, or apathy overshadow God's command to love and defend one another.[55] We can break this cycle by allowing God's Word to renew our minds and heal our hearts.[56] When women are restored by His truth and love, only then can we truly uplift one another, dismantle generational patterns of harm, and reflect Christ's love in every sphere of life.

God's wisdom promotes peace and goodness.[57] Women are called to walk in this wisdom, showing mercy, compassion, and love toward one another, rather than allowing division to grow. In recent years, women have gained influence in areas such as entertainment, media, and entrepreneurship, demonstrating that there is still room for growth and that we can make a meaningful impact across all fields of endeavor. Yet far too often, once success is achieved, not enough are extending a helping hand to those coming up behind—despite the truth that the sky is vast enough for all to shine. A group of stars is much brighter than a solitary one in a dark sky. In God's Kingdom, we are called to rise and shine, not compete against one another.[58]

It's concerning that some women's groups promote a "survival of the fittest" mentality, where self-interest outweighs solidarity, creating a dog-eat-dog environment rather than a community of light and harmony. This only fuels conflict and distracts us from the greater mission of advancing God's Kingdom. Even within the body of Christ, division and unhealthy competition can still creep in, despite our calling to live in unity and pursue mutual edification.[59] Jesus warned of division in families and communities in Scripture, such as Luke 12:53, Matthew 10:34-35, and Micah 7:6, emphasizing the need for His followers to be vigilant against forces that seek to divide us.

Instead of fighting each other, we are called to work together. When women engage in unhealthy competition, it leads to conflict and collective loss. As believers, our focus should be on removing barriers, casting *giants* and *mountains* into the sea,[60] and confronting the root causes of injustice and inequality—rather than throwing *pebbles* at the symptoms or each other. We are the light of the world,[61] and that light should shine brighter together, driven by shared purpose, not dimmed by discord. To break these cycles of rivalry and self-preservation, we must return to God's blueprint. It begins with understanding the power of legacy—living and building beyond ourselves for God's glory.

As women seek influence, success, or even survival in male-dominated spaces, many

55. Isa. 1:17; John 13:34; Gal. 6:2
56. Ps. 107:20; Rom. 12:2
57. James 3:17
58. Eccles. 4:9-10; Phil. 2:3-4
59. Rom. 12:4–5; 1 Cor. 12:25-26
60. Mark 11:23
61. Matt. 5:14

unintentionally adopt strategies that reinforce the very systems holding them back—trading long-term transformation for short-term safety or personal gain. Some sociologists describe this idea as a "patriarchal bargain"—a survival strategy in which individuals navigate an unequal system to secure some advantage, even though their participation keeps that system intact.[62] In other words, some women adapt to unfair structures not because they agree with them, but because it seems like the only way to survive within them.

While this sociological concept reflects a human perspective on gender dynamics, Scripture calls us to something higher—not conforming to the pattern of this world but being transformed by the renewing of our minds (Rom. 12:2). When women (and men) operate from a renewed mind and a Spirit-led heart, they no longer need to negotiate within the world's power structures—they rise above them. Recognizing that not every system may change, God's way resists oppression through truth, humility, and Christlike service, allowing His light to shine even in broken structures. At its core, the *patriarchal bargain* exposes a deeper truth: Systems driven by self-preservation rather than grounded in God's design for mutual honor and love are destined to collapse under their own weight. God never intended for His daughters to bargain for their worth or merely manage broken systems; He already settled their value once and for all at the Cross.

Patriarchal bargaining is evident throughout Nigerian society and many other cultures. It cuts across all spheres and social strata. For example, some highly educated or successful women in politics may settle for "safe" behind-the-scenes roles, avoiding any action that might "rock the boat." They comply with male-dominated norms to gain perceived influence, job security, and approval from a system that rewards women who conform to and reinforce its ideals—even in the face of bullying or harassment.

Though often more qualified and experienced than their male counterparts, they remain confined to roles that do not challenge the status quo. Ultimately, the system remains unchanged, and the cycle of inequality continues, leaving many women without a voice or opportunity to lead boldly—and even fewer women ready, willing, and able to serve as role models.

Some women—particularly in middle- or upper-class circles—might turn a blind eye to their husbands' infidelity to preserve their marriage, social standing, or the image of "successful wives." They may be advised by older women to "endure, for the sake of the children" or to "stay so another woman doesn't reap the fruits of their labor." By remaining silent, they may gain continued access to their husbands' wealth, social respectability as married women, and a sense of identity as "Mrs."—but in doing so, they reinforce the system that normalizes male infidelity while expecting female fidelity and obligatory silence. They must

---

62. The concept of the patriarchal bargain was first introduced by Deniz Kandiyoti in "Bargaining with Patriarchy," Gender & Society 2, no. 3 (1988): 274-290, and has since been discussed by various sociologists in analyses of gender and social systems; https://giwps.georgetown.edu/resource/bargaining-with-patriarchy/

suppress their pain and often compete for their husbands, normalizing a system that limits women's agency.

Elements of patriarchal bargaining have subtly shaped various aspects of Nigerian society, including the church. In some Christian households, it often appears more understated and is usually wrapped in religious language or interpreted roles, revealing different levels of compromise in both modern and traditional contexts. A Christian woman in this situation may suppress her opinions or concerns to "honor" her husband and avoid being labeled contentious. She may fear that expressing her needs could be viewed as rebellion against spiritual headship, to the point where she may completely surrender decision-making or even control over her own earnings.

Such a woman may gain the approval or retain their place as a "respected" married woman in her church community and be praised as a "Proverbs 31 woman," while keeping her marriage "peaceful" and avoiding confrontation. However, in doing so, she loses her voice in the partnership and reinforces the misconception that godliness in women equates to silence or passivity. Tragically, this limits her ability to fully express her God-given gifts, ideas, and influence—both in her home and the broader community.

Others endure emotional, verbal, or even physical abuse in silence to avoid "shame" or stigmatization. Seeking counseling, church intervention, or temporary separation may feel like a threat to family honor or "the testimony of the gospel." In choosing to protect their public image, these women unintentionally sustain a culture where private pain is normalized and their right of expression is suppressed, contrary to God's heart for justice, dignity, and living an abundant life.

While patriarchal bargaining might seem wise, noble, spiritual, or even sacrificial in the short term, it leaves the underlying system unchanged and perpetuates bondage and marginalization for future generations. Women sometimes gain temporary stability, acceptance, or social approval, but often at the expense of wholeness, joy, and the freedom to fully live out their purpose[63]—through their calling, dreams, and aspirations. True transformation—both spiritual and societal—requires courage not merely to survive within the system but to challenge its distortions in love, promoting homes and communities built on mutual respect, justice, and the heart of Christ.[64]

Prayer without meaningful action falls short. James 2:26 reminds us that *"faith without works is dead."* Prayer is an unshakable foundation, but women are also called to rise—taking tangible steps through education, collaboration, and bold advocacy—to dismantle oppressive systems, pursue just laws, and defend the vulnerable.[65]

---

63. Gal. 5:1
64. Mic. 6:8; Eph. 5:21
65. Prov. 31:8-9; Isa. 1:17

Women already play crucial roles—as mothers, educators, professionals, legislators, spiritual leaders, and more. Even though they may not always occupy top-tier positions, their influence is undeniable. God is calling us beyond the belief that the success of one—or a few—is enough. We are to rise collectively—building, speaking, and acting in ways that open doors for others. Isolated achievements are not the goal; God calls us to use our collective voices, talents, and resources to bring about lasting change.

A largely underutilized force for change in Nigeria is the legal profession, especially among its female practitioners. Women in law—lawyers, judges, and legislators—have the power to draft, challenge, and reform laws that can positively impact the lives of other women and entire families. The main question is: Are we intentionally leveraging that power for lasting societal change?

The statistics are telling. In 2018, 161 first-class graduates emerged from the Nigerian Law School, with approximately 70 percent of them being female. Between 2015 and 2024, seven out of ten best graduating students were women—a testament to their consistent academic excellence.[66] Yet, despite this progress, excellence has not translated into equal representation in leadership. As of 2023, women make up around 40 percent of Nigerian lawyers, but only 33 percent of judges and only 11 percent of state attorneys general are women.[67] This leadership gap restricts their ability to prioritize or influence the very laws and systems that affect their lives and those of countless other women.

Even women in prestigious or high-paying roles are not immune from structural inequalities. Personal success does not automatically shield families or communities from the injustice and gender-based limitations that persist in society. That is why we must not become complacent or ignore the need for systemic change. Wherever God plants us, our success should serve as seed for a greater harvest—one that uplifts others and promotes righteousness for generations to come.[68]

---

66. Spottershouse Limited, "Law School Graduates: 161 First-Class Candidates; 133 Are Women," November 28, 2018, *BusinessDay.ng*;

FT Staff, "Nigerian Law School Graduates 161 First-Class Candidates, 133 of Them Women," *Financial Times*, November 28, 2018, accessed July 2025, https://www.ft.com/content/3a47bb96-f899-4628-af1f-e92a2f18562f.

67. International Bar Association, "Nigeria: New IBA Report Focused on Gender Disparity in the Legal Profession Is Published," *International Bar Association*, April 12, 2023, https://www.ibanet.org/Nigeria-New-IBA-report-focused-on-gender-disparity-in-the-legal-profession-is-published;

African Law & Business, "Report Reveals Female Lawyers Underrepresented in Nigeria," *African Law & Business*, April 13, 2023, https://www.africanlawbusiness.com/article/report-reveals-female-lawyers-underrepresented-in-nigeria;

Premium Times (Nigeria), "Report Reveals Sharp Gender Disparity in Top Positions of Nigeria's Legal Profession," *Premium Times Nigeria*, April 12, 2023, https://www.premiumtimesng.com/news/headlines/533182-report-reveals-sharp-gender-disparity-in-top-positions-of-nigerias-legal-profession.html;

Institute for African Women in Law, *Women in Leadership in the Law – Nigeria*, accessed July 2025, https://www.iawj.org/WILIL-Nigeria.

68. Prov. 14:34; 2 Cor. 9:6-10; Gal. 6:9

When we stay within our comfort zones and choose convenience over conviction, we turn a blind eye to the broader injustices around us and risk missing God's greater purpose for our lives. Silence or inaction may seem safe in the short term, but it often comes at a spiritual cost—both to us and to future generations. Scripture warns that watchmen who fail to sound the alarm share responsibility for the harm that comes to the city.[69] Likewise, if we ignore opportunities to confront oppression or defend the oppressed, we inadvertently allow the enemy to tighten his grip, while God's purposes through us remain unfulfilled or underfulfilled.

Despite entrenched cultural norms, women have stepped forward to challenge harmful traditions. On April 14, 2014, the Nigerian Supreme Court unanimously struck down the Igbo customary law that barred female children from inheriting property. The case, first filed in 1981 by Gladys Ada Ukeje against her stepmother and stepbrother, moved through two lower courts before the Supreme Court upheld their rulings, declaring the practice unconstitutional.[70]

Therefore, it would be unfair to overlook the commendable progress Nigeria has already made in strengthening legal protections for women and children. Several significant laws have been enacted to address long-standing injustices and defend the dignity and rights of vulnerable members of society.

Laws such as the *Violence Against Persons (Prohibition) Act* (VAPP), 2015, the *Child's Rights Act* (2003), and the *Matrimonial Causes Act* (1990) offer critical safeguards against abuse, exploitation, and inequality. The *1999 Nigerian Constitution (as amended)* further reinforces the national commitment to gender equity, with *Section 42* prohibiting discrimination based on gender, among other grounds. Some states have also enacted localized, state-domesticated versions of these federal laws, thereby strengthening protections for women and children at the local level.

These legal provisions provide promising tools: The VAPP Act enables protective orders and support systems for victims of abuse;[71] the Child's Rights Act strengthens safeguards for children's welfare, especially regarding custody and access;[72] and the Matrimonial Causes Act ensures equitable treatment in marital disputes. However, legislation alone is not enough.

---

69. Ezek. 33:6-7

70. Harvard International Review, "When Rights Slip Through the Cracks of Culture: Women's Rights and Justice in Nigeria (or Lack Thereof)," *Harvard International Review*, October 18, 2023, https://hir.harvard.edu/when-rights-slip-through-the-cracks-of-culture-womens-rights-and-justice-in-nigeria-or-lack-thereof/.

71. Partners Nigeria West Africa, *Domesticating the VAPP Act: VAPP Tracker*, accessed 2025, VAPP Tracker, listing the states in which the Violence Against Persons (Prohibition) Act 2015 has been domesticated, https://www.partnersnigeria.org/vapp-tracker/;

   FIDA Nigeria, *Violence Against Persons (Prohibition) Act 2015*, https://www.fida.org.ng/wp-content/uploads/2020/09/Violence-Against-Persons-Prohibition-Act-2015-1.pdf.

72. D. Ogunniyi, "The Challenge of Domesticating Children's Rights Treaties in Nigeria and Alternative Legal Avenues for Protecting Children," *Journal of African Law*, October 2, 2018, featuring information on the Child Rights Act's domestic implementation in multiple Nigerian states, https://en.wikipedia.org/wiki/Child_Rights_Act_in_Nigeria;

   Refworld, *Nigeria: Child's Rights Act, 2003*, United Nations High Commissioner for Refugees, https://www.refworld.org/docid/44e344fa4.html.

Without consistent enforcement, public education, and active involvement from women who are legally empowered, the intent of these statutes may never translate into everyday realities.

For example, laws like the VAPP and Child's Rights Act are only enforceable in states that have officially adopted them, leaving many people unprotected. Deep-rooted customary and religious laws continue to influence issues such as property rights and decisions regarding who vacates the marital home—often conflicting with statutory protections. In some instances, victims face shaming, while perpetrators evade justice. Moreover, enforcement challenges such as victim-blaming diminish the effectiveness of these laws. This is where the collective rise of female lawyers, policymakers, and advocates becomes essential—not just to draft or interpret the law, but to bring it to life in homes, courtrooms, and communities across the nation.

Amid these challenges, some state-led initiatives have stepped in to provide critical legal support and protection to at-risk groups—offering a glimpse of what is possible when the law is actively enforced and made accessible. Established on July 24, 2000, the Lagos State Office of the Public Defender (OPD) has been providing free legal services to indigent and underserved residents, with a focus on issues such as divorce proceedings, maintenance, custody, child access, guardianship, domestic violence, juvenile justice, and child abuse.[73]

While the OPD's efforts are commendable, they only address a small part of the serious challenges women face in Nigeria, especially regarding the rights and the welfare of women and children in troubled marriages. Tackling these issues requires robust laws, unwavering political will, and consistent enforcement to turn legal protections into real safety and equality for women across the country. These problems require coordinated efforts from both governmental and non-governmental organizations to ensure that laws are enforced and actually protect women in their daily lives.

Throughout Nigeria's history, remarkable women have risen to challenge oppression, demand justice, and advocate for the dignity and rights of women. The following women—across generations—remind us that change is not accidental. It is often the result of sacrificial, consistent effort by those who refuse to accept injustice as the norm. Their stories challenge us all to step up and do our part—wherever we are planted—to advance justice, amplify women's voices, and build a society where everyone can thrive. Their courage, persistence, and strategic leadership continue to shape the landscape for gender equality today.

- Funmilayo Ransome-Kuti (1900–1978): Often called the "Lioness of Lisabi," she was a trailblazing educator, political activist, and women's rights advocate. She founded the Abeokuta Women's Union, which challenged unjust colonial taxes and fought for women's political participation. She was also the mother of Afrobeat legend Fela Kuti.

---

73. Lagos State Office of the Public Defender (OPD), "Our Services," accessed February 17, 2025, https://opdlagosstate.org/services.html.

- Margaret Ekpo (1914–2006): A prominent political activist and nationalist, she fought for women's participation in politics and helped mobilize women in southeastern Nigeria. She was one of the first women elected to Nigeria's parliament.

- Hajia Gambo Sawaba (1933–2001): A passionate Northern Nigerian activist who tirelessly advocated for girl-child education, the abolition of child marriage, and women's voting rights. She was imprisoned multiple times for her bold stance against social injustice and oppressive systems.

We must continue to build on these enduring legacies of female advocacy in Nigeria to inspire future generations and drive meaningful, lasting change. There are many practical ways to ensure that protective laws for women are not only passed but also enforced and implemented in everyday realities. Here are actionable steps that individuals, communities, and institutions can take:

1. Advocate for legal reforms

- Engage lawmakers: Push for the full domestication and enforcement of the VAPP Act and similar protective laws in every Nigerian state.

- Propose legal amendments: Initiate campaigns for legal provisions that require abusive partners—typically husbands—to vacate the home during domestic conflicts, similar to laws that exist in countries like the United States and the United Kingdom.

- Collaborate with advocacy groups: Partner with women-led organizations and NGOs to strengthen advocacy and increase pressure on policymakers.

2. Raise awareness and educate

- Community outreach: Organize seminars, forums, and workshops to inform women (and men) about their legal rights.

- Leverage social media: Use digital platforms to highlight real-life cases, share legal resources, and rally support for reforms.

- Public awareness campaigns: Launch initiatives that tackle stigma, expose injustice, and encourage cultural changes regarding gender-based violence.

3. Support legal aid and access to justice

- Fund legal assistance: Offer financial or logistical support to legal aid organizations that help low-income women experiencing abuse, workplace bullying, and harassment.

- Promote counseling and mediation: Support access to conflict resolution services that protect women's dignity and rights during separation or divorce processes.

4. Strengthen enforcement mechanisms

- Train law enforcement and judiciary: Promote gender-sensitive training programs for police officers, legal practitioners, and judges.

- Establish more shelters: Collaborate with NGOs and local governments to build safe, accessible shelters for women and children fleeing violence.

5. Champion cultural and religious reform

- Engage community leaders: Work with traditional and religious leaders to challenge harmful cultural practices and promote dignity and equality.

- Promote fair dispute resolution: Support Alternative Dispute Resolution (ADR) methods that are based on legal standards and respectful to women's rights.

6. Learn from global best practices

- Adapt proven models: Study successful legal frameworks from other countries and thoughtfully tailor them to Nigeria's unique socio-cultural setting.

- Expand family court access: Support the creation and improvement of specialized family courts nationwide. While the Child's Rights Act requires family courts, their effectiveness varies widely across many states.

7. Get personally involved

- Volunteer your skills: Offer your time or expertise to women's rights groups or legal aid organizations.

- Start petitions and campaigns: Use your voice and influence to drive legislative or policy changes.

- Speak up and speak out: Share personal stories or testimonies to humanize these issues and inspire action.

8. Empower marriages through church and faith communities

The church plays a vital role in shaping attitudes and promoting marital health. As a covenant community, it needs to go beyond motivational preaching and post-marriage interventions to provide genuine, transformative support for couples. This can include:

- Enhanced pre-marital counseling: In addition to compatibility assessments (such as encouraging genotype testing), churches could offer basic psychological evaluations to help couples understand personality differences and emotional readiness.

- Discipleship groups and mentorship programs: Create small groups or pair couples with spiritually mature mentors to help strengthen marriages through biblical teaching, accountability, and shared experiences.

- Building or partnering with shelters: Churches can establish or collaborate with existing shelters to provide temporary accommodation for women (and their children) in crises.

Now is the time to rise together—empowered by faith and propelled into action—bringing wisdom, justice, and lasting transformation to our communities. This is already taking shape in Nigeria's film industry, where some are using storytelling platforms to raise awareness and advocate for women's rights.

A notable example is the movie *Wives on Strike* (2016) by Omoni Oboli— an acclaimed Nigerian filmmaker, producer, and actress. This three-part series (*Wives on Strike, Wives on Strike: The Revolution*, and *Wives on Strike: The Uprising*) follows a group of market women who, in protest against societal injustices and harmful cultural practices, unite to withhold intimacy from their husbands until real change is achieved. Through humor, drama, and sharp social commentary, the films shed light on issues such as child marriage, domestic violence, and gender inequality—demonstrating the power of collective action to confront deeply ingrained injustices.

Before anyone gets any ideas—I'm *not* endorsing a "bedroom strike" as a tool for social change! Withholding intimacy as a means of control contradicts God's design for marriage (1 Cor. 7:3-5). However, these movies offer excellent insights into how storytelling can spark critical conversations, challenge destructive traditions, and inspire genuine, lasting reform.

The challenges women face—such as inequality, discrimination, and oppressive cultural norms—aren't limited to any specific region; they are global issues. Fortunately, the film industry continues to play a significant role in shining a light on these struggles, reshaping cultural narratives, and inspiring change. Here are a few powerful examples from around the world that highlight the ongoing fight for women's rights and justice:

North Country (2005)

Starring Charlize Theron, this movie is based on the true story of a woman who filed the first major sexual harassment lawsuit in the US against the male-dominated mining industry. It sheds light on workplace discrimination and the courage needed to seek justice.

Water (2005, Bollywood)

Set in colonial India, *Water* exposes the mistreatment of widows who were cast out of society and forced to live in *ashrams* (isolated widow colonies). The film challenges oppressive traditions and advocates for the dignity and rights of women.

Made in Dagenham (2010)

This British film is based on the true story of female factory workers who went on strike for equal pay in the 1960s. Their movement led to legislative changes that improved labor rights for women in the UK.

Hidden Figures (2016)

This film tells the true story of three African-American women—Katherine Johnson, Dorothy Vaughan, and Mary Jackson—who played crucial roles in NASA's space program despite facing racial and gender discrimination. It emphasizes the importance of persistence, education, and fighting for equal opportunities.

Through prayer, obedience, faith, and purposeful actions, we can overcome spiritual and societal barriers, secure a godly future for our children, and ensure that God's Kingdom continues to advance through our homes and communities. Enough is enough! We've been rooted in wrong beliefs for far too long—and broken by what we ignore. It's time to embrace and walk boldly in God's truth, which transforms lives, restores families, strengthens societies, and ultimately, rebuilds our nation.

> [Women] Arise, shine;
> For your light has come!
> And the glory of the Lord is risen upon you.
> For behold, the darkness shall cover the earth,
> And deep darkness the people;
> But the Lord will arise over you,
> And His glory will be seen upon you.
> The Gentiles shall come to your light,
> And kings to the brightness of your rising.
> "Lift up your eyes all around, and see:
> They all gather together, they come to you;
> Your sons shall come from afar,
> And your daughters shall be nursed at your side.
> Then you shall see and become radiant,
> And your heart shall swell with joy;
> —Isaiah 60:1-5

I've written extensively about culture and the many issues in Nigerian society that impact marriages, but it's important to acknowledge that, within the same environment, there are also exemplary, thriving marriages. People and relationships face various temptations, problems, and pressures at different times and in different settings. What sets us apart as Christians is how we respond and the choices we make—whether we go along with the flow or stand out and stand up for Jesus, whether we obey or challenge the social trends and the status quo.

As soldiers of Christ Jesus,[74] we do not have the luxury of complacency or passivity. We cannot afford to be entangled in the distractions of this world.[75] We are called to vigilance—to be sober, watchful, and alert.[76] We are called to put on the shining armor of light—right living in Christ[77]—and we are called to fight! Not with carnal weapons, but with mighty weapons through God that tear down strongholds.[78]

Our enemy is cunning and relentless. He is the father of lies, a deceiver who comes in many forms, seeking to limit, restrict, stagnate, hinder, and frustrate the purposes of God. He lays traps, he plots, he schemes[79]—but he is already a defeated foe!

Through the wisdom of God, we can outwit his strategies.[80] Through steadfast faith, we can resist him and watch him flee.[81] By surrendering vengeance to the Lord, we can entrust God Himself to judge the wicked.[82] And ultimately, every enemy will be made a footstool under Christ's feet—and under ours, as we reign with Him.[83]

Hear the decree of our Commander: *"And the gates of hell shall not prevail against it"* (Matt.16:18b). The gates—every place of power, influence, and decision-making that the enemy has seized—cannot withstand the advance of Christ's Church (which includes women). They will crumble. They will fall. They cannot stand against the unstoppable victory of our King!

THROUGH SÉGUN'S LENSES

It is impossible not to be struck by the stark contrast between Nigerian society's perception and treatment of separated couples. Men with philandering proclivities have long succeeded in having their cake and eating it too, even when living with their spouses in

---

74. Phil. 2:25; 2 Tim. 2:3; Philem. 1:2

75. 2 Tim. 2:4

76. 1 Pet. 5:8

77. Rom. 13:12

78. 2 Cor. 10:3-4

79. Eph. 6:11

80. Prov. 21:22; Eccles. 9:18

81. James 4:7; 1 Pet. 5:9

82. Ps. 37:9; Rom. 12:19

83. Ps. 110:1; 1 Cor. 15:25

their matrimonial homes not to talk of during separation. Separation propels such men into even higher levels of reckless abandon where the only rule is that there are no rules.

Stereotypes and centuries of misogynistic traditions and practices have dealt Nigerian women a very poor hand which men frequently take advantage of. This leaves women in a disadvantageous position when serious problems emerge in their marriages. They are expected to absorb the pain, disrespect, and opprobrium when they decide to hit the "pause" button in their marriage, whether temporarily or permanently.

Sadly, imperfections in the country's legal framework have long converged with age-old societal prejudices against women in respect of familial disputes to put, and keep, them on the back foot. The situation is further complicated because Nigeria does not operate a unified family law system. Three systems coexist, namely Statutory, Customary law, and Islamic (Sharia) law. The common denominator across these systems is that women are unable to avoid discriminatory hurdles, which hand men an unfair advantage.

One of such hurdles is financial in nature as in many local cultures, a wife who initiates divorce is expected to return the bride price, or dowry, to the husband's family. This places an immediate and unfair burden on women which is particularly destabilizing if they do not have the means to repay the dowry and the husband's family uses the opportunity to embarrass and shame them.

The financial predicament of women who initiate, or are embroiled in, divorce is further compounded when it comes to the distribution of assets. Unless a woman can prove that she contributed significantly to her family's finances, she is unlikely to receive much from the statutory courts. The situation does not change even if she demonstrably provided a nurturing environment for her children and fully supported her husband throughout their marriage, thereby allowing him the space and conditions to thrive and prosper financially. Cases of Nigerian wives receiving a substantial portion of their husband's assets through the law courts, let alone half of it, are rare.

In matters of child custody, the guiding principle of "the best interest of the child" typically favors women in the case of young children as their mothers are usually awarded custody with fathers enjoying visitation rights. However, with older children, a woman's level of financial independence assumes greater importance, and a father may be awarded custody as the children become older if verifiable evidence suggests their mother will struggle to look after them due to financial constraints. One of the inequities of the current situation in Nigeria's family law landscape is the continued underappreciation of the tremendous contribution of women in maintaining family cohesion and directly or indirectly boosting overall economic activity.

Rearview Mirror Lesson

As the father of an absolutely amazing 15-year-old daughter, born about a year after Funké and I reconciled and who will no doubt want to get married and have a family of her own in the future, it is impossible not to lend my voice to the call for urgent legal reform in respect of women's rights. This is particularly relevant in respect of the rights of married women, not just in cases of divorce but also when they are still in their matrimonial homes where their voices are easily stifled. Patriarchal customs trample on women's rights even in the face of glaring maltreatment at the hands of their husbands. Included here are situations where, for example, they attend police stations to report domestic violence, although their default setting is usually for family members to intervene. The wealthier the husband, the less likely it is for such reports to result in arrest and prosecution, even when law enforcement officers are presented with overwhelming evidence of abuse by the husband.

Enforcement of laws is very weak; for example, women may struggle to receive rights such as child maintenance. This is particularly unfair when wives do not have the financial strength to engage legal counsel, thereby leaving them at the mercy of their husbands and an inefficient judicial system.

The love, appreciation, and respect I have for my wife, especially given the unimaginably difficult six-and-a-half-year ordeal she had to endure before our reconciliation, is reason enough for me to want to advocate for fair treatment of women throughout Nigerian society, including within the country's legal system. The birth of our daughter has made me even more circumspect and more willing to throw my hat in the ring, as it were, as evidenced by my participation in this book project.

It is difficult enough for women to have to face societal prejudices by virtue of their gender, let alone having to take on an entire justice system that is often accused of dispensing injustice, especially in terms of women's rights. This section is written in demonstration of my full love and support for my wife and children but also in recognition of the need for men to advocate for women in general.

I hope this chapter draws people in, including men and women in positions of authority within the legal system. My hope is that it will encourage them to apply greater vigor in trying to plug gaps within the justice system. Nigerian women are long overdue for a restoration of their dignity and the pride of place they deserve in their marriages and in society as a whole.

11

Journey Through the Desert

*"Don't let where you are become a prophecy
of where you're going to stay."*

UNKNOWN

FACING THE UNKNOWN

The whole separation thing wasn't working for me. My husband's decision to force me out of our home was both shocking and painful to accept. I was still in love with him and willing to do whatever it took to "make our marriage work"—a deeply flawed approach, as I would soon learn the hard way.

My recurring thoughts and deepest concerns were for my children. Through no fault of theirs, they were now faced with the possibility of navigating the awkward dynamics and painful reality of feeling like outsiders in a potential "new family" down the line. I had firsthand experience with this growing up, longing for my dad's undivided attention and yearning to be a priority in his life. The thought of our four-year-old and his baby brother, barely a year old, enduring that same emotional struggle simply because their parents couldn't get along—or didn't try hard enough—was unbearable.

Perhaps our separation was inevitable. The fights had become more frequent, and we gradually became strangers merely cohabiting. We had exhausted every reconciliation avenue, yet nothing seemed to work. No one had the right answers—not the experienced psychologists we consulted, nor the numerous family interventions which, in our culture, are often skewed to absolve the husband of wrongdoing.

Such interventions typically place the burden of a failing marriage squarely on the wife, regardless of the circumstances. Whether it's physical or emotional abuse, neglect, abandonment, infidelity, financial struggles, or even delays in childbearing—somehow, it is always the wife's fault. She didn't pamper her husband enough, present an elaborate meal spread (because, after all, "the way to a man's heart is through his stomach"), or keep him entertained in the bedroom.

The truth is that conventional marriage counseling and advice can only be effective when both parties are willing, actively engaged, and genuinely committed to restoring the relationship. In our case, Ségun had "checked out" emotionally long before our physical separation. He often told people that our marriage was over—and that there was a greater chance of it snowing in Lagos, Nigeria than of us ever reconciling.

Nothing seemed to provide quick relief from the heartbreak I was experiencing. I tried praying, praising, and pushing through the pain, but my feelings kept getting in the way. I was a whirlwind of emotions—scared, furious, devastated, and completely unprepared for the reality I was facing. I cried everywhere—at work, at weddings (so I stopped attending), during movies, in church, and even while driving when our favorite songs played on the radio. Sleep eluded me at night, so I stayed awake, running on energy drinks to get through the day. My appetite suffered, and no matter what I did, the weight of it all felt inescapable.

I might have lost my sanity were it not for my extraordinary mother's unwavering support, a dependable small circle of friends, a wonderful church family, and a fulfilling job I threw myself into. I am deeply grateful for the strong network of amazing people[1] who stood by me during this dark season. They stepped in with babysitting and school runs, legal advice, listening ears, and broad, patient shoulders to cry on. In my corner, I had truth-speakers, cheerleaders, encouragers, prayer warriors, lifters, and those I fondly call "live wires" and "spark plugs." Their passion and zest for life infused joy and laughter when I was at my lowest ebb. Years later, I learned that our separation had also been difficult for Ségun.[2] Beneath his happy-go-lucky, *moving-on-up* tough exterior and the temporary distractions or "interests," there was an underlying sadness and an emptiness that only God[3] could truly fill.

What I initially thought would be just a few weeks or months apart turned into a six-and-a-half-year roller-coaster ride! For the first three years, I clung to hope despite enduring rejection, bitterness, betrayal, resentment, accusations and counteraccusations, vindictive plots, and slander—giving as good as I got! After all, my maiden name isn't a variant of the great Kung Fu master's (Bruce Lee) for nothing! But after non-stop rounds with an unrelenting battle, the fighter in me grew weary. I decided to channel whatever strength I had left into building a new life for our boys and me. Ségun and I tried to maintain civility and

---

1. Ps. 5:12; Dan. 1:9

2. Prov. 14:13

3. Eccles. 3:11; Ps. 107:9; Jer. 2:13; John 6:35

create stability for them, but despite our love for our children, attention, chaotic co-parenting schedules, and overcompensating through gifts and holidays, it was an incredibly difficult time for them, too.

Our boys often found themselves unwilling spectators in our conflicts and, at times, were shamefully used as pawns, leverage, or weapons—by both Ségun and me—to hurt each other. Looking back, we took so much for granted, blind to the depth of pain we caused them. The true impact of our actions wasn't fully revealed until they were adults. Couples in strained relationships or bitter disputes often become so consumed by their own emotions that they fail to recognize the emotional scars they leave on their children—the very ones they should be protecting. So much time, energy, and resources were wasted in duplicating efforts, trying to outdo or outmaneuver each other, and battling over issues that, in hindsight, were often inconsequential or ephemeral.

Days turned into weeks, and weeks into months, then years. It was as though all my prayers had been wasted and gone unanswered. I felt I had waited in vain, hoping for a reconciliation. During this time, I received a flood of unsolicited advice and harsh realities from people who believed I was clinging to a lost cause, wasting my life on someone who had clearly moved on. I was summoned to countless consultations with older family members and well-meaning friends. While I appreciated their concern, I grew weary of rehashing the same painful story and sitting through hours of repetitive counsel. Some of those meetings felt more like interrogations than interventions—draining, exhausting, and, at times, painfully redundant. Yet, they helped me reach a sobering conclusion: human wisdom has limits.

By the time I started hearing consolations and criticisms such as: *All men are devils and dogs; it was your fault for not keeping your home; marriage is hard, but we women stay for the sake of our children,* I knew it was time to seek something deeper than earthly wisdom. The noise became overwhelming, drowning out my own thoughts. I began to withdraw, shutting people out.[4] Some lost patience with me, accusing me of whining and wallowing in self-pity: *What's the big deal? You're not the first, and you won't be the last—dust it off, get over it, and move on!* But it wasn't that simple.

Many of my friends and family—especially those who had been loving and supportive— struggled to understand why I suddenly pulled away. I hope they do now. The weight of everything became overwhelming, not just emotionally but physically as well. We all process grief and loss in our own way and at our own pace. It's important not to rush people through that journey. While there's no set timeline for healing, Scripture reminds us *"not to grieve as those who have no hope."*[5] Where we can, we should offer support and encouragement, helping

---

4. Isa. 30:15
5. 1 Thess. 4:13

rather than enabling self-pity and harmful or destructive behavior. Heartbreak hits hard, and it affects everyone differently. So, bear one another up in love[6] —and if you can't, then pray.

I received the divorce petition in the third year of our separation. As I read every piercing word, I was crushed—Ségun's opinion had always mattered to me, perhaps too much. I couldn't believe his description of me and our marriage; it felt like I was reading about strangers. The man I thought I knew, the one I had loved and built a life with, now painted a picture of irreconcilable differences. He said he was done trying and just wanted out before one of us got seriously hurt. I couldn't believe how easily he gave up—on me, our love, and our hopes and dreams. I had stuck with him despite his flaws, failures, and moments of weakness … yet he walked away when it was my turn to be fought for.

Ségun told me he loved me but was no longer *in love* with me … and to this day, I still don't know what that truly means! To me, real love doesn't walk away when things get tough; it doesn't prioritize fleeting emotions over commitment; it doesn't give up on people—it gives up *self*.[7] I couldn't help but wonder: Did his claim of loving me imply some lingering sense of duty or commitment to our marriage, or was it merely his conscience wrestling with guilt? On the other hand, was his declaration of being *no longer in love with me* simply a reflection of his current emotions—perhaps influenced by someone else? Was he really willing to make such a life-altering decision based on temporary feelings? Ironically, those feelings changed twice over the next three and a half years.

All my pleas for Ségun to reconsider his decision fell on deaf ears—his mind was made up. It didn't help that rumors began circulating about potential stand-ins and substitutes waiting in the wings to fill the vacancy he impulsively advertised. He wasted no time telling everyone our marriage was over. Well-meaning people, thinking they were doing me a favor, would occasionally report "sightings" of my husband, offering detailed updates they believed would jolt me back to reality. In a strange twist, perhaps the divorce proceedings served as the wake-up call I needed to finally "see the light." As the saying goes, "The prospect of death concentrates the mind wonderfully."

I struggled with my faith, the sting of rejection, and the shame of a failed marriage—especially in a society that, at the time, viewed divorce as a woman's failure, a stigma to bear. More than once, I thought about quitting, escaping from everything and everyone … maybe even for good. Yes, I seriously contemplated this when I no longer had the strength to keep going on my own. Coping with the children—mentally, emotionally, financially, and physically—was draining, especially with minimal support from Ségun. My whole life had revolved around him up to this point, and now, I had no idea where to begin. I felt lost, abandoned, and utterly exhausted.

---

6. Eph. 4:2; Gal. 6:2

7. John 13:34-35; Eph. 5:1-2; 1 John 3:16

I was too tired to hope and too cut up to see even a ray of light at the end of the tunnel. Despite my fears that I was up against far more than I could handle, I knew it was time to take a stand, end the pity parties, and stop sitting on the fence while life happened to me.[8] There had to be a purpose—some meaning to all this! Just when my self-esteem had begun to rise after securing a great job, it came crashing down again, completely shattered under the weight of rejection and uncertainty. This season was a constant tug-of-war between closeness and distance from God. I had to wrestle with faith, loneliness, bitterness, personal happiness and desires, and impatience—emotions that either slowed me down or tripped me up. I believe these are some of the struggles people fail to acknowledge or process properly when relationships fall apart, leaving wounds that, if left unattended, can fester long after the breakup itself.

In an attempt to avoid the difficulty of addressing or processing these inner struggles, some people choose to hasten the severing of ties with their spouse—the presumed source of their pain—and propel themselves into new relationships or divert their attention to other distractions. Some simply "move on" to escape having to deal with the past, which can include avoiding people or any unpleasant emotions such as guilt, shame, or regret associated with the separation or divorce.

In many cases, however, such rushed attempts at new relationships fail or end in disaster because, rather than healing, the individual who has "moved on" often ends up "bleeding" on their new partner. Real closure with one's past is essential, and sufficient time must be devoted to self-reflection—confronting and processing the pain, acknowledging one's role in the breakup, and understanding what one truly wants (or no longer wants, will tolerate, or settle for).

As Christians, our approach must align with "The Book"—God's Word. The biblical grounds for divorce include abuse, adultery, and abandonment.[9] There are various interpretations regarding romantic interests or partnerships and remarriage, and it is crucial to seek wisdom, pray earnestly, and receive godly counsel before entering a new relationship—especially on the rebound.

STUMBLING BUT SUSTAINED

Although life was challenging, my steady income from work provided me with financial leverage, granting access to credit facilities that enabled me to purchase my own car (after I sold the one Ségun magnanimously left with me). I could rent and furnish an apartment when I eventually moved out of my mother's house after eighteen months of staying with her while I found my feet. I consistently saw God's favor in action. The occasional shortfalls were met

---

8. Eph. 6:10; 13b-14

9. Matt. 5:32-33; 1 Cor. 7:15-16

by my parents, who stood firmly by me, a church family that was an extension of Jesus' arms always open toward me, and super dependable friends.

Those years taught me a profound lesson in relying on God as my ultimate Source. I understood that my ability to thrive or survive wasn't dependent on another person but on God's grace and the strength He was building within me. I didn't have to compromise or diminish my worth to meet my needs, and I found peace and joy—not in material things, but in the assurance that I was being sustained and equipped for the journey ahead.

I've had women playfully tease me, saying that Cupid must have struck me with an overdose of arrows or that I'm simply hopelessly devoted to love! Interestingly, a survey I conducted a couple of years ago across cultures revealed that many women still value love and security— fundamental emotional and physiological needs—not just in relationships but in life generally. However, the way in which these needs are pursued can vary greatly. Where we look to fulfill them, how deeply we desire them, and the choices we make to attain them are shaped by our personal experiences, cultural backgrounds, and societal influences. Love and security may be paramount for some, whereas independence, personal growth, or career development may take precedence for others. Neither path is right or wrong; what matters is that each person finds fulfillment in a way that aligns with their faith, values, and sense of purpose.

I was raised with a consciousness of the great examples of strong, selfless, and hardworking women around me. This helped me realize early in our breakup that I had to pull myself together and *"follow the path of those who obtained [many] promises through faith and patience."* [10] I endeavored to stay on that path, whether running, walking, or crawling.

As word spread that my husband and I were separated, it drew attention from all spheres: the concerned, the curious, and those covert "little foxes."[11] I was initially guarded about who I allowed into my life. I felt exposed, as if I had been left vulnerable to being taken advantage of by the person I loved most, so I viewed everyone with suspicion. Over time, I reconnected with old friends and formed new relationships, gradually building a budding social circle. I didn't realize until much later that some seemingly harmless connections were little foxes in disguise—distractions that would be potential setbacks rather than blessings.

I was still going to church, but my faith had started to wane after I received the divorce papers; I didn't know what to believe anymore. *"Holding fast to the confession of [my] hope without wavering"* [12] now seemed pointless. Everything at the time was telling me it was over—after all, I couldn't force someone to love me if he no longer wanted me. I couldn't see or believe anything beyond Ségun's attitude and his divorce petition.

But God kept reminding me to hold on to His promises and what He had specifically

---

10. Heb. 6:12

11. Song of Sol. 2:15

12. Heb. 10:23

told me from the beginning of this journey. I needed to keep speaking in faith, agreeing with His Word, regardless of my circumstances. His Word is a seed, and like any seed, it requires time to grow and bear fruit ... but I wanted an instant miracle! Yet, God never promised that everything would happen overnight. The waiting period allows us to walk in faith, please God, and—most importantly—be transformed. Just as a seed's full manifestation isn't immediate but unfolds over time with proper care, so it is with God's promises. His Word can change circumstances, but our faith activates it. If we don't believe His Word, we won't act on it, and without action, we may never see the fulfillment of what He has spoken.

I grew discouraged and impatient many times and eventually decided that, while I held on to faith, I didn't have to keep my life on hold. It felt like I had been holding my breath for years. Until then, my life revolved around work, church, and my children—nothing more. My mother grew concerned, watching me decline one invitation after another, afraid I was becoming a recluse. At some point, I began to feel I had mourned the loss of my marriage long enough. It was time for Funké to get her groove back! A part of me also wanted Ségun to see or hear that I was doing just fine without him—that I had moved on too, just as he had. So, I started spending time with a friend who had also recently separated from her husband. As they say, "Misery loves company," and we became partners in our feel-good quest. She had a group of friends who hung out at a nightclub conveniently close to my mother's house, and before long, I found myself occasionally joining them.

My mother was highly protective during our upbringing, so my brother and I had a strict curfew and didn't attend late-night parties until our late teens. Even then, she dropped us off and was there just before midnight to pick us up! It wasn't until college that I tasted a bit of that side of life. So, you can imagine how everything looked to me now—new and shiny! Yet, at first, it wasn't very appealing. I hadn't been around loud music, bright lights, and a smoke-filled, crowded space in a long time. But I persevered! I initially stuck out like a sore thumb, and I'm sure those in my friend's circle wondered where she had found the *prude*. But I got my wish when I finally bumped into some of Ségun's friends, hoping word would get back to him.

I liked the few hours of distraction the outings with my new acquaintances offered. I also enjoyed the attention from chivalrous observers; it was nice to hear someone else pay nice compliments other than my mother and some work colleagues. For a couple of months, I was out living my best "new me" life ... until God, with His signature sense of humor, arranged an incident that had *Ms. Prudy* running straight back to church!

One night at the club, we were all gathered near the bar—some standing, some dancing, while I hovered around my friend, as I often did since she was the only real connection I had in the group. People drifted in and out of her circle, and she had just made some new introductions. We were dancing and making small talk when, out of the corner of my eye, I caught sight of something hurtling toward me. A bottle. Rolling midair. Headed straight for me! Instinct kicked in, and I did a quick *step-to-the-side* shuffle and ducked just in time.

The bottle smashed into the wall behind the bar, sending glass fragments, broken bottles, and a tsunami of drinks flying in every direction. For a split second, everything froze—then chaos erupted. People scrambled, some ducking, others craning their necks to see what was happening. Right in the middle of the chaos stood a strikingly beautiful, impeccably dressed young woman—hardly the type you'd expect to be at the center of a nightclub brawl—being restrained by a few people desperately trying to keep her from unleashing even more mayhem.

Apparently, she had a score to settle, and I had almost become collateral damage. As I later discovered, she was the girlfriend of one of my friend's buddies who had just been introduced. I gathered that they had unresolved issues, and she had chosen that night, that club, and that exact moment to settle scores. I never did find out whether the bottle was meant for me or the guy, but one thing was certain—I had narrowly escaped a serious head injury or worse. Suffice it to say, I was shaken.

That was the last time I hung out with that crowd and the last time I attempted to "spread my wings" in that particular direction! I couldn't help but imagine the scandalous tabloid headline that could have emerged from the incident: "Estranged wife of…, mother of two, accidentally taken down by a flying bottle in a nightclub altercation!" Definitely not the kind of attention I had in mind for getting Ségun's notice!

What was I thinking?! What started as a seemingly harmless attempt to live, have fun, and prove—to Ségun or whoever was watching—that I wasn't just sitting at home, miserable and withering away…could have had serious consequences! I questioned why he could move on so easily while I couldn't. Why did it seem like there were different rules for men and women when it came to life after separation or divorce? But in the end, the real question wasn't about fairness or perception—it was about what truly aligned with my values and the path I wanted to walk as a woman of faith.

In any case, I wasn't cut out for a lifestyle that involved dodging flying objects or weaving through chaos on the dance floor—all in the name of having a good time! I had two children and far too much at stake to take such reckless risks. Yet, instead of realigning myself within God's guardrails, I still craved quick dopamine (happy hormone) hits—to lift my spirits and help me get through each day. I joined a social media app that was popular at the time, but the excitement and novelty soon wore off. The world has no lasting happiness—only temporary fixes, always dependent on people, things, and circumstances. Some people—even Christians—see God as a killjoy, but He isn't! He delights in His children, experiencing true joy and fulfillment.[13] His joy is free, constant, and abundant—as long as we have Jesus, we also have

---

13. Neh. 8:10; Ps. 16:11; Matt. 7:11; John 15:11

access to His joy. God's joy isn't fleeting; it's a wellspring that never runs dry. I knew I needed to quiet the noise around me again and stop searching for joy in all the wrong places.

I had tried "solitude" for three years, and the pain was unbearable because I was trying to self-heal—dressing my wounds in my own strength rather than allowing God to do the deep work within me. Finding the right balance between isolation and intentional separation had become challenging, particularly as I was struggling to distinguish between the two. I saw being "still" as loneliness rather than an invitation to spend intentional time alone with God. Process always precedes the promise, and it often occurs behind closed doors—separation from the old or familiar, a season of obscurity, setting apart, coming away from distractions, staying in God's presence, and learning to be at peace there. This has been referred to as the "wilderness experience."[14] In the Bible, it's often a place of humility, hope, supernatural provision, spiritual warfare, and restoration. It's also a time of testing, refining, and preparation.[15]

God uses such seasons to strengthen faith, build character, teach dependence on Him, and prepare His people for greater purposes. I wanted all the benefits of the "wilderness," but I didn't want the experience. I longed for a shortcut, but with God, there are none! The wilderness is never the destination—it is the pathway to the Promised Land, a journey that requires trusting His leading.[16] Over the years, my faith journey had been characterized by yo-yo Christianity—marked by immaturity, instability, lukewarmness, and a constant fluctuation between spiritual highs and lows. My commitment to God had been inconsistent—strong and passionate at times, yet weak and distant when challenges arose or distractions pulled me away.[17] This cycle often stems from emotionally based faith, a lack of spiritual discipline, or external influences that shake one's devotion. In my case, it was all of these and more! James 1:6 warns against being *"like a wave of the sea, blown and tossed by the wind,"* reminding believers that steadfast faith is essential to spiritual growth and stability.

I had no excuse not to have had a consistent walk with God. He had continually placed me among people of strong faith and in an atmosphere—whether church or fellowship—where powerful, convicting, and prayer-driven sermons emphasized repentance, revival, and total dependence on Him. I was still attending my dear friend's church, pastored by her husband. Their messages carried a sense of urgency, calling believers to a spiritual reawakening, intercessory prayer, and unwavering faith amid societal moral decline. Their ministry remains deeply rooted in scriptural truth, challenging believers to move beyond mere religious activity into a Spirit-led, transformative relationship with God.

The issue wasn't what I was being "fed" but how receptive I was to the Word—whether I was

---

14. Deut. 8:2-3
15. Exod. 3:1-2; 16:4; 1 Kings 17:2-6; Hosea 2:14-15; Matt. 4:1; Luke 1:80
16. Josh. 5:6; Ps. 78:52
17. Rev. 3:15-16

allowing it to take root in my heart, grow, and truly transform me from the inside out. Despite my struggles and striving, I'm deeply grateful for the grace of God that kept me anchored by the River.[18] Whether I was gulping in desperation or sipping in quiet surrender, what mattered most was that I was still drinking—still drawing from the Living Water (Jesus Christ)[19] who sustains and restores all who come to Him.

At every moment, our lives reflect what we nourish—whether our spirit is being strengthened or our flesh is taking control. As Galatians 6:8 warns, *"Whoever sows to please their flesh, from the flesh will reap destruction; whoever sows to please the Spirit, from the Spirit will reap eternal life."* What we feed grows, and what we neglect weakens. Our choices shape our destinies, revealing whether we remain in Christ to thrive,[20] walk in the Spirit, or yield to the flesh.[21]

"Wherefore lay apart all filthiness and superfluity of naughtiness, and receive with meekness the engrafted word, which is able to save your souls." (James 1:21 KJV) In horticulture, *grafting* involves inserting a branch from one tree into another so it can draw life and nourishment from it. A successfully grafted branch, open to pruning and growth, will produce fruit,[22] and God will remove dead branches so we can grow.[23]

I sometimes wonder if my journey through the desert would have been shorter or easier had I fully yielded my life to God. Many times, I took my trust, worries, and battles out of His hands—thinking He was too slow or busy to help me. The Israelites' journey from Egypt to the Promised Land, which should have taken just eleven days, stretched into forty years due to their stubbornness and disobedience.[24] God decreed that the entire generation—except Joshua and Caleb—would perish in the wilderness because of their rebellion and unbelief. Consequently, Israel wandered for forty years, one year for each day the spies spent scouting the land![25]

The Christian journey is not one of perfection but of perseverance. Though we may stumble, God's sustaining grace upholds us—not as a license for reckless living, but as an assurance that He is faithful even in our weakness. As Proverbs 24:16 (NIV) reminds us, *"for though the righteous fall seven times, they rise again, but the wicked stumble when calamity strikes."* This is not an invitation to abuse God's grace,[26] but a call to trust in His mercy while striving toward righteousness. His grace strengthens us to rise, not to remain in sin.

---

18. Ps. 1:3
19. John 4:13-14; 7:37-38; 2 Cor. 12:9
20. John 15:4-5
21. Rom. 8:5-6
22. Gal. 5:22-23
23. John 15:2
24. Num. 14:26-35; Deut. 1:2-3
25. Num. 14:34
26. Rom. 6:1-2

TESTED, TRIED, TORN ... YET STILL TRUSTING

I knew the journey might be long and difficult, and I needed more than just positive think-ing or a strong conviction that everything would work out in the end. Though I resisted for a while, I eventually took practical steps and secured the services of a lawyer—even though I wasn't ready to grant Ségun the divorce or give up on our marriage without a last-ditch effort. He was seeking full custody of our children, and I refused to sit back and let that happen. I thought, *No one is going to punish me for standing up for myself by taking my children away!*

Months passed as the lawyers handled the divorce proceedings, and the battle for custody of our children became our primary focus. Then came the year 2007 ... and I discovered that my mother had cancer. I was stunned—she had kept the news from me for months, and I had no idea how long she had been quietly battling the disease. She said she hadn't told me because she didn't want to add to my worries.

Yet, despite her deteriorating health, my mother had remained steadfast—picking up my boys from school and caring for them until I got off work. She adored her grandchildren and doted on them like a mother hen shielding her chicks. I cherished our time together, often lingering at her place for dinner as we talked and laughed, waiting for the rush-hour traffic to ease before making the grueling one-and-a-half to two-hour drive home—depending on traffic.

My mother did everything she could to lift my spirits and distract me from the challenges I was facing at the time. From the very beginning, she took my boys and me in without a moment of hesitation. She embraced the sudden change without complaint, never minding the inconvenience of our prolonged stay—one she hadn't even been given time to prepare for properly. While I operated on autopilot for nearly two years, she took charge, providing unwav-ering support both while we lived with her and even after we moved out.

The separation weighed heavily on her. She practically gave up her own life to be there for us 24/7. Her social life faded—she rarely visited family or friends, entirely dedicated to my boys and me. Many nights, when I couldn't sleep or was overwhelmed with tears, she stayed up with me, listening, talking, and praying through the endless twists and turns of a journey she had walked before. Determined to see our family restored, Mom sought the support of both family and pastors in an effort to reconcile Ségun and me. She endured disrespect and humiliation in the process but never wavered. She gave everything. She held nothing back.

I learned about my mother's condition from her brother, a doctor. She had given him per-mission to tell me only when she could no longer cope physically, and the prognosis from the specialists they had seen was grim. I was upset with my uncle for not telling me sooner and angry at my mother for feeling the need to shield and protect me—even in her own greatest time of need.

I couldn't shake the feeling that my brother and I had been denied the chance to explore alternative treatment options through our own networks. If I had known earlier, I would have pulled myself together faster, been stronger for her, and prayerfully stood in the gap on her behalf. After leaving my uncle's house, I couldn't face my mother immediately. Instead, I drove to my friend's house and broke down in tears. I had no idea how to process the news or what the next steps should be. In that dark season, I will always be grateful for my band of sisters who surrounded me with love and rock-solid support.

How could I have missed the signs that she was ill? I had been so consumed by my own struggles that I failed to see the changes she was going through. I blamed myself for burdening her—emotionally, spiritually, physically, and financially. I had been deeply concerned about her drastic weight loss and frequent exhaustion after I moved in with her, but I convinced myself it was due to the long fasting periods she undertook on my behalf. My worries only grew as she embarked on extended fasts, some lasting seventy to ninety days at a stretch. We argued about it many times, but I couldn't stop her. My mother and my grandmother were women of deep, unshakable faith who fought and won countless battles on their knees. She carried my burdens as if they were her own and gave everything she had—until she simply couldn't give anymore.

That was her way—passed down by her mother—to solve any problem, you begin with prayer. My mother taught me how to fight the good fight of faith on my knees. She had endured her own share of heartbreaks, raising my older brother and me primarily on her own, with some support from both her family and my dad. You can't begin to imagine the depth of her joy when I got married and settled into motherhood—or how devastating the breakup was for her.

In a society that can be cruel, where whispers of "like mother, like daughter" carry a sting, she bore it all with relentless grace. My mother's strength was phenomenal. From a young age, she taught me how to walk life's journey—hand in hand with God. She showed me the importance of faith, forgiveness, optimism, grace, dignity, and discernment. She modeled hard work, compassion, introspection, the spirit of generosity, integrity, and sacrificial love—qualities she instilled in me.

Like most mothers, "self-care" was seldom on her never-ending list of to-dos. She always put herself last. Women aren't gluttons for punishment, nor were they designed to endure perpetual hardship or serve as pain sponges. Yet, many still find themselves perpetuating this deep injustice against themselves. My mother was very hands-on and preferred to do everything herself. I had hired a few nannies, but they didn't like shuttling between our two homes. So, Mom decided it wasn't necessary, and we could save money for other things if she helped me with the children instead of hiring a nanny. I quickly moved my boys and me back to her house to look after her. We hired a live-in nanny and, with the help of her cousin, arranged for an older lady to supervise and assist with cooking.

I was devastated. It felt like the world came crashing down. Not my mother! My backbone!

She wasn't perfect and was quick to admit when she was wrong. When we had disagreements—though rare—she was usually the first to call for a truce, always with grace. She was everything to me—my confidant, my number-one cheerleader, my prayer partner, and my prayer covering. I was so confident in her prayers that I always leaned on them to carry me through. I took so much for granted, believing she would always be there … but her prayers outlived her.[27] I'm so grateful that I'm reaping the fruits of her prayers, love, and goodwill—seeds she consistently and tirelessly sowed into the lives of her loved ones.

Her health deteriorated rapidly after an investigative surgery, so I took as much time as I could off work to be with her until she entered palliative care. Anyone who has either watched from afar or cared for a loved one battling cancer knows how ravaging the disease is. It leaves you feeling helpless as you watch them struggle to hold on to life. The only way I knew to cope was to shut down emotionally—it felt as if I was having an out-of-body experience.

I couldn't imagine the pain my mother endured. She and I avoided discussing the possibility of her not making it through, choosing to treat each day as a gift. Making her comfortable meant she was sedated most of the time, so such conversations were nearly impossible. But my mother knew she was loved, and I held on to hope for a miracle every time I went to see her after work. There were no goodbyes—everything just stopped. One of her cousins, who stayed with her during the day, said she was rubbing her legs to improve circulation when my mother asked her to stop. She sat up unassisted, gazed ahead with a serene smile, and waved gently at no one in particular—things she hadn't done in a long time. Then, she lay back down and peacefully slipped into eternity. That memory of my beloved mother remains a source of comfort to me to this day.

I received the dreaded call at work and didn't handle the news well. Thankfully, Ségun agreed to take the children that evening, and they stayed with him while funeral arrangements were made. I hadn't shared the full extent of my mother's illness with him, so I had been juggling the ongoing developments with the divorce, meetings with my lawyers, and preparing my response to his petition on the sidelines. I didn't know what to expect, but he attended my mother's funeral with our children.

As I watched the coffin being lowered into the ground, I wept uncontrollably in my father's arms. Ségun stood beside him, and for a moment, I hoped he would reach out to comfort me somehow. In the midst of my grief, I was reminded of the two "signposts" that God had impressed on my heart the day I was moved out of my home: John 12:24 and 2 Samuel 14:14. God had used those verses to remind me of the fleeting nature of life, a reality that was painfully clear at that moment. Life is indeed transient—like the seed that must fall to the ground and die to bear fruit, we, too—whether through death or the rapture (the second coming of

---

27. Acts 10:4b

Christ and the gathering of believers),[28] will all face the end of this earthly journey[29] and meet our Maker.[30]

After the dust-to-dust rites, Ségun stretched his hand toward me and pulled me close. As I lay my head against his chest, a stillness washed over me. The reverend's closing prayers faded into the background, drowned out by the rhythm of his heartbeat and my own quiet sobs. In that moment, the weight of over three years of anguish—perhaps even longer—rose to the surface. But no amount of comfort in those fleeting minutes could soothe the depths of my sorrow.

I wanted to stay there. That was my rightful place—by my husband's side. That's where I had been cut from, where I belonged.[31] But so many things had pulled us apart, and wounds had gone unhealed.

I returned to the house in Ségun's car, where he stayed with me until I headed to the reception to join the guests. He didn't say much; he just sat there, watching me cry, his presence speaking louder than words ever could. I didn't know what to expect from him, but those few minutes in his arms did something I hadn't anticipated. They didn't change the past or promise a future, but in that moment, they provided comfort—a flicker of warmth in the cold, hollow grief. And maybe, just maybe, they ignited a spark of hope…a faith-booster even in the ruins, that something sacred might still be rebuilt, and something beautiful might still rise.

Funerals are peculiar gatherings—friends and family come together to offer condolences and honor the departed. One would think such moments would serve as sobering reminders of life's brevity and the certainty of what lies beyond. Yet, too often, we walk away unchanged, mourning for the bereaved and grieving for the dead but failing to reflect on our own mortality. We seldom pause to consider the eternity that awaits us all—the possibility of spending forever either in the presence of God or in eternal separation from Him. Our choices in this fleeting life determine our destination in the unending afterlife. *"I have set before you life and death…therefore choose life…"* (Deuteronomy 30:19)

It's a profound truth that we often lose ourselves in this world's temporary struggles, triumphs, and distractions, yet in the grand scheme, they are but passing moments. The real questions are: How are we living our lives now? Are we living in a way that will impact where we spend eternity? It's easy to think we have all the time in the world, but life is fragile and uncertain. Today (right now), God offers His mercy, grace, and the gift of redemption through Jesus Christ to all who would receive it.

Every decision we make, every relationship we build, and every moment we spend shape our eternity. We cannot afford to live with the illusion of endless time. Each day is a gift, a

---

28. Matt. 24:30-31; John 14:2-3; 1 Cor. 15:51-52; 1 Thess. 4:16-17; Rev. 22:12

29. Gen. 3:19; Job 34:14-15; Ps. 90:12; 103:14; Eccles. 3:1; 12:7; James 4:14; Heb. 9:27

30. Rom. 14:10-12; 2 Cor. 5:10; Heb. 9:27

31. Gen. 2:23-24

chance to choose the eternal over the temporary. As we face the inevitable truth of death, let it serve as a wake-up call, urging us to live purposefully, seeking God's will in every area of our lives—ensuring that our lives reflect the love and redemption He offers. What legacy will you leave? The time to decide is now, for eternity awaits.

This has been the most difficult portion of the book for me to write. It's been eighteen years since my exceptional mother passed, and not a day goes by that I don't miss her. She was a true pillar of strength—wise, selfless, and unwavering in her faith. Indeed, she was a *"mother in Israel!"*

FROM MISSTEPS TO MERCY

Adjusting to life after my mother's passing was agonizing. The pain and regrets felt unbearable. I couldn't understand why God was stripping me of yet another cherished relationship. I thought my heart would shatter, but it didn't. I thought I would lose my mind, but I didn't. I thought the world had ended, but it kept spinning. I thought the weight of it all would crush me, but God sustained me![32] I carried immense guilt, blaming myself for overburdening my mother with my struggles—making her worry about me without considering her own frailty. I shared everything with her, taking it all to my mother so she could *take it to the Lord in prayer.* That guilt consumed me for years, but I also blamed Ségun and his family. If the breakup had never happened, my mother wouldn't have been under so much stress...or so I believed.

I was already hanging by a thread, but after my mom's passing, I completely unraveled—almost spiraling out of control. I stopped caring. It felt like all my efforts to be the "good girl" had been wasted, only to be met with pain and loss. So, what was the point? Maybe it was true after all—*good girls finish last.* I started believing those lies, letting my circumstances shape my perspective rather than standing on God's truth. Instead of holding onto His Word, I was swayed by what my senses told me. The enemy kept intensifying his attacks, determined to shake my faith and sever my grip on God's promises.[33]

My interactions and communication with Ségun became more civil, to the point that he agreed to have our children stay with him while I took a short trip abroad after my mom's funeral. I desperately needed a break. But when I returned, getting our boys back to live with me became an issue. I couldn't understand why he would do this—especially so soon after everything I had just endured. Speaking to or seeing my sons became a struggle, with obstacles at every turn. It was inexplicable, and I had reached my breaking point. I was done. I contacted my lawyers and made it clear—I was now fully committed to fighting for full custody of my children.

With more time on my hands, I began reconnecting with friends and, much like Ségun,

---

32. Ps. 34:18; 55:22; Isa. 41:10; Lam. 3:22-23; 2 Cor. 4:8-9
33. Mark 4:15

openly acknowledged to anyone who asked that we had been separated for almost four years. I started socializing more, spending time with colleagues who had perfected the typical British after-work pub routine, and even accepting invitations to go on dates. At first, it felt like reclaiming a part of myself that had been buried under years of disappointment and heartache. But beneath the surface was a restlessness—an emptiness that no amount of socializing could truly fill. Men and women face the same temptations in times of loneliness and transition, but our responses often differ, shaped by religious beliefs, cultural expectations, and family responsibilities.

Looking back, there's no doubt that Ségun and I made mistakes while attempting to self-heal amid our turmoil. We sought to numb the pain of a marriage gone sour in all the wrong places—chasing happiness, attention, validation, and respect—everything we had stopped giving each other. Many of our choices, which seemed justified at the time, were, in truth, thoughtless and, at times, even cruel. The hurt we carried spilled over onto those around us, dragging others into the collateral damage of our brokenness. We were trapped in a vicious cycle of pain, in which those closest to us became unintentional casualties of our missteps. It's true what they say—hurt people often end up hurting others.

There were moments when I should have been stronger and wiser. Instead, I allowed myself to drift into indiscretions that led to entanglements, complications, and wounds that cut deep. I still carry the weight and regrets of the past, but I'm grateful for the humbling and sobering lessons I learned in the blind spots—lessons that revealed I wasn't as faultless as I had believed.

So, I was also capable of slipping up? I had held Ségun's affair over his head from the moment I found out—much like the prodigal son's older brother resented his sibling for straying and then being welcomed back so readily, or the Pharisees, who boasted in their own righteousness. I had always seen myself as the "better" spouse—the faithful one, the wounded one, the wronged one—especially since Ségun never admitted to his unfaithfulness or expressed any remorse until after our reconciliation.

But now, we were on a level playing field. Without Jesus occupying the position of Savior *and Lord* in our hearts, we were both sinners in different ways all along. I had been blind to my own vulnerabilities. Now, I understood—none of us is above falling. In my bitterness and self-righteousness, I had naively and confidently believed I was "cleaner" than he was. I justified my hurt and reactions, convinced my suffering validated my judgments. But as Scripture warns, *"So beware if you think it could never happen to you, lest your pride becomes your downfall."* (1 Cor. 10:12 TPT)

> *"Therefore let the one who thinks he stands firm [immune to temptation, being over-confident and self-righteous], take care that he does not fall [into sin and condemnation]. No temptation [regardless of its source] has overtaken or enticed you that is*

not common to human experience [nor is any temptation unusual or beyond human resistance]; but God is faithful [to His word—He is compassionate and trustworthy], and He will not let you be tempted beyond your ability [to resist], but along with the temptation He [has in the past and is now and] will [always] provide the way out as well, so that you will be able to endure it [without yielding, and will overcome temptation with joy]. " (1 Cor. 10:12-13 AMP)

"Dear brothers and sisters, if another believer is overcome by some sin, you who are godly should gently and humbly help that person back onto the right path. And be careful not to fall into the same temptation yourself." (Gal. 6:1 NLT)

Some may say I'm being too hard on myself—that after years of separation, with a divorce already in court and a husband who had clearly moved on, I had every right to seek love again. But marriage is more than a legal contract; it is a covenant, and in the eyes of God, Ségun and I were and remain one. I wrestled with this truth, trying to silence the tension between my longing for companionship and the conviction that I was still bound to my husband. The world would have justified my choices, and perhaps even I did at the time, but deep down, I knew that my heart—still bruised, still searching—was seeking healing in the wrong ways.

Looking back, I realize that pain, loneliness, and disappointment can push even the strongest of us into justifications that feel right in the moment but leave us emptier in the end. I wasn't just searching for love but affirmation, proof that I was still desirable and worthy of devotion. But no earthly relationship could ever fill the void that only God was meant to heal. So, yes, I may have been too hard on myself. But I also know that my convictions were not misplaced. The weight of my past choices is not just about right or wrong but about the realization that I had allowed my pain to lead me rather than my faith. And that, more than anything, is my deepest regret.

LITTLE FOXES LURK

Seeking affection, attention, flattery, or feeding one's ego through seemingly harmless conversations or even direct flirtatious behavior can be the starting point of a slippery slope, gradually pulling one away from faith, trust, and healthy boundaries. Whether rekindling old friendships, revisiting past relationships, or forming new interests, these seemingly innocent exchanges can quickly lead to indiscretion or regret. Often clouded by pride, insecurities, or vulnerability, people sometimes let their guard down in moments of weakness or overconfidence in themselves.

Vulnerability, though a natural human experience, can be dangerously attractive to others, and both men and women can fall prey to temptation anywhere—at work, in social settings, or even within the church. These blind spots are setups and distractions that disrupt the spiritual walk and can derail destinies. Any pursuit of happiness that appears valid, justifiable, or innocent but leads one off God's path is a trap. *"There is a way that seems right to a man, but its end is the way to death."* (Prov. 14:12)

In Romans 8:4-14, Paul contrasts living according to the flesh with living according to the Spirit. While the flesh leads to death, living in the Spirit brings life and peace. A life governed by the flesh cannot please God, and as believers, we are called to live according to the Spirit, putting to death the misdeeds of the body and honoring God with our lives. Christ's presence in us empowers us to live righteously, and those led by the Spirit are children of God.

Living according to the flesh doesn't honor God. This doesn't imply that God doesn't love us, but rather that He cannot accept behavior driven by our carnal desires and impulses. Instead, we are called to be sensitive and reverent before Him, seeking to obey and please Him through His strength (Phil. 2:12-13). It's not about a marriage's physical or emotional status but about honoring God and recognizing that our bodies are His temple (1 Cor. 6:19-20). We are called to live in a way that reflects His holiness and righteousness.

According to Scripture, even looking at someone with lustful intent is equivalent to committing adultery in the heart (Matt. 5:27-30). As followers of Christ, we are called to live according to His way, His will, and His Word—for they are all one. While it's easy to justify our actions based on circumstances like separation, loneliness, or unmet needs, these reasons don't change the fact that we are stepping outside the boundaries that protect the sanctity of marriage.

Ultimately, what matters is not our circumstances or justifications but our faithfulness to God's standards and God Himself. External factors may tempt us to excuse our behavior, but God calls us to honor Him in every aspect of our lives, including our marriages. Only by walking in the Spirit, aligning our hearts with His Word, and seeking His strength can we navigate the challenges of life and relationships in a way that pleases God and reflects His love.

Environments, circumstances, and people play a significant role in shaping who we become. We are either influencing them, or they are influencing us. Throughout the Bible, God calls individuals and groups to separate themselves for purification, preservation, or preparation for His divine promises and purposes. Examples of this include God's call to Abraham in Genesis 12:1, Noah in Genesis 6:13-18, Lot and his family in Genesis 19:12-17, and the Israelites in Exodus 3:10.

Other examples include Numbers 16:23-26 and Leviticus 20:24, 26. In Matthew 4:18-22, Jesus calls His disciples—Peter, Andrew, James, and John—to leave their familiar lives and follow Him, giving them a new identity and purpose beyond mere survival. Similarly, in Luke 14:26, Jesus teaches that following Him requires a willingness to leave everything behind. Paul echoes this as he quotes Isaiah in 2 Corinthians 6:17, calling believers to be set apart: *"Come out from among them and be separate, says the Lord. Do not touch what is unclean, and I will receive you."*

I had walked this path of "settling" before—making choices that prioritized my desires, no matter how valid they seemed (like the pursuit of happiness), over God and His ways. At first, it appeared to serve me well, bringing to life the marriage and future I had envisioned. But in the end, it cost me far more than I ever anticipated. Trying to sustain everything in my own wisdom and strength only led to exhaustion and near ruin. Yet, grace intervened—just in time—pulling me back before I strayed too far again. It helped me wait for God's original plan and timing. The options before me were enticing, beautifully laid out, and seemingly fulfilling[34]—but so are counterfeits, and so is the enemy, who disguises himself as an angel of light.[35]

Where we stumble, God steadies us, and grace leads the way.[36] Recognizing this, I felt compelled to create distance from certain people, relationships, and environments—not because they were inherently bad, but because they had the potential to pull me off course. Letting go wasn't always easy, and I didn't always navigate it with the grace, wisdom, or tact I would have hoped for. Some ties were loosened, while others were severed—not out of malice, but because I was fighting for my life. Relationships shift, perspectives expand, and friendships are tested—some withstand the changes, while others naturally drift apart. Growth happens at different times for each of us; not everyone is meant to walk with us through every chapter of our journey. Along the way, our understanding of what truly matters can be refined. I hope that, even in the transitions, I honored those around me with kindness and sincerity, trusting God to guide each of us along the paths He has set before us.

I also eagerly pursued courses through my office's Learning and Development program, taking advantage of every opportunity to learn and grow. It wasn't just a way to keep myself occupied—it became a means of rediscovering my strengths, broadening my perspective, and equipping myself for the future. Each course challenged me in different ways, sharpening my skills, building my confidence, and reminding me that even in seasons of uncertainty, there was always room to grow, evolve, and prepare for what lay ahead.

Believe me, challenges related to infidelity are incredibly difficult to navigate in any marriage. The pain and broken trust can feel insurmountable. Yet, through it all, we have seen the hand of God at work—bringing healing where there were wounds, restoration where there was brokenness, and hope where things once seemed beyond repair. Only by His grace have we been able to rise from the mess we made, not just surviving but thriving, learning, growing, and moving forward with renewed faith. For that, we are truly grateful to God.

---

34. Gen. 3:6
35. 2 Cor. 11:14
36. Ps. 5:8; 25:5; 27:11; 143:10

THROUGH SÉGUN'S LENSES

Although I knew my insistence on separation would be an extremely consequential decision, the repercussions went far beyond anything I could ever have imagined. Four closely intertwined lives were suddenly untangled in the space of just a few hours. Despite the difficult circumstances, Funké and I did our best to ensure our children felt loved and secure while the two of us tried to find our feet.

My work kept me busy, and I was traveling a lot. On the surface, I seemed to be doing okay, but in reality, I was fighting many internal battles that I waged throughout the separation. During that time, despite several attempts, new relationships could not fill the void in my marriage. Despite my best efforts at shutting them out, I was wracked with feelings of guilt as I struggled with the prospect of beginning a serious relationship that my children would eventually be forced into. What if it didn't work? What if I made the wrong choice? This made it virtually impossible for me to confidently engage with anyone romantically, as there was a part of me that I had cordoned off.

I spent the early years of the separation trying to settle into a new routine—professionally and socially. However, attention to any spiritual growth was conspicuously absent. As a result, I lost a golden opportunity to take a deep look at myself and understand how I had arrived at this point. I continued to live each day through the prism of a husband and father who had been forced to make hard decisions involving his family's future due to factors beyond his control. My decision to ignore any dissenting voices made it impossible for me to change course, which perpetuated the process of drifting like a rudderless ship despite everything seeming to be under control.

Rearview Mirror Lesson

In the build-up to our separation, I allowed myself to be swept along by a wave of self-assuredness I believed would free me from the shackles of a marriage I had concluded was teetering on the edge of a precipice. However, nothing could have prepared me for what lay ahead, particularly as I simply replaced my self-imposed restraints with a pair of heavy-duty blinkers.

All that did was guarantee I would lose my bearings by forcing me to look in one direction, and one direction only—straight ahead. That was a fail-proof way of ensuring I lost perspective regarding my role in the breakdown of my marriage. There was little or no incentive to question my decision other than the impact the separation might have on our children.

In the following years, I refused to believe there was any sense in contemplating retracing my steps and trying to salvage my marriage. I convinced myself that I had done everything humanly possible in that regard, which made it easier to continue my emotional detachment from Funké in anticipation of an eventual countdown to a divorce in some shape or form.

Reaching the proverbial tipping point in a marriage is dangerous, as it can cloud judgment and create countless justifications for losing interest in a spouse. In doing so, a person can downplay or entirely dismiss their own role in causing or contributing to a marital rift. Getting back on an even keel afterward becomes progressively harder as pride and acquired habits prevent love, respect, and patience from taking root, especially when one spouse decides to play the role of judge and jury regarding any marital challenges they may be experiencing.

12

Fight the Good Fight of Faith, Not of Fury

"Fight the good fight of faith, lay hold on eternal life, to which you were also called and have confessed the good confession in the presence of many witnesses."

1 TIMOTHY 6:12

ECHOES OF BITTERNESS

Living together during the first five years of our marriage—and even living apart during our separation—brought out the worst in both Ségun and me. Yet, through it all, God shielded and upheld us, even when we tried to wriggle free—clinging to Him by the thinnest thread of faith.[1]

As the divorce proceedings unfolded, I tried to fight fairly, but our animosity only intensified. I felt the need to prove that I wasn't a pushover, especially as Ségun remained unrelenting in his attempts to break my resolve. The instructions I gave to my lawyers were clear—stick to the facts. I constantly had to resist their pressure to dig up dirt or disclose the "receipts" I had in response to his petition just to counter his claims or build a stronger case.

In his claims, he went as far as stating that I was an "unfit mother"—that was the final straw! I knew people on the sidelines were fanning the flames, but this? I had already endured so much from him, but I was not about to let him take my children from me and raise them

---

1. Isa. 43:2; Rom. 8:35; Heb. 13:5b

with whomever he had in mind. He had unrestricted access to them, taking them on trips abroad with whomever he chose. Yet now, I was suddenly being denied access to my own five- and eight-year-old boys—it was beyond belief!

Ségun's fixation on my mental health began when our fights escalated while we were still living together. Even after we separated, he continued to harp on this—sending emails and texts about mental health conditions as if diagnosing me through his online research. He repeatedly assigned me personality disorders, almost as though he were trying to convince me that something was truly wrong with me. He insisted I needed to see a psychiatrist for our safety and that of our children. I couldn't comprehend why he was so determined to wear me down—going to such lengths just to pressure me into signing the divorce papers and giving him full custody of our children. It made me wonder what kind of deep-seated resentment or vendetta could drive him to work so relentlessly to separate two young children from the mother who had always loved and cared for them.

While we were together, I now recognize that some of my actions or unconventional reactions may have given Ségun reasons to question or misunderstand me—perhaps because they were beyond his scope of experience or comprehension. When a person is repeatedly made to doubt what they heard, saw, or felt, it can be profoundly disorienting, even to the point of questioning their own reality. At times, it felt like I was living in an alternate universe! In my attempt to make sense of things, I found myself unintentionally taking on the role of an investigator—constantly searching for clarity and confirmation of what I instinctively knew to be true.

Rather than openly acknowledging any wrongdoing, Ségun seemed to find ways to justify his choices and the betrayal of my trust. Difficult conversations were avoided, often dismissed as overreactions on my part, which made any meaningful dialogue nearly impossible. His focus appeared to be on deflecting, denying, and keeping certain truths hidden. As a result, we never truly addressed his affair when he moved out of the house for three months or the circumstances leading up to it, nor did we confront the emotional scars it caused or the impact it had on our family. Instead, it felt as though I was expected to either dismiss my concerns as unfounded or simply accept and move forward without resolution. Looking back, I realize I was struggling to navigate this season without turning to the one source that could have provided true wisdom and healing—God's Word.

For me, it wasn't just the unfaithfulness—it was the deeper wounds that came with it: the dishonesty, the distance, and the way he seemed to shut me out emotionally, leaving me feeling unheard and uncertain. The trust and openness I had shared over the years felt as though they had been turned against me, making me question my own perceptions. I second-guessed everything—even when I tried to voice my concerns or make sense of the changes I saw. Instead of reassurance or understanding, his response was often frustrating: "If things are so bad, and I'm such a terrible husband, why stay? Why not just leave?" Those words only deepened my confusion, making it even harder to find clarity in an already painful situation. And now, twisting things and using my vulnerabilities as ammunition to label me felt deeply disheartening and profoundly unjust.

As long as we have labels and classifications for behavior, people are likely to exhibit some form or degree of deviance at one point or another. Psychologically speaking, deviance refers to behaviors, impulses, or personality traits that diverge from societal norms, though they are not necessarily harmful or indicative of criminal intent. In hindsight, I recognize that during the early years of our marriage, I sometimes responded in immature and regrettable ways. Stress, worry, and emotional struggles are part of the human experience, and while they can affect our behavior, they do not automatically indicate a psychological disorder.

Although I have intentionally refrained from using clinical terminology in this book, those familiar with psychological frameworks may recognize patterns that align with certain behavioral tendencies. The reality is that human behavior exists on a spectrum—from typical, everyday actions to more extreme or unusual behaviors—and at some point, most people will display actions or reactions that fall outside conventional expectations. These behaviors can vary depending on the situation, context, and personal experiences, highlighting the complexity and diversity of human actions. Our willingness to acknowledge, understand, and grow from these experiences matters most.

We are often quick to judge, label, categorize, or "diagnose" people—based on emotional reactions—especially when their behavior is challenging or uncomfortable. When someone's actions make us uneasy or seem inexplicable, we may hastily label them as toxic, strange, or even abnormal. This tendency can prevent us from considering the deeper causes of their behavior and, in turn, hinder our ability to empathize with their struggles. Labels and categories are useful for identifying or describing behavior patterns that may need attention but should never define a person's identity. Rather than focusing on labels that can limit understanding, we should use them as tools to encourage empathy and foster a more compassionate, open-minded view of one another.

As Christians, we're called to look past labels (1 Samuel 16:7) and prayerfully discern the real spiritual influences at work, remembering that "we wrestle not against flesh and blood" (Ephesians 6:12). This means responding—not with condemnation—but with the same compassion and spiritual authority Jesus demonstrated. When He encountered those afflicted by unclean spirits, He addressed the spirit behind the behavior (Mark 1:23–27; Acts 16:16–18). Even with Peter, whom He deeply loved, Jesus rebuked not the man but the wrong influence speaking through him: "Get behind Me, Satan!" (Matthew 16:23; Mark 8:33). This teaches us to see people with grace while confronting, in prayer and wisdom, the unseen forces that distort their actions. Such an approach creates space for healing, growth, and the opportunity to develop and sustain more meaningful and authentic connections.

To me, it seemed as though Ségun was trying to find reasons to justify his chosen path and his decision to start a new life for himself. At the same time, he was seeking ways to pressure me into signing the divorce papers and gain full custody of our children—a part of the situation that still puzzles me. If he truly believed I posed a threat to them, why did he leave them in my care when he moved us out of our home? Did he prioritize his own convenience over their safety at that moment? It appeared that his perception of me shifted during that time to align with his purpose. How did I go from the young woman who once fell madly in love with him to the one he would later suggest was unstable? How did I go from being praised as the "best mother and wife" in words, letters, and cards to being labeled "unfit"? Interestingly, about a year later, during our first attempt at reconciliation in 2008, I was again described as an "exceptional mother," along with other encomiums.

No doubt, there are serious mental health conditions that require proper assessment and treatment. However, it's both wrong and deeply unfair to mislabel someone for personal gain or to further one's own interests. If a loved one exhibits unusual or concerning behavior, the best course of action is to seek timely professional help rather than resorting to assumptions or making unfounded diagnoses.

As believers, we must be careful not to fall into the cultural trend of carelessly and hastily judging one another—whether in the form of exaggerated labels or misguided declarations. The power of life and death is in the tongue, and our words hold great weight. Sometimes, what's needed isn't a label but a shift in perspective. Adjusting how we think or interpret situations can often lead to deeper understanding and, ultimately, change how people respond and relate to one another.

Romans 12:1-2 reminds us of the importance of renewing our minds so that we can discern God's will rather than conforming to worldly patterns of thinking. 2 Timothy 1:7 reassures us that *"God has not given us a spirit of fear, but of power and love and a sound mind."* When we operate from this premise, we approach challenges—including those concerning mental and emotional well-being—with wisdom, discernment, and grace.

I came to realize that I had anger issues, which I had unknowingly nurtured and "fed" for years. A turning point came when I heard a sermon that completely changed my approach to dealing with this struggle head-on. An analogy about two prize-fighting dogs was used, and the lesson stuck with me. The story was about a man with a foolproof strategy for ensuring his bets always won whenever his dogs fought. People assumed it was a special training method or sheer luck, but the secret lay in something much simpler—food. Each week leading up to a fight, he would feed the dog he wanted to win and starve the one he wanted to lose. When the fight began, the stronger, well-fed dog would inevitably overpower the weaker, starving one.

That simple yet profound example really hit home. I realized that the anger I was carrying and my "stinking thinking" were fueled by years of feeding my flesh—my unchecked emotions, natural inclinations, and negative thought patterns. If I truly wanted to change, I had to starve these tendencies and instead nourish my spirit. I returned to the Word of God as my daily sustenance, taking it in like vital nourishment for my soul. The more I immersed myself in Scripture and allowed it to cleanse and renew me—like water washing away impurities—the stronger my spirit became. Over time, I gained the strength to resist the impulses that once controlled me. Galatians 5:22-23 speaks of the fruit of the Spirit—love, joy, peace, patience, kindness, goodness, faithfulness, gentleness, and self-control. As I fed my spirit with God's truth, these qualities began to take root in my life, gradually replacing the anger and negativity that once dictated my reactions.

Many things Ségun said and did during this period made me feel that there was more going on than just fleeting emotions—it often seemed like a deeper undercurrent at play. At one point, he saw so much to admire and love in me, but over time, his focus shifted to things that frustrated him, which he continued to express even after we lived apart. Despite my efforts to make our interactions more amicable, they often went unnoticed.

Perhaps, in his eyes, I was no match for him. But I saw it differently. It was a "David and Goliath" battle, and instead of fighting with conventional weapons, I leaned on the one thing I knew had true power—the Word of God. With every challenge he threw at me, I responded by standing firm in faith, sending slingshots of love and scriptures through emails and text messages, and even in our conversations... when I wasn't hurling insults back at him! It was the only way I knew to anchor myself when everything felt like it was crumbling around me. I didn't always get it right, but I kept pressing forward, trusting that God would strengthen and guide me even in my moments of weakness or relapse.

Ségun went as far as contacting our children's school to request their absentee and lateness records. He also convinced the boys' pediatrician and the hospitals we frequented to provide reports on their treatments and details of missed appointments while they lived with me. Thankfully, the health issues were minor—just colds and flu, nothing unusual. The missed appointments were mainly follow-up visits I couldn't attend, either because the boys were already feeling better and I called the doctor instead, or due to financial constraints. However, those appointments were typically rescheduled and kept.

The most baffling part of this situation was that I had registered the children at these hospitals, which were covered under my health insurance. I had no idea that such letters or reports had been provided to support Ségun's case until he told me what he had done during a phone conversation. Naturally, I immediately sprang into action to investigate. I obtained a copy of a letter he was given from one of the hospitals. This was a real eye-opener for me, as I hadn't anticipated the lengths he would go to get what he wanted.

What I found most upsetting about his actions in "collecting dirt on me" was how deeply patriarchal Nigerian society remains, often supporting men in such situations. Many women in that part of the world face similar struggles—or worse. I've heard stories where schools have handed children over to an estranged spouse without any court orders or injunctions. There are also accounts of police officers colluding with husbands to cover up reports of physical abuse. What's even more disturbing is that some of those perpetuating these injustices against women are other women. We can do better as a community and support one another more. When it comes to sensitive issues between estranged couples, it's not about being partial to either side but about avoiding bias. People must be professional, fair, compassionate, and empathetic, always putting the well-being of the children first when making decisions. *"And as you wish that others would do to you, do so to them."* (Luke 6:31)

There were other instances where Ségun tried to undermine me during our separation, but it was through the intervention, support, and assistance of women that I was able to navigate these challenges and ensure that such situations didn't have a negative impact on me. One significant example was when a female friend brought my attention to a form he had filled out and sent to a foreign mission that would have prevented me from traveling alone with our children without his consent. She worked in the processing department for entry clearance documents and happened to come across our applications. I'm not sure if she was aware that we were separated at the time, but she found it odd that the forms listed only my husband and a member of his family as the authorized individuals to accompany our children on overseas trips.

Maybe I was too naïve and trusting, but I never imagined that Ségun would go to such lengths—especially knowing it could have long-term consequences on my travel record and create difficulties for everyone down the line. Thankfully, God intervened, and the information on the forms was corrected. Honestly, it took nothing short of a miracle to move past some of Ségun's actions. These were deep wounds, and only God could—and did—heal.

These are just a few examples of Ségun's mindset during our separation, along with incidents for which I did not receive clear answers or closure for a long time. I was relieved to hear Ségun admit many years after we reconciled that some of what I saw, heard, and felt wasn't all in my head. However, I had to reach a place where I was ready to release them and move forward. True reconciliation and restoration require a heart willing to trust God and focus on the road ahead rather than dwelling on every detour, setback, or obstacle from the past. Getting where we are today has been a long and painful journey. One key factor that helped us overcome the initial hurdles was deciding what was essential to know or clarify, letting go of things that no longer mattered, and casting them into the sea of forgetfulness, just as God does for us.[2] Those things no longer hold any weight in who we are today or in the relationship we've rebuilt over the past sixteen years.

---

2. Isa. 43:25; Mic. 7:19

I can't fully explain my resolve to keep pressing forward despite the odds stacked against me, except to say that God expanded my capacity to love my husband. This became easier as I grew to love God even more and desired to please Him above all else. Beyond my natural inclination to persevere and stand against injustice, I deeply believed the battle wasn't just for myself or my children—I was also fighting for Ségun. Many of his actions after problems began in our marriage seemed out of character and didn't reflect the man I had known for years. It was as if he couldn't see beyond the alternative life he had chosen over his family.

The Bible tells us that *"… the god of this world has blinded the minds of the unbelievers, to keep them from seeing the light of the gospel of the glory of Christ, who is the image of God"* (2 Cor. 4:4). Spouses in this situation must understand early in the "fight" that they aren't just dealing with human choices and emotions but are contending with spiritual influences that cloud judgment and harden hearts. The enemy's strategy is to get people lost in deception and lies they can't even recognize. Through my hurts, I also felt a deep sorrow for my husband. I knew that if I had any hope of restoration—for myself, my children, or even for him—it wouldn't come from fighting in the flesh. It had to be through faith, prayer, and standing firmly on God's truth, even when everything around me contradicted what I prayed or hoped.

Yes, Ségun was making deliberate, self-serving choices, but he wasn't born again or deeply rooted in the Word at the time. I recognized that he probably didn't fully grasp the gravity of his actions or their consequences. It also seemed that no one around him was speaking the truth.[3] He may not have known the way of escape that God provides[4] or understood that redemption was still possible through mercy, repentance, and transformation—the same grace I had experienced firsthand. It all came down to perspective. Just as God had shifted my focus back to Him, I knew He could do the same for Ségun. This is the same God who got hold of Saul on the road to Damascus where he encountered Jesus, dramatically transforming his life and calling him to a greater purpose.[5]

I'm almost certain some people reading this are already giving me the *bombastic side-eye*, wondering why I chose to respond this way—as if I were excusing a grown man from taking responsibility for his actions. Some of my friends felt I should let my estranged husband lie in the bed he had so comfortably made rather than act like a savior on a rescue mission. But that wasn't the case, nor was it how I saw myself! True love—the kind that reflects God's love— doesn't stand back with folded arms, waiting for justice to run its course, especially when danger is near.

Time and again, Love has stepped in, interceded, and restored, even when we've been most undeserving. I did contemplate granting Ségun the divorce he wanted, thinking it might put

3. Prov. 5:3-5; 6:26-29, 32; Mal. 2:14-16; 1 Cor. 6:9-11; Eph. 5:25; Heb. 13:4

4. 1 Cor. 10:13

5. Ezek. 36:26; Prov. 21:1; Acts 9:1-19

an end to the pain and allow me to move on. But I couldn't until I was sure I had done all my Heavenly Father asked of me. We fought when we were together, and even after the separation, the conflict remained. Surely, there had to be a better way!

The world often operates on the principle of *an eye for an eye*, but Jesus demonstrated a different standard. When Peter denied Him three times, Jesus didn't say, "Well, that's what you get for your betrayal." Instead, He restored him and reaffirmed his purpose.[6] The father of the prodigal son didn't wait for his wayward child to crawl back in shame—he ran to meet him with open arms.[7] The woman caught in adultery and brought before Jesus was surrounded by accusers ready to condemn her, but instead of affirming their judgment, Jesus extended mercy. He challenged the self-righteousness of her accusers, saying, *"Let him who is without sin among you be the first to throw a stone at her"* (John 8:7). One by one, they left, and Jesus—though the only one truly without sin—chose not to condemn her. Instead, He forgave her and instructed her to go and sin no more.[8]

Like Peter, the prodigal son, and the adulterous woman, none of us are without fault, yet Christ offers grace rather than abandonment. True love is not about leaving people to suffer the full weight of their poor choices or missteps but about offering a hand of restoration, just as God has done for us. While the world may say, "You made your bed, now lie in it," Christ teaches us a higher way—one of redemption, restoration, and love that covers a multitude of sins.[9] That's the nature of true love: it doesn't condone wrongdoing, but it also doesn't abandon a person to destruction when there's still hope for redemption.

Love, as described in 1 Corinthians 13:7, *"bears all things, believes all things, hopes all things, endures all things."* It doesn't mean ignoring reality, enabling bad behavior, or refusing to hold someone accountable. But it does mean standing in faith, even when it doesn't make sense, and trusting that God's redemptive power is greater than any mistake or even willful negative actions. Sometimes, the best and only thing we can do is lift our concerns to God in prayer, standing in the gap for others and trusting that He will step into the situations we surrender to Him.

As long as I still had jurisdiction as Ségun's wife and remained responsive to the guidance of the Holy Spirit, I was willing to be a vessel through which God could work to bring him back to alignment with His will.[10] Deep down, I just knew—I had a conviction—that I wasn't meant to give up but fight for my family.[11] I didn't always get it right; I stumbled many times.

---

6. John 21:15-17

7. Luke 15:20

8. John 8:11

9. Mic. 6:8 (AMP); Eph. 4:31-32 (AMP); 1 Pet. 4:8

10. 2 Cor. 5:18-20; Gal. 6:1 (AMP); Heb. 12:15-17

11. 2 Cor. 10:3-6

But every time I veered off course, God was faithful to catch me and set me back on the path to recovering all the enemy had stolen. *"Pursue, overtake, and recover all."* (1 Sam. 30:8)

I had vivid dreams that revealed glimpses of our family together in the future, reinforcing my resolve. I didn't know how or when, but I knew without a doubt that God is the Promise Keeper—He can be trusted! The more Ségun acted out, the clearer it became that this was spiritual warfare, and I couldn't fight it alone—I needed Aarons and Hurs to hold up my hands in the battle.[12] In His faithfulness, God sent people to encourage me, often just when I was on the verge of giving up.

In the course of writing this book, I revisited my journals and old emails and rediscovered letters from wonderful people who had stood by me throughout different seasons of my life. Many prayed for me, and some had sent emails during our six-and-a-half-year separation, urging me not to give in while sharing specific scriptures and words of encouragement that reignited my faith. One aunt in the United States was especially committed to seeing us restored—she sent emails nearly every day and spoke life into my situation every time we talked, often several times a week.

I can't overemphasize the importance of surrounding ourselves with the right people—those who align with God's Word when facing challenges. Job's friends—Eliphaz, Bildad, and Zophar—serve as examples of the kind of people one should not have around during difficult times. Initially, they sat with Job in silence, which was an appropriate and compassionate response to his suffering. However, when they began to speak, rather than offering comfort, they accused him of wrongdoing, insisting that his suffering must have been a punishment for sin. Instead of uplifting him, they added to his distress by misjudging his situation and failing to offer real support. Job's friends serve as a reminder of the value of filling one's life with people who bring encouragement, wisdom, and understanding rather than judgment or misplaced criticism during life's challenges.

I believed that God was fighting my battles,[13] but to be honest, there were many times I struggled to fully surrender to Him—trusting that He is just and would ultimately do what was best for all of us—even if our reconciliation wasn't part of His plan. As the months passed and we spent more birthdays, anniversaries, milestones, holidays, and celebrations apart, it became increasingly clear that Ségun wasn't looking back—he had moved on. I, on the other hand, was miserable without my children and my mother, and I couldn't deny the lingering resentment I felt toward him for that.

I wrestled with the frustration of appearing vulnerable in his eyes, knowing he often took advantage of my accommodating nature. One of the things that irked me after moving out of my mother's house was how freely Ségun could enter the apartment I had rented whenever he

12. Exod. 17:12
13. Exod. 14:14; 2 Chron. 20:15

wanted to see our children, while I, on the other hand, was not permitted past the gate of the home we had once shared. It felt unfair, but I chose to focus on what mattered most—ensuring our children had both parents in their lives.

After enduring his actions and excesses for a couple of years, I found it increasingly difficult to hold my peace in the face of provocation—and I failed many times. As a result, he and I had several tense exchanges, including a few public confrontations over the children returning to stay with me. Things had been stable while they were with me for over three years, and the boys and I were finally settling into our new rhythm after my mother's passing. But just as we were adjusting, he once again made the sudden decision to keep our children with him, which disrupted everything.

FITS OF FURY!

In the midst of it all, Ségun asked me to come to the home we had once shared as a family to discuss how we would break the news of the imminent divorce to our children. We had talked about this numerous times but could never agree on how best to manage the conversation. I strongly believed they needed to be shielded from unnecessary details that their young minds might struggle to understand or process properly.

They were young and impressionable, and I worried about the possibility of them being influenced or turned against me. No matter how much hurt I carried, I was intentional about never speaking ill of their father. Instead, we prayed for him together, asking God to make all of us happy. Their innocent hearts often expressed a deep longing for mommy and daddy to be back together—a hope that mirrored my own. And so, we placed that before God, too.

I was under the impression that Ségun debriefed the boys when they were with him because he repeatedly told me, at every opportunity, to stop "building castles in the sky." It is possible that he wanted both the children and me to face his version of reality and the finality of the situation as he saw it. I, however, didn't feel I was creating unrealistic expectations or setting the children up for heartbreak. I simply told them what I felt they could handle, consistently reassuring them that their parents loved them and always would, despite our living apart. We didn't see eye to eye on this matter, as we both wanted different things at that point.[14]

Because I still wasn't allowed on the premises at the house, which only fueled my emotions, the conversation took place in my car outside the gate. Things quickly went downhill when I confronted Ségun with some information I believed to be factual, and he vehemently denied it. In an attempt to prove he was being truthful, he swore using our children's names (which is a deeply significant cultural gesture). But before he could finish his statement, something inside

---

14. Amos 3:3

me snapped. All the pent-up anger I had been holding onto suddenly turned into full-blown rage. In an instant, I lunged at Ségun to strike him. To put it mildly, he scrambled out of the car in a desperate attempt to protect himself! His shirt tore open, and his glasses fell into the car!

I had never been that angry in my life! I wanted so badly to hurt him the way he had hurt me. At that moment, it felt like I had nothing left to lose. All I had were my children, and now he was trying to take them away from me, too. I wanted him to feel every ounce of the pain, heartache, and instability he had caused me. I could tell it took a great deal of restraint on Ségun's part to avoid hitting back—thankfully, either my "shock and awe" tactic froze him in place, or God intervened, sparing me from what could have been a disaster. I couldn't believe it! Here I was, *Miss Prim and Proper*, transformed into a *street (car) fighter* in a moment of incandescent fury!

My heart was racing as I drove away, overwhelmed with shame and disappointment in myself. My reaction was the result of everything that had built up—from the physical gates that had been shut against me, keeping me away from my children, to the public humiliation of being denied access to my own home and Ségun's unacceptable behavior toward me since our separation. Those gates symbolized the emotional wall between us, his hardened heart, and the painful truth that the man I once knew was no longer there, replaced by a stranger I had to deal with. There was also the unresolved issue of not having been able to retrieve some of my belongings from the house. Later that night, I called him to apologize and broke down on the phone. It was clear he, too, was shaken by what had happened.

During our separation, I tried to stay grounded in peace and kept my distance from the house. There were many moments when I considered forcefully entering to retrieve my belongings, but common sense prevailed. Still, I felt cheated, robbed, and, in some ways, like a sucker for tolerating everything he was throwing my way without resisting or retaliating. My children were in the house that day, and he wouldn't even let me see them. That night, I couldn't help but mourn the person I was becoming amid the crisis—especially when I thought I had been making progress in growing spiritually.

The unpleasant incident only gave Ségun more reasons to stand by his decision. He believed and was reinforced by the many naysayers, critics, and advisers around him that I could never change the flaws he had pointed out. To these "voices," nothing I did was ever pleasing or acceptable, and I had most likely exhausted any grace they had ever extended to me. The truth is: If they were done with me, God wasn't. He delights in showing His power where others give up. God is in the habit of completing the work He begins and specializes in creating masterpieces! He is the Author, (Preserver), and Finisher of our faith.[15] I couldn't stay down; I had to get back up and keep at it![16]

---

15. Phil. 1:6; 2:13; Heb. 12:2; 13:21

16. Prov. 24:16

There were a few more encounters where discussions quickly escalated into heated arguments. The main point of contention continued to be access to our children. Since our divorce hadn't been finalized, their visits with each of us had remained unregulated since our separation, but now Ségun didn't want our boys to come to spend time with me. People reached out to Ségun, and I kept praying. Then, unexpectedly, I received a text with just one day's notice: He had to travel and would drop the children off with me the following day. It was ironic—after all the past restrictions, I was now entrusted with their care again when it suited his plans.

Even that arrangement and interaction with him before his trip was unsettling, making me realize we needed to establish healthy boundaries for everyone's well-being. So, upon his arrival, I didn't let the children return to him and avoided unnecessary contact with him (at least for a period). I hadn't yet found the balance between being *"sheep in the midst of wolves"* and being *"as wise as serpents and harmless as doves."* [17] It's difficult to admit that I sometimes acted *"like a senseless horse or mule that needs a bit and bridle to keep it under control."* [18] These *bit and bridle* situations were definitely set up to catch my attention and guide me into submission or position. It felt like the more I resisted, the more the pressure mounted until I finally surrendered to our All-Knowing, All-Wise, and All-Powerful Father. Despite my many failures, I persevered, striving to be and do better. [19]

THE "RIGHTEOUS" FALL TOO!

It felt as though I had run out of options and had no choice but to trust and stay committed to the "processing" God was doing within me. This includes the refining, shaping, spiritual growth, character development, and inner healing—the transformative work He does when we give Him access. It's a period where God molds us through challenges to align more closely with His will and purpose. Sometimes, I became disillusioned by the "falls" and slip-ups, which made it hard to focus or understand exactly what I was being prepared for. Why me? Why did I have to be the one making sacrifices or paying the price for the sake of peace? Why did I have to endure the fire and water to reach the other side—the "Promised Land"?

Sometimes, it felt like I was drowning in deep water, and at other times, the heat felt so intense that I feared it would consume me. But now, with hindsight, I can confidently say it was all necessary. It was in the "fire" and the "flood" that the dross, which had clung to me for years, was burned and washed away. As Isaiah 43:2 (NLT) says, *"When you go through deep waters, I will be with you. When you go through rivers of difficulty, you will not drown. When you walk through the fire of oppression, you will not be burned up; the flames will not consume you."*

---

17. Matt. 10:16-20
18. Ps. 32:9 (NLT)
19. Rom. 6:12-14 (MSG); James 1:13-15 (MSG)

At this juncture, it was clear that I had to get a grip and avoid "triggers." The skirmish in the car was a sobering revelation of how much things had deteriorated between Ségun and me, prompting us to give each other a wide berth for a while. I became more intentional about limiting my interactions with him and ending my impulsive phone calls that alternated between pleading with him to come back and lashing out whenever I felt he was being unreasonable.

Each time I reacted in anger, I struggled to believe I was still a Christian, let alone capable of truly expressing the life of Christ. His intelligent, extravagant, yet discerning love and affection[20] were already within me. However, I couldn't fully and continuously express them because I was still living by the lies that I had internalized, reacting in the flesh to every "punch" thrown at me. There were moments when, instead of turning the proverbial "other cheek," I wanted Ségun's cheek, coat, and more![21] Bearing the name "Christian" is more than a label—it is a call to a lifestyle of love, sacrifice, and consistently demonstrating the fruit of the Holy Spirit to everyone, not just those we find easy to love.

When problems escalate, it's essential to examine your methods—and then examine yourself. Focusing on other people or circumstances often blinds us to how we respond and the strategies we employ. These factors determine whether we navigate challenges wisely or make matters worse. If someone finds themselves repeatedly facing the same struggles—carrying unresolved issues into new relationships, marriages, or jobs—it's time for self-reflection. The one constant in all these situations is you![22]

> *"So then, my dear ones, just as you have always obeyed [my instructions with enthusiasm], not only in my presence, but now much more in my absence, continue to work out your salvation [that is, cultivate it, bring it to full effect, actively pursue spiritual maturity] with awe-inspired fear and trembling [using serious caution and critical self-evaluation to avoid anything that might offend God or discredit the name of Christ]. For it is [not your strength, but it is] God who is effectively at work in you, both to will and to work [that is, strengthening, energizing, and creating in you the longing and the ability to fulfill your purpose] for His good pleasure."* (Phil. 2:12-13 AMP)

God is pure light—there is no trace of darkness in Him. If we claim to share life with Him yet continue to stumble in the dark, we are deceiving ourselves and not living out the truth. But if we walk in the light, with God Himself as our light, we will align our daily lives with His precepts. I had a choice: I could either stay disappointed in myself and give up on the progress

---

20. Phil. 1:8 (MSG)

21. Matt. 5:38-42; John 3:30; 1 Pet. 2:19-23

22. Prov. 4:23; Lam. 3:40; Matt. 7:3-5; 2 Cor. 13:5; Gal. 6:4-5; James 1:22-25

I was making—no matter how much it felt like one step forward and ten steps backward—or I could turn this setback into an opportunity to confront and uproot unbridled emotions from my life before they consumed me.

There was some truth in Ségun's accusations—I admit that I still struggled with strong emotions. But it wasn't just "anger." At times, it escalated into rage when I felt exasperated, betrayed, or burdened by deep emotional wounds. *"Human anger does not produce the righteousness God desires."* (James 1:20 NLT) Yet, despite his own imperfections, he wasn't in a place where he could walk through it with me. It became my burden, my cross to bear—not his. The differences in our inclinations and approaches to life, which we once navigated with understanding, suddenly felt insurmountable to him. The "oneness" of marriage[23] seemed to apply only to the pleasant and easy moments. Looking back, it felt like an unspoken exit clause had been added to his vows: ...*for better, but not for worse*....

Even if I had wanted to speak with a professional to help me navigate my emotional challenges, I simply couldn't afford one. On top of that, I feared that if Ségun found out, he might use it as ammunition to support his claim that I was an "unfit mother" in his custody battle for our children. Weighing all these factors, I refused to validate his claims by accepting the derogatory labels he used—labels that often discourage people from seeking the help they truly need. My temper had been hard to control, but more than ever, I was determined to confront and overcome this struggle.

I finally turned to the only Divine Therapist and Counselor—the Holy Spirit.[24] His service is free and available 24/7. He works on a deeper, spiritual level to help us process our struggles, aligning our hearts and minds with God's truth for ultimate healing and transformation. He had already provided the comfort, guidance, and healing I needed, and I was extremely confident that He would complete His work if I remained faithful to the process and kept showing up.

I had to be open, honest, and willing to surrender to experience the change I desperately wanted and needed. Who knows me better than God?[25] His plans and thoughts toward us are good, designed for a prosperous future, and His purpose will stand.[26] Our mind is where renewal occurs as we allow the Holy Spirit to transform our thoughts, attitudes, and behaviors to align more with God's will. This process teaches us to live from a place of love, peace, wisdom, and sound judgment—guided by the Holy Spirit and The Word of God.[27] The Holy Spirit led me on the path to freedom from rage—a deep, overwhelming anger. In and through Him, I discovered not only the following aspects of His character but so much more:

---

23. Gen. 2:24; Mark 10:8
24. Ps. 34:18 (TPT); 41:3-4 (TPT); 103:3; 107:19-21; 116:4-14 (TPT); Isa. 53:5; Jer. 33:3; John 14:26-28; Rom. 12:2; Gal. 5:16; Phil. 4:7
25. Ps. 139:13; Isa. 46:10
26. Eccles. 3:11; Isa. 46:10 (TPT and NLT); Jer. 29:11
27. Isa. 26:3; Rom. 12:2; 1 Cor. 2:10-12; Phil. 4:7; James 1:22-24 (AMP)

- **Counselor and Comforter:** Jesus introduced the Holy Spirit to us as our Counselor—Helper, Advocate, Comforter[28]—who teaches, reminds, and guides believers into all truth.[29] More than a therapist, He provides wisdom and reassurance in times of distress. He fulfills these roles when we choose to step away from our default tendency to search for answers elsewhere—seeking and relying on people who, as I learned, sometimes have a limited perspective or are unknowingly projecting their own unresolved struggles.[30] His stability and direction help us break free from the negative choices we often make to temporarily ease pain or fill emotional voids.

- **Heart Healer:** The Holy Spirit works within us to heal emotional wounds, offering a peace that surpasses understanding[31] and restores broken hearts.[32]

- **Spirit of Conviction and Renewal:** Just as therapy helps people confront unhealthy patterns, the Holy Spirit convicts us of sin,[33] leading us to repentance and transformation.[34]

- **Source of Strength and Empowerment:** He strengthens believers in our weaknesses,[35] interceding for us when we don't know what to pray. He helps us to live victorious lives through His power.

- **Bringer of Joy, Peace, and Clarity:** The Holy Spirit provides divine insight, peace, and discernment, helping believers make sound decisions.[36]

Please take mental health seriously. Seek and get the appropriate help you need from a licensed and experienced mental health professional. We are all wired differently; while one person may need a little encouragement to reconnect with core beliefs, another may require specialized treatment or a trained guide to walk them through specific techniques. In contrast, others may require a combination of therapies and interventions to effectively address emotional, psychological, or behavioral challenges.

When Ségun and I were going through our marital storm, there weren't as many resources on "anger management" as there are now. There is free access to online faith-based devotional guides that offer scriptural insight into managing our emotions and stress. Additionally, many

28. John 14:16-17, 26; 15:26

29. John 14:26; 16:13

30. Jer. 17:5

31. Phil. 4:7

32. Ps. 147:3

33. John 16:8

34. Rom. 12:2

35. Rom. 8:26

36. Isa. 26:3 (NLT); 30:21; 1 Cor. 2:10-12

safe online channels and platforms are available for emotional support and faith-based mental health advice. Nowadays, people are becoming more comfortable discussing such issues, so no one has to face difficulties alone.

FORMIDABLE FORCE OF FAITH

I resolved to take my eyes off all the chaos—the divorce process, Ségun, and everything else—and trust the One who knows every detail of our lives. Even when we are blinded by emotions, overwhelmed by the weight of unpleasant or unexpected circumstances, or burdened with new challenges or responsibilities, God remains constant and all-powerful in the midst of our storms—just waiting for us to call out to Him.[37] He wants us to persevere, be consistent, rely on His strength, and fully commit to our walk of faith with Him.[38]

Faith is not merely a belief but a powerful, unwavering force capable of overcoming obstacles, withstanding challenges, and bringing about transformation. Though we may face struggles, opposition, and challenges in our Christian walk, God equips us for victory[39] and assures us of triumph in Christ.[40] Our commitment to Him will be rewarded.[41] Life's struggles often test and strengthen our faith, and overcoming them requires a deep trust in God and His purposes for our lives.[42]

The enemy's strategy is to weaken our faith, causing it to wither by filling our minds with lies, especially in the face of negative circumstances. He works to keep these lies in the forefront of our thoughts, affecting how we view our challenges. But we must make the conscious choice to feed our minds with the truth of God's Word, knowing that this will keep our faith strong. When we actively believe and receive the promises of God, His Word brings change and fulfillment to our lives.[43]

Fighting the good fight of faith[44] means remaining steadfast in our commitment to Christ—holding firmly to our Christian faith, principles, and values. It involves resisting anything that seeks to weaken our faith and persistently pressing forward toward the eternal reward God has promised us. *Agōnizomai*, the Greek word for "fight," from which the English word "agonize" is derived, refers to a spiritual struggle, contest, or striving with effort—much like an athlete competing or a soldier engaged in warfare. Paul uses this metaphor to emphasize that

---

37. Ps. 50:5; 55:16; 116:1
38. Rev. 3:5-6
39. 2 Cor. 10:3-5
40. 1 Cor. 15:57
41. 2 Tim. 4:7-8
42. Rom. 5:3-5; 2 Cor. 12:9-10; Eph. 6:12; James 1:2-4; 1 Pet. 1:6-7
43. Rom. 10:17; Heb. 10:23
44. 1 Tim. 6:12

faith is not passive; it requires effort, endurance, discipline, focus, and resilience in the face of trials, tests, and temptations. It is a call to confront these challenges with courage, relying on God's strength. The Christian life is filled with opposition, and believers must actively contend for their faith.[45]

This fight is not against flesh and blood,[46] but against:

- Temptation and sin (Heb. 12:1-2)
- False teachings (1 Tim. 6:3-5)
- Doubt and spiritual complacency (James 1:6-8)
- Worldly influences that pull us away from God (Rom. 12:2)

HOW DO WE FIGHT THE GOOD FIGHT?

1. Stay rooted in God's Word.

- The Bible is our weapon against deception and doubt.
- The Word of God is our sword in spiritual battles. (Eph. 6:17)
- *"Your word is a lamp to my feet and a light to my path."* (Ps. 119:105)

2. Maintain a consistent prayer life.

- Prayer strengthens our connection with God and empowers us.
- Prayer is a powerful weapon to sustain us. (1 Thess. 5:17)
- *"The prayer of a righteous person is powerful and effective."* (James 5:16)

3. Stand firm against spiritual opposition.

- Recognize that we battle not against flesh and blood but spiritual forces.
- *"Put on the full armor of God so that you can take your stand against the devil's schemes…"* (Eph. 6:11-12)

4. Walk by faith, not by sight.

- Trusting God beyond what we see helps us persevere.
- *"For we live by faith, not by sight."* (2 Cor. 5:7)

---

45. Jude 1:3
46. Eph. 6:12

5. *Keep your eyes on Christ.*

- Focusing on Jesus helps us endure trials.

- *"… Let us run with perseverance the race marked out for us, fixing our eyes on Jesus…"* (Heb. 12:1-2)

6. *Guard your heart and mind.*

- What we think and believe affects how we fight.

- *"Above all else, guard your heart, for everything you do flows from it."* (Prov. 4:23)

- *"Do not conform to the pattern of this world, but be transformed by the renewing of your mind."* (Rom. 12:2)

7. *Endure hardships with faith.*

- Challenges are part of the fight; endurance is key.

- *"Endure hardship as discipline; God is treating you as his children…"* (Heb. 12:7)

- *"Blessed is the one who perseveres under trial…"* (James 1:12)

8. *Stay in fellowship with other believers.*

- Community provides strength and encouragement.

- *"And let us consider how we may spur one another on toward love and good deeds…"* (Heb. 10:24-25)

9. *Walk in love and forgiveness.*

- Love is the foundation of our faith.

- *"Above all, love each other deeply…"* (1 Pet. 4:8)

- *"… Forgive as the Lord forgave you."* (Col. 3:13)

10. *Keep an eternal perspective.*

- Remember, our fight is not just for today but for eternity.

- *"I have fought the good fight, I have finished the race, I have kept the faith."* (2 Tim. 4:7)

⤲⚬⚭

THROUGH SÉGUN'S LENSES

Understandably, there was little room for constructive discussions between Funké and me during the initial stages of our separation, given how it happened. Our conversations revolved around our children in some shape or form as they were living with her. We worked out a routine whereby I could speak with them, usually on their way to school in the mornings and in the evenings. Over time, we made arrangements for me to spend time with them while doing our best to shield them from any simmering tensions between their parents.

My face-to-face interactions with Funké during this time were limited and, apart from issues concerning our children, largely superficial because of the wall I had erected in my mind and my heart. It was clear that I had placed her on one side of that barrier and our children on the other. All I could see were Funké's qualities that I told myself I could not live with while choosing to ignore her more numerous attributes that I could not live without.

While I could never have imagined on my wedding day that I would eventually contemplate divorce, I had to come to terms with the reality that was staring me in the face. I did not know what the future would bring, but I knew I had to begin preparing for it and that tough decisions would have to be made.

However, by allowing myself to be led by my feelings and working backward from the premise that separation was the only feasible solution, my decision-making process was severely flawed. I ended up shoehorning my decisions into my pre-determined outcome, leaving little or no room for objectivity.

Rearview Mirror Lesson

Rearview and side mirrors have a vital purpose in vehicles, aiding navigation and preventing accidents. If a vehicle is used as a metaphor for marriage—a means by which couples navigate their journey together—then through my actions and inactions, I effectively sabotaged it by removing every mirror, relying solely on my own instincts and becoming less cautious in the process. This was particularly evident during the months leading up to the filing of the divorce petition.

13

Turn the Searchlight on Me

"Examine and test and evaluate your own selves to see whether you are holding to your faith and showing the proper fruits of it. Test and prove yourselves [not Christ]. Do you not yourselves realize and know [thoroughly by an ever-increasing experience] that Jesus Christ is in you—unless you are [counterfeits] disapproved on trial and rejected?"

2 CORINTHIANS 13:5 AMPC

"THE UNEXAMINED LIFE IS NOT WORTH LIVING" —SOCRATES

"Test yourselves to make sure you are solid in the faith. Don't drift along taking everything for granted. Give yourselves regular checkups. You need firsthand evidence, not mere hearsay, that Jesus Christ is in you. Test it out. If you fail the test, do something about it." (2 Cor. 13:5-9 MSG)

"...continue to work out your salvation [that is, cultivate it, bring it to full effect, actively pursue spiritual maturity] with awe-inspired fear and trembling [using serious caution and critical self-evaluation to avoid anything that might offend God or discredit the name of Christ]. For it is [not your strength, but it is] God who is effectively at work in you, both to will and to work [that is, strengthening, energizing, and creating in you the longing and the ability to fulfill your purpose] for His good pleasure." (Phil. 2:12-13 AMP)

It is easy to get caught up in the busyness of life—becoming comfortable when things are going well or distracted when they're not. Many Christians, without realizing it, slip into autopilot mode, going through the motions of faith while gradually disconnecting from God. This often becomes a "comfort zone" where a Christian lifestyle is maintained externally—showing up at church, speaking fluent "Christianese," quoting scriptures, and doing all the right things—yet the heart remains distant from God. As Jesus warned, it is possible to honor God with our lips while our hearts are far from Him.[1] At this point, faith can shift from an intimate walk with God to a performance before others.

Neglecting regular self-examination is like failing to check a car's engine oil or fuel gauge—eventually, it runs on empty, breaking down at the most inconvenient time. Life's trials have a way of forcing us to stop, reflect, and realign or repent, but waiting for a crisis is neither wise nor necessary. Focusing solely on appearances and maintaining an image, rather than cultivating a genuine relationship with God, risks falling into cycles of sin, frustration, stagnation, and unnecessary delays. But Scripture calls us to examine ourselves and cast off everything that hinders us, especially sin that so easily entangles and weighs us down.[2]

Actual spiritual growth requires intentionality—consistently allowing God to search our hearts,[3] realigning with His truth, and refusing to settle for an empty shell of faith. A life of true intimacy with God isn't about routine or performance but about daily surrender, transformation, and walking closely with Him.[4]

The Bible repeatedly urges us to examine our hearts, align our lives with God's truth, and pursue genuine righteousness, not just outward appearances. Jesus sharply rebuked the religious leaders of His time for their sanctimonious moral superiority—clean on the outside but corrupt within.[5] He warned that a person's true nature is revealed not by their words or religious acts but by the fruit of their heart.[6] To avoid such blind spots, believers should heed God's instruction to live for Him with the help of the Holy Spirit, maintain an eternal perspective, and approach Scripture with fresh eyes—actively applying it in their lives.[7]

Regular, honest self-assessment is essential for spiritual growth and personal development. This means evaluating ourselves in light of God's Word rather than comparing ourselves to others.[8] There is always more to learn about ourselves, as life experiences shape and refine us. Self-awareness requires asking hard questions about our choices, motives, and responses. It

---

1. Isa. 29:13; Jer. 17:9-10; Matt. 15:8-9

2. Heb. 12:1-2

3. Ps. 139:23-24

4. John 15:4-5; Rom. 12:1-2

5. Matt. 23:25-28; 2 Cor. 7:1; Heb. 10:22

6. Matt. 12:33; Luke 6:45

7. James 1:22-25

8. 2 Cor. 10:12

shifts the focus from blaming others—especially those who have wronged us—to personal responsibility and accountability before God.[9]

Investing time in understanding our inner world—our emotions, triggers, thought patterns, dreams, values, and beliefs—helps us grow in wisdom and maturity. The more we allow God's truth to penetrate our hearts,[10] the more we recognize areas that need transformation. True spiritual growth happens when we surrender to God's refining work, allowing Him to shape us into His likeness.[11]

Understanding ourselves better leads to a deeper insight into others. Recognizing our flaws and limitations fosters humility and patience, essential virtues for healthy relationships. Jesus reminds us in Matthew 7:3-5 to first examine the plank in our own eye before addressing the speck in another's. This self-awareness allows us to extend grace to our spouses, embracing their imperfections and differences with love rather than criticism. It encourages a thoughtful approach to our actions, emotions, and decisions—helping us assess our motivations and understand how our behavior affects us and those around us.

Self-reflection and self-awareness are cornerstones of strong, healthy, resilient relationships. They empower individuals to navigate the complexities of intimacy with wisdom and compassion.[12] Introspection promotes deeper connections, allowing couples to approach disagreements with empathy rather than hostility.

Self-assessment involves evaluating oneself against established standards, values, principles, or goals to identify strengths, progress, and areas for growth and improvement. In 2 Corinthians 13:5, the Bible admonishes us to examine ourselves to see whether we are walking in faith and to test ourselves.

Self-reflection is a deeper, more intentional process that requires looking inward to assess thoughts, emotions, and experiences. It helps us recognize patterns, learn from past actions, and make necessary adjustments to align our lives with God's will. As Lamentations 3:40 urges, *"Let us examine our ways and test them, and let us return to the Lord."* Reflection fosters repentance, wisdom, and a renewed commitment to God's path.

Self-awareness is the ability to see ourselves clearly and objectively through introspection and observation. It is a continuous process of understanding our strengths, weaknesses, beliefs, emotions, and motivations. Proverbs 20:5 highlights this: *"The purposes of a person's heart are deep waters, but one who has insight draws them out."* The more we cultivate self-awareness, the better we can make informed decisions, grow in wisdom, and navigate life's challenges with grace. Furthermore, self-awareness enhances emotional intelligence, leading to greater self-regulation

---

9. Rom. 14:12

10. Heb. 4:12; James 4:8

11. 2 Cor. 3:18; Phil. 1:6

12. Prov. 4:7

and social awareness. By understanding our own emotions, we become more attuned to others' emotions, developing empathy and improving communication.

Recognizing and acknowledging negative emotions is the first step toward managing them effectively, allowing us to face life's ups and downs with greater confidence and clarity. Awareness alone, however, is not enough—it requires action. I admitted that I had anger issues, but I needed to move beyond mere acknowledgment to actively confront and overcome them.

Anger itself is not inherently sinful or negative. It's a natural human emotion that can serve a righteous purpose when controlled and channeled correctly. Even God expresses anger, yet His anger is always just and directed at sin and injustice. His patience and slowness to anger remind us that anger can and should be controlled and used for good rather than destruction.[13] Jesus' anger in the temple was not rooted in sin but in a zeal for God's house, demonstrating that righteous anger can be a force for correction and justice when aligned with God's will.[14]

The key is how we handle and respond to anger. Left unchecked, it can lead to sin,[15] division, rash decisions, and broken relationships. However, when surrendered to God, it can refine our character and fuel positive change. Learning to manage anger in a godly way is part of spiritual maturity and self-discipline.[16]

When we yield our emotions to God, we learn to respond to challenges in ways that honor Him rather than react out of unchecked feelings. When anger becomes unrestrained, it can escalate into rage—an intense, often destructive expression of it. Unlike righteous anger, which is measured and purposeful, rage is typically impulsive, aggressive, and fueled by personal grievances, pride, or a lack of self-restraint. It often leads to words, actions, and decisions that one comes to regret as they do not reflect God's will.[17]

Scripture warns against rage, often described as "outbursts of wrath," as part of the sinful nature that opposes the Spirit of God.[18] However, through the Holy Spirit, we can overcome negative emotions by practicing self-control,[19] letting go of grudges and bitterness,[20] and surrendering to God's wisdom. Jesus Himself demonstrated restraint in the face of provocation, responding with patience and grace.[21]

Even well into our separation, I was deeply frustrated and angry with Ségun for a long time. I wanted us to work on our marriage together under the same roof, but he made it abundantly

---

13. Ps. 5:8; Nah. 1:3
14. Mark 3:5; John 2:14-16
15. Prov. 29:11; Eph. 4:26-27
16. Prov. 16:32
17. Ps. 37:8; James 1:20
18. Gal. 5:19-23
19. Prov. 29:11
20. Eph. 4:31
21. 1 Pet. 2:20-23

clear to me—and to anyone who broached the subject—that he had no intention of doing so. I struggled to understand why he couldn't see the obvious: All relationships, without exception, go through trials, but with commitment, intentional effort, and intervention, they can emerge stronger.

I believed I hadn't done anything to deserve how he treated me, and the lack of effort on his part felt like confirmation that he had no genuine desire for reconciliation. I became convinced that separation had only ever been a stepping stone for him to file for divorce eventually, and I voiced this fear to him often. The more time, space, and distance stretched between us, the more it seemed to reinforce our divide rather than bridge it. Instead of serving as a path to healing, separation felt like a slow unraveling of everything, leaving us to pick up the pieces as we deemed fit.

With the last bit of dignity I had left, I retreated into self-preservation mode, which seemed like a good way to protect myself at the time. However, I didn't realize I was slipping back into an inflated sense of self—pride and ego. While pride and ego are not essentially bad, they become negative when they lead to self-centeredness, arrogance, entitlement, or resistance to correction. Cultivating humility and a Christ-centered identity helps keep them in check. When left unchecked, they stifle growth and development, make us unteachable, blind us to our flaws, and set us up for a fall.[22] Proverbs 16:18 reminds us, *"Pride goes before destruction, a haughty spirit before a fall,"* and Isaiah 2:11 also speaks of pride's danger. When we rise above pride and ego and aren't overly sensitive to others' opinions, we demonstrate humility—a true mark of personal transformation. "The fuller a vessel becomes, the deeper it sinks in the water."—Charles Spurgeon

The challenges I faced in the "fire," the "flood," and my "desert" experiences were humbling. They exposed truths about me that I had long overlooked or misunderstood. These trials didn't just reveal who I was, but more importantly, who God is. I realized that God is patient with us and doesn't humiliate us in a bid to force us to learn, as people might. His purpose is never to shame or degrade but to refine us, helping us grow in wisdom, character, and grace.[23] God draws us closer to Him through His discipline, shaping our hearts in love, as Ecclesiastes 7:25 states. His humbling work isn't to push us away but to transform us into the people He created us to be, conformed to the image of Christ.[24]

I once heard an analogy comparing life's challenges to hot water—it reveals the strength or weakness of a tea bag and the true essence of the tea within. Similarly, trials expose our character, authenticity, faith, and resilience.[25] When I surrendered control and allowed God

---

22. Prov. 11:2; James 4:6
23. Ps. 51:17; Heb. 12:6; James 4:6-7
24. Rom. 8:29
25. James 1:2-4 (MSG)

to intervene, guiding me through this new chapter of my life, a process of self-(re)discovery began. My perspective started to shift as I conducted an honest, non-defensive examination of my decisions and conduct—not only in my marriage but throughout my adult years. I began focusing more on my own growth, taking responsibility for and being accountable for my choices.

One of the first things I did was objectively revisit Ségun's divorce petition, a stark contrast to my initial reaction of dismissing it outright. Although I disagreed with 99.5 percent of his statements, particularly his justification for our separation based on irreconcilable differences, I gained a deeper understanding of his perspective. This gave me insight into how we arrived at this point and, perhaps, some of the fears that had influenced many of his decisions since our separation. By opening myself to honest reflection, I approached the situation with greater clarity and empathy, aligning myself with God's guidance in navigating the challenges ahead.

While I couldn't reconcile all the different sides of Ségun that had surfaced throughout our relationship—from the time we met until our separation—this time, I genuinely listened to his perspective. I heard his views about the pre- and post-marriage versions of me, the issues arising from our differences, and the conflicts we allowed. I began to see that some of his actions against me were likely shaped by what he anticipated from my past responses. However, since separation and divorce were new territory for both of us, he didn't know how I would react in those circumstances. I believe he was protecting himself in many ways, responding with a "strike before you're struck" approach.

I took a bold, honest step by confronting areas of my life that were at variance with my desires and expectations, especially my identity as a Christian. There were parts of my life where I wasn't fully living out my faith, where I wasn't producing the fruits of righteousness or walking in alignment with God's will. In many instances, I blamed others or external circumstances for my shortcomings instead of reflecting on my faith and spiritual condition. I realized that it was essential to ensure my relationship with Christ was genuine, not just in words but in a transformed life. This was my moment to stop deflecting and to honestly evaluate the state of my heart.

The roller coaster of emotions I experienced throughout this journey highlighted different dominant character traits in me at various stages. Seeing myself through God's lens helped me to adjust or eliminate the negative thought patterns that had triggered emotions I hadn't properly managed. Trusting God meant inviting Him into the closed areas of my heart where I had been nursing and justifying past hurts, exposing them to His Light (His Word). This became one of the biggest hurdles to overcome, as I couldn't do it in my own strength. Peeling back layers of self-protection and defense was hard.

I had to move past reactionary living, driven by circumstances, and shift toward living in a personal relationship with Jesus Christ. This positive move enabled me to experience and embrace triumphant living, reflecting the abundant life He promises us.[26]

SPIRITUAL CHECK-UP— UNCOVERING OUR TRUE CONDITION

"Let us therefore be diligent to enter that rest, lest anyone fall according to the same example of disobedience. For the word of God is living and powerful, and sharper than any two-edged sword, piercing even to the division of soul and spirit, and of joints and marrow, and is a discerner of the thoughts and intents of the heart. And there is no creature hidden from His sight, but all things are naked and open to the eyes of Him to whom we must give account." (Heb. 4:11-13)

Submitting myself to a "spiritual check-up" under God's "Searchlight" (His Word and Holy Spirit) forced me to look deeper—beyond the superficial and over-inflated opinions I had about my intellect, looks, pedigree, career, and what I believed was a thriving relationship with God. Scripture reminds us that no one truly knows the thoughts and motives of a person except the spirit within them.[27] Our self-perception is often skewed, driven by self-reliance, self-focus, pride, and self-righteousness. Rather than seeking and fully embracing God's wisdom, we can become trapped in a bubble, only listening to our own thoughts and beliefs about who we are, believing that the reality we create for ourselves is the only truth.[28]

This self-centered perspective causes people to believe their own press—becoming overly confident or self-important based on praise, reputation, or personal perception. Rather than considering objective views, they buy into their own hype, assuming they are better, more capable, or more righteous than they are. Shedding self-promotion and turning to God for guidance allows us to see ourselves through His eyes, uncover our true identity in Him, and live more freely and purposefully.

Jesus is the ultimate Soul Searcher; He knows the true condition of every heart. He examines the mind[29] and sees beyond outward appearances, searching the depths of the soul—not to gain knowledge or find answers, but to reveal Himself (the Way, the Truth, and the Life),[30] convict, heal, restore, and lead us into righteousness.[31] He is the Light that dispels darkness

---

26. Ps. 119:105; John 10:10

27. 1 Sam. 16:7; 1 Cor. 2:10; Heb. 4:12 (TPT)

28. 1 Cor. 10:11-12 (MSG)

29. Jer. 17:10 (NIV); John 2:25

30. John 14:6

31. Ps. 23:3

and guides our steps.[32] When we seek Him with humility and sincerity—studying and applying His Word—He grants wisdom, clarity in decision-making, and spiritual growth.[33] The Bible describes God's Word as sharp as a surgeon's scalpel, penetrating beyond surface defenses and self-deception, exposing everything within us.[34] No one is impervious to God's truth, and nothing is hidden from His sight.

For physical surgery to be effective, the patient must be at rest or in a state of stillness or quietness. Similarly, God's rest refers to spiritual peace (complete trust in Christ)—eliminating distractions and hindrances that may interfere with His "surgery." Just as good lighting is essential in an operating room, exposure to God's Light (His Word) reveals whether our faith is genuine or we're merely going through the motions. It exposes the true condition of our hearts, especially when we surrender daily to His leading and walk in His obedience. God's Word penetrates the deepest parts of our being, revealing areas in need of His transformation. When we resist His refining work, our actions will eventually expose what we truly value—whether we prioritize pleasing Him over our own desires or the approval of others. *"So you see, we are shown to be right with God by what we do, not by faith alone."* (James 2:24 NLT)

This two-edged sword—the Word of God—*"judges the thoughts and attitudes of the heart"* (Heb. 4:12), exposing our innermost desires, intentions, and everything that hinders our effectiveness in walking with God. Like a skilled surgeon's scalpel, it cuts away pride, jealousy, envy, strife, malice, selfishness, bitterness, unforgiveness, anger, hypocrisy, and stubbornness—fickle emotions often triggered by temporary circumstances. These attitudes and behaviors displease God and create barriers in our hearts and minds. Through His refining process, they are replaced as we cultivate *the fruit of the Spirit—love, joy, peace, patience, kindness, goodness, faithfulness, gentleness, and self-control* (Gal. 5:22-23). We are all a work in progress, living daily in God's transforming and perfecting grace.[35]

The light of God's Word uncovers hidden struggles—things we may not even realize are influencing our patterns of behavior, including addictions, toxic habits, destructive emotions, and external influences that pull us away from Him. Just as surgery isn't always pleasant but is sometimes necessary for healing, spiritual surgery requires going deep, cutting through hardened areas of our hearts, freeing us from sin and burdens—enabling us to fully surrender to God's correction. *"I will give you a new heart and put a new spirit in you; I will remove from you your heart of stone and give you a heart of flesh."* (Ezek. 36:26)

Sometimes, we opt for quick fixes—superficial solutions that mask our struggles rather than address them at the root. We may try to "nip and tuck" our flaws, enhancing the more

---

32. Ps. 119:105; Isa. 9:2; John 1:4-5, 9; 8:12; 9:5; Luke 2:30-32; Rev. 21:23
33. Ps. 119:130
34. Heb. 4:12-13 (MSG)
35. 2 Cor. 3:18; Phil. 1:6

appealing sides of our character while avoiding deep divine makeovers. But God calls us to lasting change, not temporary modifications. Only when we allow His Word to do its full work in us will we experience true freedom and renewal.[36]

As a child, I had a few cameras. One of my favorites was a Polaroid, which instantly produced a photo once the film was exposed to light. It was easy to use, but the photos didn't last long—they faded over time. With my other cameras, I had to be careful not to expose the film after taking all the photos. The used film had to be dropped off at a photo lab, where it was carefully processed in a darkroom. If the film was accidentally exposed to light too soon, all the "negatives" would be ruined. That's what hiding in the dark does—it allows "negatives" to develop and take shape. In contrast, God calls us to walk in His light, where deliverance,[37] healing,[38] and transformation[39] happen.

One author notes, "The world mistakenly thinks that intimacy occurs in the dark, but God says it happens in the light." This aligns with Scripture, which teaches that true fellowship and genuine connection are found in openness and truth. *"But if we walk in the light, as He is in the light, we have fellowship with one another, and the blood of Jesus, His Son, purifies us from all sin."* (1 John 1:7 NIV) When we allow God's light to expose the hidden areas of our lives, we experience His grace, redemption, and the depth of real relationships—with Him and others.

When we allow Jesus to shine His light on us, the darkness hiding our struggles dissipates. In His presence, we find forgiveness, and our wounded areas are healed. But stepping into the light requires courage—confronting fears, challenging limiting beliefs, and stepping out of comfort zones that may have served as cocoons or fortresses for decades. Yet, God's Word (Light) lovingly breaks through those barriers, offering redemption and the freedom to live in His truth and salvation.

Some people fear the dark, yet surprisingly, many are afraid of the light. The exposure of truth can be unsettling, and people often resist it, fearing what may be uncovered. This hesitation reveals a deeper struggle—an avoidance of stillness in God's presence, where self-examination occurs. Scripture warns of this tendency: *"Light has come into the world, but people loved darkness instead of light because their deeds were evil… Everyone who does evil hates the light, and will not come into the light for fear that their deeds will be exposed"* (John 3:19-20 NIV).

However, acknowledging and bringing our struggles before God is a major step toward repentance.[40] James 5:16 urges us to *"… confess your sins to each other and pray for each other so that you may be healed…"* Living in the light minimizes the tempter's power—when we walk

---

36. John 8:32

37. John 8:36; Rom. 6:22; 8:2; Col. 1:13; 2 Tim. 4:18

38. Ps. 107:20; Prov. 4:20-22; Mal. 4:2

39. Ps. 19:8; Isa. 55:11; 60:1

40. 1 John 1:8-10

in truth, the enemy loses his grip. *"… But whoever practices truth [and does what is right—morally, ethically, spiritually] comes to the Light, so that his works may be plainly shown to be what they are—accomplished in God [divinely prompted, done with God's help, in dependence on Him]."* (John 3:19-21 AMP)

The Bible encourages us to let the Holy Spirit guide our lives so we don't give in to sinful desires. *"The sinful nature wants to do evil, which is just the opposite of what the Spirit wants … These two forces are constantly fighting each other, so you are not free to carry out your good intentions."* (Gal. 5:17 NLT) Instead of striving in our own strength, we are called to depend on God fully: *"Your salvation requires you to turn back to me and stop your silly efforts to save yourselves. Your strength will come from settling down in complete dependence on me—the very thing you've been unwilling to do"* (Isa. 30:15 MSG).

THE DECEPTIVENESS OF SPOTLIGHTS

"For if anyone thinks he is something [special] when [in fact] he is nothing [special except in his own eyes], he deceives himself. But each one must carefully scrutinize his own work [examining his actions, attitudes, and behavior], and then he can have the personal satisfaction and inner joy of doing something commendable without comparing himself to another. For every person will have to bear [with patience] his own burden [of faults and shortcomings for which he alone is responsible]." (Gal. 6:3-5 AMP)

God calls us to arise and shine, for His glory has risen upon us.[41] As the light of the world, we are meant to reflect God's truth and love, guiding others toward Jesus rather than drawing attention to ourselves.[42] Like a city set on a hill, our lives should be visible testimonies of God's grace, not for self-promotion but to point others to Him. Jesus reminds us not to hide our light under a bushel but, at the same time, not to let worldly recognition become our motivation. Instead, we are called to live in a way that radiates His presence, allowing His light—not our own—to draw people in … even an unbelieving or backslidden spouse.[43]

In today's social media-driven world, many believers are embracing a different kind of light—the spotlight. The allure of "Camera! Lights! Action!" tempts people to focus on themselves, crafting images, narratives, and carefully curated personas that may not reflect God's truth. It's easy to start believing our own hype, but self-promotion and worldly validation can blind us to the deeper reality of who we are before God.

---

41. Isa. 60:1
42. Matt. 5:14-16
43. 1 Pet. 3:1-5

Satan himself is described as an "angel of light" (2 Cor. 11:14), meaning he often disguises deception as something good, wise, or even divine. He doesn't always come in obvious darkness but operates subtly, distorting the truth and leading people astray through false teachings, counterfeit spirituality, and misleading ideologies. Jesus warned that even the elect could be deceived,[44] and Revelation 12:9 describes how the enemy *"deceives the whole world."* This is why believers must stay anchored in God's Word and the Holy Spirit to discern truth from deception.[45] True light doesn't seek self-glory but reflects God's glory. The more we immerse ourselves in His truth, the less we'll be swayed by the world's illusions.

The world often equates visibility with value, applause with approval, and influence with integrity. But Scripture reminds us that the pursuit of recognition can be misleading. It's easy to be influenced by popularity, trends, and the desire for followers, but God's will is revealed through prayer and obedience, not by chasing after the crowd's approval. The spotlight can sometimes blur our true identity, inflate our ego, and lead us to compromise, making public perception seem more important than God's purpose for our lives.

Jesus, when tempted by the spotlight, chose a different path. When satan offered Him all the kingdoms of the world and their glory,[46] He rejected the allure of fame. Instead, He taught us that true greatness isn't found in being seen but in humility, servanthood, and obedience to the Father.[47] The Bible gives examples of those who fell into the trap of seeking external validation—such as Saul, who craved the approval of men over obedience to God,[48] and the Pharisees, who sought honor from people rather than from God.[49] In contrast, those who walked in true purpose—like John the Baptist—declared, *"He must increase, but I must decrease"* (John 3:30), showing that the goal is not self-promotion but Christ-exaltation.

The Pharisees were called "blind guides" (Matt. 23:16, 24), not only because they failed to recognize Jesus' true identity but also because they were blind to their own spiritual condition (John 9:39-41). As long as we fail to acknowledge our sinfulness, we cannot receive the cure—God's love and redemption—for only those who recognize their need for salvation will accept it. *"Don't be so naïve and self-confident. You're not exempt. You could fall flat on your face as easily as anyone else. Forget about self-confidence; it's useless. Cultivate God-confidence."* (1 Cor. 10:12 MSG)

The deception of the spotlight is that it can blind us to what truly matters. It can make performance more important than authenticity, accolades more desirable than alignment with God, and status more significant than sanctification. However, God calls us to walk in His light,

---

44. Mark 13:22
45. Heb. 5:14; 1 John 4:1
46. Matt. 4:8-10
47. Mark 10:43-45
48. 1 Sam. 15:24
49. John 12:43

not the world's fleeting spotlight.[50] When we seek Him and His approval first,[51] our purpose, identity, and influence will be shaped by His truth rather than public opinion or influence—leading to eternal impact rather than temporary human recognition.

The glamor, attention, or success associated with being in the limelight can be misleading, particularly in today's era of social media and influencers. It's easy for people to derive their sense of security or identity from visibility, status, and applause, unaware of the pressures, temptations, and dangers that come with public attention. Worldly success often distracts from God's truth, leading to misplaced priorities and a superficial sense of worth.

Many people seek validation through careers, businesses, degrees, social acceptance, accolades, and approval, yet these pursuits often leave them unfulfilled. True worth and genuine fellowship with others extend beyond earthly achievements—they are found in Christ as we live out His purpose and reflect His truth in every facet of life. *"Instead, we will speak the truth in love, growing in every way more and more like Christ, who is the head of his body, the church. He makes the whole body fit together perfectly. As each part does its own special work, it helps the other parts grow, so that the whole body is healthy and growing and full of love."* (Eph. 4:15-16 NLT)

"Processing" (spiritual growth and transformation) takes time, often unfolding in seasons of obscurity—where our weaknesses are refined—or in a state of quietness with God. It is here that we hear His voice more clearly as He prepares us for His purpose. When we eventually step into visibility, the image revealed should be that of Jesus, who shines brighter each day as we are renewed from one degree of glory to another.[52] As we surrender to the Holy Spirit, our lives become increasingly radiant and more aligned with His will.

If visibility comes prematurely—before Christ fully forms in us—the exposure can distort or hinder our witness. God continually calls us into His marvelous light[53]—not as a one-time invitation, but as an ongoing journey of walking in Him, allowing His perfecting grace to shape us. No one reaches a point of complete perfection, but with each passing day, the resemblance to Christ becomes clearer. Through this process, those who encounter us should unmistakably see that we belong to Him. We must be filled with Jesus to reflect Him accurately. While humans often settle for what looks good, God probes for what is good (Prov. 16:2 MSG).

Several people in the Bible underwent a season of being "processed in obscurity" (being set apart) before stepping into their God-ordained purpose. Each of these individuals grew in character, faith, and dependence on God during their hidden seasons before being revealed for their divine assignment. Here are a few examples:

---

50. Eph. 5:8
51. Matt. 6:33
52. 2 Cor. 3:18
53. 1 Pet. 2:9

1. **Moses (Exodus 2-3):** After killing an Egyptian, Moses fled to the wilderness of Midian, where he spent 40 years as a shepherd. During this time, God prepared him for his mission to lead Israel out of Egypt.

2. **Joseph (Genesis 37-41):** Before becoming Egypt's second-in-command, Joseph endured betrayal, slavery, and imprisonment. His years in obscurity refined his character and prepared him for leadership.

3. **David (1 Samuel 16-31):** Anointed as king while still a young shepherd, David spent years hiding from Saul before finally ascending to the throne. His time in the wilderness shaped him into a humble and God-dependent leader.

4. **Elijah (1 Kings 17-19):** After boldly declaring a drought, Elijah was sent to hide by the Brook Cherith, where God provided for him. This season of isolation strengthened his faith before his powerful ministry on Mount Carmel.

5. **John the Baptist (Luke 1:80):** *"And the child grew and became strong in spirit; and he was in the wilderness until the day of his public appearance to Israel."* His time in solitude prepared him for his role as the forerunner of Christ.

6. **Jesus (Luke 2:52; Matthew 4:1-11):** Though fully God, Jesus spent 30 years in obscurity before beginning His public ministry. Even after His baptism, He spent 40 days in the wilderness, resisting temptation and preparing for His calling.

7. **Paul (Galatians 1:15-18):** Paul didn't immediately start preaching after his dramatic conversion. Instead, he went to Arabia for three years, where he received revelation from God before stepping into his apostolic ministry.

WHO DO YOU SAY THAT I AM?

In the past, I didn't get very far on this "processing" journey because I got discouraged and stopped whenever I didn't see the desired change in me or couldn't sustain it. Jesus had been my Savior since age eleven, but I hadn't always allowed Him to be Lord over my life. I sometimes compartmentalized Him or took the reins from Him, choosing to follow my own will when it seemed more convenient or His way felt too challenging. As I made progress in curbing my angry outbursts—even before our separation—there were times I became a bit smug about the steps I was taking toward becoming a "better me." Instead of focusing on God's Light and my transformation, I'd shift my attention to Ségun's wrongdoings and shortcomings. As he pointed out, I often expressed my "superior wisdom" at the slightest opportunity. My impatience would get the best of me, and I was eager to showcase the "new and improved me." On many occasions, I rushed out of the Potter's hands and away from the Refiner's fire half-baked!

I thought I had aced all the tests, learned everything I needed to, and was ready for reconciliation and the restoration of our marriage.[54] But I was proven wrong by the many humbling situations I faced. Through these hard lessons, I learned to be more patient with the process and realized that the timing and outcome were best left in God's hands.[55] Having fewer interactions with Ségun during this season allowed me to stay focused and remain in God's refinement process.[56]

One of the most significant shifts we must experience—especially in marriage or any relationship—is a change in perspective. The way we see ourselves, our significant others, and our shared experiences shapes how we respond to challenges and growth. True transformation occurs when we are open to fresh insights and instructions, particularly through God's Word, and prayerfully and honestly evaluate ourselves and others. Feedback, critiques, and even difficult conversations often reveal our character and behavior. This process begins with the renewal of our minds, as Scripture teaches: *"Fix your attention on God. You'll be changed from the inside out"* (Rom. 12:2 MSG). I desperately needed a complete mind overhaul at that point in my life, so I paid close attention!

I had been at the mercy of my emotions for too long, reacting rather than responding with wisdom. But the more I surrendered to the Holy Spirit, the clearer I saw the areas where God was calling me to grow. He gently revealed His expectations for me, shifting my focus from demanding change in others to allowing Him to transform me. I also became more open to honest assessments—carefully weighing feedback against who I believed I was and who God was shaping me to be. Even work appraisals became part of this refining process, offering me a comprehensive perspective on my interactions and relationships. Through it all, I learned that true growth requires self-awareness and a willingness to let God do deep, lasting work in my heart.

It's natural to become defensive or sensitive when confronted with our weaknesses or faults. In those moments, we might shut people down, distance ourselves, or suppress our conscience, rationalizing our actions to justify or explain them away. However, truly listening to feedback—especially from people with different backgrounds and experiences—can challenge our mindset and expose us to new ways of thinking. This approach helps us stay open to diverse perspectives while remembering that our viewpoint is only one among many—not the ultimate truth. Only God's Word holds that authority.

When we look through distorted lenses, seeing everything and everyone in one-dimensional ways, we miss opportunities to grow from constructive criticism. As followers of Christ,

---

54. Job 23:10; Isa. 64:8; Mal. 3:3; Mark 9:49-50; Phil. 1:6; 1 Pet. 5:5b
55. Eccles. 3:1-15
56. 1 Pet. 5:6-11 (AMP)

our desire should be to seek His guidance in every situation, asking ourselves how He would respond. Let us not be quick to dismiss what others say about us—especially those who work or live closely with us. Sometimes, even the words that hurt or seem offensive can reveal something about our character, providing the opportunity for God's truth to take root and transform us.

Feedback, even from those we sometimes label as "haters," "enemies of progress," "trolls," "discouragers," or "critics," is just as valuable as the more positive feedback or favorable comments we receive. These individuals are often allowed into our lives for a reason or purpose. God uses different situations and people—spouses, exes, children, siblings, in-laws, friends, acquaintances, neighbors, employees, bosses, and colleagues—as tools for refinement, much like sandpaper or buffers, to help smooth away our rough edges. Instead of brooding over negative comments or criticisms and dismissing them, filtering them through God's Word and seeking His perspective is best. His wisdom will help us discern what is helpful for our growth and what we need to discard.

During my time in a male-dominated workplace, I earned the nickname "Iron Lady" in the early years. That period coincided with the time when my husband and I were separated, and I found myself transferring some of my anger and frustration onto my team. Managing male egos, cultural biases, and leading in a patriarchal society demanded a lot of Emotional Intelligence (EI)—which wasn't my strength at the time! However, listening to my team's feedback gave me valuable insights. Their perspectives helped me become more introspective, refining my management style and creating a more supportive work environment. This shift in perspective benefited my team and contributed to personal and professional growth, leading to overall success at work.

Some people seek to confine others to the shadow of their past—defined by their sins, missteps, or mistakes—while others genuinely desire to see growth and transformation into Christlikeness.[57] Instead of allowing others' opinions to become permanent labels that limit us, we should use them as stepping stones—bridges that help us transition from our self-perception (whether real or distorted) to God's ideal. Our goal should not be to meet human expectations but to please God, aligning our lives with His Word and yielding to the guidance of the Holy Spirit—*"His divine power has given us everything we need for a godly life…"* (2 Pet. 1:3). As we walk in obedience, God shapes us into who He says we are,[58] enabling us to fulfill the destiny He has planned for us by His grace.

To grow effectively, we must surround ourselves with people who speak the truth in love.[59] Those who have walked with us through highs and lows are often best positioned to offer meaningful and fair feedback. While their words may not always be pleasant, listening with a discerning heart is important. Even Jesus asked His disciples, *"Who do people say the Son of*

---

57. Gal. 4:19
58. Eph. 2:10
59. Eph. 4:15

Man is?" (Matt. 16:13-17). He was intentional about discovering what His disciples and others thought about Him—not for His own validation but to clarify their understanding, affirm what was true, and correct any misconceptions.

Jesus first asked about people's general perception of Him, knowing that public opinion varied widely. Some saw Him as John the Baptist, others as Elijah, Jeremiah, or another prophet. However, Peter, speaking on behalf of the disciples who had walked closely with Jesus, declared, *"You are the Messiah, the Son of the living God."* Peter's revelation of Christ's true identity did not come from human reasoning but from God. Similarly, God can open people's eyes to see us as He does, correcting false impressions and refining our character through wise counsel. Instead of dismissing unflattering feedback outright, we should prayerfully weigh it against God's perspective (His Word), allowing His truth to shape our growth.

God's Word reveals His nature and His will for our lives. The more we study Scripture, the clearer our understanding becomes—not only of Him but also of ourselves and the transformation He desires in us.[60] Like a mirror, the Word exposes our true state and calls us to change.[61] As Christians, we are not meant to live by the world's philosophy of "to thine own self be true," which prioritizes personal truth over divine truth. Instead, we are called to stay true to Jesus Christ, aligning our identity and purpose with His will.

We must constantly find a healthy balance between our self-perception, the opinions of others, and, most importantly, God's truth about us. Above all, the opinion that holds the greatest weight is God's, and our primary aim should be to please Him rather than ourselves or anyone else.[62] A true reflection of who we are is seen in the fruit we produce.[63] The fruit of the Spirit— *love, joy, peace, patience, kindness, goodness, faithfulness, gentleness, and self-control* (Gal. 5:22-23)—becomes especially evident when we are under pressure or facing difficult situations. How we treat others, particularly those who cannot offer us anything in return, is a good indication of our character. Similarly, our responses in crisis expose the depth of our spiritual growth. In relationships, people sometimes alter their behavior to fit into a mold created by their spouse or the expectations of others. But any change made solely to please another person—without God's transformation—will not be sustainable.[64] Rather than reshaping ourselves to meet human expectations, living to honor and please God is much more fulfilling and rewarding.[65]

Many live in altered realities of their self-image and how others perceive them. Some have worn so many masks and lived superficially for so long that they have lost sight of their true

---

60. 2 Tim. 2:15
61. James 1:23-25
62. Prov. 3:6; Gal. 1:10
63. Matt. 7:16
64. Zech. 4:6
65. Prov. 16:7; Jer. 17:5-8

identity. We live in a time of moral relativism, where absolute standards of truth[66] and morality are increasingly rejected. A growing number of people now believe they can define right and wrong for themselves, shaping their own concepts of love, marriage, family, sin, and righteousness. As accountability to God and even societal structures diminish, more people are creating their own rules and adapting to trends, circumstances, experiences, and relationships.

We frequently hear phrases like "Orange is the new black" or "Live your truth," which encourage people to embrace their own version of authenticity. But Scripture teaches that our original and truest identity is found in being created in God's image: *"So God created mankind in His own image, in the image of God He created them; male and female He created them"* (Gen. 1:27). Since the fall of man in the Garden of Eden, sin has distorted that image, and God's redemptive plan through Jesus Christ is to restore us—not to a self-defined authenticity, but to conformity with His image: *"For those God foreknew He also predestined to be conformed to the image of His Son"* (Rom. 8:29).

Anything outside of this divine restoration of order is ultimately rooted in selfishness: *"For where you have envy and selfish ambition, there you find disorder and every evil practice"* (James 3:16). However, God isn't against personal growth or happiness—He desires both for us, but within the framework of His will: *"Delight yourself in the Lord, and He will give you the desires of your heart"* (Ps. 37:4). True fulfillment is found not in self-invention or self-centeredness but in surrendering to God's transforming work in us.

THROUGH SÉGUN'S LENSES

Time spent apart during a prolonged marital separation can, and should, be used constructively for deep introspection. Six and a half years presented ample opportunity to retrace my steps and gain valuable insights about myself through frank self-examination with a view to undergoing meaningful self-improvement in some shape or form. However, my conviction about being the wronged party ensured the scales were always tipped in my favor in terms of limiting any actions I felt I needed to take in that regard.

Although I had always trusted in my resilience under pressure, this was a very different situation. It took a while for me to fully appreciate the weight of my decision that my marriage had run its course and the mental, emotional, and physical toll it would take on me, Funké, and our children. Some signs were obvious, while others were more subtle. While I might have appeared calm on the surface, I was waging an internal

---

66. Mal. 3:6, Heb. 13:8

battle that I failed to recognize for a long time. Walking past my children's unoccupied room was a daily reminder of how dramatically our lives had changed. Inasmuch as I tried not to dwell on the negative aspects of the separation, there was no "pause" or "stop" button to press to prevent my heart and head from continuing to process what was going on around and within me.

Nothing could fill the deep feeling of emptiness. Finding things to do or people to spend time with only provided temporary solutions. During my quiet times, it was impossible to pretend that all was well and that I was completely on top of things. I became self-employed during the separation, and there was a period when I would not leave the house or even draw the curtains as I wrestled with different aspects of what my family life had become.

Fortunately for me, I have never had the urge to experiment with drugs or over-consume alcohol, but I can understand the appeal of quick fixes when one is trying to numb deep-seated pain or to forget tough times one is going through. No matter how much blame I apportioned to Funké for the separation, there was no escaping the fact that a deliberate and premeditated action I took initiated it.

Rearview Mirror Lesson

There is a Nigerian proverb that says when a person is pointing at someone in an accusatory manner, the other fingers on that hand end up pointing back at the accuser. In the build-up to and during the separation, it was easier to point and blame instead of being brutally honest with myself.

I spent a lot of time doing superficial things instead of focusing on the more important process of examining myself under a microscope. This undeniably contributed to the length and complexity of the separation and my unwillingness to consider any type of reconciliation with Funké.

PART 3

The Reliable
Roadmap

A Glimpse Into My Journey: From Childhood to Womanhood.

Mom bringing my older brother for his Christening.

Dad and me at his first grandchild's Christening.

The greatest gift parents can give their children is a foundation of faith in God.

Little Funké: Mood-swing specialist—from sulk to swagger!

Dad by my hospital bedside at age nine—he wasn't there every time I needed him, but he was there when it mattered most.

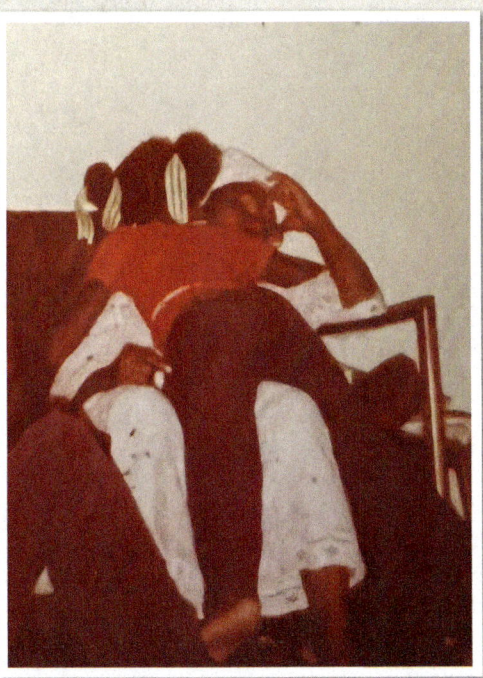

Mom, exhausted... but never too tired for cuddles.

Mom and Dad at my maternal Grandma's 80th birthday party.

With my parents and older brother at Grandma's 80th.

A classic Nigerian party—Dad celebrating Mom at Grandma's 80th.

On holiday with Dad during his work assignment in the US.

Arriving at church with my Dad on my wedding day.

14

Putting the Ways of Childhood Behind

*"The first step in solving a problem
is to recognize that it does exist."*

ZIG ZIGLAR

NAVIGATING GROWING PAINS

People make decisions based on what they know—or don't know—at any given moment in life. However, God, in His mercy, calls us to grow in wisdom and do better as we learn from our experiences and those of others.[1] Each of us is on a unique journey, and while the paths we take may differ—some longer, some more challenging—what matters most is following the right way, guided by the Holy Spirit, so we arrive at God's intended destination for our lives.[2] God's directions are readily available—through His Word, wise counsel, and inner conviction—but we must pay attention and trust His leading.

Growth and change often come with discomfort—much like planting, rooting, weeding, pruning, and grafting in a garden—yet they are necessary processes that enable us to bear good fruit and lead lives that honor God.[3] In relationships, particularly when they begin to

---

1. James 1:5
2. Prov. 3:5-6; Isa. 30:21
3. John 15:1-2

deteriorate, couples must be intentional about prioritizing their children's well-being. Parenting should not be reactive but forward-looking, recognizing that children are deeply affected by how their parents navigate life's struggles. As couples live out their relationship in full view of their children, they must consider the impact of their actions and decisions on the children's emotional and spiritual growth.[4]

We all carry baggage from our past, often dragging it into relationships like cherished collector's items. However, we must recognize and acknowledge these burdens through honest soul-searching and surrender them at the door. Nothing should be allowed to cast a shadow over the beautiful future God has planned for us.[5] Taking responsibility for our own mistakes is vital, but we must also discern the negative influences and wounds caused by others—choosing to break free from cycles of pain instead of allowing them to define us.[6] We have the choice to let unresolved trauma and generational patterns complicate our lives, or we can, by God's grace, choose healing and restoration, correcting wrongs instead of perpetuating them.[7]

As captured in the photo collage, I was a feisty, happy, playful, and affectionate toddler with a sunny disposition. Yet, there was another side to that adorable little girl—an alter ego that was moody, easily offended, and strong-willed, emerging whenever I was unhappy or didn't get my way. Growing up with my mother and older brother after my parents' separation was a journey of mixed emotions. My earliest memories of their split, which occurred when I was about eighteen months old, mainly come from photos and family conversations.

My relationship with my father during my childhood was not as close as I had hoped; it often felt distant, defined more by duty than by deep emotional connection. I was extremely sensitive and often angry when he failed to keep his promises or didn't show up for scheduled visits with my brother and me. There were frequent excuses for arriving hours late or not showing up at all, followed by attempts to compensate for his absence with gifts. In fact, for a long time, I was convinced that he owned a toy shop or even the Raleigh Bicycle Company simply because my maiden name, Leigh, bore a resemblance to the name of the brand. But I didn't want toys. I wanted my daddy!

Repeated cycles of disappointment, hurt, broken promises, and feeling as though I was receiving the short end of the stick began to shape my young mind, influencing how I viewed myself and others. From an incredibly early age, I wrestled with uncertainties, rejection, distrust, fear of abandonment, and deep-seated resentment. Each time my dad failed to show up, or when days stretched into weeks without a visit or phone call, I would cry or sulk for hours—sometimes withdrawing into a shell for days. At other times, I lashed out, blaming

4. Prov. 22:6
5. Jer. 29:11
6. 2 Cor. 5:17
7. Matt. 11:28-30

those around me rather than confronting the true source of my pain. In my innocent mind, I feared that if I ever expressed my hurt or frustration, I might drive him further away, making him disappear from my life completely. I carried this unspoken burden, trying to process emotions that were far beyond my understanding. It wasn't until I faced similar struggles during my own season of marital separation that I truly understood the weight of their impact on the entire family.

As I grew older, tantrums and outbursts were no longer considered cute or acceptable. The "rod of discipline"[8] was used when necessary to curb such behavior. Since adaptation is a natural response to changing circumstances or environments, I developed a new defense mechanism—a razor-sharp tongue. Unlike my earlier outbursts, this wasn't immediately curtailed by the adults in my life. Perhaps they found my new form of expression preferable to sulking and pouting. Occasionally, I was teased or warned about being "cheeky" or "saucy," and I was told that my attitude could get me into trouble one day. But without firm correction, my tendency to be outspoken—sometimes crossing the line into rudeness—only grew stronger.

I was aware of my "big mouth," but I justified it as a sign of boldness, confidence, and standing up for myself, regardless of the age or authority of the person I was addressing. However, unchecked behavior, no matter how small, takes root and grows when left unchallenged. Proverbs 29:15 warns, *"The rod and reproof give wisdom, but a child left to himself brings shame to his mother."* While my "sweet" side often overshadowed my sharp tongue, I learned that indulging harmful habits only strengthens them. Seemingly small undesirable attitudes, when ignored, can become deep-seated struggles later in life.[9] God, in His wisdom, calls us (both young and old) to correction and transformation, shaping us into vessels that reflect His grace and character.[10]

At that age, my view of the world was simplistic—it was either love or rejection. To me, a "real" family had both parents present, and anything less felt incomplete. No one expected me to fully understand our situation, but that didn't stop me from searching for answers on my own. My mother did her best to balance her emotions while adjusting to a reality she had never envisioned, but I was left to piece together the little I could rationalize. In hindsight, the thoughts and conclusions that were shaped at such a young age now seem short-sighted.

As a child, my emotions were easily swayed—moments of joy quickly overshadowed by deep pain. I bottled up my true feelings, too afraid of appearing ungrateful and insensitive or of upsetting my mother and making her feel inadequate. Yet, the turmoil within me found other outlets, often surfacing as misplaced anger toward those around me. Looking back, I can now see how unchecked emotions and misguided perceptions can lead to cycles of pain.

---

8. Prov. 22:15

9. Gal. 6:7-8

10. Rom. 12:2

Thankfully, God calls us to release our burdens to Him: *"Cast all your anxiety on Him because He cares for you"* (1 Pet. 5:7). The wounds of our childhood don't have to define our future, and healing begins when we allow God's truth to reshape our perspectives.

I attended boarding school from the age of eleven, where I was quite reserved. I had a small but closely knit group of friends and didn't get into fights or serious arguments. During this time, I became a born-again Christian, and I am forever grateful that God found me[11] and filled any void I may have felt in a way that only He can. I spent much of my spare time deepening my faith through religious activities—singing in the choir and engaging in covert evangelism, as any religious activity outside Sunday services and choir practice was prohibited. Living in a small, structured community made it easier to uphold the expected standards, as I was constantly surrounded by peers who shared my faith and values. The fear of serious consequences for misbehavior also helped reinforce discipline.

Beyond faith-based activities, I was deeply involved in sports, which provided a positive outlet for my energy and kept me active and focused. My efforts even earned me an award as the best sports girl for my House. I wasn't one to break the rules, but there were a few real tests—like the horrid school meals and a handful of mean senior students who sometimes tempted my natural inclination to retaliate with my "razor-sharp tongue!" At our mock award ceremonies, I often received titles like "Ms. Prim and Proper" or "Tidiest Girl," and a recurring comment on my report card was that I was "well-behaved." However, holidays were the only times I resumed my old habits, struggling with unprocessed emotions and questioning the realities of my family situation.

Being away from home also helped me channel my emotions through writing. I wrote numerous letters to family and friends to stay connected, which deepened my relationship with my parents—especially my father. I still treasure the handwritten letters, cards, and postcards they sent me while I was in school. Through their words, I gained a better understanding of their feelings and perspectives. We were a family of letter writers—my parents, who once exchanged heartfelt correspondence during their courtship, continued to write to each other even after their relationship unraveled. My mother saved these priceless pieces for my brother and me, allowing us to observe both of them in *living color*—without the subjective lens of either party. Many years later, reading those letters gave me deeper insights into their relationship, enabling me to see their journey more clearly. It helped me piece together a more complete and honest picture—one that revealed their humanity in ways I hadn't fully grasped as a child.

Initially, there was considerable animosity between my parents due to the reasons behind their breakup. However, my mother was intentional about shielding my brother and me from their disagreements. She refused to let bitterness take root and did not tolerate anyone

---

11. John 15:16

speaking ill of my father in our presence. Instead, she chose to walk that difficult journey with love, peace, and civility, ensuring that we could maintain a relationship with him. She handled it with grace, wisdom, humility, restraint, and sacrifice—qualities that deepened as she grew older and her relationship with God strengthened.[12]

In my early teens, I often found myself frustrated with my mother's approach. I couldn't understand why she tolerated some of my father's actions or why she didn't challenge him when I thought she should. I wished she would stand her ground, demand more, and react. At times, her displeasure was evident, but she quickly regained her composure and perspective. Mom saw the bigger picture and understood that reacting in anger would only cause more harm, so she chose a different path—one of patience, perseverance, and discernment.

Over time, my mother's approach bore fruit. I watched the hostility between my parents diminish as they made intentional efforts to show mutual respect, which became evident in the way they communicated. My father honored her in ways I hadn't expected—for instance, by attending her milestone birthdays, significant family events, and celebrations. My mother reciprocated by participating in his important family events, such as his mother's memorial service. Looking back, I now see how those choices, along with the examples they set, shaped and prepared me for my own path—helping me extend grace to my husband during our separation. Mom sacrificed temporary hurts and emotions for the sake of something greater—ensuring that my brother and I had a fighting chance to build and sustain a meaningful relationship with our father.[13]

University was my gateway to independence and self-discovery. For the first time, I truly had to self-regulate—practicing self-control, guarding my emotions, and testing boundaries. It was also a time when I confronted emotional struggles I hadn't fully processed—self-doubt, unresolved pain, and unhealthy coping mechanisms. This was when I met Ségun, at a time I was still embarking on a journey toward self-awareness, healing, and wholeness. Looking back, I now see that I carried some of the scars and unhealed wounds from my past into my marriage. Throwing temper tantrums might have been tolerable as a little girl, but as an adult, it was destructive. These emotions had been nurtured for so long—excused, indulged, or even protected from consequences—that they became difficult to tame.

Yes, while my parents made choices that undoubtedly shaped parts of my life, the decisions I made as an adult were entirely *my* responsibility. It takes the grace of God and a willingness to see beyond the distorted lens of past pain. There was so much about my life that was immature and carnal. In truth, some of us don't just need to adjust our lenses—we need to discard them completely and adopt God's vision for our lives. Holding on to bitterness or blaming others for past wounds serves no purpose—neither for us nor for future generations.

---

12. Rom. 12:18

13. Prov. 14:29; Eccles. 7:8; Gal. 6:9

Healing begins with a single, crucial step: forgiveness.[14] God wants us to mature into the likeness of Christ, which comes through knowing Him. Jesus is our standard of spiritual maturity.

> *"Now our knowledge is partial and incomplete, and even the gift of prophecy reveals only part of the whole picture! But when the time of perfection comes, these partial things will become useless. When I was a child, I spoke and thought and reasoned as a child. But when I grew up, I put away childish things. Now we see things imperfectly, like puzzling reflections in a mirror, but then we will see everything with perfect clarity. All that I know now is partial and incomplete, but then I will know everything completely, just as God now knows me completely. Three things will last forever—faith, hope, and love—and the greatest of these is love."* (1 Cor. 13:9-13 NLT)

My parents did their best—especially my mother, who always prioritized peace over conflict. My father, like many men, took a little longer to come around, perhaps due to guilt stemming from the way their relationship ended. Once it was clear that my father had moved on, Mom taught my brother and me early on that we had to share him with his new family—we wouldn't always have his full attention, but that was okay. As his two eldest children, we never felt the need to compete for position or assert our place whenever we were all together. My mother ensured that we felt secure in her love so that we never saw members of our blended family as competition or a threat.

Although there were times when we felt overlooked or shortchanged, my mother's unwavering trust in God shaped our perspective. She lived out her faith intentionally, teaching us—through her words and actions—to always look to God as our ultimate Source. Earthly parents may falter, be distant, or even be neglectful, but God never fails. He is a just and loving Father who always does right by His children.[15]

Long before I became aware of these biblical principles, my mother exemplified the fruit of the Spirit and made allowances for others' faults.[16] She believed in "stooping to conquer" and trusted that things would ultimately work out for good.[17] She demonstrated these virtues in her relationship with my father, even when he wasn't always a willing participant in being fair or reasonable. Change takes time, and their journey to a more cordial and civil relationship didn't happen overnight. My mother made countless sacrifices—some of which went unnoticed at the time—but the fruits of her choices blessed my brother and me long after her passing.

This doesn't mean she blindly accepted unfair treatment. Instead, she prayed, trusted in

---

14. Col. 3:13-15
15. Deut. 10:17-18; Ps. 27:10
16. Gal. 5:22; Col. 3:13
17. Rom. 8:28

God's ability to transform, and leaned on His wisdom rather than reacting in the flesh. It's tempting to write off an estranged or ex-spouse—some make it very easy to do! However, I've discovered that there are many ways, especially with the advancement of technology, to establish healthy boundaries without severing a child's connection with their non-resident parent. If you're in this situation, it's worth exploring those options.

I would like to believe that no one sets out to be an absent or irresponsible parent, though some may inadvertently or willingly play that role. Instead of assuming or expecting the worst, consider that a spouse who struggled in marriage may still have the potential to be present and engaged in his or her children's lives. It doesn't have to be all or nothing—one parent's way or the highway. With godly wisdom and cooperation, it may be possible to foster their involvement for the benefit of the children. After all, the goal isn't just personal comfort or convenience—it's raising whole and secure children who see reconciliation, forgiveness, and grace in action. It's about the legacy parents leave behind for their children!

It was after my mother's passing that my father truly stepped up, and for the first time, my brother and I felt the depth of his love, protection, and unwavering support. I experienced a closeness with him that I had longed for but had never fully known before. He drew me in, and our conversations became deeper and more personal. In those moments, years of emotional distance seemed to fade. I confided in him in ways I never had, and he, in turn, opened up to us. For the first time, he allowed himself to be vulnerable, sharing how deeply he understood our pain—having experienced the loss of his own mother at around the same age as us. Grief has a way of connecting people, but it can also bring up unresolved emotions and unspoken wounds.

My father's love and protectiveness became even more evident when he stood up for me during my marital problems. He did not remain silent or passive. Instead, he rose with strength, hiring lawyers on my behalf and meeting with me repeatedly to encourage me to respond appropriately to Ségun's petition for divorce and full custody of our children. When the situation became unbearable, he took the bold step of writing a firm letter to my father-in-law, urging him to rein in his son. My father went beyond his duty as a parent—he willingly and joyfully embraced his role as my defender, offering the kind of love that provides both security and healing.

Another chapter of our relationship, one that brought even deeper healing and closure, unfolded during his final year on this side of eternity. It was a gift from God, a sacred time when we connected on a spiritual level like never before. My father even began calling me his pastor, which was most unexpected. We prayed together, laughed, cried, and shared moments of profound understanding. I felt both his sadness and his joy—his pain in saying goodbye, yet his pride in the person I had become, which he expressed to me in our discussions, text messages, and emails that I will cherish forever.

For the first time, he entrusted me with responsibilities, sought my advice, and relied on me in ways that made me feel needed and cherished. It was everything I had always hoped for and desired from him. In many ways, life had come full circle. Yet, a part of me wrestled with the feeling that it was too little, too late. But who has time to dwell on regrets when facing the reality of eternity? I knew my father wished he had more time—perhaps to mend broken relationships—but when you are fighting for your life, where do you even begin?

I reassured him that he had done what he knew best, and I believe God provided him solace. He made peace with his Maker, and now it is left to me, and to those of us still here, to seek and embrace God's perfect peace (John 14:27 AMP). There is no point in carrying burdens of resentment or presumed injustices on behalf of others. The past cannot be rewritten, but we can choose to move forward in love.

My father wasn't perfect, but he tried faithfully. He was brilliant, hardworking, and deeply driven by success—always striving to achieve the best in life. Yet, in doing so, he often spread himself thin—not only in his work but also with his affections. Still, I know his heart was full of love for his family, even if it wasn't always expressed in ways we expected. Although he didn't get the chance to right every wrong or mend every broken relationship before he departed this earth, I am grateful that, in the end, he chose to put God first. Not everyone gets that opportunity, but he did—a grace I do not take for granted.[18] In the grand scheme of things, success fades, achievements lose their shine, but eternity remains. And in his final days, my father embraced what truly mattered.

FORMATIVE YEARS MATTER

Despite our differences during our separation, Ségun was—and still is—an excellent father. In my frustration back then, I sarcastically referred to him as "Mr. Mom" because of how fully he committed himself to parenting—even as he tried to alienate me and seek full custody of our boys. But in hindsight, I see that his love for our children was genuine, unwavering, and expressed in the best way he knew how—even if, at the time, some of his decisions seemed misguided and were unfair to me.

We all make choices based on what rules our hearts—be it faith, fear, suspicion, envy, pride, guilt, or selfishness. However, the kind of wisdom that transcends human reasoning is what we need when making decisions that shape not only our own lives but the destinies of our children. In Proverbs 4:5 (AMP), the Bible urges us to *"Get [skillful and godly] wisdom! Acquire understanding [actively seek spiritual discernment, mature comprehension, and logical interpretation]! Do not forget nor turn away from the words of my mouth."*

---

18. Isa. 55:6

The truth is, we all believe we're doing what's right most of the time—*"Every way of a man is right in his own eyes, but the Lord weighs the heart"* (Prov. 21:2). However, only God can provide true discernment. When we ask, He grants wisdom that leads to success[19] and the ability to learn from experience.[20] The sooner we turn to God and teach our children the same, the better their chances of navigating life wisely despite our own mistakes. The Bible warns that the opposite of wisdom is foolishness—*"A fool trusts in his own heart"* (Prov. 28:26) and *"despises wisdom"* (Prov. 23:9).

During a marital crisis, it's easy to get so caught up in "self-preservation mode" that we overlook the most vulnerable—our children. But this is precisely when we need the sharpest vision, the kind that sees beyond the immediate struggle and aims for long-term victory. When life throws us curveballs, we must have the wisdom to step up and hit a home run—not just for ourselves but for the whole team. This is because, ultimately, true success isn't about winning alone; it's about ensuring that everyone entrusted to us—especially our children— crosses the finish line strong.

Sometimes, despite one's best efforts at reconciliation and intervention, the healthiest option is to leave a harmful situation. Such circumstances don't necessarily spell defeat or disqualification from the "race;"[21] instead, they often signify divine redirection.[22] Even when the road takes an unexpected turn, God's plan remains intact, and He is faithful to complete the good work He has begun.[23] In those moments, it's essential to trust that God is still in control.[24]

When children are involved, their well-being must be a top priority—not just in the immediate aftermath but also in the long term. The emotional, mental, and spiritual impacts of such transitions can shape their self-perception, faith, and future relationships. It's not just about how much love the custodial parent shows or how hard they try to fill the gaps left by the other parent. What truly makes a difference from the outset of the separation is how information is managed and communicated to the child. Parents can't completely control how children feel or process fast-evolving situations around them, but they can ease the transition by having age-appropriate, truthful, and objective conversations.[25] What and how we communicate with our children matters—it influences their perception of the situation, themselves, and even their relationship with God. We must take the time to think things through—prayerfully weighing every option with a clear mind, filtering our choices through godly counsel and God's Word (His will), and scrutinizing our motives. Life-altering or destiny-defining

---

19. Eccles. 10:10
20. Prov. 15:31
21. 1 Cor. 9:24; Phil. 3:13-14
22. Ps. 37:23-24
23. Phil. 1:6
24. Rom. 8:28
25. Prov. 12:18-19

decisions should never be made on a whim or based solely on temporary circumstances or fleeting emotions.[26]

There's no perfect parent or flawless parenting style, but we must be intentional about how we raise our children, ensuring that our choices don't burden them with unnecessary complications. Before switching into "survival mode" and justifying decisions with sentiments like "I have to do what I have to do," we should pause and ask: *What impact will this have—not just on my children today but on future generations and even ourselves?* In today's culture, including within the church, people are often quick to cut others off, a phenomenon sometimes referred to as "cancel culture," rather than seeking healing or restoration. But we are called to a higher standard. Instead of striving in our own strength, we must lean on God's grace—it's the only way to handle life, parenting, and relationships with wisdom, patience, and love.

Many speak of love without fully grasping its depth and commitment—qualities that require patience, resilience, endurance, perseverance, and self-sacrifice (the willingness to put others before oneself)—P.R.E.P.S.[27] Love is not just an emotion; it's a divine command and the very essence of God Himself.[28] When we truly know Him and allow His Spirit to transform us, our lives will bear witness to it.

> *"Our actions will show that we belong to the truth, so we will be confident when we stand before God. Even if we feel guilty, God is greater than our feelings, and he knows everything. Dear friends, if we don't feel guilty, we can come to God with bold confidence. And we will receive from him whatever we ask because we obey him and do the things that please him. And this is his commandment: We must believe in the name of his Son, Jesus Christ, and love one another, just as he commanded us. Those who obey God's commandments remain in fellowship with him, and he with them. And we know he lives in us because the Spirit he gave us lives in us."* (1 John 3:18-24 NLT)

If parents truly understood the weight of their actions—the generational impact, the direct link to answered prayers, longevity, success, their children's future marriages, health, and well-being, and even the stability of society as a whole (since families are its bedrock)—they would likely pause, reconsider, and make more intentional choices. *"A prudent person foresees danger and takes precautions. The simpleton goes blindly on and suffers the consequences."* (Prov. 22:3 NLT)

Navigating life's uncharted waters requires preparation, especially when dealing with challenges such as parental separation or divorce. Research indicates that such family disruptions

---

26. Prov. 19:2; Luke 14:28; Phil. 4:6-7

27. John 15:13; Rom. 12:10; 1 Cor. 13:4-7; 2 Cor. 4:8-9; Phil. 2:3-4

28. 1 John 4:8

can lead to adverse outcomes for children and adolescents. For instance, a study published in *Demographic Research* found that across fourteen countries, children of separated parents were seven percent less likely to attain a university degree compared to their peers from two-parent families. Additionally, a comprehensive review in the *Journal of the American Academy of Child & Adolescent Psychiatry* revealed that significant numbers of children experience long-term psychological and social difficulties following parental divorce, including heightened anxiety in forming enduring attachments later in life.[29]

Given these potential challenges, it's essential not to assume that children, regardless of age, will simply adapt following such changes. Proactive measures and interventions are critical in helping children process their emotions and experiences while guiding them through difficult times with wisdom and care.[30]

Implementing thoughtful and supportive strategies can significantly enhance a child's ability to cope and thrive despite changes in their family. By fostering open communication, providing counseling resources, and maintaining a stable environment, parents can help mitigate some of the negative impacts of separation or divorce. Remember, the early years are pivotal, and the support that children receive during these times can shape their future resilience and well-being.

Research[31] highlights several factors that negatively impact children's well-being after their parents' break-up. These include ongoing—or even increased—parental conflict, a decline in parenting quality before and after the split, economic stressors, reduced contact and meaningful interactions with the non-residential parent, and frequent changes in living arrangements. Children raised in a stable, two-parent home with both biological parents often fare better across multiple life outcomes than those raised in single-parent households. However, single parenthood is not the sole or most significant cause of issues such as school dropout, teenage pregnancy, or juvenile delinquency—it is just one of many contributing factors. At the same time, being raised by a single parent does not doom a child to failure; countless children from single-parent homes go on to thrive.

Several factors contribute to children's positive adjustment to parental separation or divorce. These include dedicated and nurturing parenting, stable mental health in parents, low parental conflict, cooperative parenting post-separation, and social support. Research shows that

---

29. Judith S. Wallerstein, "The Long-Term Effects of Divorce on Children: A Review," *Journal of the American Academy of Child & Adolescent Psychiatry* 24, no. 5 (1985): 518–530, https://doi.org/10.1016/S0002-7138(09)60052-2;

Fabrizio Bernardi and Jan Radl, "The Long-Term Consequences of Parental Divorce for Children's Educational Attainment," *Demographic Research* 30, no. 61 (2014): 1653–1680, https://doi.org/10.4054/DemRes.2014.30.61;

Paul R. Amato, "The Consequences of Divorce for Adults and Children," *Journal of Marriage and Family* 62, no. 4 (2000): 1269–1287, https://doi.org/10.1111/j.1741-3737.2000.01269.x.

30. Deut. 6:6-7; Prov. 3:11-12; 4:11-12; 22:6; Eph. 6:4

31. Paul R. Amato and Bruce Keith, "Parental Divorce and the Well-Being of Children: A Meta-Analysis," *Psychological Bulletin* 110, no. 1 (1991): 26–46, https://doi.org/10.1037/0033-2909.110.1.26;

E. Mavis Hetherington and Julie Kelly, *For Better or For Worse: Divorce Reconsidered* (New York: W. W. Norton & Company, 2002).

children generally experience fewer adjustment problems when the resident parent (typically the mother) has a robust support system and provides consistent, nurturing care. I can attest to this. My mother had a dependable support structure built around her, which included her mother, siblings, trusted friends, and compassionate bosses. Likewise, I don't know how I would have survived my six-and-a-half-year ordeal without my own reliable network of support.

Furthermore, positive outcomes are linked to children maintaining a strong relationship with their non-residential parent, typically the father. While the quality of this relationship matters more than the frequency of contact, regular interactions often strengthen these connections, ultimately benefiting the child's overall well-being.

When parental conflict is high, a positive relationship with at least one parent can serve as a stabilizing factor for children. Additionally, having trusted and supportive figures, such as grandparents and close friends, helps children transition with minimal disruption. These relationships act as a buffer, providing the emotional support that children need during times of upheaval. On the other hand, parental discord can cause tension, sometimes leading to contempt or resentment toward one or both parents. The way each parent manages their emotions and interacts with the other can have a profound impact on how children perceive and process the separation. Children are particularly sensitive to these dynamics during their formative years. When it comes to minors—who cannot advocate for themselves—I urge parents to set aside pride, malice, past hurts, or grievances, and be intentional about prioritizing their children's well-being. Many avoidable hardships, such as neglect and abuse, could be prevented if parents made choices rooted in love, wisdom, and their children's best interests.

The Bible acknowledges the importance of peace in the home. Proverbs 17:1 states, *"Better a dry crust with peace and quiet than a house full of feasting, with strife."* This highlights the importance of creating a peaceful environment, even during challenging times. Helping children manage changes and transitions, particularly by improving their coping skills and resilience, can provide long-term benefits. For children who are experiencing or will experience parental separation, learning these skills is invaluable. As parents and caregivers, it's our responsibility to support them on this journey, guided by love, patience, wisdom—and most importantly, prayer.

BREAKING GENERATIONAL CYCLES

The foundation we lay matters! The choices we make today have generational consequences, whether for good or evil. Longitudinal studies[32] show that divorce can have a ripple

---

32. Joan B. Kelly and Robert E. Emery, "Children's Adjustment in Conflicted Marriages and Divorce: A Decade of Research," *Journal of the American Academy of Child & Adolescent Psychiatry* 42, no. 3 (2003): 343–350, https://doi.org/10.1097/01. CHI.0000046871.66656.98;

Megan M. Sweeney, "Remarriage and Stepfamilies: Strategic Approaches to Family Life," *Annual Review of Sociology* 36 (2010): 391–412, https://doi.org/10.1146/annurev.soc.012809.102610.

effect—emotionally, psychologically, physically, and socioeconomically. The same is true for every strong, godly marriage, but in a positive direction. With God's help and a firm commitment, we can break negative cycles and build a legacy of faithfulness and blessings. Scripture reminds us that *"a good man leaves an inheritance for his children's children"* (Prov. 13:22) and that God's desire is for us to raise a godly generation (Mal. 2:15). What we build today shapes not only our own lives but also the lives of those to come. Let's choose wisely!

The intergenerational cycle of family problems refers to issues—ranging from divorce to emotional or behavioral struggles—that, when left unaddressed, can have a lasting impact on the lives of children, grandchildren, and future generations. These inherited traits can be deeply ingrained, often passed down unconsciously or reinforced through learned behavior. For instance, patterns of fear, anxiety, anger, and depression may be transmitted through generations, along with inexpressiveness, lack of affection, and an absence of empathy or compassion.

Other traits may include selfishness, mean-spiritedness, mistrust, or even a strong aversion toward marriage and commitment. Emotional wounds, such as low self-esteem, and destructive behaviors like substance abuse, promiscuity, philandering, cheating, stealing, violence, and abuse can also be passed down across generations. Moreover, negative values, such as the absence of moral codes and irreligious attitudes, can take root, distorting how individuals perceive relationships, love, family, and God.

Emerging research in epigenetics suggests that trauma and prolonged stress can alter gene expression, potentially influencing the biological makeup of future generations. These changes are not merely theoretical—they have been observed in the descendants of Holocaust survivors (Yehuda et al., 2016) and in individuals prenatally exposed to the atrocities of the Rwandan genocide (Perroud et al., 2014). A study conducted by the University of South Florida revealed that the children of survivors often display altered levels of cortisol, a key stress hormone, making them more vulnerable to anxiety and PTSD-like symptoms. This suggests that the trauma experienced by one generation can leave a biological imprint on the next, reinforcing the reality of inherited burdens.

Although this may seem distant from typical everyday struggles, the principle also applies to more familiar contexts, such as parental separation or divorce. Studies indicate that children of divorced or separated parents often experience prolonged stress, which can influence their emotional resilience and overall well-being. Research suggests that sustained elevated cortisol levels in such children may lead to genetic modifications over time, which can affect their emotional regulation and immune function (Essex et al., 2013).

In addition to this, research on adverse childhood experiences (ACEs) indicates that early-life stress can lead to long-lasting changes in genes linked to anxiety, depression, and even chronic illnesses (McGowan et al., 2009). While not every child of divorce experiences these biological effects, the risk is heightened in cases where separation involves high conflict, emotional neglect, or insufficient support. This highlights the crucial importance of stability, nurturing, and healthy co-parenting practices in safeguarding a child's emotional and physical well-being.

Generational trauma refers to the transmission of emotional wounds, pain, or negative behavior patterns from one generation to another. It often originates from profoundly impactful experiences such as war, genocide, slavery, abuse, discrimination, poverty, or dysfunctional family dynamics. These unresolved traumas can influence people's beliefs, coping mechanisms, and emotional responses, shaping their approach to relationships, self-worth, and life challenges within a family or community. From a spiritual standpoint, generational trauma can also be associated with habitual sin, strongholds, or negative cycles that persist until they are addressed and healed.

In Exodus 20:5-6 and Deuteronomy 5:9-10, God speaks of visiting the iniquity of the fathers upon the children to the third and fourth generations of those who hate Him, highlighting how the consequences of sin can transcend multiple generations. However, God also promises to show love and mercy to thousands of generations of those who love Him and keep His commandments.[33] While the consequences of iniquity can affect future generations (Exod. 20:5), Ezekiel 18:19-20 emphasizes that spiritual judgment on sin is based on personal actions, not inherited guilt. Sin means missing the mark or falling short,[34] whereas iniquity refers to gross injustice, wickedness, or deep moral corruption. It signifies persistent, intentional wrongdoing—a state of moral depravity or rebellion against God.

Regardless of the perspective one adopts, whether biblical (generational curse) or psychological (intergenerational trauma), the struggles stemming from historical trauma or family breakdown need not define us. Science may reveal the patterns, but God's Word provides the solution—healing, restoration, and a new legacy of blessings for future generations. Through Christ, God offered freedom from the curse of the law, including family strongholds (Gal. 3:13-14). By His power and grace, God has rescued believers from the control of darkness—including cycles of dysfunction—and transferred us into the Kingdom of His beloved Son, granting us a new identity and liberty in Christ.[35] For those seeking healing, it's important to recognize that while these patterns may be deeply ingrained, they are not irreversible.

God's grace and knowledge of His truth bring about a paradigm shift in our hearts and minds, prompting a willingness to change. *"Through Christ Jesus, God has blessed the Gentiles with the same blessing he promised to Abraham, so that we who are believers might receive the promised Holy Spirit through faith."* (Gal. 3:14) Through His finished work on the cross, we are no longer bound by the weight of sin and condemnation (Rom. 8:1-2) but now live in the

---

33. Deut. 7:9; 28:1-14; 30:19-20
34. Rom. 3:23
35. Rom. 5:18; Eph. 2:8-9; Col. 1:13-14; Titus 2:11-14

freedom and righteousness He has secured for us (2 Cor. 5:21). In Christ, we are free indeed (John 8:36) and empowered to walk in the newness of life (Rom. 6:4).

This process of renewal isn't about willpower, positive thinking, mere behavior modification, avoidance, or physical distance from the family or community that perpetuates or triggers those negative patterns—although the latter may be necessary in some cases. It's about relying on God's strength and committing to His plan for our lives. True transformation isn't magic; it comes from God's supernatural intervention that delivers us from sin and undesirable behavior. These patterns often take root in the mind and heart before manifesting in actions. *"A good person produces good things from the treasury of a good heart, and an evil person produces evil things from the treasury of an evil heart. What you say flows from what is in your heart."* (Luke 6:45 NLT) God is our Maker and has the power to uncover any dark, distressing secrets that may be hidden in our hearts, bringing them into His light for healing.

Lasting change occurs through discipleship—an ongoing journey of spiritual development in which a believer commits to following Jesus, learning from His teachings, and applying biblical principles in daily life. It involves not only personal transformation through prayer, study, and obedience but also mentoring and encouraging others in their faith. True discipleship emphasizes the development of Christ-like character, deepening one's relationship with God, and actively serving others to advance His Kingdom.

One's early years shape the trajectory of one's life, and dedicating children to God while training them in His ways protects both them and their parents from unnecessary suffering and regret. A strong example of seeking God in one's formative years is Josiah, who became king at the tender age of eight. Instead of indulging in fleeting pleasures or following destructive paths, he pursued righteousness, which resulted in personal transformation and the revival of an entire nation.[36] True wisdom is found in guiding our children to develop a relationship with God from an early age. By sharing His truth—His Word, teachings, and principles—we guard their hearts against deception.[37] This helps keep them rooted in God's love, allowing Him to shape their character and guide their decisions for His purpose.

God is never mocked; ignoring His call to repentance leads to destruction, while responding to Him in humility brings renewal. Just as Josiah's heart was tender toward God, prompting him to reform a nation, we, too, are called to turn to Christ, allowing Him to renew our hearts and guide our steps. As God's people are being built up, the goal is that *"we all come to a perfect [mature] man, to the measure of the stature of the fullness of Christ; that we should no longer be children … but … may grow up in all things into Him who is the head—Christ"* (Eph. 4:13-15). God doesn't want us to remain spiritually immature but to grow into the likeness of Christ's character.

---

36. 2 Chr. 34:1-3; Eccles. 12:1

37. Prov. 4:23; Jer. 17:9

CONFRONTING AND HEALING
GENERATIONAL TRAUMA[38]

1. Deliberate and targeted effort to break the cycle:

The first step to healing is awareness and recognition of the patterns of trauma and dysfunction that have been passed down. This requires sincere introspection and the identification of recurring harmful behaviors, emotional scars, or toxic attitudes within the family or community. While we may not be responsible for the trauma inherited from our predecessors, we are accountable for our reactions to it. Making a conscious decision to break unhealthy cycles demands commitment, humility, and a willingness to change. Seeking beneficial coping strategies or developing healthier ways to process pain—such as prayer, meditation, and journaling—helps prevent trauma from further impacting one's life and relationships.

2. Counseling–Professional guidance for healing:

Christian or secular therapy and counseling can help individuals process past wounds, reframe negative thought patterns, and develop more positive ways to relate to themselves and others. However, in any childhood intervention, parents should not abdicate or outsource their responsibility to nurture, train, raise, guide, coach, and equip their children at every stage of life to therapists and counselors. While professional support can be beneficial, God has entrusted parents with the primary responsibility of caring for their children. Let's be faithful stewards of this precious gift.

Many generational traumas stem from childhood wounds; therefore, healing the inner child is essential. A therapist can help individuals work through repressed feelings and unmet needs from their past. Holding onto bitterness toward previous generations only prolongs the suffering. Counseling can provide tools to genuinely forgive—not to justify past wrongs, but to free oneself from resentment. Support groups, mentorship, and healthy friendships can offer encouragement and accountability during the healing process.

3. Faith-based renewal:

Spiritual restoration and freedom emerge from breaking spiritual strongholds[39] and embracing God's truth. Some generational trauma correlates with spiritual bondage, negative patterns, or destructive family cycles. These cycles can be dismantled through prayer, fasting, and receiving God's power. Healing necessitates a transformation in thinking patterns through God's Word. Meditating on Scripture shifts one's perspective from pain-driven to purpose-driven. Jesus provides us with inner healing, which we can receive by laying our burdens at His feet.[40] Faith

---

38. Exod. 34:7a; Rom. 12:1-2; 2 Cor. 5:17

39. 2 Cor. 10:4-5

40. 1 Pet. 5:7

empowers individuals to experience profound spiritual and emotional healing.[41] Believers can intentionally cultivate generational blessings[42] by obeying God and instilling faith, love, and godly values in future generations, rather than being hindered by past trauma.

Healing from generational trauma is a process. However, with self-awareness, professional support, and spiritual renewal, individuals and families can rewrite their stories and confidently step into freedom, wholeness, and purpose. When poor decisions have already been made or when one has strayed from God's plan, His compassion and mercy can transform circumstances for the better.

> *"This means that anyone who belongs to Christ has become a new person. The old life is gone; a new life has begun! And all of this is a gift from God, who brought us back to himself through Christ. And God has given us this task of reconciling people to him. For God was in Christ, reconciling the world to himself, no longer counting people's sins against them. And he gave us this wonderful message of reconciliation."* (2 Cor. 5:17-19 NLT)

THROUGH SÉGUN'S LENSES

Barely a few weeks into the separation, I had already begun to feel like I was trapped in a maze. With each passing year, it became more obvious that the more seemingly confident I was in the decisions I was making on behalf of four individuals, the less certain I was of the outcome. This was largely because the knowledge and tools I had at my disposal were wholly inadequate for the complex and dynamic situation I was dealing with. I adopted a short-sighted and fleshly approach to what was essentially a spiritual matter that required a godly intervention.

The Bible specifically instructs Christians to wage spiritual battle with spiritual weapons. Particular emphasis is attached to relying on God's strength while wearing His full armor that comprises truth, righteousness, peace, faith, salvation, and the sword of the Spirit. Instead, I wholeheartedly placed my trust in myself, what I knew, and any information I managed to pick up along the way. The combination of all those things could not even scratch the surface of what needed to be done at the time.

There were days when I was overcome by an almost indescribable feeling of helplessness

---

41. Ps. 147:3
42. Deut. 7:9

and debilitating sadness due to my inability to make sense of, or change for the better, what was happening to me and my family. The feeling worsened whenever I saw our children in their innocence and Funké in her pain, as I had no idea what our future would look like, but I had to keep forging ahead. However, each step I took exposed just how spiritually ill-equipped I was for the process I was driving. My inability to realize this took me further adrift in terms of my thought process, my words, and my actions. Even with the best intentions in the world, neither Funké nor I could, on our own, provide our children with the emotional support they needed. Our efforts fell short of the more effective outcomes for children that are typically achieved when co-parenting is done in unison, even amidst marital difficulties.

Rearview Mirror Lesson

Attempting to replace godly wisdom with earthly knowledge creates an automatic imbalance every single time. For the greater part of six and a half years, I backed myself in terms of my intentions, my thought process, and my decision-making skills.

This guaranteed that the results achieved would always be at variance with God's will. Fortunately, His patience and mercy are inexhaustible, and He is always prepared to intervene and quell our storms when we call on Him.

15

Divine Makeover

"And yet, O Lord, you are our Father. We are the clay,
and you are the potter. We all are formed by your hand."

ISAIAH 64:8 NLT

SKIN-DEEP VS. SOUL-DEEP

A divine makeover is a complete spiritual, emotional, and character transformation powered by God's grace. It's a renewal (spiritual rebirth) that transcends surface-level change, beginning in the heart and radiating outward—reshaping our thoughts, actions, and identity in Christ. It's not merely about becoming a better version of oneself; it's about redemption, restoration, and being made whole in Christ...for our good and the glory of our Father. This transformation is profound and lasting, unlike a physical makeover that fades with time. It involves surrendering to God, allowing His Word and Spirit to refine, heal, and mold us into His likeness.[1]

Like any makeover, there's a common thread of removing something, adding something, or incorporating something new. Spiritually, this signifies shedding the old self—our previous way of thinking and living—renewing our minds through God's truth, and putting on Christ.[2] The Word of God isn't merely a book we read—it's living truth that we internalize,

---

1. Rom. 8:29
2. Deut. 11:18; Ps. 119:11; Eph. 4:22-24; Col. 3:10, 16

allowing it to guide and shape us daily. This transformation is God's work in us. However, we participate by yielding to Him.[3]

Donning the new self—regenerated in the likeness of Christ[4]—is similar to wearing new spiritual clothing that embodies Jesus' character, mindset, and holiness. *"You were taught, with regard to your former way of life, to **put off your old self**, which is being corrupted by its deceitful desires; to be made new in the attitude of your minds; and to **put on the new self**, created to be like God in true righteousness and holiness."* (Eph. 4:22-24 NIV) These "deceitful desires"— which can include needs, ambitions, habits, or even good things and activities we prioritize above God—may seem harmless or justified. However, over time, they can conceal "inordinate affections,"[5] cravings and attachments that subtly draw us away from a Christ-centered life. It often begins with small compromises: rationalizing certain behaviors, ignoring convictions, or adjusting the truth for comfort. If left unchecked, these seemingly minor steps can lead us off the "straight and narrow,"[6] ultimately influencing our values, principles, and character.

In our pursuit of happiness or self-fulfillment, we can unintentionally replace God's truth with temporary substitutes—people or things that cannot truly satisfy or love us as He does.[7] The Bible describes this as trading the truth about God for a lie while worshiping and serving the things God created instead of the Creator Himself.[8] It reminds us how easy it is to lose sight of God when we chase what the world promises but cannot deliver. That's why immersing ourselves in the Word is essential. Scripture doesn't just teach us about God—it reveals His heart, sharpens our discernment,[9] and shows us who we are in light of who He is. The more we feed on His truth, the more attuned we become to His voice and the more empowered we are to surrender to His will and walk in the newness of life.

None of us have "arrived" yet! As followers of Jesus Christ, we're all on a journey—growing, learning, and being transformed daily. Spiritual maturity doesn't happen overnight; it's a process marked by intentional pursuit, honest self-reflection, and continually leaning into God's grace.[10] The apostle Paul captured this beautifully in Philippians 3:12-14 (NIV):

> *"Not that I have already obtained all this, or have already arrived at my goal, but I press on to take hold of that for which Christ Jesus took hold of me. Brothers and sisters, I do not consider myself yet to have taken hold of it. But one thing I do: Forgetting*

---

3. Deut. 30:6; Ps. 51:10; Ezek. 36:26; Rom. 12:1-2

4. Rom. 13:14; Gal. 3:27

5. Col. 3:5

6. Matt. 7:13-14

7. John 3:16; James 1:22-25

8. Rom. 1:25 (NLT)

9. Heb. 4:12

10. Ps. 119:9-16 (MSG)

what is behind and straining toward what is ahead, I press on toward the goal to
win the prize for which God has called me heavenward in Christ Jesus."

In other words, growth in Christ means pressing forward—letting go of the past, and actively pursuing the life God has designed for us. It's about progress, not perfection. There's a striking verse in Proverbs 11:22 (AMP) that says: *"As a ring of gold in a swine's snout, So is a beautiful woman who is without discretion [her lack of character mocks her beauty]."* Without wisdom, even beauty loses its value and dignity. God desires inner transformation that aligns with His truth and character, not just outward appearances. A spiritual makeover isn't like the glamorous reveal we see on TV. While a new hairstyle, outfit, or makeup can drastically change our outward appearance, inner renewal—becoming more like Christ—requires something deeper. It often begins with brokenness, which is not always comfortable or pleasant.

As Psalm 51:17 says, *"The sacrifices of God are a broken spirit; a broken and contrite heart, O God, you will not despise."* Unlike surface-level changes that disappear with time, a divine transformation impacts more than our outward appearance—it reshapes how we think, speak, love, and live.

Many unyielding Christians don't pray soul-deep prayers like, "Change me! Break me! Mold me, Lord," because such prayers may be difficult to express as they often cause discomfort. Yet, many yearn for transformation without the pain, inconvenience, or deep soul work it requires. We desire change but would prefer not to endure the sacrifice of "dying to ourselves." Scripture reminds us in Colossians 3:3-9 that our old selves have died as believers, and our lives are now hidden with Christ in God. We are called to put to death whatever belongs to our earthly nature—things like anger, lust, greed, and deceit—and to shed our old way of living. True transformation means laying down our will, desires, preferences, comfort zones, and control at the altar of obedience.[11]

Too often, our prayers focus on asking God to change others, fix our circumstances, or remove our challenges—rather than seeking change in ourselves.[12] *Change around us often begins with change within us.* Sometimes, a challenging situation seems prolonged because God allows it to work within us first. Just as the Israelites wandered in the wilderness, God may lead us through dry, uncomfortable places to humble us, test us, and reveal what truly lies in our hearts.[13] The deeper the resistance or the layers of self-reliance, fear, pride, or hurt that need to be stripped away, the longer the healing and transformation process may take.

We've all heard the phrase: "Be the change you want to see in others." It's more than just a motivational quote—it's a principle rooted in Scripture. Jesus consistently modeled change

---

11. Luke 9:23
12. Matt. 7:3-4
13. Deut. 8:2

by example. If we want to see more kindness, forgiveness, honesty, or humility in others, we must first embody those qualities ourselves. Galatians 6:4-5 (NIV) reminds us to focus on our own conduct: *"Each one should test their own actions … for each one should carry their own load."* Allowing God to start the process within us instead of waiting for others to get it right is how we lead by example—and that's where genuine revival begins!

A quick visit to the barber or a few hours of pampering at the beauty salon or spa can enhance our physical appearance and sense of well-being. However, when it comes to lasting results in life and health, the truth is that real transformation requires effort. Exercise, detoxing, intermittent fasting, and a disciplined lifestyle don't always feel good at first, but the long-term benefits far outweigh the temporary discomfort. As the saying goes, "No pain, no gain." Yet many of us still prefer shortcuts and instant results, sometimes turning to risky or artificial alternatives for quick fixes—physically, emotionally, or even spiritually.

The Bible describes transformation not as a luxury experience but as a refining process that includes pruning, testing, sacrificing, and the trial of our faith.[14] Following biblical patterns, God didn't use resorts, exotic islands, or comfortable locations to train His children. Although there were a few palace scenarios, most sites for refinement and preparation were deserts, wildernesses, valleys, storms, famines, prisons, the Red Sea, and fires. They may be harsh settings, but they're purposeful.[15]

Just as diamonds are formed under intense heat and pressure, our training or divine makeover often occurs in difficult environments or situations. However, God is always present— He is our Strength, Defender, Shield, Provider, Healer, and Shepherd.[16] While our character is forged amid upheavals,[17] He watches over us closely. And when the refining process is complete, He brings us out—not a moment too soon or too late—but right on time![18] We emerge stronger, wiser, more grounded in truth, and better equipped to walk in purpose—for our good and His glory.

Like the Israelites on their journey from Egypt to the Promised Land, when God chooses to "process" us—refining and preparing us for purpose or promotion—we sometimes follow reluctantly, burdened by a sense of entitlement. We grumble, complain, and allow fear, impatience, and self-will to cloud our faith. Instead of embracing the journey with trust, we resist and complain that we don't want to perish in our "wilderness" like those who disobeyed God. Scripture warns us: *"Let us, therefore, make every effort to enter that rest, so that no one will perish by following their example of disobedience"* (Heb. 4:11).

---

14. John 15:2; James 1:2-4; 1 Pet. 1:6-7

15. Gen. 39-41; Deut. 8:2-14; Ps. 23:4; Dan. 3; Matt. 4:1-11

16. Exod. 15:26; Ps. 18:1-2; 23:1; 103:3

17. Rom. 5:3-5

18. 1 Pet. 5:10

When we question God's every move and refuse to surrender fully, we miss the opportunity to experience His best. Yet, time and again, Scripture reminds us that God knows what He's doing—even when we don't understand.[19] Total dependence on God is not weakness—it's wisdom. He sees the full picture, and nothing is hidden from Him.[20] Yes, the places God leads us through can be daunting—the unknowns, the delays, the pain—but isn't it far better to follow the Good Shepherd,[21] the Way Maker,[22] the Way, and the One who knows the end from the beginning?[23] Job grasped this truth during his suffering. He didn't know when or how his trial would end, but he trusted the One leading him through it and believed that he would emerge purified—like gold refined by fire. *"But he knows where I am going. And when he tests me, I will come out as pure as gold."* (Job 23:10 NLT)

MADE FOR MORE

Sometimes, the noise of life—its busyness, expectations, heartaches, and pressures—can drown out the quiet truth etched into the core of our being: We aren't meant to simply exist or survive. We all yearn for purpose, meaning, and reassurance that our lives matter beyond the daily grind. This longing arises because eternity has been planted in the human heart.[24] We were created on purpose, for a purpose, and it's through fulfilling that divine purpose that we find true joy and satisfaction.

Our identity isn't defined by what we do, what we have, or how others perceive us—it's rooted in the One who made us. He fashioned each of us intentionally, in His image, and for His glory.[25] Your life is not an accident; it's a divine assignment. His purpose for you is woven into your design. Before fear, failure, or falsehoods took hold, the original version of you and me was *very good*.[26] We are fearfully and wonderfully made.[27] But then life happened. Sin entered the world,[28] and with it came pain, distractions, distorted truths, and perhaps deep wounds from broken relationships, betrayal, or disappointment. These things can blur our true identity, making us forget who we really are in Christ. But here's the good news: Jesus came

---

19. Prov. 3:5-6
20. Heb. 4:13
21. John 10:11-16
22. Exod. 14:21-22; Isa. 43:16, 19; John 14:6
23. Isa. 46:10
24. Eccles. 3:11
25. Gen. 1:27; Isa. 43:7
26. Gen. 1:31
27. Ps. 139:14
28. Rom. 5:12

to restore us—to bring us back to God's original blueprint. Through Him, we are made new. *"For we are God's masterpiece. He has created us anew in Christ Jesus, so we can do the good things He planned for us long ago."* (Eph. 2:10 NLT)

Each of us carries a unique blend of personality and God-given gifts and talents that define us. These distinct qualities make us vital parts of the Body of Christ, each with its own special function.[29] Life experiences have molded our uniqueness—both good and bad—shaping our strengths and highlighting areas that need growth. But God doesn't leave us to navigate this alone.

When we yield to the Holy Spirit, He empowers us to overcome our weaknesses. For example, boldness can be channeled to share the gospel, defend what is right, and stand for justice—not to intimidate or dominate others. A tendency to be talkative can serve as a gift of encouragement and a voice of hope rather than a source of gossip, nagging, or belittling others. A critical or analytical mind can discern issues and proffer solutions—not to condemn but to uplift and bring clarity where there's confusion.

As we transition from our old nature to a new life in Christ, we must attune our hearts to hear the voice of Jesus.[30] He teaches us to walk in new ways, gently replacing old patterns with godly habits. He may even lead us into "deep waters"—challenging or unfamiliar territories. However, when we trust God, consistently commit our paths, and allow Him to direct our steps,[31] the results exceed anything we could achieve by doing it our way.[32] No half-measures; no half-baked lives! The God who makes all things new[33] has invited us into a Spirit-empowered life with Him. His thoughts are higher, and His ways are far beyond anything we can imagine.[34]

"Jesus Christ is the same yesterday, today, and forever." (Heb. 13:8) While our world continues to evolve—growing more advanced, fast-paced, and complex—His Word remains constant. God's standards, values, and precepts are not subject to cultural trends, personal preferences, or shifting societal norms. We must align ourselves with His unadulterated truth rather than distorting it to satisfy our appetites, selfish ambitions, lusts, or acts of rebellion. *"I am the LORD, and I do not change…"* (Mal. 3:6 NLT) *"For in him we live and move and have our being…"* (Acts 17:28) He alone is our unchanging anchor in an ever-changing world. No part of God's Word is outdated!

During difficult times, it's tempting to seek quick answers in blog posts, tweets, podcasts, or trending hashtags. While some of these may provide valuable insights, none can compare to the enduring wisdom and power found in Scripture. God's Word is our firm foundation—a

---

29. Matt. 25:14–30; Rom. 12:4–6; 1 Cor. 12: 4–7, 12–14, 27; 1 Pet. 4:10
30. John 10:27
31. Prov. 3:5-6
32. Luke 5:4-6
33. Rev. 21:5
34. Isa. 55:8-9

solid rock for building every aspect of our lives, including marriage, parenting, decision-making, relationships, finances, leadership, identity, and purpose.[35]

To remain steadfast and deeply rooted amid life's storms, we must fully engage with God's Word beyond superficial interactions. A quick dip into Psalms for comfort or a motivational verse from Proverbs may soothe us momentarily, but it isn't enough. We need complete immersion—a deep, continuous exploration of the living waters of Scripture.[36] Only then can we correctly interpret, teach, and apply God's Word with humility, diligence, and reverence—committed to knowing the truth and living it out. It's not about cherry-picking verses to suit our preferences but allowing His Word to prepare and equip us for every good work.[37]

When we are double-minded—wavering, inconsistent, and torn between worldly ideologies and godly principles—it becomes difficult to receive from God or grow spiritually.[38] Nothing compares to God's Word. It is living and active, sharper than any double-edged sword. It exposes our innermost thoughts and desires, bringing conviction, correction, and clarity—not confusion.[39]

Sometimes, we hurriedly make our own independent plans or seek advice from others before turning to God for guidance—first going to the phone instead of the throne! In Isaiah 30:1-2 (NLT), the prophet sharply rebukes the people of Judah for this type of behavior: *"What sorrow awaits my rebellious children," says the Lord. "You make plans that are contrary to mine. You make alliances not directed by my Spirit, thus piling up your sins. For without consulting me, you have gone down to Egypt for help. You have put your trust in Pharaoh's protection. You have tried to hide in his shade."* Their disobedience led them astray, down a path that ultimately resulted in bondage and defeat.

Who's on speed dial as our spiritual "first responder"? Friends? Mentors? Coaches? Therapists? Self-proclaimed gurus? Clerics? Preachers? And whose example are we following in our daily lives? Celebrities? Influencers? Reality show stars? It's important to pause and evaluate these relationships and influences. Who is currently shaping our mindset and decisions? Where are these substitutes leading us? Are their lives rooted in Christ—or the shifting values of the world? What is their testimony? More importantly, what will ours be?

Apostle Paul challenges our motivations in Galatians 1:10: *"For am I now seeking the approval of man, or of God? Or am I trying to please man? If I were still trying to please man, I would not be a servant of Christ."* This highlights what God desires us to remember: not every voice is worthy of our trust unless they are following Christ. Scripture also cautions us in 1 John 4:1:

---

35. Ps. 119:105; Matt. 7:24-27

36. John 17:17; Eph. 5:26

37. 2 Tim. 3:16-17 (NLT)

38. James 1:6–8; 4:8

39. Heb. 4:12

"Beloved, do not believe every spirit, but test the spirits to see whether they are from God, for many false prophets have gone out into the world." We must be discerning—popularity doesn't equal truth, and charisma doesn't equal character.

Our ultimate example is Jesus Christ. He is the only perfect Guide, and our Heavenly Father, has called us to model our lives after Him.[40] God knows the full cost of disobedience and the traps the enemy sets to lure us into sin—that's why He forewarns us. In His mercy, He made a way for us to be reconciled to Him through His salvation plan in Christ. He requires our submission—our willingness to believe and follow Him as He lovingly realigns us with His original design for our lives.[41] God is always more concerned with our character than our comfort. That's why He uses life's circumstances—*the good, bad, and ugly*—to shape us into Christ's image.[42] True rest, the kind that brings peace even in uncertainty, is found not in ease, but in obedience to His Word.[43]

Our brokenness can become a canvas for God's beauty—but only to the extent that we yield to Him. Surrender isn't passive—it calls for trust and cooperation. When we let go of our understanding and allow Him to direct our paths, He leads us in lasting and true ways.[44]

God's intent is not for us to plateau or drift spiritually. His desire is for us to grow—from glory to glory.[45] Yet many have lost focus—entangled by the cares of this world and distracted by comparison, competition, or spiritual complacency.[46] We were never meant to blend in or become lukewarm in our devotion.[47] Jesus gave everything—enduring the cross—for us to live fully awake to His call. When we lose sight of that, we risk becoming less of the *soldier, athlete, farmer, laborer in the vineyard, and fisher of men* He has called us to be.[48]

Some reach a certain point in life and start believing they're self-made—independent of God's hand. "Why change now?" they may ask. "Why surrender control when I've come this far on my own?" But Scripture warns us against relying solely on human strength: *"Cursed is the man who trusts in man and makes flesh his strength ... Blessed is the man who trusts in the Lord ... "* (Jer. 17:5–8). We weren't created to chase our own whims or merely seek comfort. The true purpose of life is to glorify God and enjoy a deep, fulfilling, and eternal relationship with Him.[49]

Destiny is calling! Your God-ordained assignment still awaits you. Beyond past disappointments,

---

40. John 13:15; Eph. 5:1-2; 1 Cor. 11:1; 1 Pet. 2:21; 1 John 2:6
41. Jer. 29:11
42. Heb. 12:10-11
43. Matt. 11:28–30; Heb. 4:9–11
44. Ps. 25:4-5; 86:11; Prov. 3:5–6 (MSG and NLT)
45. 2 Cor. 3:18
46. Luke 8:14; 2 Tim. 2:4
47. Rev. 3:15-16
48. Matt. 4:19; 20:1-16; 25:14–30; 2 Tim. 2:3–6
49. Matt. 22:37; 1 Pet. 4:1–2

heartaches, and delays, there's something greater ahead. Now is the time to rise in faith and embrace it. *"Blessed are those who hunger and thirst for righteousness, for they shall be satisfied."* (Matt. 5:6) This promise isn't just for the "qualified" or "perfect"—it's for the hungry, the willing, the seekers ... those who desire more!

THE MAKING OF A PEARL

I'm constantly in awe of God's intentionality—how He consistently places "signposts" along our paths. During my season of separation from Ségun, I encountered several of these divine markers: timely scriptures, wise counsel, and unexpected moments of insight. One that stood out was a segment on a seemingly "random" TV program about how pearls are formed. That moment still lingers with me—it became a vivid illustration of how God works through discomfort to create something truly remarkable.

Nature itself points us to God and His infinite wisdom.[50] If we pay close attention, even the natural world reflects the spiritual truths of transformation and growth. One such natural treasure and wonder is the pearl—a gem formed inside the soft tissue of a mollusk, such as an oyster or mussel. It develops when an irritant, like a grain of sand or a parasite, gets lodged within the mollusk's shell. In response, the creature secretes a smooth, hard, crystalline substance called nacre—also known as mother-of-pearl—which coats the intruder layer by layer until, over time, a beautiful, luminous gem is formed.

Interestingly, in freshwater pearl farming, an external irritant isn't always necessary—simply cutting into the oyster's soft tissue is enough to begin the pearl-making process. The deeper lesson here is that transformation doesn't always require an obvious wound or offense—such as difficult situations or people who get under one's skin. Sometimes, it's the internal cuts—life's hidden pressures and painful moments—that God uses to reshape us. What matters most is how we respond to life's challenges and what we allow God to do with our pain. Just as the pearl is formed quietly in darkness through discomfort or injury, so are we spiritually changed in the hidden places of struggle. God never wastes pain. Instead, He draws out purpose, purifies us, and reveals Christ in us through it all.[51]

Our divine makeover doesn't begin in comfort but often in disruption. God uses what was meant to harm us as the very substance for promoting self-growth and blessing other lives.[52] Just as the mollusk doesn't reject the irritant but encases it with beauty, God invites us to surrender our pain, let Him work through it, and allow His grace to do the layering—transforming our inner wounds into spiritual gems that glorify Him. Like many God-ordained processes

---

50. Ps. 19:1-4; John 1:3; Rom. 1:20; Col. 1:16

51. 2 Cor. 3:18

52. Gen. 50:20

in creation, the formation of a pearl is unseen and often gradual. But each divine makeover is distinct, and the outcome is priceless, just as yours is designed to be.

A pearl's formation is a powerful illustration of resilience and inner transformation. Just as a pearl begins as an irritant within the oyster, life's hardships can feel uncomfortable, painful, or even unjust. However, when we surrender to God, these difficulties become the very process through which He cultivates beauty, wisdom, grit, and strength in us. A particularly striking detail is the structure of the pearl itself—its coating consists of microscopic crystals that reflect and refract light, giving it its radiant shine. Similarly, as God layers our lives with grace, truth, and transformation through adversity, we begin to reflect His glory.[53] We become lights in a dark world,[54] drawing others to Him through the brilliance of our lives.

When we allow God to tend to and cover our wounds, we don't just survive pain—we heal and emerge in ways we never could have without the refining process. While watching the segment on how pearls are formed that day, I couldn't shake the image of the "nacre" as symbolic of the Word of God. It reminded me that healing begins when we intentionally apply God's Word to the "irritants" in our hearts—those hidden areas where currents of anger, anxiety, bitterness, unforgiveness, or unbelief have swept through and left scars or harmful residues.

Nacre, the precious coating found in mollusks, doesn't stop after the first layer. It continues to envelop the irritant or intruder until a pearl is fully formed. In the same way, when we persist in coating our struggles with Scripture—layer upon layer, the Word grows mightily and prevails.[55] Watching that program helped me to pause and reflect on some fundamental questions: What "pearl-forming" process am I currently experiencing? Am I allowing the love of God to recreate something beautiful from the mess and pressure points in my life? Or am I nurturing "thorns"—bitterness, fear, resentment—that choke the Word and prevent it from bearing fruit in me?[56] God wants to mold us into vessels of purpose in Christ, sons and daughters who radiate His glory, and fulfill the unique purpose He's defined for our lives.[57]

Let's imagine the human heart or mind as the soft tissue of an oyster—sensitive and exposed—where all kinds of intrusions and disruptions can slip in unchecked. These may include unresolved hurts, disappointments, betrayals, or daily frustrations. Without proper protection or healing, they rub against our innermost being, leaving emotional wounds that fester and spread over time. Without the "nacre"—the Word of God—the person has no defenses, no layer of truth or comfort to shield them. They may become irritable, restless, quick to lash out, or withdrawn. Constant agitation becomes the norm, and peace seems out of reach.

---

53. Isa. 61:3
54. Matt. 5:14-16
55. John 1:5; Acts 19:20
56. Matt. 13:22 (NIV)
57. Jer. 29:11; 2 Cor. 5:17

God's Word does far more for us than nacre does for the oyster. Just as it slowly coats an irritant to form a pearl, the Word of God serves as our healing balm and anchor—sanctifying and transforming us from within.[58] This illustrates Christ's ongoing work of purifying His bride—the Church—through the truth of Scripture. As believers, we are that bride,[59] and Christ lovingly washes us clean—layer by layer—removing worldly residue, spiritual impurities, and emotional clutter. Without it, we're left trying to self-soothe with temporary fixes: avoidance, addictions, busyness, or empty affirmations. These options may seem helpful at first, but they sometimes trigger frustrations, deeper issues, harmful patterns, or toxic responses—like a venomous defense mechanism that spills over into our relationships and decisions.

Scripture reminds us, *"Above all else, guard your heart, for everything you do flows from it"* (Prov. 4:23 NIV). The heart is the wellspring of life—it holds our thoughts, emotions, and intentions. What we allow into it—be it truth or lies, peace or chaos—determines how we think, feel, respond, and ultimately, who we become. If our hearts are filled with God's truth, our lives will exude the fruit of the Spirit—showing that even the most painful intrusions can, through surrender, become the very material God uses to form something even more precious than the pearl in our lives.

JEWEL OR JUNK?

Just as receiving the gift of salvation through faith in Jesus Christ is a personal choice,[60] pursuing holiness and living a life set apart for God is also intentional. It doesn't happen by default. God calls every believer to live in a way that reflects His character—resisting sin, rejecting falsehood, and shining as lights in a dark world.[61] However, transformation only occurs when we let go of our own desires and allow God's truth to permeate and work in our lives. As we yield, the Word does its refining work, helping us become *"vessels for honor, sanctified and useful to the Master, prepared for every good work"* (2 Tim. 2:20-21).

We all know that jewels are treasures, but using "junk" as a contrast may seem harsh when describing our best efforts or righteousness before a holy God.[62] Yet in Philippians 3:7-8, Apostle Paul boldly calls everything in life "garbage" compared to the surpassing worth of knowing Christ. Junk refers to items regarded as having little or no value, quality, or relevance—often outdated, discarded, or no longer useful.

In God's eyes, we are not junk. However, whether or not we become jewels depends on

---

58. Ps. 107:20; Eph. 5:26
59. Rev. 19:7-8
60. Eph. 2:8-9
61. Phil. 2:15; Heb. 12:1-2
62. Phil. 3:3-9

our response to Him. Are we allowing God to polish and shape us into precious, enduring jewels? Or are we resisting His touch, settling into patterns that diminish our worth and usefulness? What are we putting on or into ourselves? Are we filling our lives with superficial fillers that mask the deeper longing only God can satisfy? Are we filling our hearts and minds with beliefs, habits, mindsets, or influences that unknowingly hinder our spiritual growth?[63] Sometimes, these are the things we hold onto—like toxic thoughts, lies we've believed, negative habits, or behavior patterns. They might not seem significant initially, but they cloud the heart over time and stifle transformation.

In Isaiah 64:6, the phrase "filthy rags" is a sobering metaphor that describes human righteousness as impure and inadequate before God. The original Hebrew term points to something unclean or defiled, emphasizing that even our best efforts—apart from God—fall drastically short of His holiness. *Rags* typically refer to old, torn, or worn-out pieces of cloth. God invites sinners to come just as they are, but true sons and daughters do not remain as they were. Instead, they are being transformed into the image of Jesus Christ with ever-increasing glory[64]—through God's perfecting and sustaining grace. Although God loves all His children and sees each one through the eyes of mercy and compassion, He also expects growth—not only in spiritual maturity, but also in usefulness, fruitfulness, purpose, and impact[65]—all through faith in Christ.[66]

Another powerful comparison to a treasure is found in 2 Corinthians 4:7: *"But we have this treasure in earthen vessels, that the excellence of the power may be of God and not of us."* The "treasure" here refers to the glorious gospel—the message of Christ's salvation and the revelation of God's glory through Jesus, who is the Treasure Chest—the Source and Keeper of all wisdom and knowledge.[67] We have more than enough when we have Jesus. In Psalm 63:1-3, David declares that God's love and presence are better than life itself, and that knowing Him brings a satisfaction that nothing else can offer.

Apostle Paul also uses the comparison of a *great house* in 2 Timothy 2:20-21 to describe the Church or God's Kingdom. The vessels—containers or instruments—represent believers. Some vessels, like gold and silver, are used for noble or honorable purposes, while others, like wood and clay, are used for common or dishonorable ones. The distinction here is not about material value, but about spiritual usefulness. These verses emphasize the different kinds of vessels and their purpose in God.

In Paul's time, clay jars were inexpensive, fragile, and unremarkable; yet, they were often used to hold items of great value—such as hidden treasures or precious substances. *"Earthen*

---

63. Eph. 5:8-10
64. 2 Cor. 3:18
65. Eph. 2:10; Col. 1:10; Heb. 5:12-14; 2 Pet. 3:18
66. Phil. 3:9
67. Col. 2:3

vessels" symbolize our frail human nature: weak, imperfect, and easily broken. The contrast in 2 Corinthians 4:7 highlights the fact that the power comes from God, not us. It's not about our abilities, strength, or status, but about God working through us—despite our weaknesses. Our brokenness doesn't disqualify us; we may feel unworthy or inadequate, but God displays His power through our human limitations.[68]

Titus 3:5 (NIV) reminds us that *"He saved us, not because of righteous things we had done, but because of his mercy—through the washing of rebirth and renewal by the Holy Spirit."* We are valuable to God not because of our perfection but because of His purpose and love. He places immense worth on His children.[69] Throughout Scripture, God's people, His wisdom, and the Kingdom of Heaven are described as His treasured possessions, likened to jewels.[70]

2 Corinthians 4:7 is a call to humility and dependence on God. It also reminds us of the need to extend grace to others when they fall short of our expectations, just as we rely on God's strength in our own weakness. Our expectations of others—spouses, children, in-laws, friends, and co-workers—are often unrealistically high and inevitably lead to disappointment. Only God is perfect and fully able to meet our deepest needs. We find true hope, love, peace, joy, purpose, and the satisfaction of our hearts' desires in Him alone. We are all a work in progress.

Marriage is one of God's refining tools. Proverbs 18:22 (NLT) describes the immense value of a godly wife: *"The man who finds a good wife finds a treasure, and he receives favor from the Lord."* A good wife is a precious and rare gift—her presence in a man's life signifies God's blessing. A healthy, loving marriage—especially with a wise and godly partner—is part of God's favor and provision. Contrary to some beliefs, marriage isn't merely a social or romantic arrangement or simply about happiness or identity. At its core, it's a spiritual blessing—designed by God to shape and refine the couple, reflecting His covenant love.

A Christ-centered marriage also reflects God's sanctifying love for His Church. *"Husbands, love your wives, just as Christ loved the church and gave himself up for her to make her holy..."* (Eph. 5:25-27) This process of sanctification is a divine makeover that changes us into radiant reflections of our Bridegroom. And one day, we will give an account—not just of what we believed, but of how we lived and how our lives pointed others to Christ.[71]

Spouses often serve as each other's most consistent sharpening agents—especially in areas such as patience, forgiveness, and unconditional love. Marriage may not always be pleasant or problem-free, but a husband and wife are called to be trusted companions who speak the truth in love. Challenges within a marriage can serve as a divine testing ground for spiritual growth and maturity. *"As iron sharpens iron, so one person sharpens another."* (Prov. 27:17)

---

68. 2 Cor. 2:15; Phil. 4:18

69. Ps. 139:14; Isa. 43:4 (AMP); 1 Pet. 2:9

70. Prov. 3:15; 18:22 (NLT); Isa. 62:3; Mal. 3:17; Matt. 13:45-46

71. Rom. 14:12

Iron is sharpened through contact with iron—an intentional friction that refines, restores, and strengthens. Similarly, spouses undergo growth phases where imperfect or messy parts are exposed, acknowledged, and addressed through honest conversations, constructive feedback, and mutual accountability. A strong, godly marriage builds character, cultivates wisdom, and nurtures maturity in faith, knowledge, and purpose.

"For everyone will be tested with fire. Salt is good for seasoning. But if it loses its flavor, how do you make it salty again? You must have the qualities of salt among yourselves and live in peace with each other" (Mark 9:49-50 NLT). In Matthew 5:13-16, Jesus calls His followers the salt and light of the world. As salt, we preserve what is good and bring godly influence to the world. However, if we lose our "flavor"—our distinctiveness and impact—we lose our usefulness. Living in peace with one another, especially in marriage, requires us to remain spiritually "salty": grounded in truth, seasoned with grace, and surrendered to God's refining work.

We are meant to shine brightly amid gross darkness—like a city on a hill that cannot be hidden.[72] Just as no one lights a lamp only to cover it with a basket, our lives aren't meant to be concealed. Instead, our light should be visible and purposeful, like a lamp on a stand to brighten an entire room. In the same way, God's goodness in our lives should radiate through our actions, so others may see and be drawn to honor and glorify our Heavenly Father.[73] Light illuminates, brings clarity, and shows the way. When we walk in His light, we become beacons of hope in a dark world.

UNLEARN TO RELEARN

Everything I've encountered and experienced thus far in life has been significant and used by God to mold and build me into who I am today. Nothing has been wasted. I'm still on a journey of becoming, and God isn't finished with me yet. He's been with me every step of the way, even when I didn't feel His presence, especially in the seasons when I chose to go my own way. Looking back, I realize how often I was blindsided simply because I wasn't paying attention to what He was doing around me. God allowed me to experience certain situations and interact with specific people, not to harm me, but to gain wisdom, learn deeper truths, and become more aligned with His purpose for my life.

God sees the end from the beginning and knows exactly what we need to change to become who He designed us to be. He has promised never to leave nor forsake us, and He often reveals His presence through people and circumstances, speaking to us each day—sometimes in a still, small voice. But we must stay attentive to the signposts—those divine instructions and nudges that redirect our focus back to Him. God can use anything—situations, conversations, even

---

72. Matt. 5:14

73. Isa. 60:1-3; Matt. 5:15-16

interruptions—to get our attention. There are teaching moments around us if we're willing to see them.

Not every undesired thing that happens is coming *at* you or *against* you. Yes, God corrects and disciplines those He loves.[74] Even in times of adversity, God works through those situations—not as punishment, but as part of His redemptive plan.[75] With hindsight, I now recognize moments—especially during my toughest seasons—when I missed opportunities to learn, grow, or listen more closely. Yet, even in those times, He was—and remains—merciful.

For instance, while I was pregnant with our two sons, I had to be away from home for a few months each time to access better medical care. During those times, I stayed in the homes of Christian families—homes rich with love and godly example. God is intentional, and nothing with Him is ever happenstance. This was within the first five years of our marriage when Ségun and I faced some of our most intense challenges. I now realize how much I could have benefited from sound advice and mentorship if I had opened up to the older couples I spent time with. However, at that time, I didn't recognize the opportunity. It wasn't until after our breakup that God used two amazing aunts from those same families as strong pillars of support—and I'm grateful they continue to walk with me to this day.[76]

In addition, I've had the immense privilege of having a couple of outstanding mentoring mother figures—childhood friends of my late mother—standing firmly by my side and offering loving counsel since her passing. Truly, Solomon was right: *"Where there is no [wise, intelligent] guidance, the people fall [and go off course like a ship without a helm], but in the abundance of [wise and godly] counselors there is victory"* (Prov. 11:14 AMP).

God intentionally places us in communities—families, friendships, churches, and other circles of influence—for support, growth, and mutual strengthening. Don't isolate yourself in an attempt to avoid the "irons" or "sandpapers." The truth is, growth often happens in uncomfortable spaces. *"To learn the truth you must long to be teachable, or you can despise correction and remain ignorant."* (Prov. 12:1 TPT) God never intended for you to fight your battles or navigate life alone. He called you to be part of a strong, healthy, vibrant, and growing community—the Body of Christ. None of us is perfect, but together, we can stand firm in truth and persevere through every trial with grace and strength.

Some people only listen to their own voice or seek counsel that aligns with their desires, rejecting anything that challenges or convicts them. But the Word of God warns: *"What sorrow awaits those who try to hide their plans from the Lord, who do their evil deeds in the dark! 'The Lord can't see us,' they say. 'He doesn't know what's going on!' How foolish can you be? He is the Potter,*

---

74. Heb. 12:6

75. Lam. 3:33; James 1:13

76. Titus 2:3-5

and he is certainly greater than you, the clay! Should the created thing say of the one who made it, 'He didn't make me?' Does a jar ever say, 'The potter who made me is stupid?'" (Isa. 29:15–16 NLT).

A real spiritual makeover, though internal, should be visible in how we treat others—not just the people we like or those who treat us well, but everyone. We're called to live in a way that reflects our new life in Christ and demonstrates that we belong to Him. Stripping off our old self and "putting on" godly character means intentionally embracing and expressing virtues like compassion (tenderhearted mercy), kindness, humility, gentleness, patience, and forgiveness in our daily lives and relationships.

Jesus went about doing good—actively demonstrating God's love through kindness, healing, and deliverance throughout His earthly ministry.[77] In the parable of the Good Samaritan (Luke 10:25-37), He teaches that love for our neighbor isn't based on proximity, race, or religion—it's about compassion in action. He calls us to show mercy and kindness just like the Samaritan did. In verse 37, Jesus said, *"You go, and do likewise."* We grow in Christ by following His example of understanding the pain of others, their weaknesses, and struggles.[78] Jesus understands us—He knows what it's like to feel physical pain, hunger, grief, rejection, and temptation. Compassion isn't just sympathy; it's empathy. It means sharing someone else's pain and responding as if it were our own.

The Holy Spirit helps us to steward our pain wisely—not as a weapon to lash out, but as a tool in God's hands to bring comfort to others and reveal His redemptive power through our healing.[79] Every pain prompts us to make a choice, and every trial holds an opportunity. The hardships we face can turn us inward in self-pity, or outward in mercy. They can make us victims—or merciful victors—as we overcome through Christ.[80] Compassion isn't our natural response, but God calls us to a higher way. He's not asking us to be super-human, but rather to be more Spirit-filled so we can exude Christ even in adversity.

Just like physical makeovers require proper, age-appropriate nutrition and exercise for the body to grow and thrive, spiritual renewal also calls for the right nourishment and discipline for both soul and spirit. In 1 Corinthians 3:2-3, the metaphor of spiritual food—*milk* versus *solid food*—illustrates different stages of spiritual maturity. This scripture reminds us that spiritual growth should reflect how we live and relate to others, not just how much Scripture we know. Paul addressed the Corinthians for their lack of maturity. Despite their access to the Word and the Spirit, they were still driven by jealousy, strife, and division—worldly behaviors that revealed their spiritual stagnation. He said he had to feed them "milk" (the basic teachings of the faith) because they weren't ready for "solid food" (the deeper truths and insights that come with maturity).

---

77. Acts 10:38
78. Isa. 53:3-4; Heb. 4:15
79. Gen. 50:20; Isa. 61:1-3; 2 Cor. 1:3-4
80. Gal. 6:2

Similarly, Hebrews 5:11-14 rebukes the believers for their spiritual sluggishness, pointing out that they ought to have been teaching others by then, but instead, they still needed to be taught the foundational truths all over again. They hadn't grown in discernment or depth, even though they'd had the time and exposure to do so. These reproofs aren't meant to shame us but to awaken us. They represent a call to leave behind spiritual infancy and grow in discernment, understanding, and the capacity to lead and disciple others. Maturity in Christ goes beyond knowledge; it's measured by obedience, consistency, and fruitfulness. It's about practicing the Word—not just hearing it.

MIND MAKEOVER IN MOTION

God continued to melt my heart—the more I read His Word, the more I got to know Him, His unimaginable love, and His plans for me. I was strengthened by God's power to do what He required of me.[81] One significant step I took during this period was resetting some boundaries between Ségun and me. Our interactions often stirred intense reactions and emotions, so I limited phone calls and physical contact. Instead, I chose to communicate mainly through texts and emails, which allowed me to be more thoughtful and prayerful in my responses. I made sure to lace each message with Scripture—declaring God's promises, offering encouragement, and sending prophetic prayers. I didn't know then what kind of fruit these "seeds" would bear; all I knew was that they would not fall to the ground and wither away.[82]

In this seemingly simple act of obedience to the Holy Spirit's leading, something was also happening in me. I was letting go—surrendering my desires, pride, and comfort. I was *dying to self*.[83] Sometimes, what we lay down or lose for God's sake becomes what He uses to produce something far greater in and through us. This unconventional step I took regarding my communications with Ségun—one that felt counterintuitive at the time—proved to be one of the best decisions I ever made.[84]

Unbeknownst to me, I was planting seeds of life in the hard places God had already gone ahead to till in preparation for harvest. I began to see the tangible fruits of God's Word in my life—and others started to notice and testify to this as well.[85] I had fallen in love again with Jesus. It felt like I was *born again, again*—fresh, exciting, and all-consuming. All I wanted to do was share this joy with everyone around me.[86] Soon enough, I began to experience an

---

81. Josh. 1:8
82. 1 Cor. 15:36-41
83. Matt. 16:24; Luke 9:23-24; Rom. 6:6; 7:6; Col. 3:3
84. Isa. 55:8-9
85. Luke 6:43-45
86. Eph. 5:19; Col. 3:10, 16

all-around turnaround—a kind of favor and peace that only happens when our focus shifts from ourselves to God—when we live to please Him above all else.[87]

> *"What a God we have! And how fortunate we are to have him, this Father of our Master Jesus! Because Jesus was raised from the dead, we've been given a brand-new life and have everything to live for, including a future in heaven—and the future starts now! God is keeping careful watch over us and the future. The Day is coming when you'll have it all—life healed and whole.*
>
> *I know how great this makes you feel, even though you have to put up with every kind of aggravation in the meantime. Pure gold put in the fire comes out of it proved pure; genuine faith put through this suffering comes out proved genuine. When Jesus wraps this all up, it's your faith, not your gold, that God will have on display as evidence of his victory.*
>
> *You never saw him, yet you love him. You still don't see him, yet you trust him—with laughter and singing. Because you kept on believing, you'll get what you're looking forward to: total salvation."* (1 Pet. 1:3-9 MSG)

THROUGH SÉGUN'S LENSES

Coming to terms with the fact that I was becoming increasingly unsure of which way to turn in terms of my family's future was a rude awakening. Until then, I had been confidently operating on the basis that I would figure everything out as time went by, but that turned out not to be the case.

I really missed my children and wanted nothing more than to be permanently reunited with them. However, I still could not see any path toward reconciliation for Funké and me.

There was no escaping the crushing sense of guilt that my actions had put two wonderful little boys in the middle of a crisis they had nothing to do with. At the same time, I could not help thinking that they might have felt responsible for their parents living apart. This added greatly to the feeling that I had let them down.

Around the same time, things had suddenly started to unravel on the business front, which increased my uncertainty. This was fueled by some vivid dreams, including one

---

87. Prov. 16:7

where I was the prodigal son described in the Bible in Luke Chapter 15. The fact that I remembered the dream at all was uncharacteristic for me, and the subject of the dream made it particularly poignant.

After successfully completing a pilot training program for a Nigerian government agency, I received the agency's in-principle nod for a nationwide rollout of the program. We agreed that, at the next board meeting, a resolution would be passed to approve the national rollout. Taking this as a fait accompli and having worked relentlessly on the pilot program for close to three months, I decided to take a short break in the United Kingdom.

Imagine my shock when, a few days into my arrival in London, I learned that the entire board of the government agency had been dissolved during a television news bulletin announcement. The new agency head placed a blanket ban on any new contracts, eventually throwing out my project, which never saw the light of day. Despite the huge social impact the project would have had nationwide, the consolation is that I would almost certainly not be married to Funké today had it gone ahead, as I had already filed for divorce and was in a serious relationship. This "hand of God" prevented the trajectory of so many lives from being forever altered.

Rearview Mirror Lesson

It was much later, after this difficult period, that I learned firsthand how some people truly need to experience adversity for God to get their attention. The fact that I was busy with work and things had been going well on the business front turned my attention even further away from considering the possibility of reconciling with Funké.

I was completely blindsided by the abrupt cancellation of my project. The experience began the process of stripping me of various forms of shortsightedness, selfishness, and pride, which interfere with the Holy Spirit's ability to do His transformative work within us.

Before the storm settled...
and after restoration

2006—wandering through dry sands.

2013—finally settled in sweet lands.

16

Waiting Well

MY JOURNEY FROM DRY SANDS[1] TO SWEET LANDS[2] WAS PAVED BY GRACE.

"I waited patiently and expectantly for the Lord; And He inclined to me and heard my cry. He brought me up out of a horrible pit [of tumult and of destruction], out of the miry clay, And He set my feet upon a rock, steadying my footsteps and establishing my path. He put a new song in my mouth, a song of praise to our God; Many will see and fear [with great reverence] And will trust confidently in the Lord." (Ps. 40:1-3 AMP)

This scripture captures the heart of what it means to *wait well*. God doesn't ignore our cries or abandon us in the dark. He hears, He lifts, He steadies—and ultimately, He renews. However, amid hardship or uncertainty, it's easy to forget that the season we're in has an expiration date and will give way to another. One of the most valuable facts I've learned—often through pain—is that trials are temporary.[3]

---

1. Deut. 8:2; Hosea 2:14-16

2. Ps. 23:5-6; 34:8-9; 126:5-6; John 10:10; 1 Pet. 5:10

3. Ps. 30:5; Rom 8:18; 2 Cor. 4:17; 1 Pet. 5:10

If there's one takeaway I want you to hold on to, it's this: *This too shall pass.* I wish some-one had instilled this truth in me more deeply, with greater clarity and conviction—anchored in Scripture and layered with lived experience—when I felt overwhelmed by pain. Perhaps I would have handled our separation journey (and marriage) differently! Instead, I was so fix-ated on the storm that I missed the pocket of supernatural peace and protection in its eye.[4] God was there all along, but I was too focused on the waves to see the Rock beneath me. So, I kept circling the same mountains, getting stuck in prolonged delays and avoidable suffering.

Waiting well also means recognizing that the weight of our struggles can burden our bod-ies and minds. I learned the hard way that trauma—those deeply distressing experiences that overwhelm a person's natural ability to cope—may not fade over time. Trauma can linger and hide in the background, eventually manifesting as exhaustion, chronic symptoms, mood swings, or even changes in our physical appearance. Unhealed soul wounds express themselves in ways we may not immediately associate with their source. But even here, God is our healer. *"He heals the brokenhearted and binds up their wounds."* (Ps. 147:3)

For many years, I lived in survival mode. The emotional, mental, and physical toll of our mari-tal crisis—and eventual separation—left deep imprints. I had internalized so much pain that it qui-etly, but noticeably, reshaped who I was. Looking through old photos while preparing this chapter was a sobering experience. I barely recognized the woman in them—gaunt, frail, and hollow. My frame had shrunk so drastically that a favorite bespoke outfit I'd had made a year after our sepa-ration hung loosely on me until seven years later, when it finally fit me perfectly again! I couldn't eat or sleep. I felt extremely unattractive, like a mere shell of my former self. That's what unpro-cessed pain can do: It drains you and distorts both self-perception and how you relate to others.

By the time I reached the proverbial "darkest hour before dawn," I felt emotionally drained and spiritually worn out. Before I discovered the roadmap to navigate the latter part of this journey effectively and truly surrender to God, my chosen path to healing had become more performative than substantive. I had developed an addiction to long, aimless fasts—not always out of faith or devotion, but from frustration. My coping mechanism now involved self-indul-gent prayers[5] stemming from desperation, giving, and serving in the hope of earning wholeness. God never asked for performance or self-punishment—He asked for surrender. And in that quiet place of letting go, He gently reminded me: *You are made for more.* More than merely surviving. More than shrinking into the shadows of my former self.

We all experience seasons of waiting, but how we wait determines what we gain from the process. Purposeful waiting involves being hopeful while seeking God's will and entrusting our lives to His love—even when we don't understand His timing. It requires us to refuse to let a pause become a permanent stop or detour, or to trigger a cycle of delay. The problem

---

4. Isa. 26:3; Ps. 46:1-3; Mark 4:39; Phil. 4:7

5. James 4:3

isn't having dreams or desires; rather, it arises when, due to our impatience, we try to control outcomes or insist on things that may not align with God's will. Many waste valuable time or even their entire lives in this futile endeavor! This is why we must invite the Holy Spirit (the Spirit of discernment) to help us recognize when God is speaking, moving, or redirecting us—especially when the road ahead is unclear.[6]

Challenges—trials, difficulties, and unexpected interruptions—are often God's way of getting our attention. While not all hardships are sent by God or meant as punishment, they can be His gentle (and sometimes not-so-gentle) invitation to draw us closer, realign our priorities, or remind us of His sufficiency. In His mercy, God sometimes allows disruption—not to crush us, but to awaken us spiritually or rescue us from distraction, sin, or misplaced trust.

During those difficult seasons, many of us come to know God in ways we hadn't before—not just as Savior, but as Father, Redeemer, Deliverer, Provider, Restorer, Healer, Comforter, Vindicator, Righteous Judge, and so much more. These aren't just names we read in Scripture—they become real, personal, and deeply transformative when we yield to Him in the waiting. Like the psalmist, Jonah, and Paul, we discover that affliction can lead us back to God (Ps. 119:67; Jonah 2; 2 Cor. 12:7–10), that His discipline is a sign of His love (Heb. 12:7), and that He is always ready to heal and restore when we return to Him (Hosea 6:1). Joseph's story echoes this truth: God can turn even the direst circumstances around for good and for His divine purpose. His long ordeal in Egypt ended with a powerful realization—God had been at work all along, guiding, positioning, and ultimately redeeming it all for good (Gen. 45:7; 50:20).

Our lives are not defined by a single unresolved issue, an unanswered prayer request, or a prolonged trial. God's incomparable love, extraordinary kindness, and purpose extend far beyond any temporary hardship we may encounter.[7] Yet, when we become consumed by pain, we risk missing what God wants to teach and produce in us through it. Those dark, lonely seasons often hold treasures—invaluable lessons that shape our character, strengthen our faith, and equip us to help others. If we remain open, those experiences can refine us into the likeness of Christ, bringing glory to God.

Personally, it took hitting rock bottom for me to enter God's "waiting room." My dreams crumbled, and my carefully laid plans unraveled; I had exhausted every effort to fix things on my own. Isn't that often the case? We rarely pause or seek stillness when life unfolds according to our expectations, and everything seems to fall perfectly into place. Yet Lamentations 3:25 reminds us that ... *"The LORD is good to those who wait for him, to the soul who seeks him."* In the discomfort of delay, God often reveals His strength most clearly.[8]

God does not orchestrate evil but allows the shaking of our comfort zones for a divine

---

6. Ps. 32:8

7. Rom. 8:35-39

8. 2 Cor. 12:9

purpose. Much of the hardship we experience comes from poor choices, granting access to the devil and his cohorts, or the brokenness of this fallen world. Yet God, in His mercy, steps into our mess and redeems it—if we let Him.[9] He specializes in turning mourning into dancing and trials into testimonies.

Waiting well is both a spiritual discipline and a sign of emotional maturity. It's not about keeping up appearances in a strained marriage, enduring pressure from family or society, or passively suffering in silence. It's not about marking time—instead, it's about how we position ourselves during seasons of transition. The Bible teaches that what we do during the *wait* matters. Growth, strength, and breakthrough are often the result of our response to delay and difficulty—not just the passage of time itself, but the faith-filled, obedient, and patient attitude we choose along the way.[10]

The key to overcoming life's trials lies in our posture when God says, "Be still." We see this in Joseph, who waited *faithfully* in prison while serving others, until God promoted him.[11] David, though anointed king as a youth, *endured* years of persecution and wilderness trials while fleeing Saul for many years before taking the throne. He waited *patiently* and *trusted* God's timing.[12] Even Jesus waited thirty years, growing in wisdom and stature, before beginning His public ministry.[13] These are the paths and examples we are encouraged to follow, not shortcuts and quick fixes.[14] Divine waiting is never wasted time—it's preparing us for what's ahead.

Nothing catches God off guard. He's never unaware of our circumstances or at a loss about how to help us! Sometimes, we often wrongly attribute delays in our breakthroughs to others—whether family, friends, or even perceived enemies. However, we must be willing to examine ourselves honestly to see how we've contributed to our situations. More often than not, we find ourselves lying in the beds we've made, or those we've allowed others to make for us. True freedom and restoration begin when we stop striving in our own strength and hand the reins back to God. His wisdom far exceeds ours,[15] and He desires full, not partial, obedience in every area of our lives.[16] God has an eternal perspective that includes our children. Our decisions don't just affect us; they ripple into future generations. So, it's crucial to rest in God's plan for their sake and ours, walk in His ways,[17] and commit to faithfully staying on the path He's set before us.

---

9. Ps. 126:1-3

10. Isa. 40:31; Rom. 8:25; James 1:2-4

11. Gen. 39:20-23; 40:14, 23; 41:1, 14

12. 1 Sam. 16:13; 19–30; 2 Sam. 2:4

13. Luke 2:42-52; 3:21-23; 4:1-13

14. Heb. 6:11-12, 15

15. Prov. 3:5-6

16. Prov. 4:10-13

17. Ps. 17:4-5

We often find ourselves weary during seasons of divine preparation—not necessarily because God's process is too difficult, but because we overextend ourselves in trying to accomplish what only He can do. Isaiah 43:1-2 reminds us that it is God who saves and keeps us. Yet many of us take on more than we are meant to carry, often believing—subconsciously—that if we don't hold everything together (our marriage, family, work, life), it will all fall apart. However, Colossians 1:17 clearly states: *"In Him all things hold together,"* not in us.

This burden often weighs heaviest on women. In many homes, it is the wives who attend church services and prayer meetings and consistently intercede for their spouses and children. They remain spiritually alert, discerning attacks and waging war in prayer. While these actions are noble and necessary, the imbalance can be draining when the effort is one-sided. Marriage is meant to be a partnership—spiritually, emotionally, and practically. When one partner feels solely responsible for carrying the family burdens to God, or when spiritual roles are reversed, resentment can quietly grow, especially if their spouse seems passive or indifferent.

This is part of the enemy's strategy: to wear us out, frustrate our faith, and discredit our testimony as children of God. Sadly, "for the sake of the children," many have remained in difficult marriages without a clear word from God or a plan—hoping that things will change for the better. However, waiting without direction can cause more harm than good. This often creates emotional scars, deep disappointment, and lost years, instead of transformation. That's not God's will. Stories like these have left many observers disillusioned, skeptical, cautious, or afraid to trust such decisions again. Some even blame God!

Our journeys aren't identical. Destinies and paths differ, and some people succeed in situations where others struggle. Seek God, and faithfully follow His direction to your own provision, promise, and purpose. In Genesis 26, the story of Isaac offers a powerful illustration of perseverance and thriving in the face of resistance. He obeyed God's instruction to stay in Gerar, where there was a famine, instead of fleeing to Egypt. It made no sense, but he reopened the wells his father Abraham had dug—wells the Philistines had blocked out of envy. Every attempt to reclaim those wells was met with conflict at Esek and Sitnah.

Despite facing repeated opposition, Isaac didn't fight back; he moved forward and continued digging until he reached a point where the conflict ended. He named the place Rehoboth, declaring, *"For now the Lord has made room for us, and we shall be fruitful in the land"* (Gen. 26:22). Isaac succeeded where others might have given up—he pressed on in faith, re-dug what had been obstructed, and was led into a spacious and prosperous land. His story reminds us that success or breakthrough often comes not from striving in our own strength or wisdom, but from steadfast obedience, quiet resilience, and knowing when to remain or push forward as God leads.[18] The waiting season often involves conflict, resistance, and emotional weariness.

---

18. Gen. 26:2-3, 12-13

282 • Trilogy Refining Decisions

But when we follow God's direction instead of our own assumptions or cultural pressures, we find the strength to endure and the clarity to take the next right step.

Regardless of our challenges, maintaining a connection with God and aligning with His timing remains vital. Even when situations seem dire or we encounter disappointment, we must stay steadfast in our faith. Galatians 6:9 reminds us, *"Let us not grow weary in doing good, for at the proper time we will reap a harvest if we do not give up."* Many people complain or give up too soon—not because God didn't show up, but due to a lack of perseverance before the breakthrough. With God, the process is just as important as the promise. He prioritizes who we are becoming over what we are waiting for.[19]

The discipline and practices we cultivate during hidden seasons—prayer, studying the Word of God, and obedience—prepare us for the visible victories ahead. Waiting isn't wasted time when we engage with it intentionally. Psalm 27:14 encourages us: *"Wait for the Lord; be strong, and let your heart take courage; wait for the Lord!"* Through my own journey, I discovered thirteen biblically rooted, actionable principles that refined, strengthened, and prepared me, helping me persevere and thrive in seasons of uncertainty.

Numerous books and opinions exist on topics such as faith, forgiveness, prayer, and others. I'm simply adding my voice—not as an authority but as a fellow traveler, someone who has wrestled with doubt, waited in silence, and learned to rely on God's Word amid real-life trials. My perspective is shaped by experience and anchored in Scripture—not to pontificate from a pedestal, but to walk alongside you. More like a friend saying, "Hey, I've been there too, and here's what helped me through."

Think of these spiritual principles as function keys on a keyboard—each "F" representing a Kingdom key, rooted in Scripture, that unlocks God's promises, gives access to spiritual breakthroughs, insight, clarity, or strength for the journey ahead, and alignment with God's will. These "13 Fs" aren't passive postures but active choices—tools that help us grow stronger, not bitter; focused, not frantic; and faithful, not faint-hearted in the face of delay or uncertainty.

13 Fs FOR WAITING WELL: USING FUNCTION KEYS OF FAITH IN DELAY

1. Faithful facilitator:

Seasons of waiting often stir up fear, worry, despair, and at times, a fragile hope that clings to the possibility of change. Now more than ever, we need wisdom and strength to trust the Holy Spirit as our faithful Guide. He isn't just present—He's active: strengthening our hearts

---

19. Rom. 5:3-5

when patience wears thin and reminding us of God's promises when doubt tries to take root.[20] Even when we don't know what to pray, the Holy Spirit intercedes on our behalf, aligning our groanings with the will of God.[21] As we yield to Him, He works in us to produce lasting fruit—perseverance, character, and renewed hope.[22] Waiting well isn't passive resignation; it's purposeful trust. The Holy Spirit empowers us to remain anchored in God's unchanging faithfulness, steadily guiding us toward deeper surrender.[23]

But God also works through people—His support team for our journey. Trusted advisers, counselors, mentors, and Spirit-led coaches often serve as tangible extensions of His wisdom and love. These Christ-centered companions help bridge troubled waters, provide encouragement when we are weary, and walk alongside us during seasons of healing, self-discovery, and preparation for purpose. Be prayerful and intentional about finding the right support—a certified professional, a spiritual mentor, or someone who has walked a similar path and is willing to share their story, strategies, and insights. Sometimes, what you need most is someone who can simply point you in the right direction.[24]

As 1 Corinthians 12:6-8 (MSG) beautifully illustrates, *"God's various expressions of power are in action everywhere; but God himself is behind it all... Each person is given something to do that shows who God is: Everyone gets in on it, everyone benefits."* Whether through gifts of wisdom, healing, faith, or discernment, God equips His people to support one another—especially during times of waiting.

2. Focused, vision-led living:

In moments of divine instruction, God asked prophets like Jeremiah, Amos, and Zechariah a simple yet powerful question: *What do you see?*[25] This wasn't a casual inquiry—it was a spiritual prompt, an invitation to look beyond the natural and discern what God was revealing about His plans. During seasons of waiting or uncertainty, God often shifts our perspective, calling us to see through the lens of faith rather than fear or frustration.

When delays arise or circumstances seem stagnant, it's easy to focus on what's lacking. But God redirects our gaze and asks, *What do you see?*—not with physical eyes, but with spiritual insight—a faith-filled vision. Waiting well requires us to perceive not only our current position, but also where God is leading us. Vision often precedes fulfillment. That's why those lacking

---

20. John 14:26
21. Rom. 8:26-27
22. Rom. 5:3-5
23. John 16:13
24. 1 Cor. 12:4-11 (MSG)
25. Jer. 1:11, Amos 7:8, Zech. 4:2

spiritual sight or divine insight may wander aimlessly—relying solely on physical senses or instincts, reacting to life instead of seeking God's guidance.

God's question is more than a test of awareness; it's a call to discernment and surrender. He isn't testing our eyesight—He's awakening our vision and aligning it with His purposes. Our faith and reliance on the Holy Spirit help us recognize what God is doing—even when it's not yet fully visible. Waiting becomes purposeful when we ask God to open our eyes to His plans and prepare our hearts to receive His promises, before they unfold.[26]

Living with focused, vision-led clarity—especially during periods of marital strain or other circumstances that create doubt and confusion—requires a deep commitment to God. It involves persevering with unwavering trust, even when the path is difficult to discern. James reminds us that *a double-minded person is unstable in all they do*" (James 1:6-8). True focus demands single-hearted devotion to God.

Feelings or distractions don't drive this kind of intentional living; instead, it's anchored in faith rooted in God's Word. Jesus taught that effective faith is unwavering,[27] and Scripture urges us to keep our eyes fixed—on purpose, not pressure.[28] When we set our hearts on God's direction, we wait not with anxiety, but with assurance.

Isaiah 40:31 promises that those who hope, trust, and wait on the Lord—not on circumstances, people, or outcomes—will find renewed strength. They will soar on wings like eagles, rise above challenges, run and not grow weary, walk and not faint. This verse highlights a vital truth: Waiting on God brings supernatural endurance, fresh perspective, and deep restoration. Those who keep pace with God's timing begin to see life from a different (higher) viewpoint—above fear, defeat, or discouragement. Like an eagle that soars above the storm, our strength and outlook are renewed when we choose to trust in God's plan. Height determines sight. The higher we go with God, the clearer our understanding of what we face below. We stop fixating on the devil's narrative of defeat and instead focus on God's promise of victory.[29]

This reference to the eagle in Isaiah 40 symbolizes supernatural strength (grace), divine renewal, and the extraordinary lifting that comes from trusting God's timing instead of relying on human effort. Known for its strength and exceptional vision—and estimated to have an acuity 4 to 8 times sharper than that of humans—the eagle maintains sharp focus, accurate perception, and clarity as it descends upon its target. This mirrors what it means to *set our faces like flint*, as stated in Isaiah 50:7. Such determined focus empowers us to remain anchored in truth, even when the journey is long.

A focused vision allows us to see the *bigger picture* and interpret all our experiences (good

---

26. Jer. 29:11
27. Mark 11:23
28. Prov. 4:25-27; Phil. 3:13-14; Col. 3:2
29. 2 Cor. 2:14

and bad) through God's perspective.[30] This outlook fosters healthy thoughts and habits that help people live with greater strength and stability, view setbacks as setups for divine outcomes, and approach tough situations as new challenges rather than threats. A renewed mind chooses healthy, faith-filled thoughts such as: "This will build me, not break or destroy me." "God is in control—I'm safe with Him." "This will end in victory." We learn to speak God's truth over our lives, instead of defaulting to defeatist thoughts like: "I'm damaged goods … this is it for me." "No one loves or cares about me."

Sometimes, hindsight offers us 20/20 vision—a clarity that emerges after the trial—but even while we wait, we can ask God to help us see now what we'll later understand. After all, God sees the end from the beginning,[31] and walking with Him provides the perspective and peace to wait well and speak well—using the Word of God—while we wait. It's important to voice your expectations—not your fears. This isn't mind-over-matter or pop psychology. It's standing on God's Word and declaring, *"I can do all things through Christ who strengthens me"* (Phil. 4:13).

We may never receive all the answers we desire to fully understand our circumstances;[32] yet, God provides glimpses. These insights inspired the early believers, including the Apostle Paul, who wrote in Ephesians 1:9-10: *"Making known to us the mystery of his will, according to his purpose, which he set forth in Christ as a plan for the fullness of time, to unite all things in him, things in heaven and things on earth."* We, too, can seek the plans God chooses to reveal to us. Even when there are no sneak previews or clear roadmaps, we can rest assured … *"that in all things God works for the good of those who love Him, who have been called according to his purpose"* (Rom. 8:28). It will end in praise and victory![33] What that victory looks like may vary from person to person, but Scripture defines what is truly praiseworthy: namely, growth in godly character, peace that surpasses understanding, and the fulfillment of God's will.[34]

Perspective is key. While our worldview is often shaped by personal experiences, emotions, and upbringing, as believers, our lens should be continually renewed by the Word of God.[35] Looking back at past events, particularly in my marriage, I now realize how differently I might have approached certain frustrations if I had been more attuned to God's perspective. Some of the things I once stressed over were resolved effortlessly when I shifted my focus from striving to trusting—allowing God to be my Source and maturing me in faith.[36]

For instance, I once lamented not being able to furnish our first home with my husband.

---

30. Gen. 50:20; 2 Cor. 12:7-10

31. Isa. 46:10

32. Isa. 55:9

33. 1 Cor. 15:57

34. Rom. 12:2; Gal. 5:22-23; Phil. 4:7

35. Rom. 12:2

36. Phil. 1:6

But in God's timing, I transitioned from being a "domestic engineer" to overseeing the renovation and redecoration of over eighty properties while managing a multi-million-pound portfolio. The very concerns I had about personal development were addressed as I gained professional training and international exposure. Truly, God did *"immeasurably more than all I could ask or imagine!"* [37]

Regarding the issues that weren't resolved as I had hoped, I received the grace to release them and move forward with the lessons learned. If your life isn't what you wish it to be, it doesn't mean it will remain that way. Sometimes we fear that people will never change or that circumstances won't work in our favor, but we need to understand what God says about such situations and then put the Word to work—trusting that He makes all things beautiful in their time.[38] Waiting well doesn't mean everything works out exactly as we want—but that everything works together according to *His* plan. Waiting with vision involves trusting God's pace and process, believing He who began a good work in you *will* complete it.[39]

Vision-led living is essential for waiting well. I call it "Focus and Follow"—focus on Christ and follow His lead. Waiting without vision breeds frustration, but when we wait with focused faith, we're not idle, stagnant, or disconnected from God—instead, we're actively engaged and aligned with God's plan. It's a time of purposeful growth, spiritual alertness, and obedience. We're not just sitting around hoping something happens; we're trusting, preparing, praying, seeking, and obeying God's instructions—fully immersed in His Word while anticipating His timing for peace, settlement, or justice.

Hebrews encourages us to imitate those who inherited the promises through faith and patience.[40] These men and women remained steadfast—some witnessed fulfillment, while others died still believing God's promises.[41] Yet all lived with forward-looking faith. We can either fixate on our lack or focus on God's sufficiency. Scripture reminds us: *"The Lord is my helper; I will not be afraid;"* [42] *"Greater is He who is in you;"* [43] *"I can do all things through Christ who strengthens me."* [44] These truths anchor our perspective. God's presence and promises empower us to persevere with purpose. When we focus on Him—our constant Helper—we see life through His capability, not our limitations.

Proverbs 29:18 warns that without vision—whether it is prophetic insight or divine guidance—people perish. In this context, the Hebrew term for "perish" signifies casting off restraint

---

37. Eph. 3:20

38. Eccles. 3:11; Isa. 55:11; Hab. 2:3; Rom. 8:28

39. Phil. 1:6

40. Heb. 6:12-15

41. Heb. 11:13; 1 Pet. 2:21

42. Heb. 13:5-6

43. 1 John 4:4

44. Phil. 4:13

or living recklessly. In other words, without a defined purpose or spiritual direction, individuals tend to wander, react impulsively, and squander their potential. Vision provides structure to our waiting, offering a perspective that informs our choices and guides our daily lives.

When we look up to God instead of around at others, we shield our hearts from the inclination to be unnecessarily competitive, from anxiety, the fear of missing out, and feelings of being left behind, especially when others seem to be enjoying themselves and making progress—particularly at our expense.[45] God's timeline is not a race against others but a personal journey of trust and growth. As Ecclesiastes 9:11 reminds us, *"The race is not to the swift ... but time and chance happen to them all."* It's not about speed but direction and stamina. As Jim Rohn aptly said, "You cannot change your destination overnight, but you can change your direction overnight." With God, that shift occurs the moment we surrender. By His mercy, He allows us to course-correct and realign at any stage—walking with us every step of the way, so that when we arrive, we are not merely reaching a goal—we are arriving transformed for His glory.

3. Foundational faith:

"So then faith comes by hearing, and hearing by the word of God." (Rom. 10:17) Faith isn't something we create on our own—it begins and grows through continuous exposure to God's Word. Whether it comes through Scripture, sound teaching, preaching, or the quiet voice of the Holy Spirit, true faith is grounded in divine truth. It's not about passive listening but about receiving God's Word with an open and expectant heart. We can't believe what we haven't heard. The more we immerse ourselves in God's Word, the stronger and more resilient our faith becomes—especially in times of waiting, uncertainty, or decision-making.

Waiting seasons test our faith while inviting us to deepen it. Our confidence in God grows as we consistently receive and respond to His voice, primarily through Scripture. We begin to hear more clearly, believe more boldly, and persevere more patiently. In a world filled with noise and distractions, God's Word serves as a steady anchor for our souls,[46] helping us remain confident even when answers are delayed.[47]

Just as God asked the prophets, *What do you see?*, He also invited Abraham into a life of vision-led faith. In Genesis 13:14-15, after Lot departed, God told Abram: *"Lift your eyes now and look from the place where you are—northward, southward, eastward, and westward; for all the land which you see I give to you and your descendants forever."* Even though Abram had no land in hand, he believed God and acted on what was promised. Later, in Genesis 15:5 (NIV), God asked him to *"look up at the sky and count the stars—if indeed you can count them. Then he said to him, So shall your offspring be."* He asked Abram to envision countless descendants

---

45. Psalm 37:7; 73:2-3; Prov. 23:17-18

46. Heb. 11:1

47. Ps. 27:13-14; 130:5

while he was still childless. These were not just visual illustrations, but faith-building moments. In time, even his name was changed to match the vision: from Abram to Abraham, "father of many nations" (Gen. 17:5).

Like Abraham, we are often called to see beyond our current circumstances and realities—to trust God's promises even when there's no visible evidence of change. Whether it involves a broken relationship, financial strain, or a health challenge, foundational faith responds, "God is still working." Romans 4:18, 20–21 reminds us that Abraham hoped against hope and was fully persuaded that God had the power to do what He had promised.

Our Father, who is the same yesterday, today, and forever,[48] still invites us into faith-stretching moments, much like He did with Abraham. While He may not speak the exact words today, the essence of His call remains: "Lift your eyes; look from where you are; what you see—by faith—I will give you." During our seasons of waiting, it's as if God gently whispers, "Look up. See what I see." He invites us to imagine, believe, and trust in His unseen hand at work—because *we live by faith, not by sight.* [49]

4. Freedom through forgiveness:

"But I say to you, love your enemies, bless those who curse you, do good to those who hate you, and pray for those who spitefully use you and persecute you." (Matt. 5:44) Jesus introduces a radical and countercultural way to respond to offense with this command. Instead of repaying hurt with hurt, He calls us to reflect God's grace and mercy—even toward those who've wronged us. Forgiveness doesn't imply that they deserve it. We forgive because God desires transformation—for them and us. Prayer becomes the tool that softens our hearts and protects us from bitterness. It breaks the cycle of offense and opens the door for God's redemptive work: *"…that you may be children of your Father in heaven."* (Matt. 5:45)

Forgiveness is freedom. It lifts burdens, cultivates patience, and helps us walk in gratitude. Embracing the liberty Christ has purchased breaks every shackle of fear, resentment, and the emotional weight of holding on to unforgiveness. When we choose mercy over retaliation, we free ourselves and others to enter God's healing hands. You cannot pray effectively for someone you resent or who has hurt you. *"And when you stand praying, if you hold anything against anyone, forgive them, so that your Father in heaven may forgive you your sins."* (Mark 11:25 NIV)

Jesus made it clear: Our willingness to forgive others directly impacts our ability to obtain and walk in God's forgiveness.[50] It's not just something we receive—we're also called to extend it. Forgiveness isn't optional in the kingdom of God; it's central to the heart of the Gospel. In Matthew 18:21-22 (NIV), Peter came to Jesus and asked, *"'Lord, how many times shall I forgive*

---

48. Heb. 13:8
49. 2 Cor. 5:7 (NIV)
50. Matt. 6:14-15

my brother or sister who sins against me? Up to seven times?' Jesus answered, 'I tell you, not seven times, but seventy times seven.'" That's 490 times—for the same person!

Let's be honest: Many of us struggle to forgive once, let alone twice. Some of us are still giving the silent treatment over an offense from three birthdays ago or the last Thanksgiving gathering! And yet, Jesus didn't lower the bar—He raised it beyond human logic, calling us to a forgiveness that mirrors God's own grace. It's as if He's saying, "You're keeping score, but I'm watching hearts." *"For the Lord does not see as man sees; for a man looks at the outward appearance, but the Lord looks at the heart."* (1 Sam. 16:7b) Spiritual maturity isn't about "being right," but about being right *with God.*

Holding onto unforgiveness often reveals a disconnect in our understanding of God's mercy—the very mercy we have received ourselves. This doesn't mean God's love is withdrawn; rather, our fellowship with Him is hindered when our hearts are hardened. When we truly grasp the depth of God's forgiveness toward us, it becomes unthinkable to withhold that same grace from others.

Research shows that unforgiveness—characterized by chronic resentment, bitterness, and rumination—can result in serious health consequences. Studies have linked it to a range of physical and mental health issues. These negative emotions can trigger prolonged stress responses that contribute to high blood pressure, heart disease, and even stroke.[51] Additionally, it weakens the immune system, exacerbates mental health conditions, and may lead to depression, anxiety, chronic pain, inflammation, and sleep disturbances.[52] Conversely, practicing forgiveness has been shown to reduce many of these health risks. One study in the Journal of Health Psychology even concluded that forgiveness can buffer the impact of stress on mental illness.[53] Learning to forgive not only fosters spiritual growth but also enhances emotional and physical well-being.

Forgiveness doesn't excuse the offense—it releases its hold on your life. In God's economy, forgiveness isn't a sign of weakness; it's a demonstration of strength. It's how we keep our hearts pure, maintain unhindered prayers, and sustain unbroken fellowship with Him: *"Be kind and compassionate to one another, forgiving each other, just as in Christ God forgave you"* (Eph. 4:32). Forgiveness also helps us emerge from our emotional cocoon. We break free and step into fresh possibilities—new peace, renewed relationships, and a clear path forward in our waiting. It's a choice that keeps us spiritually light and emotionally free to follow wherever God leads.

---

51. Steven R. McEvoy, "The Effects of Forgiveness and Resentment," *The Table*, Biola University Center for Christian Thought, October 26, 2015, https://cct.biola.edu/effects-forgiveness-resentment/.

52. Laura van Dernoot Lipsky, "Grudge Match: Can Unforgiveness Be Bad for Our Health?" *Psychology Today*, September 18, 2013, https://www.psychologytoday.com/us/blog/supersurvivors/201309/grudge-match-can-unforgiveness-be-bad-our-health.

53. Mandy Oaklander, "Why Forgiveness Is Powerfully Good for Your Health," *Time*, June 30, 2016, https://time.com/4370463/forgiveness-stress-health/.

5. Fervency in prayer:

Scripture urges us to *pray without ceasing,* and to *always pray and not give up.*[54] These aren't calls to empty ritual but invitations to remain spiritually connected—anchored in the unwavering truth that nothing is too hard or impossible for our God.[55] Prayer isn't a monologue; it's a two-way lifeline with our Father, where we communicate with Him and listen for His guidance, comfort, and correction through His Word and Spirit.[56]

To pray fervently means to pray with sincerity, deep passion, and focused faith—not halfheartedly or mechanically, but with a heart fully engaged and confident in God's power to respond. God isn't impressed by eloquence; He responds to humility and honesty.[57] James 5:16b (NLT) affirms this: *"The earnest prayer of a righteous person has great power and produces wonderful results."* That kind of prayer isn't passive or routine—it's persistent and Spirit-led—refusing to give up at the first sign of delay or contradictions. It's not about many words or merely going through the motions; it reflects a soul truly seeking God and determined to persevere until a breakthrough comes.[58] It's prayer that flows from a heart that believes God hears, sees, and will fulfill what He has promised—according to His perfect wisdom, love, and timing.[59]

Hannah's story in 1 Samuel 1 exemplifies this prayer. She prayed so earnestly for a child that Eli, the priest, thought she was drunk. Yet her tears and silent lips signified a soul crying out to God with profound faith—and God answered.[60] Jesus Himself affirmed persistent prayer in Luke 18:1-8, while cautioning against vain repetition in Matthew 6:7. The concern isn't repetition itself but rather vain or empty prayer that is mindless, formulaic, or performance-based, rather than sincere. In times when we feel too weary or confused to express our needs, the Holy Spirit assists us. He teaches, reminds, and intercedes on our behalf with groanings too deep for words, aligning our prayers with God's will.[61]

Instead of succumbing to anxiety, God invites us to bring everything to Him in prayer—with thanksgiving and trust.[62] This posture brings a peace that surpasses all understanding, calming our hearts and minds in Christ. Make prayer your first response, not your last resort. Present your worries, hopes, and even doubts to God before discussing them with anyone else. God is not hard of hearing and is eager to bless His children.[63] Ecclesiastes 5:2-3 reminds us

---

54. Luke 18:1; 1 Thess. 5:17
55. Ps. 147:5
56. James 4:8
57. Ps. 51:17
58. Jer. 29:13
59. Luke 1:45
60. 1 Sam. 1:10-13
61. John 14:26; 16:13-15; Rom. 8:26-27
62. Phil. 4:6
63. Ps. 34:15; Isa. 59:1; Matt. 7:11

not to be hasty with our words or make careless promises before God—so speak honestly, but with reverence.

God sees the whole picture. His will is perfect,[64] and He knows what's best for us even more than we do.[65] As the One who knows the end from the beginning,[66] God alone holds the wisdom, timing, and strategy for our lives. Jeremiah 33:3 reminds us that when we call Him, He responds with insight that far exceeds our understanding. Trusting God means resting in the assurance that even delays serve a purpose in His greater plan.

Like incense, prayer rises continually before God.[67] Just as incense is fueled by fire, certain heart postures—such as gratitude, patience, and surrender—stir and sustain a fervent prayer life. A *thankful heart* keeps us grounded in what God has already done, building confidence for what He's yet to do. Instead of rushing ahead or trying to force outcomes, *patience* allows us to wait with hope, trusting that God is working behind the scenes, even when nothing seems to be shifting.[68] A *surrendered heart* releases our illusion of control, helping us yield to God's perfect will and timing, rather than striving to force results. Psalm 27:13-14 urges us to wait with courage and confidence. True faith isn't just belief—it's the fuel that drives us to pray with conviction and expectation.[69]

When it comes to marriage, praying fervently isn't always easy, especially during times of disappointment. However, we're called to intercede for our spouses not merely out of obligation, but as an act of obedience and love for God. If Jesus calls us to pray for our enemies,[70] how much more should we intercede for the person with whom we've entered into a covenant through marriage? God's mercy triumphs over judgment,[71] and Jesus continues to advocate for us despite our flaws. Therefore, when we refuse to pray for our spouse, we're not just giving up on them—we're doubting God's transforming power.

I've had women tell me, "Go ask his mother to pray for him!" Honestly, I completely understand. When you're hurting, it's easier to focus on your children and concentrate on your healing than to pray for the one who caused the pain. But here's the truth: Choosing to stand in the gap for your spouse—even during times of brokenness—isn't a sign of weakness; it's warfare. It's a bold declaration of faith and surrender that says, "God, I trust You more than I trust what I see. Please give me the desire and the power to do what pleases You."[72]

---

64. Matt. 6:10
65. Isa. 48:17-18
66. Isa. 46:9-10; Rev. 22:13
67. 1 Thess. 5:17; Rev. 5:8
68. Prov. 23:18 (AMP)
69. Heb. 11:1
70. Matt. 5:44
71. James 2:13
72. Phil. 2:13 (NLT)

As women, perhaps because we tend to carry so much emotionally, we may struggle more in this area. We find it easier to retreat or protect ourselves, particularly in prayer. However, fervor in prayer requires vulnerability. It means bringing God our raw, honest emotions while believing He can restore, redeem, and make all things new.[73]

I remember the Holy Spirit asking me hard but heart-searching questions: "How deeply do you love Me, Ségun, and your children? Can I trust you to look beyond your pain and pray for your husband—my son?" Those questions pierced me. In that moment, committing to consistent prayer for Ségun felt like the last thing I wanted to do. Yet I sensed God wasn't asking me to pray from a place of strength or understanding—He was inviting me to lean on His grace to do what I couldn't do on my own.[74]

To make this possible, I had to start seeing Ségun not through the lens of offense, but as God's child and the father of our children. That shift didn't come easily. I often reminded myself that, when we married, God became the third strand in our cord—our divine bond.[75] If we were truly one, as Scripture affirms, then whatever affected my husband could impact me, too. Even if he seemed distant from God at that time, I understood that it only takes one willing heart to partner with God for restoration—and what that ultimately looks like for our marriage is entirely in His hands.

The Holy Spirit kept nudging me, "Don't rush. Tarry in the place of prayer." And though I can't fully explain it, the more I read God's Word and surrendered to His will, the more my anger gave way to compassion. A burden to intercede replaced the bitterness I once carried. I found myself no longer praying for justice or vengeance, but for mercy—mercy for Ségun, for myself, and our family. I stopped imagining scenarios in which he might "slip on a banana peel and learn his lesson," and started believing in a heart transformation that only God could orchestrate in both of us.

We often impose deadlines on God: "If things don't change in three months, I'm done." But God doesn't operate on our timelines. What He considers is the posture of our hearts. Are we surrendered, or are we still trying to control the outcome? Proverbs 19:3 reminds us that we can ruin our own lives through foolish choices and then blame God or the devil for the results. Pride blinds us to truth. When we ignore godly wisdom and insist on our own way, we set ourselves up for pain—and then we turn around and point fingers at the only One who could've helped us all along.[76]

Being a praying spouse isn't easy! Too many emotions get in the way. It requires a heart that remains pure before God, even when it feels broken. More than the time or effort involved,

---

73. Rom. 8:28
74. Matt. 5:7; Phil. 2:2-5, 12-15
75. Eccles. 4:12
76. Prov. 12:15

the real challenge lies in praying for someone who has hurt us deeply. Staying humble, obedient, and yielding to God while harboring bitterness is almost impossible in our own strength. But Jesus didn't mince words: *"If you love Me, you will keep My commandments."* [77] Bitterness and rebellion taint our prayers. Often, God begins the transformation not with our spouse, but within us—softening our hearts, humbling our pride, and reshaping us to become His vessels of hope and redemption. [78]

Things started to shift when I stopped venting to others and began taking my pain and frustrations directly to God. I continued speaking His Word over my life and marriage—not just reciting scripture but declaring His truth in faith. It wasn't pretense; it was positioning. Even when Ségun's actions didn't change, I chose not to tear him down in conversations. I distanced myself from circles that mocked or belittled imperfect men and gravitated toward those who sought to honor God through their marriages. By choosing praise, faith, and obedience over fear, frustration, and gossip, I made room for God to move.

Over time, God gave me new eyes—eyes to see who Ségun could become in God's hands. He revealed vulnerabilities, not for me to exploit or weaponize, but to cover in prayer. [79] I was still his wife and held a unique spiritual role in His life. Because we are one flesh, I carried the authority to intercede with purpose and insight. Love finds ways and reasons to stay together—not out of naivety, but conviction. In truth, most relationship decisions stem from the heart long before advice or counseling is sought. People often seek support to reinforce what they've already decided—whether to forgive or to walk away.

Prayers began to rebuild trust long before reconciliation occurred for us. At one point during our separation, I learned—through someone else—that Ségun was facing some business-related challenges. He never communicated this to me directly, perhaps out of pride or fear that it might affect the custody situation regarding our children. Honestly, Ségun gave me plenty of reasons to use any unfavorable information I received against him. But the Holy Spirit kept me in check and reminded me to walk in the Spirit, not the flesh. [80] So I continued praying. I brought everything to God, trusting Him with the whole picture. Nothing is hidden from Him. He knows our struggles intimately, and because Jesus endured the same temptations, He offers grace and help in our times of need. [81]

I had so many "what ifs" that scared me, especially as I began praying intentionally for my husband's heart to return to the Father. What if nothing changed? What if I looked foolish in the end? However, I soon realized that my decision to persevere in prayer wasn't for public

---

77. John 14:15, 21

78. Isa. 52:7; Rom. 10:14-15; 2 Cor. 5:20

79. Isa. 43:26; Rom. 8:26-27; Heb. 4:16

80. Gal. 5:16-17 (NLT)

81. Heb. 4:13-16

approval—it was between me and God. In the moments when I felt afraid or unsure, I found comfort in knowing that I wasn't risking mockery or shame because I hadn't made a spectacle of my faith. My stand wasn't secretive or a showy display—it was a quiet, steady resolve rooted in trust.

Even so, I understood that my prayers needed to align with my words. Those who graciously stood with me in prayer also required clarity and direction, and I owed it to them—and to God—not to send mixed signals. Ultimately, He is the One we're accountable to, not people.[82] I didn't need to explain or justify why I believed our marriage could be restored. I knew God was trustworthy. I had nothing to lose and everything to gain. I refused to shrink back in the very areas where I had declared His goodness and what He promised.[83] *"Because the Sovereign Lord helps me, I will not be disgraced. Therefore, I have set my face like a stone, determined to do his will. And I know that I will not be put to shame."* (Isa. 50:7 NLT)

From then on, I diligently sent Ségun scriptures, encouragement, and prayers—every day. Even when he asked me to stop, even when he called my efforts "hypocritical" or dismissed them as a waste of time, I persisted—not to prove a point, but because I trusted God's Word to do what only it can. *"So shall My word be that goes forth from My mouth; it shall not return to Me void, But it shall accomplish what I please, And it shall prosper in the thing for which I sent it."* (Isa. 55:11) Eventually, I began to see the fruit of obedience. Ségun's walls started to come down, and he gradually opened up. Our conversations became more frequent—still cautious, but sincere. Trust, though fragile, began to take root again.[84]

That period taught me that fervent, Word-based prayer significantly changes things—but not always instantly. There is a process between prayer and the promise, and that's where many give up. Waiting well means staying faithful in the in-between. It involves praying even when we don't see results, speaking God's Word even when emotions scream otherwise, and surrendering our expectations while holding on to hope.[85]

We can't sustain this kind of faithful, hope-filled waiting in our own strength. It requires God-given faith and grace—what I like to call staying power—to maintain a posture of "praying without ceasing." It's more than willpower; it's Spirit-empowered perseverance that keeps you anchored in God's promises—through trials, silence, and doubts. Luke 15 provides a powerful glimpse of God's heart through the parables of the lost sheep, the lost coin, and the lost son (the prodigal son). In each story, what was lost mattered deeply—and was actively pursued and joyfully restored. That's the God we serve, not one who gives up on people, but One who seeks and saves with relentless love.

82. Rom. 14:12
83. Ps. 34:5; 121:1-2; Isa.50:7; Mic. 7:7; 1 John 5:14
84. Prov. 18:19-20 (NLT and TPT)
85. Mark 14:38; Heb. 11:6

As long as there is breath, there is hope—and as long as there is grace, there is strength to keep praying. But if you're struggling to keep praying for that relationship or partner, take time to examine your heart. Do you still desire restoration? Be honest with yourself and with God. Whatever the answer, ask Him for the grace to pray—not from a place of striving, but from a heart that's healing.

After five long years of separation, the seeds planted in faith and watered with tears began to germinate. During that extended period, most of my prayers centered around my marriage: I longed for Ségun to return to the children and me. I asked God for the tangible and visible— the healing and the restoration. While there was nothing wrong with that, over time, the Holy Spirit gently shifted my perspective through James 4:3: *"You ask and do not receive, because you ask amiss, that you may spend it on your pleasures."* I realized that I had been so focused on res- toration that I overlooked what mattered most—Ségun's reconciliation with God. The deeper need wasn't just for him to reunite with his family, but for his heart to return to the Father.

That conviction deepened as Matthew 6:33 began to resonate in a new way: *"Seek first the kingdom of God and His righteousness, and all these things shall be added to you."* I wasn't deny- ing reality or pretending everything was fine—I was simply learning to reorder my priorities. Like Abraham, who *"… did not consider his own body, already dead … but was strengthened in faith, giving glory to God …"* (Rom. 4:19-22), I had to trust God beyond what I could see. That kind of faith shifted my posture—from desperation and begging God to boldly believing Him.

Intercessory prayer isn't about persuading God—it's about yielding to Him and partner- ing with Him to release His will on earth in mercy and love.[86] God loves us. He listens, and He cares. Matthew 6:9-13 (The Lord's Prayer) became more than just a popular scripture I had memorized and recited since I was a toddler—it became a revelation. When I stopped praying from a place of anxiety and surrendered my will to God's will, everything began to shift—not instantly, but progressively—and it began with me. It became more important for His plans and purposes to prevail in my life and family, and I was willing to fulfill my part.[87]

It felt as if I had been fumbling with a bunch of unlabeled keys for five years, desperately trying to unlock several doors. But once I embraced God's priorities—salvation, surrender, and spiritual transformation—it was as if I had received the master key. The "gates and doors" that had been sealed for years began to open with surprising ease. Grace replaced striving, and peace displaced fear. The story didn't end there. In fact, it was just beginning!

> *"I would have lost heart, unless I had believed that I would see the goodness of the Lord in the land of the living. Wait on the Lord; Be of good courage, And He shall strengthen your heart; Wait, I say, on the Lord!"* (Ps. 27:13-14)

---

86. 2 Chron. 7:14-15

87. Luke 22:42

With these first five "Fs" of Waiting Well, it's possible to establish a solid spiritual foundation for navigating seasons of delay, uncertainty, and preparation. By partnering with the Holy Spirit as our Faithful Facilitator and engaging fervently in prayer, these practices can help shape our inner world and align our hearts through grace with God's purposes.

But this is only the beginning. These inward postures prepare us to wait well; yet, waiting also has an outward expression. It's not just about what happens within us—it's how we live through it. In the next chapter, we'll explore the remaining eight "Fs"—practical, emotional, and relational dimensions that empower us to wait with wisdom, intentionality, and hope.

THROUGH SÉGUN'S LENSES

After recovering from the shock of learning that a major business project of mine had been canceled, I had to pick up the pieces and move on. It was clear that I had to focus on the things I could control and not allow myself to be consumed by the unexpected circumstances in which I found myself.

I had begun to spend an increasing amount of time by myself, and the stillness forced me to become more introspective amid the uncertainty I was dealing with. It was only later on that I realized that, by being knocked off balance and humbled during that period of uncertainty, I was becoming more receptive to what God had in store for me.

Rearview Mirror Lesson

I learned, firsthand, how some people truly need to experience adversity for God to get their attention. The fact that I had been fully immersed in my work, which had been going well, turned my attention even further away from Him until things went awry. The following "Five Rs" sum up how I was able to make it through those tough times.

Rest: It is vital to find a natural way to maintain one's energy levels when in the eye of the storm given the amount of emotional and mental anguish one is going through. Fortunately for me, I have seldom found it hard to fall asleep even when in pressure-laden, emotionally distressing situations.

Reflect: Given the amount of time I had to myself during the separation, I eventually managed to put myself in the witness box instead of constantly pointing an accusing finger at Funké. After many years of convincing myself that my share of the blame was minimal, I was able to think deeply about my missteps and misconceptions while recognizing the role I had played that resulted in the separation. This was a slow process, but the penny finally dropped for me.

Reconnect: When things became stressful, I shut down and withdrew from my normal social routine. The difference was clear when I focused on getting fit and resumed a reasonable level of social activities, which made me feel a lot better about myself.

Remember: By reminding myself that everything happens for a reason and that tough times last for a season, I was able to dig myself out of a deep hole with the help of the Holy Spirit. God redeems even painful experiences and can bring meaning out of them.

Receive: Unbeknownst to me, I was a continual recipient of God's grace during my wilderness period. He kept me from losing myself in the darkness and gave me the strength not to throw in the towel.

17

Still Waiting, Still Well

"You're blessed when you stay on course,
walking steadily on the road revealed by God."

PSALM 119:1 MSG

In the first half of our journey through the 13 "Fs" of Waiting Well, we explored the quiet, internal heart work—the hidden postures that steady us when life feels suspended between promise and fulfillment. These truths provide a deep spiritual anchor, holding us firm in seasons that test both our patience and our faith.

Now, we step into the second half—the outward expression of waiting. These next "Fs" speak to how we care for our physical health, manage our time and resources, protect our emotional well-being, nurture and navigate relationships, grow with and respond to feedback, and ultimately, how we finish well. Because waiting well isn't just about getting through; it's about growing through it. It's living with purpose, even in the in-between.

"Let us not grow weary in doing good, for at the proper time we will reap a harvest
if we do not give up." (Gal. 6:9 NIV)

6. Fit for purpose:

Embracing the waiting periods—which we all experience at one point or another—as preparation rather than a punishment, is a sign of spiritual maturity and trust in God's perfect timing.[1]

---

1. James 1:12

Being fit for purpose means becoming equipped—spiritually, emotionally, and physically—for the journey or unique assignment God has entrusted to us. It's not just about activity or outward service in the body of Christ, but about being aligned and whole—ready in heart, mind, and body to effectively fulfill our calling. This readiness is found in Christ. Spiritually, it involves being rooted in God's Word, led by the Holy Spirit, and strengthened through consistent prayer and obedience. Emotionally, it means cultivating resilience, maturity, and a sound mind—responding to life not with fear but with faith, love, and self-discipline.[2] Physically, it's about stewarding our bodies not for vanity, but for vitality—so we can endure and serve with strength and longevity.

God desires our total well-being: *"Beloved, I pray that you may prosper in all things and be in health, just as your soul prospers."* (3 John 1:2) When our body, soul, and spirit are aligned, we become sharpened vessels—fit for the Master's use and energized for the road ahead.[3] Our bodies are temples—not shrines or dumpsters—for the Holy Spirit to dwell in. We are called to offer ourselves as living sacrifices—holy, acceptable, and set apart for His purposes.[4] This requires clearing out anything that competes with His presence—whether toxic habits, self-indulgence, destructive patterns, or spiritual complacency—so we remain sensitive, surrendered, and ready. Waiting isn't wasted when it prepares you to carry His glory well.

There are numerous references in the Bible to holistic fitness—spirit, soul, and body—so we can live well and serve faithfully. Caring for our physical bodies isn't about superficial appearance—it's about taking responsibility. Scripture encourages moderation in what we eat and drink,[5] self-control in our habits,[6] and readiness for every good work.[7] While spiritual training is of greater value, physical discipline also holds importance.[8] In all things, our lives should reflect balance, reverence, and the awareness that we are God's dwelling place.[9]

Getting fit—spiritually, emotionally, and physically—doesn't happen without intention. Real, lasting change, especially the type that shapes our character, mindset, habits, or faith, requires conscious effort and purposeful direction. It doesn't just occur by accident or wishful thinking; it happens through deliberate choices and actions aligned with a clear goal. People often change in response to a crisis or the promise of a reward. However, many resist growth due to a lack of understanding or motivation. Without a compelling "why" or a meaningful "what for," it's easy to remain stuck—even when transformation would move us forward.

---

2. 2 Tim. 1:7

3. Deut. 6:5

4. Rom. 12:1; 1 Cor. 6:19-20

5. Prov. 23:20-21; 25:16

6. 1 Cor. 9:27; Gal. 5:22-23

7. 2 Tim. 2:21

8. 1 Tim. 4:7-8

9. 2 Cor. 6:16; Phil. 4:5

This is especially true when fear or anxiety creeps in. These aren't just fleeting emotions—they can mentally, emotionally, and spiritually derail people. Jesus warned against worry in Matthew 6:25-34, reminding us that it undermines trust in God. Fear clouds spiritual sensitivity, distracts us from prayer, and fosters self-reliance over surrender.[10] And the effects aren't only spiritual. Chronic fear and stress trigger the body's fight-or-flight response, resulting in hormonal imbalances, sleep disturbances, inflammation, digestive issues, and fatigue. Over time, this can physically wear a person down, making it even more difficult to endure waiting seasons with strength and purpose.

On an emotional level, anxiety distorts one's thinking, drains joy, and fuels cycles of dread. Proverbs 17:22 says, *"A cheerful heart is good medicine, but a crushed spirit dries up the bones."* Emotional wellness isn't optional—it's deeply connected to physical and spiritual wholeness. But God didn't design us to carry fear. Instead, He invites us to cast all our cares on Him.[11] When we surrender our burdens, He exchanges our anxiety for peace that surpasses understanding.[12] That peace sustains us through the waiting.

Over time, I realized that many of the delays, struggles, and stress-related symptoms I experienced were often linked to being out of alignment with God's will. Obedience isn't intended to be a heavy burden but rather a life-giving pathway to peace, fulfillment, and stability. Isaiah 48:18 reflects this beautifully: *"If only you had paid attention to my commands, your peace would have been like a river, your well-being like the waves of the sea."* When we walk in God's ways, we remain under God's covering[13]—come what may!

One of those commands is to *"love your neighbor as yourself"* (Mark 12:31). This implies a healthy love for oneself and care for one's own well-being as a foundation for loving others from a place of wholeness. The Bible doesn't promote self-love in the modern self-indulgent sense, but it assumes we nourish and care for ourselves in ways that honor God.[14] That kind of stewardship is essential to serve others effectively.

Obedience leads to spiritual and emotional stability[15] while disobedience opens the door to restlessness and distress.[16] During seasons of intense stress, I felt God nudging me to care for myself more intentionally—but I didn't always listen. I underestimated the emotional and physical weight I had been carrying. For years, I was on autopilot—functioning but not flourishing. I didn't pay much attention to my mental or physical well-being. Although I've always been naturally slim, there was a time during our separation when I weighed nearly 10 to 15

10. Phil. 4:6-7; 2 Tim. 1:7

11. 1 Pet. 5:7

12. Phil. 4:6-7

13. Ps. 91:1

14. Eph. 5:29

15. Deut. 28:1-2; Ps. 119:165; Prov. 3:5-8

16. Jer. 7:23-24

kilograms below the healthy range for my age and frame. Outwardly, I still looked fine—some even said I looked pretty—but in truth, I was *pretty hungry* and deeply depleted in every sense!

Reflecting on the past, that neglect remains one of my biggest regrets. I've seen many others do the same during a crisis—praying fervently for healing, restoration, or breakthrough—yet overlooking the inner work that builds strength for the journey. We separate our petitions from our practices, but faith must encompass every part of us—our habits, mindset, health, and attitude. God desires wholeness, not just results.

In many cultures, women are often seen as "pain sponges"—a reflection of the social expectation to absorb emotional turmoil, manage relational stress, and quietly endure for the sake of peace at home, work, or within the community. Rather than releasing their emotions, they internalize them, soaking up not only their own feelings but also those of others.

For men, the pattern tends to differ. They're more often "pain vaults"—storing pain silently and locking it away rather than expressing or processing it. This kind of suppression is frequently mistaken for strength. Although the pain may be concealed, it still weighs heavily and is often redirected into work, performance, or pleasure as a coping mechanism.

Some men become "pressure cookers," containing emotional buildup until it either drives productivity or erupts in frustration. Others carry pain like "armor-bearers," shielding those around them while denying their own vulnerability, which can be misinterpreted as weakness because culture has taught them to hide it. Unfortunately, this isolation can have a negative impact on their spiritual and emotional well-being over time.

These metaphors capture deeply ingrained gendered responses to pain—absorption versus suppression.[17] While they may reflect common human tendencies, Scripture calls both men and women to bring their burdens to God rather than carry them alone. *"Cast your cares on the Lord and He will sustain you."* (Psalm 55:22a) God never intended pain to be silently endured or secretly stored. He invites us to lay it down so that we can be made whole.

Medical professionals acknowledge that traumatic or prolonged stress—particularly from significant life events such as pregnancy, childbirth, grief, divorce, serious illness, job loss, financial difficulties, relocation, legal issues, and abuse—can trigger or exacerbate chronic health conditions, especially for individuals already predisposed to stress. These conditions include hypertension, IBS, chronic fatigue syndrome, fibromyalgia, anxiety and depression, insomnia, autoimmune diseases, migraines, heart disease, metabolic disorders, and weakened immunity.

The birth of our daughter in 2010—a year after our reconciliation—signified a fresh start. Physically, it was my smoothest pregnancy, but emotionally, I felt deeply anxious about financial

---

17. Arlie Russell Hochschild, *The Managed Heart: Commercialization of Human Feeling* (Berkeley: University of California Press, 1983) https://en.wikipedia.org/wiki/The_Managed_Heart;

Niobe Way, *Deep Secrets: Boys' Friendships and the Crisis of Connection* (Cambridge, MA: Harvard University Press, 2011);

Terry Real, *I Don't Want to Talk About It: Overcoming the Secret Legacy of Male Depression* (New York: Scribner, 1997).

uncertainties. Our relationship was still healing, family dynamics were tense, and I carried unresolved stress from years of marital strain into that season. What I didn't realize then was how profoundly the emotional burden I carried would affect my physical health.

Shortly after giving birth, I began to experience intense, widespread, and unexplained joint and muscle pain, accompanied by persistent fatigue. Simple activities became a struggle—driving, kneeling to pray, and keeping up with work felt almost impossible. The pain was relentless, and I relied on prescription steroids, red light therapy, and a combination of medications, although they only provided temporary relief. I had survived, but I neglected my health. My body was signaling what my spirit had long been trying to express: I was drained. And while I prayed for restoration, I was learning—sometimes painfully—that healing isn't always instant, and rest is not weakness, but an act of obedience that acknowledges our dependence on God.[18]

For the next six years, I struggled with symptoms that doctors were unable to diagnose. The intensity varied, often worsening due to stress, changes in indoor temperature, physical activity, or even weather conditions. I endured relentless musculoskeletal pain, profound fatigue, disrupted sleep, morning stiffness, numbness, and tingling in my hands and feet, increased sensitivity to touch, headaches … and even severe hair loss!

In 2016, the diagnosis was finally identified as a borderline autoimmune condition. It was a sobering moment—one that made me fully realize just how poorly I had been taking care of myself. While external factors, such as environmental toxins and processed foods, contribute to illness, one cannot overlook the impact of lifestyle choices. Many health issues today are worsened by dehydration, chronic stress, poor sleep, unhealthy diets, vitamin deficiencies, sedentary habits, substance abuse, and internalized anxiety.

Most autoimmune conditions have no known cure in conventional medicine. At best, symptoms are managed with long-term medications—often accompanied by severe side effects. I chose a different path: combining integrative, functional, and naturopathic medicine. With this approach, healing wasn't just about relieving symptoms; it was about addressing root causes and supporting the realignment of body, mind, and spirit. It resonated with me, reminding me of the way God designed me—fearfully and wonderfully made, not in disconnected parts, but as a whole person.[19] This "enemy" called sickness appeared stronger than the options I had tried so far. So, I cried out to God for strength to fight what felt like overwhelming opposition to my well-being.[20] Sickness is not God's will. Scripture reveals it as an enemy to be resisted,[21] and God equips us for the fight. *"Blessed be the Lord, my rock, who trains my hands for war, and my fingers for battle."* (Ps. 144:1)

---

18. Exod. 20:8-10; Ps. 23:1-3; Mark 6:31; Heb.4:9-11
19. Ps. 139:13-16
20. Ps. 18:16-17; John 10:10
21. James 4:7; 1 Pet. 5:8-9

Through prayer, a complete lifestyle overhaul, and the expert care of a gifted husband-and-wife specialist team in Nigeria—along with the unwavering support of Ségun—every symptom I had battled for six years was reversed in just six months. This recovery was made possible by God's grace and a healing strategy focused on restoring the body's natural function, which included nutritious food, detoxification, restful sleep, stress reduction, regular cardio workouts like dance aerobics, spinning, and swimming, as well as complementary therapies such as lymphatic massages, stretching, steam rooms, and more. It reminded me that when we partner with God and take care of our health, healing is possible. The pursuit of wellness drew us closer as a family, as we engaged in physical activities together and explored healthier food choices.

However, healing isn't always a one-time event; it must be sustained over time. Around the time I began to feel better, we were also navigating a difficult financial situation. To cut costs, I withdrew from the wellness program, and regrettably, I slipped back into old stress patterns during yet another long and trying waiting season. The progress I had made began to unravel. It wasn't until a family vacation in 2019 that I realized something was wrong. Our daughter pointed out light patches on the back of my neck. Within weeks, the discoloration had spread. Once we returned home, we consulted several dermatologists. After a series of tests, the doctors confirmed it was vitiligo—an autoimmune condition with no known cure. By then, it had appeared on my neck, back, arms, face, and scalp.

Vitiligo is an autoimmune condition in which the immune system mistakenly attacks melanocytes—the cells responsible for producing skin pigment—leading to well-defined white patches that can appear anywhere on the body. Although it isn't contagious or life-threatening, its visible nature can result in emotional and psychological strain.

While I could cover the lighter patches on my face with makeup, other areas were more difficult to conceal. Out of curiosity—or insensitivity—some people made thoughtless remarks that cut deep. Whether real or imagined, the stares made me self-conscious. I adjusted my wardrobe and began to withdraw socially. But in His faithfulness, God has brought significant re-pigmentation over time. He truly restores health and heals wounds.[22]

The chronic stress I once internalized had not only affected my body, but it also dulled my spiritual vitality. Yet by God's mercy, I now possess the strength to be present for my family, contribute meaningfully to the body of Christ, and engage with my community—free from the physical limitations that once held me back.

These health battles have served as teachers, revealing the significant cost of not waiting well. When we ignore God's nudges or fail to care for ourselves during stressful seasons, the consequences can be severe. Our bodies are not just vessels—they are messengers, warning us when we're misaligned, and responding when we align them with God's Word in faith. The Word of

---

22. Jer. 30:17

God isn't merely a collection of inspirational sayings; it's a living truth that holds power. Speak it over yourself and your circumstances consistently. In it, we find wisdom, strategy, insight, and divine guidance for defending and protecting our bodies and overall well-being from external threats, invasions, and spiritual oppositions.

We weren't created in fragments or compartments, but as fully integrated beings. God intricately wove our physical, mental, and spiritual dimensions into one beautifully unified whole—working together in harmony—as part of the body of Christ. As explicitly affirmed in 1 Thessalonians 5:23, God cares about every part of us and desires wholeness, not just survival. *"Now may the God of peace Himself sanctify you completely; and may your whole spirit, soul, and body be preserved blameless at the coming of our Lord Jesus Christ."*

7. Fueling with food for the soul:

Waiting seasons can stretch us in ways we never imagined. They expose deep fears, magnify doubts, and can leave us feeling vulnerable and unseen. Yet, in those quiet, in-between spaces, and throughout our emotional journeys, God offers us something unshakable—His Word. These roads are often lonely—but they're also where we walk most intimately with the One who truly knows us.[23] It's in this personal space that Proverbs 14:10 rings true: *"Each heart knows its own bitterness, and no one else can fully share its joy."*

Choosing to nourish our body and spirit is crucial for providing both physical and spiritual sustenance on our journey. What we consume, listen to, watch, and dwell upon matters—not just in the moment, but over time, as these inputs shape not only our habits but also our convictions and responses. Our real "soul food" is the Word of God; the more we feed on it, the better equipped we are to stand firm against uncertainty and temptation.

God fed the Israelites with manna—bread from heaven—during their wilderness journey to the Promised Land,[24] teaching them to rely on Him daily. However, when they grew dissatisfied and craved meat instead, grumbling and complaining against His provision, God granted their request. And it came with a sobering lesson: Not all cravings lead to fulfillment, and not every alternative to God's provision nourishes the soul.[25]

In response, God told Moses that He would provide meat for the people—not just for a day, but for a whole month—until it came out of their nostrils and they loathed it.[26] This was a form of divine irony and discipline. God sent a wind that brought quail from the sea, and the people gathered excessive amounts—driven by greed and craving.[27] But while the meat

---

23. Ps. 139:1-3
24. Exod. 16:4, 35
25. Num. 11:4-34
26. Num. 11:18-20
27. Num. 11:31-32

was still in their mouths, before it could even be digested, a severe plague broke out, and many died at the place they named Kibroth Hattaavah, meaning "graves of craving," because many died there in their indulgence.[28] Their story serves as a sober warning: Unchecked cravings can lead us away from God's best and open the door to consequences we didn't bargain for. Their physical appetite reflected a deeper spiritual void and lack of trust in God's provision.

This pattern echoes in the New Testament. When people repeatedly reject God and His ways, and choose to follow their own desires, He allows them to do so—even if it leads to spiritual ruin. As Paul writes, *"God gave them up to the lusts of their hearts… to dishonorable passions… And since they did not see fit to acknowledge God, God gave them up to a debased mind…"* (Rom. 1:24, 26, 28).

When we refuse to be nourished by what truly satisfies (especially God's Word) and instead feed on the wrong things in pursuit of temporary cravings—whether food, social media content, or false promises—we risk missing out on the sustaining grace He offers daily, becoming spiritually malnourished, vulnerable, and distant from Him. Unlike fleeting fixes, the Word of God nourishes us wholly. When everything else feels uncertain, God's promises remain our sure foundation. His Word doesn't just inform—it is our daily bread that comforts, preserves, revives, and fuels our weary souls.[29]

Watch out for cravings! These intense desires or longings—often sudden and urgent—can manifest in physical, emotional, or spiritual ways. Most commonly, we think of food cravings (like sweets or salty snacks), but cravings can also be for things like comfort, attention, intimacy, sex, success, or control. In a spiritual context, cravings often reflect a deeper inner hunger or unmet need, which we sometimes try to fill with temporary or unhealthy solutions instead of turning to God for lasting satisfaction. James 1:14-15 speaks to this: *"But each person is tempted when he is drawn away by his own desires and enticed. Then, when desire has conceived, it gives birth to sin; and sin, when it is full-grown, brings forth death."* Cravings aren't always wrong—but they become dangerous when we allow them to rule our decisions, lead us away from God's will, and try to fill a spiritual void with quick substitutes or fleshly indulgences. The Israelites' craving for meat in Numbers 11 wasn't just about food—it revealed a deeper ingratitude, discontentment, and lack of trust in God's provision (manna) and care. This displeased God and kindled His anger.[30]

Everyone responds to pain differently. While I was barely eating, others might overeat or emotionally shut down. These are survival mechanisms. Either way, our bodies sometimes pay the price and absorb the brokenness when our spirit tank is forced to run on empty. Whether through under-eating, over-indulging, or other destructive responses to pain, a crushed spirit

---

28. Num. 11:4, 18-20, 33-34

29. Ps. 19:7; 119:25, 50, 52; 1 Tim. 4:6; Heb. 6:19

30. Num. 11:1, 10

finds expression. Scripture calls us to *buffet (BUF-fit)* the body (to discipline it and bring it under control), not to *buffet (boo-FAY)* it with excess or self-gratification.[31] There must be a balance! In my case, I wasn't just neglecting physical nourishment—I was hungry for healing, peace, and restoration that only God could give. I had to surrender everything—every emotion, heartbreak, and burden—to Him.[32]

Scripture is more than ink on a page—it is life-giving, soul-sustaining nourishment that brings hope to those who meditate on it and allow God's unchanging truth to sink deep into their hearts.[33] When we are tempted to despair, the Word of God calls us to remember—but we can only recall what we've first stored within. As Romans 15:4 reminds us, *"For whatever was written in former days was written for our instruction, that through endurance and through the encouragement of the Scriptures we might have hope."*

These sacred texts were not written in a vacuum. They reflect the struggles, triumphs, and faith of real people who waited too—Abraham, Hannah, Joseph, David, and many others. Their testimonies aren't just part of history; they demonstrate that God always keeps His Word, and His timing can be trusted. So let God fill your heart and whole being with His Word[34] and the *zoe* life it brings—life that's rooted in Christ and empowered by His Spirit.[35] This life is not just for seasons of waiting or hardship; it is eternal, sustaining, and transformative. It enables us to rise above mere survival and step into joyful obedience, spiritual strength, and deep communion with God.

8. Fruitful finances:

I'm not a financial expert, but one thing I know for certain is that being gainfully employed and financially independent boosted my confidence and provided me with flexibility in making decisions during our marital transition. One cannot overemphasize the importance of financial literacy and preparedness for both men and women, especially when navigating challenges like separation or divorce while trusting God for direction, peace, and next steps. Understanding and planning for potential financial implications can help mitigate the risks associated with unexpected or significant changes.

Financial instability can have significant consequences, and the best way to avoid it is by developing sound money-management skills. This is particularly important in contexts where the legal system offers limited protection for financially dependent spouses. In Nigeria, the legal framework does not mandate the division of marital property upon divorce. Courts typically

---

31. 1 Cor. 9:27
32. 1 Pet. 5:7
33. Prov. 4:20-22
34. Eph. 5:18-19; Col. 3:16; 1 Pet. 2:2
35. John 1:4; 3:16; 10:10

adhere to a strict property rights approach, meaning only the spouse whose name appears on the title has legal ownership, unless the other spouse can prove a financial contribution. This situation leaves the financially weaker spouse—often the wife—at a considerable disadvantage, with no automatic claim to shared assets.[36] In contrast, English family law allows courts to recognize both financial and nonfinancial contributions such as homemaking and childcare when dividing assets, facilitating equitable redistribution during divorce.

Cultural practices, outdated laws, and patriarchal legal interpretations further hinder women's financial stability post-divorce or separation. These practices perpetuate economic dependency and limit women's autonomy.[37] Advocates argue for legal reforms to address these disparities, suggesting that Nigerian courts should consider non-financial contributions during marriage when determining property settlements. Such changes could provide fairer outcomes for women and help mitigate the economic hardships they face after separation or divorce.

According to a 2023 *US Government Accountability Office* report, women's household income decreases by an average of 41 percent after divorce—compared to 23 percent for men. Nearly one in five divorced women experience poverty, often losing access to health insurance, stable housing, or steady income. A 2020 study by *Legal Templates* also revealed that 64 percent of divorced individuals face unexpected financial challenges. These realities highlight the importance of prudence, stewardship, financial planning, God-led diligence, and honest communication regarding money matters well before marriage[38]—not concealment of assets, fear-driven hoarding, or self-protective independence, which often erode trust and unity in the marital relationship.

Scripture reminds us that it is God who gives us the power to produce wealth.[39] He provides the wisdom, strength, and resources—not just through hustle, but by His grace. While relationships may change, our Source remains faithful. Trusting God while taking practical and responsible steps—such as earning, saving, investing, and living within our means—helps us honor Him, even during uncertain times. It's wise to establish multiple streams of income, enroll in healthcare and car insurance, and plan for the future with a pension or retirement fund. Don't let fear push you to hoard or overspend; instead, live within your means.

Sadly, many women—especially those raising children without support—are left to carry heavy burdens alone. This pressure can sometimes drive them to "settle" or move from one relationship to another, simply as a means of survival. But God is always a present help, and He never demands unhealthy terms or unrealistic payback. He showed up for me through people,

36. Chinedu J. Efe and Esther E. Eberechi, "Property Rights of Nigerian Women at Divorce: A Case for a Redistribution Order," *Potchefstroom Electronic Law Journal* 23, no. 1 (2020): 1–39, https://doi.org/10.17159/1727-3781/2020/v23i0a5306.

37. Wikipedia contributors, "Feminization of poverty," *Wikipedia, The Free Encyclopedia*, last modified July 22, 2025, https://en.wikipedia.org/wiki/Feminization_of_poverty.

38. Prov. 21:5; 1 Cor. 4:2

39. Deut. 8:18

opportunities, sound advice, and even unexpected harvests from seeds I'd sown—whether through generosity, service, or wise investments.

I've witnessed how financial vulnerability can lead to compromising situations—emotional dependence, unhealthy relationships, or even moral concessions—but that's not God's way. During times when I felt overwhelmed with fear, uncertainty, and the weight of responsibility, like Hagar, God opened my eyes to see what was already present: a well full of water.[40] He has equipped us with everything we need for life and godliness,[41] and as we grow in our relationship with Him, we begin to walk in the fullness of His provision[42]—both in lean times and in plenty. Just ask, seek, and knock—God is a generous Father who gives good gifts to His children.[43] Fruitful finances begin with faith in His ability to provide, stewarding what we have with diligence, contentment, and trust in His timing.[44]

9. Framed or filtered feelings:

This is the intentional practice of viewing emotions through the lens of faith and truth rather than impulse or circumstance. It means acknowledging our feelings while refusing to let those emotions run wild, define our reality, or dictate our decisions. It encourages emotional maturity—bringing raw emotions under the authority of God's Word so that feelings are processed (not suppressed), sifted through His truth, and shaped by hope and faith, rather than fear and despair.[45]

One significant external influence I noticed during our breakup was music. It became both a comfort and a trigger. I found solace in songs—they eased my pain, distracted my mind, and at times, articulated emotions I couldn't express. However, music also had the power to intensify my feelings. Rather than help me heal, it sometimes deepened my sadness or anger. It didn't just reflect my emotions—it began to direct them.

Music is powerful! It creates an atmosphere that engages the soul. Depending on the genre or the spirit behind it, music can uplift or unnerve. Every element—rhythm, lyric, frequency, and tone—evokes something within us. That's why intentional listening is important, especially during times of emotional vulnerability. Studies have shown that music can enhance emotional well-being and resilience, particularly when curated thoughtfully and intentionally.

David understood this. He encouraged himself in the Lord through music, composing many of the Psalms during times of deep distress.[46] When Saul was tormented, he called for

---

40. Gen. 21:19
41. 2 Pet. 1:3
42. Phil. 4:19
43. Matt. 7:7-11
44. Prov. 3:9-10; Luke 16:10-11; 1 Tim. 6:6-8
45. Ps. 42:5; 2 Cor. 10:5
46. 1 Sam. 30:6

David to play, and the music brought relief.[47] The psalmist wrote, *"Let me remember my song in the night"* (Ps. 77:6), reminding us that worship can coexist with weeping. Even Job's friend Elihu observed that God "gives songs in the night" to those in distress[48]—a beautiful image of divine comfort and praise in dark seasons.

For a long time, I unknowingly allowed the "voices of strangers"[49] to influence my emotions, thoughts, and decisions. Music played a significant role in this—especially R&B, from the late '90s to the mid-2000s. These songs became the soundtrack of heartbreak, voicing pain and replaying disappointments on an endless loop. I absorbed their lyrics and, without realizing it, began to agree with their messages—messages that often fostered sorrow, bitterness, and longing rather than hope or healing.

Some of my favorite tracks back then included raw, emotional, and deeply relatable lines like: *"I'm going down, my whole world is upside down…," "Seven whole days without a word from you…, I can't eat, can't sleep…" "Un-break my heart…, without you, I can't go on…" "Another sad love song…," "I don't want to be here alone…," "…I'm going crazy…,"* and *"When you left, I lost a part of me…."* These weren't just songs; they were echoes of my feelings. They stirred my emotions—heightening my sadness and reinforcing the notion that I was broken, abandoned, unloved, and hopeless. Even our wedding song—*All My Life* by K-Ci & JoJo—could completely unravel me if I heard it unexpectedly. At that time, I was essentially the DJ of my own emotional spiral, hosting full-blown pity parties on demand!

Now, I'm not saying all secular music is bad—some songs do highlight healing and strength. However, most tend to point to self or others as the source, which can be limiting when true wholeness comes from God. For a long time, I leaned more toward songs that mirrored my brokenness, not my breakthrough. As Proverbs 23:7 says, *"As a man thinks in his heart, so is he."* What we feed our minds and emotions matters. That's why God calls us to *"guard our hearts above all else, for everything we do flows from it"* (Prov. 4:23). What we listen to becomes part of how we live. If we're not careful, we can reinforce despair instead of filtering our feelings through the hope and truth of God's Word.

Many believers understand the power of words, so the enemy takes a subtler route—through music. Proverbs 6:2 reminds us: *"You are snared by the words of your mouth,"* but sometimes, we're trapped not by what we say aloud, but by what we sing or even hum without thinking. Lyrics can quietly open doors to heartache, anxiety, despair, sickness, or even violence—especially when they echo pain or glorify harmful emotions. And once we step into those emotional portals, finding the way out isn't always easy.

Romans 10:17 says, *"Faith comes by hearing, and hearing by the word of God."* If faith is built

---

47. 1 Sam. 16:23
48. Job 35:10
49. John 10:5

through hearing God's Word, what happens when we're constantly exposed to words of fear, lust, sadness, or fantasy? Our hearts absorb what we listen to. Our senses act as gateways, and what passes through them can influence our thoughts, feelings, and even our physical responses. Over the years, numerous studies have demonstrated the significant neurological impact of music on mood, memory, and behavior.

I had to wean myself off songs (and voices) that fueled my pain. While comforting at first, they accentuated feelings of grief, despair, and emotional vulnerability. That part of me had been overindulged and left unchecked for too long. So, I made a shift—replacing my old playlists with Spirit-filled, Scripture-rich music, the audio Bible, and sermons that heightened my sensitivity to hear the Holy Spirit and kept my heart enveloped in truth. These deliberate choices created an environment that aligned with my faith, not my feelings. Remember, God inhabits the praises of His people, and it is in His presence that we experience the fullness of joy!

We must be mindful of what's playing in the background of our lives. What we listen to leaves an imprint on our minds, shaping our inner thoughts and conversations. 1 Thessalonians 5:22-23 (AMP) urges us to *"abstain from every form of evil [withdraw and keep away from it]. Now may the God of peace Himself sanctify you through and through [that is, separate you from profane and vulgar things, make you pure and whole and undamaged—consecrated to Him—set apart for His purpose]; and may your spirit and soul and body be kept complete and [be found] blameless at the coming of our Lord Jesus Christ."* The Message translation puts it plainly: *"Check out everything, and keep only what is good. Throw out anything tainted with evil."*

Feelings or moods can be influenced by creating the right atmosphere around you—calm, joyful, and conducive to emotional well-being. God still gives us songs—not to ignore the pain, but to guide us through it. In waiting seasons, music can become a sacred space—not to stir despair, but to anchor us in truth. So, let your playlist, like your heart, be filtered through God's Word. Spirit-filled, Christ-centered songs can provide a lifeline, fostering peace, strength, and reflection.

Your environment matters—be intentional about experiencing God's presence each day through worship, the beauty of His creation, gentle spiritual rhythms like prayer walks, or unhurried moments in Scripture where you can hear from Him.[50] Paul encouraged believers to focus on what is true, noble, lovely, and praiseworthy.[51] We, too, can process our emotions daily in the light of God's truth.[52]

10. Fortified friendships:

Some friendships are like sandcastles—easily washed away by the tide. But others are built like fortresses: fortified, tested, and able to withstand storms. These are life-giving,

---

50. Ps. 19:1-4; 105:4; Mark 1:35; Luke 5:16; John 15:4; James 4:8

51. Phil. 4:8

52. Ps. 16:11; Isa. 26:3

Christ-centered relationships shaped by loyalty, protected by love, and nourished by grace. They've endured trials, misunderstandings, distance, and change, yet remain resilient because they're rooted in godly values. True covenant friendships are honest, forgiving, and covered in prayer—beautiful reflections of God's design in a world of disposable connections and fleeting alliances.

God calls us to cultivate intentional relationships that can withstand the test of time—not fleeting, seasonal connections, but secure bonds that reflect His steadfast love. Friendship isn't just about what we can receive; it's also about what we're willing to give. When we extend our love—time, resources, encouragement, and care—it shifts our focus from our burdens to helping others improve their lives. Redirecting our attention from "me, myself, and I" toward serving others not only blesses them but also uplifts us. Philippians 2:4 states that we shouldn't look out only for our own interests, but we should take an interest in others.

The last thing one needs in challenging times is unnecessary drama or emotional drain. Surround yourself with people who sharpen and strengthen you—those who speak truth in love, respect your values, and walk in agreement with your faith. *"Can two walk together unless they are agreed?"* (Amos 3:3) Healthy relationships don't pull you off course—they anchor you in purpose and peace.

David and Jonathan's friendship exemplifies a powerful example of a fortified, covenantal bond. *"The soul of Jonathan was knit to the soul of David, and Jonathan loved him as his own soul."* (1 Sam. 18:1) Their connection was marked by deep loyalty and selfless love—proof that God-given friendships can be stronger than even familial ties.

At times, God prunes our circle—not to punish, but to protect His plan and maintain our dependence on Him. Just as He did with Gideon in Judges 7, it's not always about quantity, but quality—and alignment with God's purpose. Jesus Himself had many followers, yet He chose twelve to walk closely with Him. Within that group, there was an inner circle of three: Peter, James, and John.[53] Even among that trusted circle, Peter—perhaps the boldest—often faltered. Jesus had to rebuke him sharply when he opposed the path to the cross, saying, *"Get behind Me, Satan!"* (Matt. 16:23). Although Peter meant well, his human perspective was at odds with God's divine plan—revealing how even sincere intentions can become stumbling blocks when not aligned with spiritual truth.

On more than one occasion, I too had to issue my own firm "Get behind me, satan!"—especially to those who came with so-called *prophetic* words. Some claimed Ségun wasn't meant to be my husband and that our marriage was a mistake. One even said I'd remarry a pastor and have five children! Others advised me to stop believing in the impossible and move on with my life. One person flat-out declared that God couldn't possibly restore our marriage—that

---

53. Mark 9:2

it was beyond repair. That angered me. I couldn't accept the idea that anything was too hard for my God. NOTHING is too complicated for Him.[54]

I chose to believe in God's power to redeem, restore, and do the impossible—even when everything around me suggested it was over. Jesus Himself said salvation is impossible through human effort alone, but with God, even the hardest hearts can be transformed: *"With man this is impossible, but with God all things are possible"* (Matt. 19:26). I knew then—and I still believe now—that God has the power to save, especially those we label "unlikely," "unreachable," or "too far gone."[55] Just look at Saul (Paul), the thief on the cross, Mary Magdalene, etc. Honestly, you and I belong on that *sinner-to-saint* list too! We all have our own mercy-filled turnaround stories and testimonies of grace—yet, we're still works in progress.

Redemption isn't about who we are or how "good" we are; it's about who *God* is and how good *He* is—merciful, loving, and mighty to save.[56] Maybe some of those voices meant well, and maybe others had less pure intentions, but either way, I had to shut them down quickly. They didn't align with what the Holy Spirit had repeatedly whispered to my heart, nor with what God's Word clearly promises—and definitely not with the possibilities He opened my eyes to see.

Returning to Peter's relationship with Jesus, we witness another pivotal moment unfold in the Garden of Gethsemane. When Jesus needed him most, Peter fell asleep,[57] and later reacted impulsively by cutting off the ear of the high priest's servant.[58] Later, he denied even knowing Jesus three times before the rooster crowed.[59] Yet, Jesus never gave up on Peter. He forgave him and restored him,[60] continuing to entrust him with significant responsibility in the early Church. This reminds us that even close friendships require grace. Friends won't always get it right; they may speak or act out of fear, hurt, or misunderstanding. However, we must stay focused on God's purpose. We're called to bear with one another, forgive quickly, and love deeply—just as Jesus did.[61]

This is not the time to isolate completely. Yes, there are moments for solitude and stillness to hear God clearly,[62] but even during those times, He often sends help through people. Proverbs 24:6 reminds us: *"For by wise counsel you will wage your own war, And in a multitude of counselors there is safety."* God, who knows our every need, frequently answers our prayers through relationships, divine connections, or even simple nudges.

---

54. Jer. 32:17, 27
55. Isa. 1:18; 1 Tim. 2:3-4; 2 Pet. 3:9
56. Zeph. 3:17
57. Matt. 26:40-41
58. John 18:10-11
59. Luke 22:61-62
60. John 21:15-17
61. Col. 3:13-14
62. Ps. 46:10

I experienced this firsthand during a difficult health season. After trying everything to no avail, I felt prompted to reconnect with two dear friends. What started as an impromptu lunch became a divine appointment. One of them, I learned, had been facing similar health challenges, which began to improve after she followed a specific wellness protocol. Her progress encouraged her sister to embark on her own journey of healing, and through them, I was introduced to the same incredible wellness team. That one act of obedience—choosing connection over isolation—opened the door to answers I had been praying for. It reminded me that God often wraps solutions in people.

That said, spiritual insight is essential. Embracing or cultivating relationships doesn't mean being naïve. Be aware of your vulnerabilities—others can sometimes perceive your weaknesses from a distance. Unfortunately, not all environments are safe, even those that appear familiar or spiritual. The enemy can use anyone who gains your trust to plant seeds of doubt, discouragement, distraction, or to attempt to deceive you. Jesus said, *"Behold, I am sending you out as sheep in the midst of wolves, so be wise as serpents and innocent as doves"* (Matt. 10:16).

Choose your confidants prayerfully. Let Jesus remain your closest Friend and the Holy Spirit your Counselor, Guide, and Comforter.[63] While godly friendships are valuable, your primary source of strength, wisdom, and protection must be God Himself. Don't rely solely on human insight to carry you through this season. Instead, ask the Lord what He's doing in your situation and partner with Him to *wait well*—not in isolation, but in discernment and community.

During vulnerable seasons, it's wise to keep a safe and respectful distance from members of the opposite gender—regardless of their role or presentation, such as clergy, counselors, coworkers, or even comforting companions. Not everyone who appears harmless or godly has pure intentions. Jesus clearly warned in Matthew 7:15, *"Beware of false prophets, who come to you in sheep's clothing, but inwardly are ravenous wolves."* These individuals seek to exploit emotional or spiritual weaknesses, particularly within the faith community.

Paul further warns in 2 Timothy 3:6-7 about deceptive individuals who prey on vulnerable or gullible women, gaining access through manipulation, and under the guise of spiritual care. These scriptures emphasize the need for vigilance, a strong biblical foundation, and wisdom to recognize and resist those who use religious appearances to deceive and control others.[64] *"My dear friends, don't believe everything you hear. Carefully weigh and examine what people tell you. Not everyone who talks about God comes from God. There are a lot of lying preachers loose in the world."* (1 John 4:1 MSG)

God wants us to be perceptive, not paranoid! He still has faithful servants with a proven walk of integrity, grace, and reverence. Test every spirit, every voice, and every interaction, no matter how impressive or familiar they may seem. God urges discernment in all our relationships

---

63. John 14:26
64. Prov. 12:5; Isa. 30:1

because it influences what we hear and receive, which in turn has a bearing on our relationship with Him.[65]

During waiting seasons, especially when hope feels deferred and emotions run high, we must stay diligent and keep our focus on the bigger picture—our healing, growth, and destiny in Christ. This period requires concentration, and one may need to treat certain decisions as life-or-death matters to align with God's will. The frustration of delay and emotional fatigue can leave one exposed, so it's crucial to take precautions and establish clear boundaries—especially with those who seem helpful but may ultimately prove to be manipulative, spiritually distracting, or misleading.

Discernment is crucial in friendships and connections, as the people you allow to get close will influence what you hear, how you feel, and the decisions you make. Avoid staying in uncomfortable, spiritually draining environments out of guilt or obligation. Your loyalty belongs to God first. Let His wisdom, not people's opinions, guide your choices.

"In a multitude of words, sin is not lacking, but he who restrains his lips is wise." (Prov. 10:19) Loose lips sink ships! More often than not, it's during casual chats or unguarded conversations that careless words are spoken—statements that conflict with our faith and the promises we profess. You don't owe everyone an explanation. While it's wise to seek godly counsel or accountability when needed,[66] you're not obligated to share personal matters with everyone or defend your decisions—especially those involving severing ties that no longer align with where God is taking you.[67]

I found that providing honest, concise, and polite responses helped prevent unnecessary friction with those who were curious about my situation but were not necessarily meant to walk closely with me. A simple answer like, "We're working through some things, and God is helping us—please keep us in prayer," was often enough. A gentle answer steers the conversation away from pressure or gossip; just be ready to respond with grace and discretion when the need arises.[68] Ask God to help you recognize those He has placed in your life for mutual edification.[69]

Just like in the Garden of Eden, the serpent (satan) sowed a seed of doubt through a seemingly simple conversation with Eve. This powerfully illustrates how listening to the wrong voice can distort one's identity, invite shame, and lead one away from God's truth. Adam and Eve chose to believe a lie, disobeyed God, and ate the forbidden fruit—despite His clear command not to. Before the fall, they were naked and unashamed,[70] but sin altered their perception

---

65. Isa. 8:20; Matt. 7:15-16; 2 Cor. 11:13-15; 1 Thess. 5:20-21; 1 John 4:2-3
66. Prov. 11:14
67. Ps. 17:2; 35:24
68. Col. 4:6
69. Rom. 14:19
70. Gen. 2:25

of themselves. That's why God asked, *"Who told you that you were naked?"* (Gen. 3:11). It was never just about disobedience—it was about believing a voice that contradicted God's Word. That question still echoes today, reminding us to filter what we hear and believe through God's Word, not emotions or popular opinion.

No relationship is foolproof, and even the strongest friendships experience challenges. In Ephesians 4:2, the Bible encourages us to offer grace and space for one another's imperfections because of our love. We're also called in Colossians 3:12-14 to clothe ourselves with compassion, kindness, humility, gentleness, and patience… *"forgiving as the Lord forgave us. And over all these virtues **put on love**, which binds them all together in perfect unity."* These are the God-given "materials" that fortify relationships and build and sustain formidable friendships.

Micah 7:5-7 presents a sobering picture of broken trust and betrayal—even among families and close relationships. We live in similarly fragile times, filled with social injustice, relational breakdowns, and spiritual decline. The passage serves as a reminder that when society fails, and even those closest to us fall short, God remains trustworthy. He listens when others are silent, sustains when support is scarce, and restores in His perfect timing.

Rejection—especially from a spouse—can be incredibly painful and difficult to cope with. It can leave you feeling lonely and craving comfort or validation. In that vulnerable state, it's easy to rush into emotional attachments or rebound relationships in an attempt to fill the void. However, these responses don't heal the wounds or affirm your worth—to yourself or anyone else. Emotional entanglements aren't the solution. Healing comes from finding quietude in God's presence. I learned this the hard way. It wasn't instant, but over time, God showed me that I was made for more. My value didn't depend on what I lost but on whose I was. God says in Isaiah 43:4, *"…you are precious in my eyes, and honored, and I love you…"* No human affirmation can match that!

Friendships often reflect our inner needs as we seek fulfillment during various phases of life. As adults, we gravitate toward relationships that validate us—those who "see" us and support the choices we've made. Whether consciously or not, we're drawn to people who mirror our emotional, spiritual, and mental states. This isn't always negative, but it does require awareness. The company we keep often reveals the convictions we've embraced. For example, our stance on whether to stay in or leave a marriage is typically reflected in the kinds of friendships we cultivate or avoid.

One of the greatest gifts God gave me during this waiting season was the friendship of godly, married couples—some of whom I had known since our university days, back when they were still single. Their lives reflected consistent faith, kindness, and encouragement. One such relationship was with my chief bridesmaid and her husband, who later became a pastor. We often attended worship events together during the period Ségun and I were separated. One night in Lagos, Nigeria, remains unforgettable. Daniel Winans was ministering, and as he sang

"Brightness of the Moon," the lyrics struck a deep chord within me. I wept openly—not out of sadness, but conviction. I had been wrestling with whether to let go of Ségun and finally move on with my life, but in that moment, God reminded me that His love never gives up.

It's such a beautiful song that still moves me to this day whenever I listen to it. The lyrics speak of a love that remains—a guiding light that never goes out. I knew right then, without a doubt, that God had left His light on for us. Although Ségun had long since emotionally checked out and moved on, the Holy Spirit gently urged me to leave the candle burning—to keep hope alive. God's patient and unwavering love finds and rests with all of us, despite our tendency to forget or reject Him. Like the father waiting for the prodigal son,[71] God was reassuring me that His grace would do the drawing, and His promise would not fail. Despite what I could see or hear, I knew our story wasn't over. What God had written would stand—unchanging and sure![72]

This moment might never have happened if I hadn't been surrounded by faith-filled friends who continuously poured into me, prayed with me, and stood by me when I couldn't stand on my own.[73] *"A friend loves at all times, and a brother is born for adversity."* (Prov. 17:17) Their presence preserved my faith and helped me realign with God's truth at a critical crossroads. Formidable friendships are God's vessels of light and salt in our lives—carrying truth, preserving peace, and reminding us of who we are and whose we are. As Jesus said, *"Everyone will be tested by fire. Be preservatives yourselves. Preserve the peace"* (Mark 9:49-50 MSG). We all face refining seasons, but those surrounded by godly counsel endure with hope. We're called to be that kind of friend for one another.

It's also important to recognize that not everyone around you is for you. Some will quietly observe, waiting to see how long you'll endure or whether your God will truly come through. Instead of feeling anxious or self-conscious, take heart. The more such people gather, the more witnesses there will be to the testimony God is about to bring forth in your life. *"Many will see and fear the Lord and put their trust in Him."* (Ps. 40:3b) What the enemy meant for shame, God will use to showcase His power and faithfulness.

So let them watch. Let them bring their popcorn. They're about to witness the unfolding of a divine story—your story—crafted by the Author and Finisher of your faith.[74] Your sacrifices are seen, your tears are counted, and your waiting is not in vain.[75] Settle it in your heart: In Christ, your victory is assured.[76]

---

71. Luke 15:20

72. Ps. 119:89; Isa. 55:11

73. Eccles. 4:9-12

74. Heb. 12:2

75. Ps. 56:8; Rom. 8:28

76. 2 Cor. 2:14; Phil. 4:13

You're not drifting aimlessly through life. Your Heavenly Father already wrote your ending—*"all the days ordained for me were written in your book before one of them came to be."*[77] Just as Jesus stepped into the Father's will, saying, *"I have come to do Your will, O God"* (Heb. 10:7), we too are discovering—not creating—our purpose as we walk out what's already written.[78] You may be walking through a refining fire now, but you're being revealed as gold—and the brilliance of your life will point everyone (friends and frenemies) around you to the light of Christ. Remember, you're not alone.

11. Formative feedback:

This refers to the ongoing guidance that God provides to shape us as we grow into the likeness of Christ.[79] Whether through the Holy Spirit, a sermon, convicting scripture, or trusted people in our lives who speak truth in love, God uses these moments to chisel away what doesn't belong and to cultivate what does. As Proverbs reminds us, we shouldn't despise the Lord's discipline or get upset when He corrects us, *"for the Lord corrects those He loves, just as a father corrects a child in whom he delights"* (Prov. 3:11-12). And through His Spirit, who leads us into all truth, God gently instructs and refines us—not to shame us, but to encourage reflection and steady growth toward becoming all He has called us to be.[80]

Our response to feedback—especially correction—demonstrates our maturity and willingness to grow. In times of waiting, it helps us remain aligned with God's voice and purpose. *"My sheep hear my voice, and I know them, and they follow me"* (John 10:27). Like a potter shaping clay, God patiently molds us into vessels fit for His purpose.[81] This type of feedback encourages us to stay teachable and humble. If we're unapproachable or defensive, we may miss out on the very truth we need to hear. It's especially powerful when we pause to ask the Holy Spirit, "What are You showing me here?" or "How can I grow from this?" Waiting well requires us to embrace correction as a tool for transformation—not a sign of failure, but proof of our Father's care and commitment to us.[82]

Don't forget where you began or what God has accomplished along the way. *"Write the vision and make it plain…"* (Hab. 2:2) Journaling your journey—including scriptures, prayer points, and revelations—helps you track the process of transformation (before and after) and remember God's faithfulness.

God longs to speak to us, yet in prayer, we often do all the talking and forget to listen.

---

77. Ps. 139:16
78. Isa. 46:10; Eph. 2:10
79. Rom. 8:29; 2 Cor. 3:18
80. John 16:13
81. Jer. 18:1-6
82. Heb. 12:11

How can He guide or correct us if we're not listening?[83] We must intentionally spend time meditating on Scripture, where He reveals His heart and gives us His instructions.[84] This was a pivotal turning point for me—learning to sit, listen, and receive without rushing to face the world unprepared. Be honest and give yourself grace as you uncover your flaws and grow.

12. Flourishing in grace and fullness of joy

> *"Rejoice in the Lord always [delight, take pleasure in Him]; again I will say, rejoice!*
> *Let your gentle spirit [your graciousness, unselfishness, mercy, tolerance, and patience]*
> *be known to all people. The Lord is near. Do not be anxious or worried about any-*
> *thing, but in everything [every circumstance and situation] by prayer and petition*
> *with thanksgiving, continue to make your [specific] requests known to God. And the*
> *peace of God [that peace which reassures the heart, that peace] which transcends all*
> *understanding, [that peace which] stands guard over your hearts and your minds in*
> *Christ Jesus [is yours]."* (Phil. 4:4-7 AMP)

Waiting on God isn't meant to be filled with frustration. It's a sacred opportunity to grow in grace, deepen our trust in Him, and discover joy rooted in His presence—not in our circumstances.[85] When we surrender to God's timing, we don't just endure the *wait*—we thrive. He gives *"beauty for ashes, the oil of joy for mourning, and the garment of praise for the spirit of heaviness"* (Isa. 61:3).

Flourishing means choosing joy in every season, even amid uncertainty. It's allowing God's beauty to shine through your life, embracing His strength, and bringing His peace into every situation and interaction. Psalm 37:3-4 reminds us, *"Trust in the Lord and do good…Delight yourself also in the Lord, and He shall give you the desires of your heart."* Ephesians 3:18-19 calls us to experience the *width, length, depth, and height* of Christ's love and be *"filled with all the fullness of God."* Being fulfilled or content in Christ brings us to a point where loving, laughing, rejoicing, singing, and praising come easily. It's accepting His love and believing God still has a purpose for you.[86]

So, walk and talk like a true child of the Most High God. My sister, present yourself like royalty—like Queen Esther, who carried herself with grace and courage even under intense pressure.[87] Those seemingly small details in her preparation mattered—and yours do as well. My brother, lead with integrity and humility, like David, a man after God's heart. He waited,

---

83. Isa. 30:21
84. 1 John 5:3
85. Ps. 16:11
86. Prov. 17:22
87. Esther 5:1-2

worshiped, and warred in the spirit, even in hidden places, trusting in God's timing and training. God is perfecting all that concerns you.[88] Flourishing in this season is possible—and beautiful— when you stay rooted in God's presence, walk in His love, and embrace joy as your strength.[89]

Don't put your life on hold for anyone or anything.[90] Waiting on God is not a season of idleness—it's a delivery room. In this sacred space, you'll give birth to purpose, ideas, unique gifts, and new depths of intimacy with Him. This perspective not only excited me but also shifted everything for me, empowering me to embrace life again with balance, gratitude, and joy. Waiting becomes an invitation to rediscover God in richer dimensions, because *"those who know their God shall be strong and do exploits."* (Dan. 11:32b).

I remember something Ségun said after we reconciled: He told me part of the reason he was drawn back to me was that I had started glowing again—he even mentioned the weight I'd gained in my legs! I was shocked. I thought he had stopped noticing altogether, yet he was still watching—maybe even ogling! That moment reminded me that true contentment radiates from within. God's light cannot be hidden, and His love is an irresistible force that draws others—not just to us, but ultimately to Him.

> *"Be happy [in your faith] and rejoice and be glad-hearted continually (always);Be unceasing in prayer [praying perseveringly]; Thank [God] in everything [no matter what the circumstances may be, be thankful and give thanks], for this is the will of God for you [who are] in Christ Jesus [the Revealer and Mediator of that will]. Do not quench (suppress or subdue) the [Holy] Spirit"* (1 Thess. 5:16-19 AMP)

Don't delay or postpone your happiness. If you can't learn to be happy now, even while you wait, you won't suddenly become happy when the promise arrives. Joy is a decision rooted in confidence that God is at work. It's a byproduct of inner peace, not a result of perfect circumstances. It's how we renew our minds,[91] fix our thoughts,[92] and set our affections.[93]

Discontentment whispers that joy lies in what we don't have, but Scripture warns us not to be deceived: Joy in trials is part of God's design for us.[94] True strength is found when you rejoice even in sorrow, knowing *"the joy of the Lord is your strength"* (Neh. 8:10). Our ultimate aim isn't just happiness; it's fulfilling God's will—loving Him, obeying Him, and loving others

---

88. Ps. 138:8
89. Neh. 8:10
90. Ps. 62:5
91. Rom. 12:2
92. Phil. 4:8
93. Col. 3:2
94. John 16:33; 1 Pet. 4:12-13

with Christlike compassion. When we shift from "What do I want?" to "What does God want to do in me and through me?"—we experience true contentment.

In His presence is fullness of joy[95]—a joy that sustains us through seasons of waiting and uncertainty. To flourish in grace is to anchor yourself in that joy, live with purpose, and refuse to let delays paralyze your hope. As Psalm 1 declares, the one who delights in the Lord and meditates on His Word is like a tree planted by streams of water—steadfast, nourished, and fruitful in every season. However, flourishing is not just about outward stability; it's also about tending the heart. In anxious moments, remember: *"Anxiety weighs down the heart, but a kind word cheers it up."*[96] So let your words—both to yourself and others—be filled with grace: *"like honey, sweet to the soul and healing to the bones."*[97] This is part of your calling. You are a radiant reflection of God's glory. *"Arise, shine, for your light has come, and the glory of the Lord rises upon you."*[98] And like the morning sun, *"the path of the righteous shines ever brighter till the full light of day."*[99]

> *"... for I have learned how to be content (satisfied to the point where I am not disturbed or disquieted) in whatever state I am. I know how to be abased and live humbly in straitened circumstances, and I know also how to enjoy plenty and live in abundance. I have learned in any and all circumstances the secret of facing every situation, whether well-fed or going hungry, having a sufficiency and enough to spare or going without and being in want. I have strength for all things in Christ Who empowers me [I am ready for anything and equal to anything through Him Who infuses inner strength into me; I am self-sufficient in Christ's sufficiency]."* (Phil. 4:11-13 AMP)

13. Finishing strong and well:

Running your race with perseverance and crossing the finish line with joy, faithfulness, and victory isn't just a hopeful outcome—it's a deliberate result of how you choose to *wait*. How we navigate and endure the process determines how we finish. Waiting isn't just about patience— it's about preparation, perseverance, and character. Those who wait well—anchored in faith, obedient in action, and surrendered in spirit—are more likely to complete their journey with joy, purpose, and peace. As Paul said in 2 Timothy 4:7, *"I have fought the good fight, I have finished the race, I have kept the faith."*

Finishing strong is the result of waiting well. Looking back, our journey might not have needed to last six and a half years. If we had tackled specific issues and utilized these "13 Functional

---

95. Ps. 16:11
96. Prov. 12:25
97. Prov. 16:24
98. Isa. 60:1
99. Prov. 4:18

Keys" earlier—opting for faith and patience over pride or fear—our time apart could have been shorter.[100] However, what truly matters is that, at some point, Ségun and I chose to prioritize God once again. We gave Him His rightful place in our hearts and marriage, and that's when things began to change—when we genuinely allowed His will to shape our story.

Hebrews 12:1 reminds us to lay aside every weight and the sin that so easily entangles, allowing us to run our race with endurance, focus, and freedom—just as God intended. This journey of faith isn't a casual stroll or a competition for show. We're not running just to say we tried or to receive a participation award—we're running to win the eternal prize.[101] That means we can't let anything—fear, bitterness, selfishness, insecurity, or even the pressure to perform or please others[102]—hold us back or knock us off course.[103] In God's eyes, victory isn't measured by speed or status—it's about steady, faithful obedience. The goal is not to impress people but to please God in every area of life—marriage, parenting, purpose, and even in the quiet, hidden places no one sees.

Yes, the nights may seem long right now, but morning always comes. There is light at the end of the tunnel, and what you're facing will eventually pass. *"Forgetting what is behind and straining toward what is ahead...I press on toward the goal to win the prize for which God has called me heavenward in Christ Jesus."* (Phil. 3:13-14 NIV) Scripture encourages us with real-life examples of how God rewards endurance with restoration—yours can be the next testimony. Your Father sees the end from the beginning. He is compassionate, full of mercy, and He loves you. So, hold on to hope. Stay the course. Don't quit. Wait well. Run to win. Finish well.[104]

> *"Take the old prophets as your mentors. They put up with anything, went through everything, and never once quit, all the time honoring God. What a gift life is to those who stay the course! You've heard, of course, of Job's staying power, and you know how God brought it all together for him at the end. That's because God cares, cares right down to the last detail."* (James 5:10-11 MSG)

---

100. Heb. 6:12
101. 1 Cor. 9:24
102. Gal. 1:10
103. Gal. 5:7
104. Ps. 84:11; Heb. 6:11

18

The Valley of Decisions

"This is what the Lord says: 'Stop at the crossroads and look around. Ask for the old, godly way, and walk in it. Travel its path, and you will find rest for your souls. But you reply, 'No, that's not the road we want!''"

JEREMIAH 6:16 NLT

BUDDING GRAPEVINES

It's important that we pay close attention to warning signs along our journey—especially at crossroads, where crucial decisions must be made that could shape or shake the course of our lives. Sadly, many treat love and marriage like a revolving door, falling in and out of them as though it were a game or a reality show! But marriage isn't a trend or an emotional whim—it's a spiritual agreement between God, man, and woman. Jeremiah 6:16-19 (MSG) reminds us that God offers a tested and true path, yet many reject His direction, dismiss His warnings, and choose instead the road of self-will and independence.

The "valley of decisions" is where the soul is tested: Will we surrender to God's leading or insist on our own? The cost of ignoring divine guidance is rarely isolated; it impacts generations. That's why the "valley" isn't a place to rush through; it's where we stop, reflect, and choose wisely before the consequences of disobedience take root.

No matter how logical or justifiable a decision might seem—especially those that could alter destiny, like choosing a spouse, initiating a separation, or contemplating divorce—we must be led by God, not by emotions.[1] Deuteronomy 28:1-6 teaches that obedience brings blessings, while disobedience results in consequences. From our limited perspective, we can't always foresee how our choices will ripple through time, relationships, and generations. That's why, if you're standing in a valley of decision right now, pause and seek the Lord. Look up, listen to godly counsel, and reflect on Jesus—the One who endured suffering with joy because He saw the greater promises ahead.[2] As Hebrews 6:12 (AMP) urges, *"… be imitators of those who through faith [lean on God with absolute trust and confidence in him and his power] and by patient endurance [even when suffering] are [now] inheriting the promises."*

While my lawyer managed the divorce proceedings, I stopped trying to convince Ségun to change his mind. Instead, I focused on walking with God and standing firm—especially in refusing to grant him sole custody of our children. Rather than respond with animosity, I was more consistent in sowing seeds of faith and love: sharing scriptures, praying earnestly for him, and refusing to be vindictive. Unknowingly, those seeds took root and continue to bear fruit in our family today. My transformation became undeniable. As I healed and grew—emotionally, spiritually, and professionally—it began to show. I wasn't the same woman anymore, and Ségun noticed. He later admitted he was drawn to my confidence, maturity, growth, and quiet strength through the storm. I was thriving—not for show, but because God was rebuilding me from the inside out. I believe this may have contributed partly to Ségun initiating a last-ditch effort to see if we could work things out in the fifth year of our separation. Indeed, *"loyalty makes a person attractive"* (Prov. 19:22a NLT).

Our first significant attempt at reconciliation began in February 2008, when Ségun's tone in his messages and phone calls became noticeably softer and more thoughtful. He asked to visit occasionally, and we'd spend time talking about the possibility of getting back together. As we grew more comfortable with each other, his calls became more frequent. He asked probing questions, and I answered honestly. Ségun asked for my forgiveness—for the lost years and the pain I endured during our separation. He affirmed me as a wonderful mother, praising the children's character and my efforts in raising them. I also sought his forgiveness for the ways I had responded to the hurt—whether through confrontations, emotional outbursts, or disrespect. His words were encouraging, but I remained cautiously hopeful. He agreed to pray with me sometimes, which helped anchor our conversations in something deeper than just emotion or nostalgia.

We agreed that it was crucial to rebuild our relationship privately and allow God to guide the process before involving others. We wanted our decision to be firm before making it public—to prevent outside interference, no matter how well-intentioned. I was particularly keen on this approach because I felt we needed to address the real issues between us, rather than

---

1. Prov. 3:5-6
2. Heb. 12:2

the noise and influences that had previously obscured God's will for our lives. We had learned the hard way how external voices, even loving ones, could distort perspective, delay healing, and drown out God's voice.

In March, Ségun arranged counseling sessions with an elderly Christian couple who were close friends of his parents. A mutual friend also hosted us for a private discussion. Although I appreciated the effort and goodwill, I found it hard to connect with the older couple. Their line of questioning felt intrusive and one-sided, often downplaying the deeper issues we needed to address. It seemed their loyalty leaned more toward Ségun, which made me feel unseen and discouraged. Thankfully, he soon realized that the approach wasn't helping us move forward. Recognizing the need for deeper, unbiased guidance, he suggested we explore professional counseling without religious overtones.

Discussing issues as a couple is helpful, but having an objective, discerning, and neutral voice present can be even more beneficial—especially in the early stages of reconciliation. Proverbs 11:14 reminds us that *"… in the multitude of counselors there is safety,"* but that safety depends on the quality and wisdom of the counsel. Nothing is more frustrating and hinders progress than being misunderstood, ignored, or misrepresented. Without the right guidance, conversations can spiral into blame or defensiveness rather than lead to healing. True reconciliation requires more than just talking—it requires truth, humility, and God's help in pruning away what no longer serves the relationship, so something new can begin to grow.[3]

Sadly, even at this stage, Ségun remained fixated on the idea that something was fundamentally wrong with me—that I was the root of our marital problems. So, he began searching for a psychologist who could address his concerns about me. Fortunately, he eventually settled on one in Harley Street, the UK, whom he thought would be the best fit, and arranged a few joint sessions to coincide with our children's summer holiday. I agreed to go along, even covering my travel costs, hopeful that with the right therapist, both of us would gain fresh perspective and identify areas where we each needed to grow. Secretly, I also wondered how he might respond if confronted with his own shortcomings—perhaps even diagnosed with a few clinical "labels" that reflected the traits I'd observed in him during our marriage. But truthfully, I was more interested in healing together than proving a point.

By mid-April 2008, we had officially—though still secretly—reconciled, and I began staying with him at our marital home. Our boys, who were still living with him, were initially unaware of the situation. Ségun felt it was best not to tell them, to avoid raising their hopes, until he was sure that the relationship was on solid ground. It was a covert arrangement—he would send a car to pick me up discreetly from my place and return me either home or to work before the children woke up.

---

3. John 15:2

In May, when Ségun had to travel on business to Accra, I officially moved in to stay with our boys. This gave us the perfect opportunity to gently tell them that we were trying to get back together, and that I would be around more often. Their joy was overwhelming—like a dream come true. You'd have thought we'd promised them a trip to Disneyland! When Ségun returned, he asked me to go back to my place, and by then, we had already started openly interacting with each other in front of our children and spending time together indoors with them. That was a huge step forward.

Ségun told me he would instruct his lawyers to halt the divorce proceedings and assured me that, after a month of inactivity, the case would be automatically dismissed. I took him at his word and didn't follow up with my lawyer, since we hadn't gone public yet. Around the same time, he confided in me about a major government contract he had been working on, which was unexpectedly shelved by the agency concerned. I saw how devastated he was, and I stood by him—encouraging him, praying with him, and even offering contacts from my net-work to help explore new business opportunities.

I supported meaningfully in running our home. This was significant for me—it felt like I was finally being given the chance to demonstrate my value as a wife, partner, and mother in ways I hadn't before our separation. I did it not to prove a point or out of pride, but with joy and a sense of accountability to God.[4] Despite his reservations about our reunion, Ségun found quiet ways to show he still cared. One moment stood out: When I expressed dissatis-faction with certain aspects of my job, he unexpectedly asked for my résumé so he could send it to a friend. I was surprised—not just by the gesture itself, but by what it suggested. It could easily raise eyebrows that he was helping his "ex-wife," or that he was back with her. But it showed effort and a willingness to support me. We both seemed open to trying again, even if we weren't fully aligned.

Although we'd agreed to treat this as a trial period, I hoped for more than reconciliation—I longed for restoration. The emotional and physical back-and-forth between two homes wasn't ideal, but I was willing to be patient. I was fully in, but Ségun seemed to be battling invisible walls. Sometimes he was distant, as if wrestling with inner fears or unspoken issues that held him back from committing at the same level as I was—or at least meeting me halfway. Our relationship began to feel strained. He said he wanted us to try again, yet some days I felt like I was forcing myself into his life. I started to hold back emotionally, too, afraid to voice my hurt over how I had been treated. Ironically, if anyone had a right to hesitate or needed more healing, it should have been me. But I had nothing left to prove or convince Ségun about. I had poured out my love openly and consistently. At that point, all I could do was watch and pray for more grace to *wait well*—with faith that God would complete what He had begun.[5]

---

4. Col. 3:23

5. Phil. 1:6

I observed a few things during this back-and-forth arrangement with Ségun. He had moved out of our old apartment and was now occupying two apartments directly opposite each other. The one we shared before our separation remained largely unchanged, which puzzled me—especially considering the financial strain he claimed to be under due to the canceled contract and unresolved disputes with a former business partner. I couldn't understand his decision to keep both properties, but I chose to give him the benefit of the doubt. Perhaps he was overwhelmed or hadn't had the time to sort out all our belongings and give up the extra property.

Most of our conversations focused on me—what I had done, where I had been, and why I had made certain choices after our separation. In contrast, he only shared what he thought I needed to know. Maybe he wasn't sure he could trust me, or he feared how I might respond to the full story of his journey during our years apart. It took a lot of restraint not to revert to my old ways of "digging for facts." Instead, I relied on God to reveal what truly mattered, in His time. I knew that the access I now had—back into my children's lives and, slowly, into my husband's—was a sacred opportunity to reconnect and rebuild. I didn't want to jeopardize it.

Before we reached this point of sheathing our swords, my lawyer told me about an unusual moment at what was meant to be our penultimate court hearing. A divorce *nisi* was to be granted on that day before the final step of the process—a divorce *absolute*. I rarely attended court, except for custody issues involving our children—I found the entire ordeal emotionally exhausting and deeply humiliating. Ségun, on the other hand, was always present, being the one actively pursuing the divorce.

That day, however, the presiding judge made an unexpected comment. Ségun later told me that she spoke directly to him, urging him to reconsider his divorce petition altogether, although she would, for the time being, grant his request for a divorce nisi. She said that she would be praying for a reconciliation ahead of the final hearing and that, at our joint appearance, we would tell her that not only were we back together, but we had arranged a holiday in an exotic location. Indeed, God can use anyone! I truly believe the judge planted a seed that day—one that God continued to water and sprout in Ségun's heart. *"The king's heart is in the hand of the Lord... He directs it like a watercourse wherever He pleases."* (Prov. 21:1)

In the summer of 2008, our children traveled to the UK with Ségun's mother. They stayed with his sister until we arrived. In a gesture that still humbles me, one of Ségun's friends offered us his home for the duration of our stay and even covered the cost of our sessions with the psychologist. His gracious mother, with whom Ségun has a close bond, kindly looked after our boys while we attended the appointments.

The sessions were incredibly helpful, providing fresh insight into how we're wired—our strengths, fears, and triggers. However, psychology has its limitations, especially when it comes to spiritual matters, covenantal responsibility, and the moral foundation of marriage. Therapy can help identify patterns, but real transformation—lasting change, healing, and course correction—comes from God. *"Unless the Lord builds the house, those who build it labor in vain."* (Ps. 127:1)

Psychology is rooted in human reasoning—careful observation, pattern recognition, and evolving theories—but such knowledge is partial and ever-changing. What seems insightful today might be revised tomorrow. In contrast, God's Word is both timeless and eternal—unchanging in truth and enduring in power. It is unwavering and discerning—offering wisdom that penetrates far deeper than any clinical tool can reach in a few therapy sessions. *"For the word of God is living and powerful … and is a discerner of the thoughts and intents of the heart."* (Heb. 4:12)

Even the best therapists can only work with what they observe or what their patient is willing and able to express. But the Holy Spirit knows what lies beneath. Where therapy explains, the Spirit transforms for good. He uncovers what is hidden and heals what is broken.[6] Sometimes, outcomes can be subjective—shaped by the therapist's values, beliefs, sensitivity, experience, and therapeutic approach. These factors can either enhance or hinder the healing process—human interventions, though often valuable, pale in comparison to God's.

After a couple of sessions, I began to lose confidence and interest in the process. I felt exposed, and I was doing most of the emotional heavy lifting. I was open, diligent with the homework, and genuinely trying to apply what we were learning. But Ségun seemed more focused on convincing the therapist that something was wrong with me, even pressing her for a formal assessment, which she wisely declined. That shifted the atmosphere. I became guarded with my words, though by then, the damage was done. I had said more than I was comfortable with, and trust—already fragile—felt even more misplaced.

One of the reasons I agreed to therapy was that Ségun claimed there were deep issues we needed to unpack together under professional guidance. During one session, he reassured me that he had instructed his lawyers to withdraw the divorce petition, insisting that this trip to the UK—despite the cost and time away from work—was proof of his seriousness. But with each passing session, I began to doubt his motives. Was this reconciliation genuine, or just a strategic move to gather evidence for court? I was deeply disappointed. I had hoped we'd use the opportunity to stop avoiding the hard stuff and finally begin to heal.

Still, it was refreshing to spend time together as a family after being apart for so many years. I had quietly hoped that being in a different environment—away from familiar pressures and routines—might spark some warmth and affection between us. But emotional distance doesn't automatically disappear with geography. The past has a way of following us, especially when lessons remain unlearned and unresolved issues are swept under the carpet.[7]

We did our best to enjoy the trip, but both of us knew things weren't quite right. Sometimes laughter filled the air—but as Scripture says, *"Laughter can conceal a heavy heart, but*

---

6. 1 Cor. 2:10–11; Rom. 8:6; 12:2; Titus 3:5

7. 1 John 1:8 (NLT)

when the laughter ends, the grief remains" (Prov. 14:13 NLT). Healing doesn't happen by pretending; it happens when we confront lingering issues head-on with courage and clarity, however uncomfortable.

THE BREAKING POINT

We returned to Lagos in August with the children, and I continued living in our apartment. Financial pressures began to mount, and soon after, the nanny Ségun had employed resigned. The reality of our situation started to sink in, affecting each of us in different ways—not just materially, but emotionally too. I began to tread softly, as everything felt like delicate ground again.

By the end of the year—around September or October—I felt it was time to take a cultural step toward reconciliation with Ségun's family. He hadn't raised the subject, but I believed it was the right thing to do: to visit his parents and ask for their forgiveness. I knew I had been blamed for our separation, and while I disagreed with that narrative, humility sometimes calls us to make peace even when we feel misunderstood.[8] Ideally, Ségun should have accompanied me, but he declined. Traditionally, an elder from my side should have led that effort—especially after formal talks between both families—but those conversations had been shut down early in our separation. That door had long closed.

In our culture, the responsibility to initiate reconciliation often falls on the spouse deemed "at fault," and in this case, that was me. I hadn't told my father that Ségun and I were back together. Given the history and the abrupt manner in which I had been uprooted from my home, it would take much more than good intentions to convince him of Ségun's sincerity. According to our custom, it was Ségun's duty to reach out to my father before I returned to our matrimonial home. Some of these traditions are designed to protect and preserve dignity; others, when misapplied, can wound and silence. It takes discernment to know which is which.[9] Since Ségun wouldn't go with me, he at least facilitated my visit to his parents. But the visit didn't go well. His reluctance to support that effort—and his refusal to honor tradition by visiting my father in return—left me questioning where we were truly headed. Were we building something new or just trying to patch over old cracks?

For safety and accountability, I confided in a few elders on my mother's side about the reconciliation and my decision to accept it. Their response? Complete shock. They thought I was out of my mind—especially since I was going against the grain of our custom. Since marriage in Nigerian society is considered a union between families rather than just individuals, both families should have been involved in the dissolution or reconciliation process, just as they were when the marriage was formalized. So, I began to inform a small circle of trusted

8. Rom. 12:18
9. Eccles. 3:1, 7

friends and family, including my pastor, my older brother, and two aunts in the US, keeping them updated on the unfolding developments.

Time moved quickly, and before I knew it, December was here. I was genuinely looking forward to spending Christmas together as a family—something that had once seemed impossible. But to my utter dismay, Ségun suddenly asked me to move back to my apartment so a friend visiting from the UK could stay with him. I felt deeply hurt. Why would a man who had just reconciled with his wife ask her to leave so that his friend—who had family, other options, and even hotels—could stay? It wasn't as if we lacked enough space to accommodate all of us.

Though my mind raced with all kinds of thoughts, I chose not to react impulsively. I moved out quietly, but things came to a head when Ségun casually remarked that we hadn't "finalized anything" and that our reconciliation was still a trial period. That comment stung. He told me about three weeks later that his friend had left and that I could return if I wanted to. And I did—though with growing reservations.

By February 2009, the pressure mounted. Ségun was now facing the harsh reality of his financial situation, and he had to give up one of the apartments, then eventually the second. It was a difficult season for him, and while I didn't have the full picture of how we got here, I knew now wasn't the time for blame but a time to act. I rolled up my sleeves—sorting, packing, and coordinating movers. It was exhausting work—mentally, emotionally, and physically draining—but necessary.

We agreed that once I had created enough space and finished cleaning and refurbishing my place, which now contained items from our decluttered old apartment, the boys would move in with me. I invited Ségun to join us, but he said he was considering other options. My mothering instincts were strong—I wanted my children with me—but one of our boys had a dust allergy, and exposing him during the clean-up phase could have caused severe breathing issues. So, I waited.

I moved back to my apartment on March 2, 2009, and continued to keep in touch. I would often visit our home after work, before heading to my place. Everything seemed relatively stable until March 9, 2009, when Ségun suddenly started avoiding my calls. He refused to let me speak with the children, and his behavior became eerily familiar—withdrawn, unpredictable, and cold. When we did speak, he vaguely said things were "too complicated to explain."

I only spoke to our boys twice after they left the apartment, and he instructed them not to tell me where they were or who they were with. Finally, on March 16, 2009, he agreed to bring them to see me briefly after school. They arrived at my office fast asleep and had to be woken up just to say a quick hello. I fought back the tears. The unnecessary emotional strain being placed on them—and on me—was heartbreaking.

Days turned into weeks, and all I received were excuses for why our agreement couldn't be honored. Eventually, Ségun stopped taking my calls altogether, and I had no idea where he or our boys were staying. It became painfully clear that the children weren't coming to live with me—I had been misled. Even more troubling, his hostility suddenly returned, and the air of peace we'd rebuilt was gone.

I was scheduled to travel to the UK on March 22, 2009, for a ten-day work-sponsored course and was desperate to see our children before leaving. I kept sending messages, pleading to at least speak with them and find out what had changed. Finally, Ségun allowed a call, and one of our sons innocently let the "secret" slip that they were staying at their paternal grandparents' house. A couple of days later, one of them whispered they had moved again. My concern deepened as I couldn't tell if Ségun was cracking under pressure or deliberately playing mind games, but either way, the instability worried me.

Just days before my trip, he called one evening with a cryptic explanation: He was "going through some things beyond his control," experiencing what he described as a spiritual awakening. He insisted that he would give me access to our boys only when the "time was right." His words were unsettling. I ended that call in tears, kneeling before God, casting all my cares . . . my children on Him.[10]

Until then, I hadn't had any real concerns about our sons being with their father—but something about Ségun's utterances didn't sit right with me. I found the courage to call my dad and tell him everything. He was understandably upset that I had kept him in the dark and delayed the legal process— by refusing to file my response to Ségun's petition in court— especially with the final hearing just a few months away. Still, he comforted me and promised to take action in the morning—reaching out to his network and writing a firm letter to Ségun's father, urging him to call his son to order and stop the bullying. He reminded me that situations like this are precisely what our culture is meant to prevent, and that things might have gone more smoothly if I had let him handle it the traditional Yorùbá way—by involving elders from both sides to ensure accountability.

Though my father's reassurance helped, I was reminded by the Holy Spirit of an even greater covering. Earthly emissaries and cultural systems have their place, but nothing surpasses the power, presence, and protection of my Heavenly Father. I didn't have to wait until morning for help to arrive. That night, I entrusted Ségun and our boys into God's capable hands,[11] and I lay down in peace, confident that He was already at work behind the scenes.[12]

The days that followed were difficult, but I chose to keep walking in faith, returning to the "holding pattern" God had placed me in—*waiting well*—until I heard His explicit instruction

---

10. 1 Pet. 5:7

11. Ps. 121:7-8; 2 Tim. 1:12

12. Isa. 26:3-6

to move forward.[13] I trusted that, just as the Holy Spirit had led me through unknown terrain before, He would continue to guide me—step by step—into the place of promise.[14]

The chance to see my children finally arrived during a school concert—just a day before my trip to the UK. Ségun initially agreed to let them spend a few hours with me afterward, but once the concert ended, he abruptly changed his mind. He asked me to say my goodbyes next to his car. I was stunned. When I asked for a reason, he offered none, simply telling the boys to get in. I told him I couldn't leave the country, not knowing where my children were or who they were with. I urged him to put himself in my shoes and told him this wasn't fair to them or me. As a compromise, I suggested we all go somewhere nearby for ice cream. He agreed— on the condition that he came with us, and only one child could ride with me! While I was still trying to understand his reasoning, he suddenly canceled the outing altogether.

Refusing to let things end that way, I got into the back seat of his car to say a proper good- bye. The boys clung to me, their eyes brimming with tears—I couldn't bear it! On impulse, I refused to get out until he gave me answers. Without a word, Ségun drove off with me in the car, making a few calls before heading to his parents' house. Sensing a potential confrontation, I quickly reached out to my childhood friend, her husband (my pastor), and my older brother in the US—just in case things escalated. They urged me to ask Ségun to stop and let me out, but by then, we were already too far along the journey—literally and emotionally. I was deter- mined to get to the bottom of this matter.

When we arrived, Ségun quickly ushered the boys into the house. There was a bit of com- motion as I tried to follow. His parents were home, and they asked me to state my mission. I explained that I wanted to spend some time with my children before my work-related trip and needed clarity on when Ségun would fulfill his promise to bring them to live with me. I wasn't there to argue—I just wanted what was best for our sons. And on that day, it simply meant seeing them, holding them, and knowing they were okay. It was a moment of deep anguish and disappointment, but also of quiet resolve—one that still grieves me to recount, even for this book.

There was a lot of back and forth, filled with hurtful, accusatory words. I was told in Yor- ùbá: *"Bàbá ló l'omo,"* which means "The father is the owner of the child." It's a phrase often thrown around to assert paternal dominance, especially in times of conflict, but rarely invoked when fathers are expected to take responsibility or actively care for their children. That night, it was weaponized to strip me of any perceived rights over my children. I was told plainly that they belonged to the Adenijis, not to me. I stood there, grappling with the weight of cultural expectations that had been twisted for convenience. It made me question—again—how eas- ily people bend both tradition and Scripture to suit their agendas. But God's truth is not to

---

13. Gen. 12:1-2; Exod. 14:15; Deut. 1:6-7
14. Josh. 1:9; 3:4b-5

be manipulated. It is powerful enough to expose and demolish every false stronghold, cultural lie, and arrogant argument raised against His knowledge and justice.[15]

Scripture doesn't support such claims but consistently affirms the vital role and value of both parents in a child's life. It doesn't promote paternal ownership or dominance over children. The Bible clearly states that children are a gift from the Lord—not the possession or property of either parent—and that both father and mother have a shared responsibility (as stewards, not hierarchical owners) to love, nurture, protect, and train them in God's ways.[16] Any cultural or traditional belief that sidelines or dismisses the mother's God-given role is not only flawed but stands in opposition to the justice and truth of God.[17]

The contributions of both parents are considered essential and balanced. God honors and affirms a mother's role as a teacher, nurturer, and moral guide. From the Ten Commandments to the stories of faithful mothers like Hannah, Mary, and Jochebed, motherhood is honored throughout Scripture. The 5th commandment in the Bible doesn't elevate or favor one parent over the other.[18] Jesus' actions and teachings were steady, intentional, and unwavering in affirming the dignity and worth of women, including mothers. He never supported cultural systems that silenced or devalued them. His interactions with Mary, his own mother, and others, such as the Syrophoenician woman, demonstrate deep respect and responsiveness.

I lost my composure and reminded them that I had equal rights as a parent—and even more, since the children were legally minors. Their response? "Let the courts decide." My sons were instructed to go upstairs, and I was asked to leave. They looked torn and scared when I called to them, but they were physically blocked from reaching me. Then came the final blow: "If you want to see your children when you return, call us."

Ségun stood there, mostly silent. I stared at him, stunned. Surely, even if his parents were being overly protective—especially during this difficult phase in his life—this wasn't how to handle any conflict or disagreement between us. It became painfully clear that, in their eyes, I never truly belonged. I wasn't part of "them," like the children were. I was the outsider—still viewed as an intruder after all these years. And it showed.

In that moment, I realized major decisions had been made about our marriage and our children—and I was the last to know. I asked Ségun to explain to his parents that we'd been living together for months and had made plans for the boys to move in with me after they vacated the apartment, but he said nothing. His silence was deafening. I refused to leave without my children and was prepared to cancel my trip and inform my employers that I had a family emergency. If they feared I might take the children away, that concern was

---

15. 2 Cor. 10:5-6 (msg, esv, and amp)

16. Ps. 127:3; Prov. 6:20; 22:6

17. Mic. 6:8

18. Exod. 20:12

unfounded—Ségun had their passports. There was simply no justification for what was unfolding before me.

Since we weren't making any progress, I called my childhood friend and her husband again, and they kindly offered to pick us up since my car was still at the concert venue. While waiting for their arrival, and before I fully understood what was happening, Ségun hurriedly left with our children! Somehow, I managed to hold myself together and walked to my friends' car. They had been waiting outside the Estate, unable to gain entry. Both were relieved to see I was relatively okay, but emotionally, I was deeply shaken. Once I sat in the car, the tears flowed freely. What had just happened—and why? I just wanted to see my sons before leaving the country. Was that too much to ask as their mother?

In that heart-wrenching moment, I gained clarity. I just saw, firsthand, some of the influences shaping my husband's actions. It was sobering and eye-opening. We all have sources we draw from: family, mentors, preachers, experts, books, celebrities, and even social media influencers. While some offer life-giving wisdom, others can lead us astray. That's why we must know God for ourselves and be rooted in His Word that never misleads. Like Eve in Eden, it's easy to trust the wrong voice, but the consequences can be far-reaching.[19]

I called Ségun on our way to get my car, but his phone was off. I called my dad and told him what had transpired. He was furious and urged me to report the incident to the police. I decided against this as I didn't want to make things worse. My dad wanted to see me that night, but I reassured him that I was in safe hands and that I needed to pick up my car before going home.

That night, I spoke with some trusted friends and family. Everyone encouraged me to follow through with my work trip. My career and income were crucial—especially now—and I couldn't afford to jeopardize that. Traveling would also give me a chance to breathe, clear my mind, and take a break from the chaos for a while. A few people promised to check in on the boys in case Ségun wouldn't answer my calls, and Dad assured me he'd handle things while I was away.

I barely slept that night. By the time the office car arrived to take me to the airport the next morning, my eyes were swollen from crying. It was Mothering Sunday (Mother's Day) in Nigeria and the UK, which only intensified the pain of the day before. I wept for most of the flight and eventually fell asleep from exhaustion. I don't recall if anyone was able to reach Ségun, but thankfully, he answered my call when I landed. He allowed me to speak to the children and continued to do so every day while I was away—never once addressing the incident at his parents' house. He simply handed the phone to our sons.

Upon my return on April 1, I went straight to the school to see my boys. Ségun was already there to pick them up. Seeing them again brought overwhelming relief, though the memory

---

19. Gen. 3:1-6

of them crying and being taken from me still haunted me. I silently prayed those moments wouldn't leave a lasting mark on them. At a much later date, Ségun and I discussed what happened that night, but he claimed he was so focused on getting the children out of his parents' house that he hadn't paid much attention to how I was being treated. That excuse offered no comfort.

Despite my return, I was still denied unaccompanied access to our children. They could not visit or sleep over at my house. One day, during a call, they mentioned Ségun was attending prayer meetings. Ordinarily, I would have rejoiced at such news. But knowing his past contempt for my faith and his mockery of my devotion,[20] I was cautious. Spiritual hunger without discernment is dangerous. While Ségun occasionally attended church, I feared that deception might take root—especially since he hadn't consistently walked in close fellowship with God, wasn't grounded in His Word, and hadn't been part of a nurturing spiritual community. I simply didn't want him to be drawn into error or the kind of spiritual manipulation that, unfortunately, is prevalent everywhere.

The first time the boys were allowed to visit me after my return was on April 10, 2009—coinciding with the second anniversary of my late mother's passing. Their next visit was on April 19. Around this time, I began journaling more intentionally. I documented every significant detail—saved messages, our conversations, the children's updates. During that period, Ségun had a growing tendency to forget details of key discussions, decisions, or events, and I usually found myself second-guessing what actually happened. For emotional clarity, healing, and careful record-keeping, journaling proved to be a trusted companion.

Children are more perceptive than we often give them credit for. By their second visit, I knew exactly where they had been, who had visited, and even about a maid who disciplined them harshly. I was stunned to learn they had been living just a few streets away—yet instead of giving them the stability of living with their mother, Ségun moved them from place to place. I sensed that decision—like many others—might not have been solely about custody but could have been influenced by deeper concerns such as fear, control, or conflicting loyalties.

Ségun and I had agreed to meet twice that April to discuss the growing tension between us, but he kept postponing until we finally sat down toward the end of the month at a nearby hotel. Providentially, it was the same venue where I had attended the worship event, where Daniel Winans ministered his song "Brightness of the Moon." I entered that meeting still tender from recent wounds and, honestly, I hadn't fully "put on" the Lord Jesus Christ that day as I should have.[21] But as I walked toward Ségun, I was suddenly filled with a sense of God's presence. The lyrics of the song flooded back, washing over my soul as a powerful reminder

---

20. 1 Cor. 2:14 (NIV)

21. Rom. 13:14

of His unwavering nearness. That moment prepared me to stay calm and listen—not from a place of hurt, but from a heart yielded to God's grace.

I asked Ségun what had gone wrong this time—why the renewed hostility, and why it now felt more intense than ever. He explained that he'd had some kind of "epiphany" two months earlier and had gained clarity over the past six weeks. Then came the shock: Part of that so-called revelation, he claimed, was that I was "evil, diabolical, and a danger to him and the children!" He wouldn't say where this came from or when it was revealed. If he truly believed all that, why did he return in the first place and express a desire to rebuild? It was deeply unsettling.

His words left me speechless. I just stared at him in total disbelief. After a while, I couldn't take it anymore—I quietly left. He remained seated, looking subdued. I walked away feeling used and foolish for trusting again. Yet, even in that moment, I could tell he wasn't himself. He seemed as confused as I felt—and in all the years I'd known Ségun, I'd never seen him like that. What became unmistakably clear to me that day was that our battle wasn't just emotional—it was spiritual.[22] There were forces at work, relentless and determined, fighting against the possibility of our restoration. And though my heart ached, I began to understand that not every budding vine will automatically bear fruit—thorns choke some, others never take root.[23]

I had toiled, tilled, and tended. But now, I wasn't sure I had the strength or desire to keep contending for the faith amid the "thorns"[24]—whether suspicion, external voices, worries and pleasures of life, or spiritual blindness—that seemed to choke what had been sown. I knew that if the vine was to bear fruit, I needed to keep showing up with earnest prayer, wisdom, humility, and grace—entrusting God to bring the supernatural growth.[25] But I was weary... and slowly losing faith. It reminded me of Proverbs 13:12: *"Hope deferred makes the heart sick...."* The budding hope I once felt was now being put to the test again.

In Nigerian society, there's a common tendency to blame spouses, in-laws, neighbors, colleagues, or even domestic staff for misfortunes one encounters in life—illness, death, job loss, miscarriage, financial setback—anything that seems beyond human understanding. Sadly, women often bear the brunt of these accusations, especially when their husband's family hasn't fully accepted them as "blood." Yet, ironically, the covenant of marriage between husband, wife, and God is much stronger (and thicker) than any human blood tie.[26]

Tragically, these narrow perspectives cause some to accuse their own spouses of witchcraft or evil. Yes, evil exists—satan does come to steal, kill, and destroy[27]—but not every challenge

---

22. Eph. 6:12
23. Luke 8:14
24. Jude 1:3b
25. John 15:1-2, 5; 1 Cor. 3:6-8
26. Gen. 2:24; Eccles. 4:12
27. John 10:10

is the result of external spiritual warfare. Sometimes, it's a call for introspection. Before blaming others, we must ask: *Could my own choices, fears, or alliances be working against me?*

Many enter marriage without spiritual discernment, only to find themselves battling imaginary or exaggerated evils—much like characters from *Percy Jackson, Van Helsing*, or *Buffy the Vampire Slayer*.[28] These fictional comparisons may be amusing, but they reveal how some people live in constant suspicion. The truth is, we don't need to emulate fictional heroes—we need the Holy Spirit and the Word of God as our guide in making wise choices. *"... By their fruit, you will recognize them..."* [29] A person's character, actions, and choices reveal who they truly are as opposed to just appearances.

A well-known Yorùbá proverb states, *"Kòkòrò tó ń je ẹ̀fọ́, inú ẹ̀fọ́ ló wà"*—"The insect that eats the vegetable lives inside it." Often, it's those closest to us, whom we blindly trust, who quietly cause the most harm—through poor counsel, divisiveness, selfishness, or hidden envy or jealousy. But let's not forget: *We* may also be the "insect"—sabotaging our own homes with pride, bitterness, or cruelty. As Proverbs 11:17 (NLT) says, *"Your kindness will reward you, but your cruelty will destroy you."*

This is why God calls for introspection. In Malachi 2:13-16 (NLT), He rebuked men who covered His altar with tears but neglected the wife of their youth. God witnessed the vows they made, yet they had become cruel and unfaithful. *"Didn't the Lord make you one with your wife?... So guard your heart; remain loyal to the wife of your youth. 'For I hate divorce!' says the Lord."* When we mistreat covenant relationships, even our worship is hindered.

God takes our relationships seriously—especially the vows we make in marriage. In Malachi 2:14-16, He rebukes men who dealt treacherously with their wives, emphasizing that marriage is not just a social contract, personal commitment, or a private affair—it's a sacred covenant made before Him. The pain of broken trust isn't just horizontal; it also disrupts our relationship with God. This call to faithfulness applies not only to men but also to women. Throughout the Bible, God calls everyone—men and women—to walk in faithfulness, honor, and love, especially in our closest relationships.[30]

Marriage vows are not to be taken lightly—they involve someone else's heart and future. God warns us not to be careless with our words or promises—especially to Him.[31] We need to understand the weight of our words before God. Whether it's in marriage, family, or community, God watches how we treat each other. He blesses integrity and loyalty, but He resists

28. *Percy Jackson & the Olympians: The Lightning Thief* (2010), directed by Chris Columbus, starring Logan Lerman; *Van Helsing* (2004), directed by Stephen Sommers, starring Hugh Jackman; *Buffy the Vampire Slayer* (1992), created and written by Joss Whedon, starring Kristy Swanson—all referenced as fictional analogies, not theological truth.

29. Matt. 7:15-20 (NIV)

30. Prov. 14:1; Matt. 19:3-9; Mark 10:2-12; Eph. 5:21-33; Col. 3:18-19 (MSG); 1 Pet. 3:1-7

31. Deut. 23:21-23; Prov. 20:25; Eccles. 5:2-5; Matt. 5:33-37

those who act unjustly or selfishly in marriage.[32] Proverbs 5:15-23 (NLT) paints a wonderful picture of marriage as a source of blessing, joy, love, grace, fulfillment, intimacy, and romance—when nurtured with wisdom and grace. When trust is broken, it affects our prayers, our peace, our worship, and our witness.

For the last six years, I had persevered in prayer and hope. And just when I thought the answer was within reach, things fell apart again. In hindsight, I realized our reconciliation was premature. Healing hadn't gone deep enough, and there were lingering conversations we hadn't had—especially the honest, uncomfortable ones Ségun kept avoiding. I also faltered: leaning on emotions instead of God's counsel and acting as if we could take over from Him. I rushed ahead, as though saying to God, "Thanks, we've got it from here!"

My prayers had waned when they should have intensified.[33] Some relational ties that needed severing were still intact, making it difficult for us to rebuild ours. I overlooked and underestimated the influence of the unresolved ties—those whose opinions still shaped our decisions and whose presence still clouded our union. Without God's love truly binding us, old wounds and baggage resurfaced—weaponized not only by us, but also by others who were still too involved. The result? Our fragile progress buckled under pressure.

Perhaps Ségun was sincere in wanting to try again, but he was still relying on his own limited strength and understanding. The pressure of unresolved issues—both relational and professional—caused friction that left little room for honest healing or rebuilding. Trying to move forward without God's full counsel often takes us right back into the very place we're trying to escape.

Things quickly took a dark turn when Ségun started sending hostile and threatening messages to my work email—twisting my words and weaponizing past conversations against me. I wasn't blameless; we exchanged many hurtful words. But amid the pain, I continued sowing seeds of God's Word into our communication, no matter how small. Still, I had reached a turning point. I loved him deeply, but I could no longer keep making excuses—or keep fighting for someone who repeatedly showed he wouldn't fight for himself, for me, or for us. Two people cannot walk together without first agreeing on which way to go and how to get there.[34]

Deep down, I had hoped that by now he'd recognize the weight of all that had been lost. So much had fallen apart, yet he seemed stuck—wavering between loyalties and listening to voices that distorted the truth of who I had always been to him since 1993. If, after all this time, he still couldn't see the *real Funké*—choosing confusion and external opinions over reality—then it was no longer my burden to prove myself. I was exhausted. The manipulation—whether he

---

32. Heb. 13:4 (AMP)

33. Prov. 3:5-6

34. Amos 3:3

allowed it knowingly or passively—had taken its toll. That night, after the meeting at the hotel, I called him and said I'd agree to the divorce he'd once demanded—and still insisted he wanted.

Even then, the Holy Spirit whispered: *"Be on guard. Stand firm in the faith. Be courageous. Be strong. And do everything with love"* (1 Cor. 16:13-14 NLT). God reminded me that He was still in control—fighting for us behind the scenes, if only I would surrender the reins to Him.[35] I still trusted God, but hearing what Ségun said that night really shook me. His words pierced something deep. I had reached my breaking point—the proverbial "deal-breaker." Yes, I once belonged to that school of thought, too. I wasn't turning away from God; I was just prepared to let go of a marriage that I felt had become emotionally unsafe. After all, I signed up for marriage, not martyrdom! I had laid nearly everything down, including my health, peace of mind, and my sense of self, in the process of *trying to save my marriage*. Pain can mold us, yes—but we're not called to enter it recklessly! As Glenn Lutjens wisely puts it, "Facing pain can certainly refine us, but we don't get extra credit for walking into it—especially when it can be avoided."

Breaking up the second time was even more painful and devastating than the first. For me, this was the last straw! I felt Ségun had taken my willingness to walk the path of peace for granted—and worse, taken advantage of it. Though I was deeply angry, I still had the presence of mind to pray—not just for myself, but for our future. I knew we both needed God's help to move forward and parent our children with wisdom. In anguish, I cried out for mercy and vindication.[36] I asked God to open Ségun's spiritual eyes, to give him a fresh revelation of Jesus Christ, and to flood every dark or confused area of his heart with the light of truth.[37]

During that season, I immersed myself in Scripture, drawing strength and clarity from passages that became lifelines and prayers—verses like 2 Samuel 14:14; Proverbs 21:1 AMP; John 3:16; Acts 16:31 TPT; Joshua 24:15 NLT; 2 Peter 3:8-9 MSG; Ephesians 1:18-20; Colossians 1:9-10; 1 Corinthians 7:13-14 TPT; Psalm 5:8; Psalm 25:5; Psalm 27:11; and Psalm 143:10.

There were many times I wrestled internally. *Had I misunderstood what God told me years ago? Did my approach make me appear weak? Was I foolish for holding on this long? Had I enabled Ségun's attitude toward me? Misheard God's promises? Misread the signs or misapplied the Scriptures?* After six long years, it felt like I had been circling the same mountain—emotionally, mentally, and spiritually drained. I wasn't prepared to waste another day. So, I instructed my lawyer to proceed with the divorce—fully and finally. Strangely, I wasn't afraid. Maybe it was the peace that comes when you know you've done all you can. I had fought the good fight with all I had.[38] Now, all I wanted was rest and stability—for my children and for myself.[39]

---

35. Exod. 14:14 (NLT); 2 Chron. 20:15b; Jer. 29:11; 2 Cor. 10:3-5

36. Isa. 54:17; Ps. 35:23-24; 37:5-6; 43:1-5 (AMP)

37. Matt. 6:22-23; Ps. 119:18 (NKJV)

38. 2 Tim. 4:7

39. Isa. 30:15

As I awaited the final hearing, I became reflective. I pondered the many confirmations I had received over the years—signposts from God, vivid dreams, prophetic words, and encouragement from people He placed around me. The day I was forced out of my home, my older brother called from the US and tried to reassure me: "Ségun will come back to beg you!" My mother wholeheartedly believed in our restoration—and until her passing, she never stopped assuring me it would come.

God surrounded me with an "army." One aunt, whom we fondly call Grandma T, was a tireless encourager. She sent regular emails filled with scriptures and guidance she believed were from the Lord. She made significant sacrifices, checking in several times a week to help me stay on course. My best friend, who had known us from the beginning, never took sides. She treated Ségun with grace, even during our separation, and lovingly welcomed him back. Her counsel was honest—sometimes rebuking me but always rooted in love. She's with the Lord now, and I miss her dearly. I'm grateful for every note, email, or phone call I received during that time, from loved ones far and near, as each one felt like a Rhema word—God's timely voice breaking through the chaos.

Using every tool my Heavenly Father placed in my hands, I hoped against hope and believed against all odds.[40] At this point, it was in God's hands. If He chose to do a last-minute miracle, I was ready. If He didn't, I would accept that too. Whether or not I bore the title of "Mrs.," I resolved to keep serving God, to raise my children well, and to live the abundant life He promised.[41] The Soul-Searcher knew my heart.[42] He knew I didn't want a divorce, but after years of resistance, I felt I had to choose it. I wasn't rejecting our marriage—I was saying no more to the pain, dysfunction, and spiritual compromise it had become. This wasn't marriage as God intended it to be. Rejection from a man is not the same as rejection from God.[43] His love never left me—even in this valley of decisions.

TURNING POINT

Time seemed to race by as our final court date drew near. I became more anxious—especially about the custody of our children. So, I took my plea once again to the *Supreme Court of Heaven*, petitioning the *Great Judge* of the universe for mercy. I asked Him to silence the enemy of my home and deliver a divine verdict that aligned with His perfect will, which would astonish

---

40. Rom. 4:18
41. John 10:10
42. Ps. 139:1
43. Rom. 8:38-39

everyone involved.[44] Though my earthly strength was fading, I reminded myself that Jesus had already secured the victory.[45] My task was simply to remain on the winning side.

As divorce increasingly felt like the path of *least resistance*, I emotionally withdrew, limited all contact with Ségun, and tried to make peace with the idea of moving on. After all, I had fought long and hard. I reasoned that God hates divorce, not the divorcée.[46] In that mindset, I began praying for a fresh start and, half-jokingly, gave God my "wish list" for a future partner—this time placing more emphasis on character—specifically, a man of faith, who feared God—rather than on appearance.

Then, just a few weeks before our final court date, "Mr. Newman" showed up—right at my door. And wouldn't you know? He looked exactly like Ségun! Looking back, I realized that God had granted my desire—but delivered it in familiar packaging, with a twist I never saw coming: a refurbished model with upgraded features. His thoughts are indeed higher than ours,[47] and He certainly has a great sense of humor! Because our vision is limited, we often pursue what we want, unaware that God knows exactly what we need.

Ségun said he'd had another epiphany—like a Damascus encounter, as he put it. He spoke with a depth and clarity I hadn't seen in years, especially about God. Something had shifted. The man who once fought to be rid of me now stood in my living room, asking for forgiveness and wondering if it was too late to salvage what we once had. There was a tangible sense of God's presence—but I was skeptical. What had I missed … and when?

It turned out that God had been working in Ségun, behind the scenes, especially during those final, silent weeks. Just when I was preparing to let go, He was completing what He started.[48] I had come to the end of myself—and that was precisely where God needed me to be. My exhaustion had cleared the way for His intervention. What I thought was a breaking point was, in fact, a turning point.

Some come to God willingly; others are driven to Him by the storms of life—kicking, screaming, and trying to stay afloat on their own. Then there are those broken by hardship, swept along by trials, who finally surrender and are carried to safety. Sadly, some remain too proud and blinded to receive God's help, rejecting His lifeline and perishing in deep waters. But make no mistake: Every knee will bow, either now in surrender or later in regret when it's too late to turn back.[49]

If Ségun expected warmth or relief that evening, he must have been disappointed. I didn't

---

44. Ps. 21:13 (MSG); Isa. 1:18; 41:21-24 (NKJV); Nah. 1:7-11; Rom. 8:31
45. Rom. 8:37 (NLT)
46. Mal. 2:16
47. Isa. 55:9
48. Phil. 1:6
49. Rom. 14:11; Phil. 2:10-11

trust him and had no intention of allowing chaos back into our lives. Although he admitted his faults and spoke well of me—as a remarkable woman, wife, and mother—I'd heard those words before. They once held weight. Now, they rang hollow. As the saying goes, "Fool me once, shame on you. Fool me twice, shame on me." A third time? That would be bordering on insanity!

I felt nothing. Unlike Joseph, who broke down in tears when he saw his brothers after years of betrayal and hardship,[50] I had no emotional response. No anger. No longing. Just emptiness and a need for peace. Joseph, although wounded, still felt the weight of family and the stirrings of compassion. I, on the other hand, couldn't relate to that tenderness anymore. But I could connect with Joseph's actions—how he orchestrated events to test whether his brothers' hearts had changed.[51]

The Bible describes the inner struggle Joseph experienced, torn between justice and mercy, truth and reconciliation.[52] His pain was raw, but mine had hardened into distance. At that moment, I didn't want reconciliation. I was craving space, clarity, stability, and the kind of healing that no longer depended on another person's remorse or empty words.

My guard went up. I had a million and one questions for Ségun and a mental checklist of hoops he'd need to jump through just to prove this wasn't another game. I was consumed with suspicion and anxiety. Nothing had prepared me for this kind of emotional *déjà vu*. Even Shalamar's hit song in 1979 was titled "The Second Time Around"—not a third! Surely, there must be some unspoken "break-up and make-up" rule that says two strikes are enough!

Despite everything God had guided me through, I was still scared—afraid that Ségun 's return was just another strategic move. I wasn't sure he fully grasped the emotional toll his unpredictability had taken on me and the children over those six long years. Why now? Was it genuine repentance—or a tactic to avoid losing custody? I didn't know. All I knew was that I couldn't afford another wrong decision that might unnecessarily prolong my stay in this valley.

So, I kept my distance. Unlike the last attempt at restoring our relationship, I didn't encourage frequent visits. I insisted on communicating only through emails, texts, and limited phone calls so there would be a record. If this was truly a turning point, it needed to be led by truth, not charm; by accountability, not emotion. I had come too far with God to turn back without clarity.

With lessons still fresh from our last failed reconciliation, I didn't keep Ségun's return a secret. I informed key people, knowing I needed both spiritual and emotional support. My father was furious and warned me that he wouldn't just stand by if I got hurt again. My lawyer suspected it might be a tactic and urged caution. Some pleaded with me to walk away for

---

50. Gen. 42:24; 43:30; 45:2

51. Gen. 44:1-2; 42-44

52. Gen. 45:4-5

good—"Run!" they said, "Kick him to the curb!" But my beloved prayer army, unwavering as ever, simply said, "We'll go with you where God leads."

Yet, I found myself alone at a familiar crossroads. Once again, everything—the future of my children and me—depended on a life-altering, time-sensitive decision. I had nothing and no one to rely on in making this decision but God. I had walked with Him long enough to know He wouldn't fail or abandon me.[53] That assurance gave me the strength to seek His Word for wisdom, direction, and courage. It was time to live what I claimed to believe.

"Do not be afraid" appears about 365 times in Scripture—a daily reminder to choose faith over fear. David's words in Psalm 23:4 anchored me: *"Even though I walk through the valley of the shadow of death, I will fear no evil, for You are with me."* It's a reminder that transitioning from waiting seasons—often filled with uncertainty and valley-like situations—doesn't have to be stressful or confusing when we maintain the right outlook. Even in the "valley of the shadow of death," God is present. The fear or anxiety doesn't come from the valley (situation) itself, but from our perspective of the problem and forgetting that the Good Shepherd is with us. His rod offers protection and gentle correction when we're tempted to stray. His staff provides guidance, care, support, and security, even in times of confusion.

Instead of being afraid of the unknown or rushing to escape discomfort, we're encouraged to trust that God is guiding us *through* the valley, not abandoning us *in* it. "Walk through" implies a temporary passage, not a permanent destination. And we're not walking alone—Goodness and Mercy follow us all the way to the table He has prepared.[54] This verse reassures us that God's presence, protection, and provision aren't delayed until problems are solved or life improves; they're sent right in the face of trials, opposition, and sometimes during an onslaught.

Keeping this in mind, we can wait peacefully, rather than feeling pressured, worried, restless, fearful, or overwhelmed. *"Don't call everything a conspiracy, like they do, and don't live in dread of what frightens them. Make the Lord of Heaven's Armies holy in your life. He is the one you should fear. He is the one who should make you tremble. He will keep you safe."* (Isa. 8:12-14a NLT)

Like Elijah—afraid, discouraged, and burned out—God reminded me to rise and return to my assignment, moving forward with renewed purpose. This was bigger than a marriage—it was about obedience to His call. Jesus came for souls, not for earthly marriages. He died to reconcile us to the Father, not to guarantee domestic bliss.[55] God's redemptive plan moves forward—with or without us. If we refuse, He'll raise others who are willing and obedient to complete the work, despite our excuses or fears. I didn't want to be replaced. I wanted God to finish what He started with us. I longed to hear Him say, "Well done, Funké." But to hear those

---

53. Isa. 43:1c-3a; 43:2; Rom. 8:35; Heb. 13:5b (NLT)

54. Ps. 23:5-6

55. 2 Cor. 5:18-20

words, I had to stay in step with His will and faithfully complete my part. *"But you need to stick it out, staying with God's plan so you'll be there for the promised completion."* (Heb. 10:36 MSG)

Thankfully, in my quiet moments, God's voice grew louder than my trepidation. I wasn't yet at the point where I felt like the Proverbs 31 woman who *"laughs without fear of the future,"* [56] but a small part of me still hoped that God would restore our marriage—perhaps even at the eleventh hour—making it sweeter and stronger than ever. Maybe that small ember of faith was all He needed to work with.

There were many nights I lay awake thinking about how God steps into dire situations, especially when all seems lost. I remembered Joseph in the Bible, who was about to quietly divorce Mary when he believed she had been unfaithful. But God sent an angel in a dream to stop him.[57] Mary carried a divine promise—a destiny far greater than anyone could comprehend—and God wasn't going to let human misunderstanding thwart His plans. At first, Joseph didn't fully see her worth or the magnitude of what God was doing through their union, but God stepped in to reveal the truth and redirect his course.

This story isn't a comparison to ours, but it reveals a powerful truth: No matter how impossible a situation appears, God can intervene—even in seemingly hopeless relational situations. Martha once said to Jesus, *"Lord, if you had been here, my brother would not have died."* But Jesus replied, *"Your brother will rise again. ...I am the resurrection and the life."* (John 11:21-25) Even when everything seems beyond repair, God can still bring dead things back to life.

Hosea—the prophet whom God instructed to marry Gomer, a promiscuous woman[58]—also had a compelling assignment that defied logic. Even when she strayed, God told Hosea to take her back as a living demonstration of His unwavering love for His people.[59] Like Joseph, Hosea had every reason to walk away, but obedience to God's higher purpose kept him rooted in a redemptive mission. **Though Hosea's experience isn't identical to Joseph's,** his obedience—despite heartbreak, public shame, and repeated betrayal—reflected a kind of sacrificial love that mirrored God's pursuit of His people. I could now see that the issue was never whether God could restore my marriage—but whether I still wanted Him to.

Ségun started visiting more frequently, usually claiming it was because the children missed me. I watched him closely—like a hawk—and made sure we prayed every time he came. I wasn't suspicious of him, but I had learned to be cautious and prayerful. Scripture reminds us that we're sent out as sheep among wolves, so we must be as wise as serpents and as harmless as doves.[60] I took that to heart—not to judge others, but to guard my heart and seek discernment

---

56. Prov. 31:25 (NLT)

57. Matt. 1:18-21

58. Hosea 1:2

59. Hosea 3:1

60. Matt. 10:16

as I navigated this delicate season. The boys began sleeping over at my house again, and eventually—of his own volition—Ségun suggested they move back in full time. I agreed. He also proposed that we work out shared custody between ourselves, but I insisted that the arrangement be formalized in court.

Even though he was now saying the right things and showing affection, I couldn't ignore everything he'd put us through, nor the damage that had been done. I was still learning not to lean on emotions but to seek wisdom and guidance from the Holy Spirit. And in His mercy, God overwhelmed me with confirmations and faith-boosters like never before!

One recurring sign was the number eight, which I explore more in the next chapter. But beyond that, I began to notice how God had been speaking all along—through signs, promptings from the Holy Spirit, and even nature. When I allowed fear in, it blurred my vision and dulled my spiritual senses. But now I was awaking to the beauty and power of God's presence. Just as He guided the Israelites through the wilderness with a cloud by day and fire by night,[61] He had been guiding me too. His leading wasn't always dramatic, but it was precise—timely words, unshakable peace, "random" scriptures, and doors that opened or shut at just the right time. For instance, there were moments when I'd be torn between reacting emotionally and waiting in silence, and then a devotional, a sermon, or an unexpected message or call from a friend would echo exactly what I needed to hear.

He delivered me from sin and sickness through signs and wonders,[62] parted seas (removed barriers),[63] sent manna (provision) from heaven,[64] and drew water from rocks (made the impossible, possible).[65] And though He may not have visibly made the sun stand still for me to win battles,[66] there were many times He sure made my day stand still long enough for grace to carry me through—especially during my most time-sensitive challenges.

As powerful as those moments and external signs were, even more precious to me is the Holy Spirit who lives in us and anchors us. He guides,[67] leads,[68] teaches and reminds,[69] comforts,[70] convicts us of sin,[71] helps us pray,[72] and empowers us in countless ways.[73] These

---

61. Exod. 13:21
62. Deut. 6:22
63. Exod. 14:21
64. Exod. 16:4
65. Num. 20:11
66. Josh. 10:13
67. John 16:13
68. Rom. 8:14
69. John 14:26
70. John 14:16; 2 Cor. 1:3-4
71. John 16:8
72. Rom. 8:26
73. Acts 1:8; 1 Cor. 12:7-11; Gal. 5:22-23; Eph, 1:13

truths strengthened my confidence—not just in God's ability to restore—but in His faithfulness to finish what He started in my life. My family was destined to reflect His glory. Hallelujah!

That was when I fell in love with Donnie McClurkin's powerful song "I'll Trust You, Lord." It became my theme song—my heart's anthem and the soundtrack of that season. I played it over and over, as if having a heart-to-heart conversation with my Heavenly Father. The lyrics echoed my struggles and helped put my doubts into perspective. Whenever I faced hard decisions or overwhelming challenges, I whispered, "Yes, Lord, I'll trust You." Like Mary, I chose to believe: *"Blessed is she who has believed that the Lord would fulfill His promises to her"* (Luke 1:45).

I believe our next court hearing was adjourned, as this gave Ségun more time to visit. Our interactions became more cordial throughout the summer. After much prayer and personal reflection, I decided to try again—cautiously—the week before our final hearing. This time, I set clear conditions: We would take things slowly, keep extended family out of our relationship decisions, attend church together, and he would be open and honest about any past, present, or future issues—no longer on a "need-to-know basis"!

Ségun met with his lawyers to formally withdraw his divorce petition. We each followed up with our own lawyers and sent joint letters, informing them that we had reconciled and no longer wished to proceed with the divorce. It was a significant act of faith, but also one of determination.

At our final court appearance, the same judge who had previously granted a divorce nisi and said she would be praying for a miraculous turnaround was visibly excited to see us reunited. The courtroom was completely full that day, packed with senior advocates of Nigeria (SAN), some of whom knew our families. While they had likely come for high-profile cases scheduled after ours, God had orchestrated it so that our declaration of reconciliation would unfold in their presence.

She (the judge) asked us to move to the middle of the courtroom, and much to our surprise, everyone stood and applauded. Many came forward to shake our hands, celebrating what they saw as courage and grace. One of the SANs—who would later become Nigeria's vice president—even offered a heartfelt prayer over us. At the judge's request, we embraced and sealed our reconciliation with a kiss. It felt like divine theatre—God showcasing His power to redeem and restore. The very place I once dreaded and avoided because of *public humiliation* was now filled with *public jubilation* over the same matter!

That was God's signature right there! It marked a turning point not just in our marriage but also in my understanding of His faithfulness. He turned my mourning into dancing and clothed me with joy, just as He promised.[74] He signed, sealed, and delivered on His Word in a way that could not be denied—boldly, publicly, and unmistakably.[75] Only God could have authored such a story.

---

74. Ps. 30:11
75. Ps. 18:30 (NLT); Dan. 9:4 (NLT)

REDEFINING LOVE

I wish I could say we immediately slipped into a fairy-tale ending after the euphoria of the courtroom celebration wore off—but real life isn't scripted that way. What we faced during the months that followed was anything but a "happily ever after." The bridge that once connected us had long been broken, and years of hurt, pride, and silence had washed away the remnants. There were no pieces to pick up. It was time to assess the damage, take stock, and rebuild—essentially from scratch.

Every part of our lives had been shaken, and years of fighting and working against each other had taken their toll, leaving our finances, trust, and emotional connection in ruins. Still, we had each other, our children, and—most importantly—God. That foundation alone gave us a reason to hope.

The road to healing and recovery wasn't easy. One of my first hurdles was letting go of the resentment I held toward Ségun for the financial struggles we were facing. We were in dire straits, and I was convinced that his choices—his secrecy and decisions driven by personal needs or pain, without considering our family as a whole—had brought us there. We had spent so much time fighting each other instead of fighting for our home. I knew I had played a role in the dysfunction, but I still felt disappointed over how he had handled his role as the head of our family.[76]

We agreed to downsize and focus on essentials while figuring out the next, more urgent steps. After several difficult conversations, Ségun moved in with the boys and me to cut costs. I'd be lying if I said I didn't feel a small sense of vindication—but not for long. I soon realized God was truly causing *"all things to work together for good."*[77] Ségun had been moving full speed ahead, convinced he was living his best life. But God allowed everything to come undone—not out of cruelty, but out of mercy. What the enemy meant for evil, God repurposed for good—bringing about a humility and awakening that nothing else could.[78]

Some people insinuated that everything unfolding was just the natural consequence of Ségun's past choices. But I saw something else. It wasn't retribution; it was redemption. God's love and mercy collided with a broken and contrite heart—something He has never despised.[79] Still, the challenges tested the boundaries of our rekindling love in new ways.

The more pressure we faced, the more I wrestled with the thought that Ségun's decisions had now made his problems mine—and our children's too. I had built an independent life during our six-and-a-half-year separation. I learned to survive—and eventually thrive—by the

---

76. Eph. 5:23
77. Rom. 8:28
78. Gen. 50:20
79. Ps. 51:17

grace of God alone. For the first time, I realized I could breathe without him. I could parent, prosper, and provide—leaning into strengths I never knew I had.[80]

But now, it felt as if I was being called to lay all that down—not because I was weak, but because I was being refined. Real love, as God was teaching me, wasn't about romance, finance, comfort, or control. It was about loyalty, sacrifice, surrender, patience, trust ... even when everything in me wanted to protect what I had rebuilt on my own. This valley became the place where love was being redefined daily—by resilience and reverence for God's will.

It took me several years to completely stop playing the blame game over our finances and fully align my perspective with God's. What once felt like punishment, I now see as preparation. God helped me accept our entire journey—not just the parts I preferred—as a gift filled with lessons that built endurance, character, and hope, just as Romans 5:3-5 reminds us.

Through our mistakes and ignorance, Ségun and I had opened the door to devourers—*consuming locusts*[81] that robbed us of peace, progress, and provision for a season. Yet we held onto God—our Provider, the Lifter of our heads, and the Restorer of fortunes.[82] *God is a healer of broken dreams and a restorer of stolen years* (Joel 2:25). He wasn't just restoring our marriage—God was doing a deep work in us—healing our hearts and helping us to reprioritize how we managed what He had entrusted to us—so we would be ready to receive the blessings He had in store, not just as gifts, but as rewards for walking in obedience.[83] When the God of Wonders restores,[84] He doesn't just patch things up—He makes everything beautiful and appropriate in its time,[85] and truly makes all things new.[86]

Another area I struggled with was unforgiveness. I thought I had checked that box long ago, but sharing space again and re-establishing relationships with family members brought buried emotions and unresolved offenses to the surface. What I once viewed as "forgiven" suddenly felt raw all over again. To his credit, Ségun would apologize each time I brought things up, but I wanted more—I wanted explanations that would make sense of it all, that would give me closure.

At some point, he withdrew into a shell, tired of what felt like nagging. However, after some honest conversations with my Heavenly Father, I realized how hypocritical I'd been. I had deeply hurt Ségun and others on my journey of self-discovery. There were things I also needed to forgive myself for. This wasn't about comparing notes or judging sins and offenses; it was about obeying God[87]—surrendering my right to be right and choosing His way instead.

---

80. Ps. 18:28-29 (MSG)

81. Joel 2:25-26 (NLT)

82. Deut. 30:3; Job 42:10; Ps. 3:3; 126:1; Zeph. 3:20; Phil. 4:19

83. Deut. 28:1-2; Isa. 1:19; Matt. 6:31-33; 7:24-25; Luke 11:28; John 14:23; Heb. 10:36; James 1:25; 1 John 3:22; Rev. 22:14

84. Ps. 77:14

85. Eccles. 3:11 (AMP)

86. Rev. 21:5

87. Luke 6:37; Col. 3:13

I took a U-turn after that, working with the Holy Spirit to release, rebuild, and restore. I had to stop expecting my husband to carry the burden of my pain—making him live under constant guilt or prolonged emotional debt. We both carried deep wounds that are still healing today. Something said or done may reopen them, but we've learned to process these sore points together, choosing to walk in grace daily. Praying together—both over and for each other—has been immensely helpful. It has allowed God's presence to penetrate the layers of our wounded hearts through the cleansing washing of water by the Word,[88] continually healing us from the inside out over time. Real forgiveness isn't just an emotional release or gesture—it's a spiritual reset. It paves the way for spiritual and relational restoration.

Isaiah 43:18-19 (MSG) says: *"Forget about what's happened; don't keep going over old history… I'm about to do something brand-new."* That scripture challenged me to stop letting unforgiveness keep me locked in the past and blind to God's present work. 2 Peter 1:5-11 (NLT) warns that when we lack virtues like love and grace, we become shortsighted—forgetting what God has already done and what He still plans to do. Redefining love meant choosing to see Ségun not just through the lens of our past, but through the eyes of Love (God), maturity, and obedience to God's higher calling for our family.

This transitional season was pivotal in reshaping how we understood and expressed love. Our version had to be realigned with God's Agape standard—sacrificial, sincere, and without hypocrisy.[89] We needed to unlearn unhealthy patterns and let go of every tradition, belief, attitude, and cultural mindset that didn't match God's Word.

Relationships, even marriages, can often become quite superficial. We all sometimes put on fronts or masks to protect ourselves. In our case, the real issue from the outset wasn't a lack of effort to be sincere; it was our approach—driven by fear, anger, and a lack of faith in the face of life's challenges.[90] Something had to change! If we wanted different results, we had to make different choices—starting with returning to God's Word and listening for the leading of His Spirit. Obedience often precedes clarity.

Like Paul, we had to forget what lay behind and press on toward the upward call of God.[91]Redefining love meant learning to trust God's truth above our emotions. In the past, relying on what I saw, felt, or heard nearly caused me to give up—right on the verge of our breakthrough.[92] But God's grace made a way. It has carried us as we humble ourselves and learn to walk in step with Him.

We're not meant to figure out life on our own. We need God's wisdom and correction to

88. Eph. 5:26
89. Rom. 12:9-10; 13:8 (AMP); 1 Pet. 1:22
90. Jer. 17:5-6 (MSG)
91. Phil. 3:12-14
92. Heb. 3:19

stay on course. *"Trust God from the bottom of your heart…listen for God's voice in everything you do…Don't assume you know it all. Run to GOD! Run from evil!…."* (Prov. 3:5-12 MSG) That shift—from self-reliance to God-dependence—marked a turning point in our journey.

By December 2009, God had started to restore joy, peace, and hope in our home. The Christmas season brought deeper meaning—we were under one roof again, the divorce chapter was finally behind us, and slowly, by God's grace, we were recovering—emotionally, spiritually, and even financially. I had begun to exhale, to trust again. Then came an unexpected but beautiful surprise: I was pregnant!

The news generated mixed emotions. We were still figuring out living arrangements, finances, and how to share our reconciliation with others. Yet I asked God for a girl—as a personal sign that He was with us and that our restoration was real. And He honored that request!

Once the "bump" began to show, and our "secret" was out, I faced a wave of criticism for accepting my husband back. Surprisingly, some of the strongest reactions came from fellow "Christians."[93] While a few were outspoken, others expressed their disapproval or skepticism through disapproving stares and subtle jabs. I even heard the word *mumu*—a Nigerian slang for someone easily fooled, or being thrown around—as if my decision somehow dishonored womanhood!

But I didn't let their ignorance sway me. I hadn't committed a crime by choosing to love again, and again, or by giving my marriage another chance. I decided to follow God's leading and trust His path to restoration.[94] As 1 John 3:16 reminds us, *"We know what real love is because Jesus gave up his life for us."* Love costs something. Real love is selfless and sacrificial, not always logical to others looking in from the outside.

Some people acted as if I owed them an explanation, but I was too focused on staying healthy and strong for the baby, maintaining my composure, and not adding to the emotional burden I was already carrying. This wasn't about proving a point or pleasing others—it was about pleasing God. He had the final say in our story, and I was determined to walk in line with His will, even when misunderstood. As Galatians 6:9 (NLT) urges, *"Let us not grow weary of doing good, for at the right time we will reap a harvest if we don't give up."*

It was never about blind optimism. I clung tightly to what God had revealed to me, even during my darkest hours. Yes, I kept my eyes wide open—watching, praying, discerning, and working. Choosing to love again didn't mean I ignored reality; it meant I refused to be ruled by fear, pride, or public opinion.

I wasn't going to let what others felt they couldn't—or wouldn't—accept in their own marriages to be projected onto mine. We each navigate our own paths and seek what feels best in

---

93. James 2:24 (NLT)

94. Deut. 28:1-6 (NLT); 30:19-20 (AMP); Prov. 4:26-27

our unique situations. But ultimately, we all must strive for God's best—because in the end, we will reap what we sow.[95]

I believed then, and still do, that some reasons given for divorce—like "irreconcilable differences" or "incompatibility"—can be modern-day covers for self-interest or emotional fatigue. In Matthew 5:32 (MSG), Jesus warns against using divorce as "a cover for selfishness and whim." That said, *redefining love* doesn't mean tolerating destruction.

Let me be clear: This is not a call to remain in abusive or life-threatening relationships. If your safety is at risk, seek help immediately—whether spiritual, professional, or legal, if necessary. Only the living can love—and only the whole can love well. Your well-being matters to God.

Ultimately, this was *our* decision—my husband's and mine—to fight for our marriage, give it everything we had, stand firm, and love without stopping—and to believe that the same God who authored our story could still redeem it.[96] God redefined love for me in that valley—not as a feeling, but as a series of daily decisions: to forgive, to trust, to hope, and to obey. Love isn't weakness; it's obedience. And when rooted in Christ, it becomes a force stronger than shame, opinion, or fear.

Our pregnancy became a public affirmation of renewed love and mutual forgiveness—especially because some of our earlier offenses had played out in public. It would've been easy to worry about what people might say, but that could have distracted us from the greater work God was doing. As Paul reminded the Galatians, *"Obviously, I'm not trying to win the approval of people, but of God. If pleasing people were my goal, I would not be Christ's servant"* (Gal. 1:10 NLT). Thankfully, that pregnancy was my smoothest: no complications, no anesthesia, no fear—just grace. God had gone ahead of our baby, preparing for every need, reminding us that His love doesn't just restore—it redeems.

I wanted my dad to hear the news from me, not from someone else. Once I brought him up to speed, he wished me well but urged me to be careful, still unsure about Ségun's intentions—especially since things hadn't yet been done the "proper" way in line with culture. I gently reminded him that our confidence wasn't in ourselves but in God, *"whose eyes range throughout the earth to strengthen those whose hearts are fully committed to Him"* (2 Chron. 16:9a NLT). I reassured him that the right things would be done concerning the wider family at the right time and that everything would work together for good. It's every good parent's desire to seek their child's welfare and to be protective, but as the adult child proves their discernment, maturity, and consistency, it becomes easier for the parent to relax, trust, and release them into God's hands.

God had shown me glimpses of His redemptive plan—just enough to encourage me to keep moving forward, even when I didn't fully understand. James 1:25 (MSG) says, *"But whoever*

---

95. Gal. 6:7-10 (NLT)

96. 1 Cor. 16:13-14 (MSG)

catches a glimpse of the revealed counsel of God—the free life!—even out of the corner of his eye, and sticks with it, is no distracted scatterbrain but a man or woman of action. That person will find delight and affirmation in the action." So, I pressed on, trusting that God would meet me in my obedience.[97]

There was nothing shameful about what we had been through or where we were. Every marriage reaches a "breaking point"—a moment of reckoning where vows are tested and character is refined. What matters is how a couple bounces back from the brink. James 1:2-4, as paraphrased by William Barclay, captures this beautifully:

> *"My brothers, you must regard it as nothing but joy when you are involved in all kinds of trials, for you must realize that when faith passes through the ordeal of testing, the result is the ability to pass the breaking point and not to break. This ability must go right on to the end, and then you will be perfect and complete, without a weak spot."* [98]

Like Simon Peter, Ségun and I had toiled in the dark—feeling empty, frustrated, and disappointed. But at the right time, Jesus said, *"Launch out into the deep and let down your nets for a catch"* (Luke 5:4). This time, we were stepping out not in our strength, but in response to God's call. We were determined to try again—together, in His timing.[99] Obedience often turns failure into overflow.

Our second chance was a refining process.[100] The first "fire" (separation and the threat of divorce) purified us individually—stripping away pride, anger, and all the excess baggage we carried. But this new furnace forged us together through shared trials[101]—financial strain, health scares, parenting challenges, delays, and unexpected losses. Then came the "quenching" and "tempering,"[102] which strengthened, unified, and shaped us by mercy. We weren't just healing through these experiences—we were being transformed into useful and fruitful vessels in Christ.[103]

Restoration didn't happen quickly. It was quiet and often hidden. But what people see now—joy, triumph, laughter, unity, resilience, peace, and faith—was birthed in fire. Through pain and surrender, we discovered our worth, redefined our love, and realigned with God's purpose. The outcome? A beautifully refined blend—a "perfect combination" only God could orchestrate.

---

97. Ps. 37:23 (NLT).
98. William Barclay, *The Letters of James and Peter*, The Daily Study Bible Series (Philadelphia: Westminster Press, 1976).
99. Eccles. 3:1
100. Isa. 48:10; Mal. 3:2-3
101. Rom. 8:18; 2 Cor. 4:17; James 1:2-4
102. Ps. 23:3; 2 Cor. 4:8-9; 1 Pet. 5:10
103. John 15:4-5 (AMP); 2 Tim. 2:21

Looking back, I realize how vital God's grace has been through every valley and decision. Endurance, wisdom, and initiative all played a part, but it was His grace that carried us. I made mistakes and took some wrong turns, but turning back to the Lord[104] and continually seeking His wisdom kept me from derailing completely off course. Through brokenness, I found wholeness—rediscovering Jesus not just as Lord and Savior, but as The Answer. In Him, I found security, purpose, and a love that has redefined EVERYTHING.[105]

THROUGH SÉGUN'S LENSES

On the day of the court hearing at which the divorce nisi was to be granted, I was laser-focused on my objective. I did not have the slightest iota of doubt that I was doing the right thing. Although represented by her lawyer, Funké was not in the courtroom on that day.

The presiding judge had reviewed our respective files which included family photographs and personal letters that Funké and I had exchanged over the years. She essentially told me that she could not understand why I was filing for divorce as, based on the information presented to her, Funké, our children, and I appeared to be a picture-perfect family. Nevertheless, she granted the divorce nisi and said that she would be praying for us in the hope that we would announce our reconciliation at the next hearing. Were I a betting man and asked to place a bet on whether there was any possibility that the judge's words could come to pass, I would have wagered my life savings that it was totally impossible. Nevertheless, I was deeply touched by the compassion with which she spoke.

A few weeks before the final hearing, I attended a church service at a popular Pentecostal church in Lagos. It was a prophetic service that was held at the end of every month with congregants numbering in the hundreds of thousands. It was very unusual for me to even contemplate going to such a service as I had been born and raised an Anglican and had never been comfortable in Pentecostal church settings. The dancing, ballistic casting, and binding prayers and speaking in tongues were not my cup of tea. However, this particular day was very different. I felt a burning desire to be there, possibly as a last roll of the dice as the next court hearing was just around the corner, and nothing Funké and I had tried until then had produced anything even remotely resembling

---

104. Lam. 3:40
105. Lam. 3:22-31; Zeph. 3:17-20 (NLT)

resolution, let alone satisfactory resolution. At various times, we had jointly and separately sought mediation from our parents, church and lay counselors, family members, friends, including those who had experienced divorce, and a celebrated psychologist. Nothing worked. On the way to the church service, my car began to overheat despite having just had the engine replaced. That did not stop me as I simply parked the car at a gas station and took a taxi to the church.

There was an altar call during the latter stages of the service, and I was one of the first people to reach the altar. On getting there, I lay down on my stomach and started crying like a baby for what felt like an eternity. Years of pent-up emotion flowed out of my tear ducts. By the time I stood up, there were hundreds of people around the altar, and my eyes went straight to an area barely six feet away from me, where people had deposited photos of loved ones and all manner of objects. There were candles, blood-soaked clothing, amulets *(juju)*, weapons, printed materials—a host of things representing people on whose behalf supplications were being made or conscious decisions of those wanting to sever ties to dark and unsavory aspects of their lives.

The thing that stood out to me the most was a piece of paper filled with symbols, which made the hairs on my arm stand on end. I knew that those symbols conveyed a very dark message, and for someone who was not well versed in the Scriptures, my mind immediately went to Ephesians 6:12, which says, "*… we wrestle not against flesh and blood, but against principalities and powers, against the rulers of the darkness of this world."* It was clear to me that I was receiving confirmation that there is a lot more to the world than what we see in the physical.

I realized that, in my ignorance and arrogance, I had been trying to bend Funké to my will with the misguided aim of molding her into the person I believed she should be. That is God's role. I met with Funké soon after and shared my experience with her and my conviction that our marriage could be restored. Although she was understandably highly skeptical given everything we had been through, she gradually lowered her guard and we began to pray together, and thus began the process toward our eventual and miraculous reconciliation.

Rearview Mirror Lesson

It was during the altar call described above that I understood for the first time that, as human beings, we cannot bring about fundamental changes within ourselves without divine help—without the grace of God—talk less of when one tries to change one's spouse. Although counterintuitive, the way to bring about a change in others is to focus on changing oneself as opposed to adopting an accusatory approach, which will almost invariably encounter resistance given the natural inclination of human beings to become defensive at such times. That was the defining realization of my life that I can confidently say has changed the rest of my life.

Memories from the road—every step a reminder that God restores and renews

Our first photoshoot together—six years after our reconciliation.

Oxbridge Ball 2017.

LASTING LOVE
INTERNATIONAL COUPLES BANQUET
LAGOS

Segun & Funke Adeniji
LASTING LOVE SPECIAL GUESTS

Sharing our story and allowing God to use us to restore hope in marriages brings us so much joy.

21st Wedding anniversary.

At a concert in 2019.

One of our date nights in 2020.

Orlando holiday in 2018—grateful for our "new beginnings" and the beautiful memories with our children.

Arabian apparel photoshoot during a holiday in Dubai.

Our family's 2019 visit to the Kigali Genocide Memorial in Rwanda.

Our visit to Rwanda left a lasting
impression—reminding us of the cost of
hatred and the power of choosing love.
Always choose love!

The Campaign Against Genocide Museum in Rwanda.

Photoshoot at the family house to celebrate my mother-in-law's 80th birthday in 2022.

Vow reaffirmation 2024.

Still savoring every moment together in 2025.

19

New Beginnings

*"Where the devil tries to take you out is where the Lord will often
send you back with bragging rights, saying: I'm back!"*

BILL YOUNT

FROM WANDER TO WONDER

God writes the best stories, and like bestselling thrillers, they're filled with suspense and unexpected twists. That's why patience is vital when our own stories are unfolding.[1] If we stay with His script—even when events don't go as we imagined—they will ultimately work for our good and His glory. Not all life shifts are negative. Some simply stretch us, forcing adjustments in our hearts, minds, and wills. As Henry Ford observed, *"Failure is the opportunity to begin again more intelligently."* When we embrace the changes God allows, we begin to see both Him and ourselves in a new light. In His hands, even our failures become lessons that *refine* us, not *define* us—preparing us for deeper faith and greater fruitfulness.

Our *New Beginning* didn't look like what I had envisioned. At the start of our reconciliation, I often asked God for signs, because it didn't look at all like the fairy-tale ending I had hoped for. I thought we had reached our "Promised Land" after years in the wilderness, but instead, we met new battles. Just as Israel discovered giants in Canaan, we too faced obstacles

---

1. Eccles. 7:8; Heb. 10:35-36

365

that had to be confronted step by step, not all at once.[2] Some challenges resurfaced because we had only swept them under the carpet instead of bringing them into the light of God's Word.[3] They remained until we finally confronted and overcame them in Christ.

At first, I imagined Ségun's return would be a season of rest and pampering, a second honeymoon with our family, and a swift healing of old wounds. Instead, it felt more like the prodigal son's homecoming[4]—a joyful return, but I had to brace myself in preparation for what I didn't know would be years of an arduous rebuilding process. Looking back, I can now draw a parallel between Nehemiah's strategy and the plans we adopted over the course of many years on our restoration journey. He didn't just rebuild Jerusalem's walls; he restored hope, order, and covenant faithfulness.[5] Likewise, our marriage required a deliberate plan rooted in Christ, built through prayer, vision, and wisdom from the Holy Spirit.

I used to wonder why rebuilding Jerusalem's wall weighed so heavily on Nehemiah. To him, a ruined city meant God's people lived in disgrace and God's name was dishonored.[6] His concern wasn't just national pride or image, but zeal for God's glory and the destiny of His people. Without walls, Jerusalem was vulnerable, ridiculed, and unable to live securely or worship freely. His grief, prayers, and bold request before the king[7] show that his burden was Spirit-led. I believe the same is true for marriage restoration. Just as Nehemiah carried a God-given burden, and Joseph had one for Israel, there's no way I could have sustained love and hope for my husband over six and a half years without God's help!

Here's how Nehemiah's story provides a powerful lens for rebuilding marriages:

1. A God-given burden and vision (Nehemiah 1:3-4):

When Nehemiah heard the report of Jerusalem's broken walls, he mourned, fasted, and prayed. That burden became a divine blueprint.

- **Marriage analogy:** In marriage, restoration often begins when one spouse dares to recognize the brokenness and carries a God-given desire for healing. In our case, I bore that burden for years until Ségun responded to God's pull, and together we sought to do what the Lord requires: *to act justly, love mercy, and walk humbly with Him* (Micah 6:8). Our healing began when we stopped blaming each other, faced our sins honestly, acknowledged the broken areas of our marriage, and surrendered completely to God.

---

2. Deut. 7:22

3. Eph. 5:14

4. Luke 15:20-24

5. Neh. 2:17-18; 6:15-16

6. Neh. 2:17

7. Neh. 2:4-5

2. *Prayer, repentance, and divine guidance (Nehemiah 1:5-11; 2:4-8):*

Before taking any action, Nehemiah earnestly sought God. He confessed the sins of his people, including his own. He began with this step, before asking God for favor as he approached the king to request letters, protection, and resources. His initial "planning table" was prayer, through which he received wisdom, favor, and courage for the work ahead.

- **Marriage analogy:** In the same way, rebuilding a marriage must start with humility and repentance—acknowledging personal faults instead of blaming others.[8] Prayer invites God's guidance into the process.[9]

3. *Quiet assessment and wise planning (Nehemiah 2:11-16):*

When Nehemiah arrived in Jerusalem, he didn't immediately reveal his plans. Instead, he went out at night and inspected the walls privately to assess the real extent of the damage before sharing his plan. This shows wisdom, foresight, and good judgment.[10]

- **Marriage analogy:** This means taking time to reflect and honestly assess the damage to understand the "cracks" before rushing to fix them. A couple must evaluate the "ruins"—whether mistrust, resentment, or communication breakdown—without shame, and without ambient noise or interference. Practical steps matter—counseling, clear boundaries, scheduling time together, but most importantly, prayer, which fuels planning.

- **Prayer is key at every stage.** For Ségun and me, those early reflections were sobering. We had lost not only time and opportunities but also joy because of pride, selfishness, and disobedience. But clarity prepared us to begin again. Like Nehemiah, we kept our rebuilding plan before God until it was time to act and share it publicly.

4. *Teamwork and shared responsibility (Nehemiah 2:17-18; 3:1-32):*

Nehemiah shared the vision with the people, motivated them, and then carefully assigned sections of the wall to families and groups. Chapter 3 reads almost like a construction project plan—who repaired what, where, and alongside whom.

- **Marriage analogy:** Marriages heal when spouses commit to repairing their "part of the wall." One person can't do it alone.[11] Restoration requires mutual effort—healing communication, rebuilding trust, renewing intimacy—always with the Holy

---

8. 1 John 1:9

9. James 5:16

10. Prov. 4:7

11. Eccles. 4:9-10

Spirit as the Chief Architect.[12] However, if only one partner is ready—as in Nehemiah's case—they can still invite the other with hope, patience, and consistent love. Small, thoughtful, persistent efforts lead to restoration. When we both submitted to God, we found the strength and willingness to build the shared vision together, for His glory.[13]

5. Overcoming opposition (Nehemiah 4:7-9, 17-18):

Nehemiah's "blueprint" wasn't just structural but also spiritual and strategic—he stationed guards, armed workers, and balanced building with defense. He adapted the plan as challenges arose. He stayed alert, set boundaries, and protected his team and project from enemies who mocked, threatened, and tried to sabotage the work.

- **Marriage analogy:** In marriage, opposition often comes from past wounds, discouragement, temptations, or spiritual attacks. Couples must "stand guard" over their marriage by staying vigilant in prayer, upholding godly standards and safeguards (Prov. 4:23; 1 Pet. 5:8), and resisting the enemy's schemes.[14] Over time, Ségun and I discovered that fighting side by side, as soldiers in the same army, strengthened our bond and protected our family.

6. Completion and dedication (Nehemiah 6:15-16; 12:27-43):

The wall was completed in record time, and the people dedicated the work to God with joy.

- **Marriage analogy:** Likewise, a restored marriage should be celebrated and dedicated to God—through thanksgiving, testimonies, or even reaffirmation of vows if desired. Ségun and I continue to testify of the great things the Lord has done for us[15] across various platforms and engagements for many years. Recently, we finally had the opportunity to rededicate our marriage to God in a small ceremony with family and friends. Our restoration isn't just for us, but for God's glory and the encouragement of others—showing that forgiveness, covenant love, and new beginnings are indeed possible through Him.[16] It's always important to acknowledge God, celebrate Him for milestones, and give thanks for progress.[17]

---

12. Ps. 127:1

13. Phil. 2:13

14. Eph. 6:11

15. Ps. 66:16; 107:2; Mark 5:19; Rev. 12:11

16. Gen. 50:20

17. Ps. 126:3

I wish we had those six steps for rebuilding laid out in front of us when we got back together; it would have made the process so much easier! Instead, we had to figure things out as we went, testing what worked, stumbling along the way, and slowly learning to trust each other again. I was mentally and physically drained, struggling both financially and health-wise, yet I leaned on Ebenezer—"my stone of help."[18] Like the prophet Samuel, I also acknowledged, "Up to this point the Lord has helped us!" and I trusted that He would not abandon us halfway.[19]

At times, I felt weary and frustrated, and I even questioned why our journey seemed harder than others'—why so many tests just to rebuild what was once broken. Yet in those moments, I was reminded that refinement is part of God's process. And who am I to complain when even Jesus was not spared suffering so that God's purpose might be fulfilled?[20]

When my faith wavered, as it did a few times, I would intentionally seek signs of God's goodness, even in the midst of painful or uncertain circumstances we faced at the time. That reassurance in Romans 8:28 reminded me that nothing I face is random, wasted, or outside of God's plan. The Lord orders my steps,[21] and I walk in His divine destiny. So, I began paying closer attention to His voice—whether through Scripture, Spirit-filled songs, sermons, or the wise counsel of trusted people He had placed around me. Gradually, I learned to stay expectant, listening for His direction at every turn.[22]

Those early months back together felt like stepping off Noah's ark after months of drifting at sea.[23] The work before us looked daunting, and I was honestly apprehensive at first, but I knew that the same God who had caused the "floodwaters" to recede and brought us safely to land[24] would also help us build back better. It reminded me that progress often begins with a single, courageous step: *"Take the first step in faith. You don't have to see the whole staircase, just take the first step"*—Martin Luther King Jr.

There were days I was tempted to ask Ségun to consider sorting himself out before coming back to me and the children, but the Spirit reminded me that we are one flesh.[25] As his helpmeet, I couldn't detach myself from his refining process; and neither was he separate from mine—we needed to walk and work it out together, especially in this critical phase of reconciliation, not simply watch from the sidelines.

It was a deeply humbling experience for our family, especially for Ségun. At times, I found it hard not to gloat or remind him of his missteps, but the Word checked my heart: *"Do nothing*

18. 1 Sam. 7:12
19. Ps. 138:8; Phil. 1:6
20. Rom. 8:32; Heb. 5:8
21. Ps. 37:23-24
22. Isa. 30:21
23. Gen. 8:13-19
24. Isa. 43:2
25. Mark 10:8-9

from selfish ambition or conceit, but in humility regard others as better than yourselves. Let the same mind be in you that was in Christ Jesus" (Phil. 2:3-5). Instead of tearing him down, I asked God for strength and wisdom to encourage and to walk beside him in humility and love.

Thank God for our supportive friends and church family, who stepped in during difficult times. I share these details not to embarrass my husband or family but to hopefully teach important lessons through our story. During our separation, there were times when I asked Ségun to contribute financially, as he had the means to do so, even in small ways, knowing my salary alone wasn't enough to cover all the boys' expenses and mine. In hindsight, perhaps that support would have been saved, not only to ease our burden when we reconciled but also to serve as an investment in his own future. After all, *what a person plants, he will harvest.*[26]

Life teaches that when you tend your own vineyard—even from afar—you'll eventually enjoy its fruit; if not directly, then your children will. And when you fill your own cistern, you'll have water to draw from during droughts. As the Yorùbás say, *"Bí a bá ń sunkún, ká máa ríran"*—"Don't let tears or distress blind your judgment." It's a wise reminder not to act impulsively or irrationally when faced with anger, grief, offense, or hardship. *Wisdom involves choosing actions today that you'll be grateful for tomorrow.* Ultimately, we all face the outcomes of the choices we once tried to ignore or evade. Sadly, many forget that their decisions impact not only themselves but also those around them. Scripture also reminds us in Proverbs 14:12 and Galatians 6:8-10 that every choice has consequences.

This is why relationships matter. Sensory experiences often leave a deeper impression than mental recollections of facts or events, which is why people may forget what you said or did, but they rarely forget how you made them feel—because emotional imprints linger long after words fade. This idea also aligns with the principle of love in action.[27] Jesus' ministry itself modeled this—He healed, touched, listened, and showed compassion that transformed hearts more deeply than words alone could. How we treat people—whether valued or dismissed, respected or ignored—often lasts longer than any deed. So, please take a moment to look around before it's too late and treat people with kindness. When life shakes or sifts us, as it surely will,[28] kindness becomes even more critical, especially toward those closest to us. Even in conflict, don't make enemies with a spouse. *"Be kind and compassionate to one another, forgiving each other, just as in Christ God forgave you."* (Eph. 4:32)

I observed this in my parents as they grew older. At the peak of his career, when making a major decision, my father sought my mother's prayers over his plans. Even though they had been separated for nearly two decades at that time, he still trusted her intercession, possibly because he had seen God work in her life. Many years later, as he battled illness, he specifically

---

26. Gal. 6:7-8 (MSG)

27. 1 Cor. 16:14

28. Luke 22:31-32

asked my children (his grandchildren), whom he loved dearly, for prayers. Had he burned those bridges with my mother and me when they parted, he wouldn't have had these additional relationships to lean on for spiritual support when he needed them most.

Looking back, I realize that even our lack of financial freedom when Ségun and I reunited was a sign of God's mercy. Too much flexibility might have become an escape route, making it easier for either of us to walk away again. Instead, that limitation narrowed our focus, forcing us to depend on God alone.[29] It humbled us, drew us together, and reminded us that trust is built not on comfort but on shared surrender through trials and tests.

I'm grateful for that season, as it prompted me to delve deeper into entrepreneurship and side hustles as potential income supplements.[30] These ventures not only uncovered untapped skills and gifts but also stretched our creativity, revealing what true partnership in marriage could be.

It took time, but gradually my apprehension about Ségun's sincerity lessened as God reassured me, showing me glimpses of His plans for us. Some of these came as dreams during our separation. One, for example, showed Ségun and me in a dimly lit room, practically empty except for a small table and the two chairs on which we sat. These dreams hinted not only at reconciliation but also at a lean season to follow. I came to see them not as random—or as bad cases of indigestion from late dinners—but as God's faith boosters, "sneak previews" of His plans, designed to strengthen my faith.[31] I was reassured that God was not caught off guard by anything we were going through.

I recorded each dream, praying over them for understanding, and some took years to unfold. Scripture affirms that God can use dreams and visions to guide and instruct us,[32] yet He never contradicts His Word, so every revelation must be tested.[33] God once used a donkey to speak to Balaam,[34] and He still uses unusual means within the boundaries of His character and Word to capture our attention and communicate His purposes.

During the period leading up to our reconciliation, something interesting began to happen. I only recognized the pattern later because I had kept a journal of events—no matter how insignificant they seemed at the time. The number eight surfaced repeatedly during our journey. After our daughter was born, Ségun shared its biblical significance—new beginnings, resurrection, and renewal. He'd come across it in a book or a teaching program, but it resonated with me. Eight often points to renewal and fresh starts—like Noah and his family, eight in total, stepping into a cleansed world after the flood (1 Pet. 3:20). God is intentional: *"He*

---

29. 2 Cor. 12:9-10

30. Eccles. 11:6

31. Matt. 9:29

32. Ps. 16:7; Job 33:14-16

33. Acts 17:11; 1 John 4:1

34. Num. 22:28–30

works out everything in conformity with the purpose of His will" (Eph. 1:11 NIV). In Scripture, not all references to numbers are random; three, seven, twelve, and forty often symbolize divine order, guidance, or a new season.

EXAMPLES OF BIBLICAL SYMBOLISM OF NUMBERS INCLUDE:

1. Three: (completion, confirmation, divine testimony)

- The Trinity: God revealed as *Father, Son, and Holy Spirit*—three Persons, yet one God (Matt. 28:19).

- Jonah in the fish: Jonah spent three days and three nights in the belly of the fish, foreshadowing Christ's burial and resurrection (Jonah 1:17; Matt. 12:40).

- Jesus' resurrection: He repeatedly told His disciples that He would rise on the third day (Luke 9:22).

- Peter's denial: Jesus foretold that Peter would deny Him three times before the rooster crowed (Matt. 26:34).

- Jesus' reinstatement of Peter: After Peter's denial, Jesus asked him three times, *"Do you love me?"* restoring him completely (John 21:15-17).

2. Seven: (perfection, covenant, completeness)

- Naaman: He was told to dip in the Jordan seven times (2 Kings 5:10) before being cleansed of leprosy.

- Jericho: The Israelites were instructed to march around Jericho for seven days, and on the seventh day, seven times before the walls fell (Josh. 6:3-4).

- Forgiveness: Jesus told Peter not just to forgive seven times, but seventy times seven (Matt. 18:22).

3. Forty: (testing, preparation, transition)

- Moses: On Mount Sinai for forty days and nights receiving the Law (Exod. 24:18).

- Israel: Wandered in the wilderness for forty years (Num. 14:33-34).

- Jesus: Fasted for forty days and nights in the wilderness before beginning His public ministry (Matt. 4:2).

4. Twelve: (government, order, authority)

- Tribes of Israel: God established the nation through twelve tribes (Gen. 49).

- Jesus' disciples: He appointed twelve apostles to lay the foundation of the Church (Matt. 10:1-2).

- Elijah: Rebuilt the altar of the Lord with twelve stones, one for each tribe (1 Kings 18:31).

Perhaps there's a deeper meaning to numbers in Scripture that scholars can unpack, but since my reflections are more personal than academic, I'll leave that work to them. My own insights barely scratched the surface during research for this book.[35] What I do know is that while some people go overboard—slipping into speculative interpretation or attributing mystical meanings to every number, even when Scripture uses them literally—that's not my approach. My references to the significance of certain signposts, such as numbers, aren't intended to lend credence to New Age practices like fortune-telling, divination, or astrology, but rather to point us back to solid, context-based Bible study and the teachings and revelations of the Holy Spirit.[36]

I also understand why some believers are cautious about this subject, since biblical symbols have often been hijacked and misused. Take the rainbow, for example. God gave it as a covenant sign, a reminder of His promise never again to destroy the earth with a flood.[37] Though its meaning has been distorted in modern times, that doesn't strip away its original purpose. We don't relinquish what God intended for good simply because the enemy distorts it; instead, we hold firm to His original meaning and promise.

As I reflect on my own journey, I see how repeated signs—whether numbers, dates, scriptures, or timely confirmations—were part of God's orchestration and His way of reassuring me of His presence, especially during the time Ségun and I were separated. In particular, the recurrence of the number eight in our story wasn't superstitious. Instead, I recognize it as God's quiet confirmation that He was guiding us into *new beginnings*—the fulfillment of His promise. Some may dismiss these moments as coincidences, but Scripture reminds us that in the last days God will speak through dreams, visions, and signs.[38] Looking back, I realize those "eights" were not situations I could have manipulated or anticipated, but God's gentle signposts of His promise that our story was not ending—it was being renewed.

It wasn't until recently that I realized God had been weaving the theme of *new beginnings* into our story from the very start, even though Ségun and I paid little attention at the time. The number eight had been carefully crafted down to the finest details—even in our wedding date, April 18, 1998. God is the Master Orchestrator, and I was reminded of this recently while

---

35. John J. Davis, *Biblical Numerology: A Basic Study of the Use of Numbers in the Bible* (Chicago: Moody Press, 1968);

    R. J. Plugge, *Biblical Numeric Keys: Interpreting Numbers in Scripture* (Bloomington, IN: WestBow Press, 2016).

36. Deut. 18:10-12; 1 Cor. 2:13-16; Col. 2:8

37. Gen. 9:12-17

38. Acts 2:17; Heb. 2:4

browsing through pictures on my phone, and I was drawn to my 2017 album. Our first family vacation abroad with our daughter was eight years after our reconciliation. That August (8th month), as we drove from Naperville—where we had visited a dear friend and his family—to Fort Wayne, where we had stayed with other family friends who have been such a blessing to us over the years, a brilliant rainbow stretched across the sky. The excitement in the car was unforgettable as our children talked over each other, eager to explain its significance and prove they had been paying attention in Sunday school.

Ségun and I told them it was more than just a natural phenomenon; the symbolic appearance of the rainbow to our family that day was a special gift and a reassuring sign from God. For us, it represented stepping out of our own "ark" into a season of *new beginnings*, especially as our sons were about to continue their studies in the US. We even connected the discussion to the birth of our daughter, which you'll read about in this chapter. Oh, you should have seen her face light up with joy at the thought of being part of God's unfolding plan for our family! Yes, science has its explanation for rainbows, but for us that day, it was a beautiful reminder from God—the Creator of the universe—of His faithfulness and the promise of a good future.

A REVELATORY INSIGHT FROM GENESIS 8

What follows is not a direct interpretation of Genesis 8, but rather a revelatory insight I received during this deeply personal season. Through divine prompting, I was able to draw lessons from this chapter because of the recurring significance of the number eight in our story, the symbolic resonance between the birds' wanderings and their return flights to the ark, and Ségun's unexpected "U-turn" at that time. Nothing and no one could have prepared me for his return; the only instruction from the Holy Spirit was simple yet profound—show mercy.

Our first attempt at reconciliation in 2008 was unsuccessful because, although the desire was there, we weren't yet ready for the new God intended. But God did not give up on us. In 2009, during the very week I was studying Genesis chapter 8, *Mr. Newman* (Ségun) reached out, asking for another chance. Interestingly, that passage describes how the rain had stopped, yet it took nearly a year for the floodwaters to fully recede before the earth was ready for a *new beginning*. Likewise, even though the "rain" had ceased in 2008, our hearts[39]—our "new land"—needed time to be softened, cleared, and prepared to receive God's Word afresh, much like the good soil Jesus described in the Parable of the Sower in Matthew 13:18-23.

Genesis 8:6-12 records how Noah sent out a raven and later a dove to see if the floodwaters had receded. The raven went to and fro until the waters dried up, while the dove, after

---

39. Ezek. 36:26; Hosea 10:12

fruitless wanderings, returned to the ark—first with nothing, then with a fresh olive leaf, and finally, not at all, once dry ground appeared.

As I reflected on this, I began to notice similarities between the birds' movements and our own journey. Both the raven and the dove, at different stages, mirrored our experience of searching for rest outside the "ark" of our marriage. Over time, however, Ségun's story aligned more closely with that of the dove—a weary soul who returned, first empty-handed, and later bearing quiet evidence of peace and hope. In marriage, reconciliation doesn't always come with explanations, apologies, or olive branches. Sometimes, the return itself is the gift—an act of surrender that makes room for God to restore what seemed lost.

Genesis 8:9 states that when the dove couldn't find a place to rest, she returned to the ark, and Noah reached out his hand and took her in. That moment became a vivid illustration to me of God's mercy.[40] The dove didn't enter by her own strength; mercy drew her in. It was a reminder that God had already woven His redemption plan into the fabric of our story— despite the wear, tear, and loose ends that once threatened to unravel our bond.

The ark had been home for the dove, just as the covenant home is meant to be a place of protection and rest for the family. And just as Noah extended his hand, God shows us how to reach out with mercy to a weary spouse who has wandered, drawing them back into safety and love.

At times, a husband or wife may drift like the raven or the dove, searching for something they cannot find outside the covenant. But if they return—even empty-handed—mercy still has the power to welcome them home. This reflects God's heart toward all of us: *"Return, O backsliding children"* (Jer. 3:14). He doesn't demand tokens of worth or proof of change—He accepts us just as we are. Jesus Himself said, *"Come to Me, all you who labor and are heavy laden, and I will give you rest"* (Matt. 11:28). In the same way, reconciliation isn't about tests, promises, undertakings, or performance—it is about one person extending mercy's hand and another responding to it.

When God called out to His beloved Israel to come home in Jeremiah 3, He did so without attaching stringent conditions. He simply asked them to admit their sin and return to Him. His faithful love is never-ending, and His mercies are new every morning.[41] That same call still reaches us today, to anyone who feels distant from Him. Jesus' arms remain open— choose life, love, and rest in Him.

For us, the most amazing of *new beginnings* came with the birth of our "union baby," Ruth, on the 8th day of the 8th month, 8 years after her brother. God had been speaking clearly and consistently through the years, ensuring we heard the message multiple times, in case we were in any doubt that He had brought us to a place of quiet rest—new life, a new covenant, a new

---

40. Jer. 3:12, 14; James 4:8
41. Lam. 3:22–23

chapter.[42] Amid the recurring signs and patterns of eights, I began to sense God awakening the psychologist within me—drawing my attention to the principle of repetition, that law of learning and conditioning. Perhaps He was showing me that what keeps repeating itself often carries a lesson He wants us to finally learn.

If you've journeyed with us through these pages, you've probably already guessed why we chose the name "Ruth" for our daughter. In Scripture, Ruth, a Moabite woman, is renowned for her loyalty, kindness, and devotion (Ruth 1:16–17). The name is of Hebrew origin and is often interpreted as "friend," "companion," "vision of beauty," or "satisfaction." Ruth is celebrated as a model of devotion, faithfulness, compassion, and integrity. For me, naming our daughter Ruth was a prophetic declaration—an act of faith over a relationship, which at the time of her birth seemed impossible!

My mother, who always believed that Ségun and I would reconcile, often teased me by calling me "Ruth" during our marital crises. I didn't realize at the time that she was planting seeds of hope in my heart. She even dreamed during my second pregnancy that I would have a daughter, although I gave birth to a son then. We both laughed, thinking her dream receptors had malfunctioned! Yet three years after my mother's passing, when our daughter was born, she looked exactly as my mother had described. Just as God allowed Moses a glimpse of the Promised Land, though he never entered it,[43] my mother was given a vision of what God had prepared for me, and her faith helped carry me closer to that promise.

God rarely reveals the full picture upfront, and for good reason. Like Israel's journey from Egypt to Canaan, we are often led step by step, because knowing everything in advance might overwhelm or discourage us.[44] Although I couldn't see how all the pieces of our story would come together—or anticipate the new challenges along the way—I knew that God could be trusted. He had already made the impossible possible, and that assurance was enough to keep me confidently moving forward with Him.

Ruth's birth became the tangible "wonder" of our journey—a living sign of God's faithfulness and the fresh start He had planned for our family. Just as the Israelites reached the Promised Land after years of wandering in the wilderness, we are now in a season of restoration, hope, and purpose. Her arrival was God's confirmation that even after seasons of drifting, pain, and uncertainty, He turns our wandering into wonder, writing a story of redemption, joy, and covenant faithfulness that only He could create.

---

42. Deut. 32:2; Ps. 62:11; Isa. 28:10-13
43. Deut. 34:4
44. Exod. 13:17

CHOOSING COVENANT AND COURAGE
OVER CULTURE AND CONVENIENCE

In today's world, marriages and relationships face challenges not only from personal struggles but also from powerful cultural narratives that influence how people see endings and new beginnings. Many societies develop philosophies and sayings to help them cope with disappointment, betrayal, or loss. Two notable examples are the *cancel culture* phenomenon in America and certain *Yorùbá proverbs* about broken relationships. While these frameworks may provide a sense of finality or closure and replacement, they can also hinder true restoration and renewal when it's needed. These views often encourage individuals to close the door on reconciliation and to find comfort in substitutes rather than seeking genuine healing.

Cancel culture, which has gained significant traction through social media since the late 2010s, operates on the premise that once a mistake is made, it cannot be undone or redeemed. A person is "canceled," excluded, and rarely gets a second chance, even after showing remorse or growth. Similarly, in many patriarchal systems (including Yorùbá culture), certain cultural sayings influence social attitudes. Yorùbá proverbs such as, *"A kìí kí wọ́n káàárọ̀ níbí tí a ti sọ pé ó dàárọ̀"* (You don't return to say good morning where you've already said goodnight), *"Okùnrin kì í sọnù aya"* (A man never lacks a wife; you can always find another woman), and *"Tọkọ bá kọni, ọkọ mìí ló máa fẹ́ni"* (If a husband leaves, another husband will marry her), suggest that relationships are replaceable, and breakups are final. These views promote moving on quickly and embracing life's natural progression rather than trying to repair what was broken or restore what was lost.

The idea that once a matter has been concluded or deemed beyond repair, it shouldn't be revisited is often applied to relationships by those who hold this belief. To them, there's no going back or pretending everything is fine; you just move on! They view this as being realistic, but it often makes reconciliation harder when mistrust or other factors seem to rule it out. Elders, family members, or friends may offer advice or gentle warnings to accept what cannot be undone or fixed *by them*—especially when they believe resolution or reconciliation isn't possible or not worth the effort. As a result, people are sometimes encouraged to give up when faced with situations that appear hopeless in marriage or relationships and to simply look for another spouse.

Interestingly, these same proverbs offer comfort or perspective, especially to women facing relationship challenges. They emphasize that destiny (*àyànmọ́ or orí*) and companionship are not limited to a single relationship but exist within a larger community and divine purpose. While Yorùbá philosophy allows for some reshaping of destiny by making extraordinary sacrifices, good character, and spiritual alignment, it parallels the concept of "divine decree" in some religions, which encourages accepting circumstances as they present themselves rather than seeking change.

Scripture, however, reminds us that God calls us to courage and covenant, not resignation. Where culture may insist on moving on or replacing a relationship, God offers redemption, restoration, and new beginnings.[45] True healing in relationships comes from obedience to His guidance, humility, and perseverance, not simply conforming to cultural expectations. Choosing covenant over convenience requires faith, patience, and courage to pursue what God has ordained, even when society signals otherwise.[46]

The following are a few permutations of selected Yorùbá proverbs that encourage women not to lose hope after divorce or abandonment. These sayings are often shared by mothers, aunts, or older women to console a woman who has experienced heartbreak or disappointment in a relationship. While these sayings promote resilience—especially in communities where abandonment carries heavy social stigma—they also affirm that rejection by one man does not diminish a woman's value or future. They emphasize that renewal and happiness are still possible, however, through another man!

- "Okùnrin tó bá fi iyawo sílé, okùnrin mîì ni yóò tún gbé e."

  » The man who leaves his wife will make way for another man.

- "Tí okùnrin bá kó obìnrin kan, okùnrin náà ni yóò tún fé ẹ."

  » If a man rejects a woman, another man will marry her.

- "Okùnrin tó bá sọ ìyàwó di èké, okùnrin mîì á rí i gégé bí wúrà."

  » If a man calls his wife worthless, another man will see her as gold.

- "Kí okùnrin tó bá fi iyawo sílè má ránti pé, obìnrin náà lè tún rí ayò ní ọwọ́ elòmîì."

  » The man who leaves his wife should remember she, too, can find joy elsewhere.

Romans 12:2 (MSG) reminds us not to copy the behavior and customs of this world, but to let God transform us into new persons by changing the way we think. We are in the world, but not defined by it, and God's standards—not human or cultural ones—are what define our worth. God never abandons His own,[47] and He calls us to choose life and trust His guidance.[48] While these cultural perspectives might seem encouraging, they can pose risks when in conflict with biblical principles and may lead to rigidity or negative outcomes such as the following:

---

45. Isa. 61:7; Joel 2:25

46. Rom. 12:2

47. Heb. 13:5b

48. Deut. 30:19

1. **Normalizing divorce or abandonment:** Proverbs like these can unintentionally make divorce or abandonment seem casual—not a big deal—diluting the Christian view of marriage as a lifelong covenant (Mark 10:9) and overemphasizing remarriage as the answer.

2. **Shifting focus away from reconciliation:** Emphasizing moving on can discourage forgiveness, patience, and restoration (Christian virtues), whereas Scripture encourages couples to seek reconciliation whenever possible and not to separate casually (1 Cor. 7:10-11).

3. **Promoting dependence on human solutions:** Hope is placed on finding a new spouse instead of God's healing, timing, and direction (Ps. 34:5, 18; Isa. 54:5). True renewal comes from Christ, not human validation (Jer. 17:5-8; 2 Cor. 5:17; Titus 3:5; Gal. 1:10).

4. **Devaluing marriage as a covenant:** Viewing marriage as a transaction of availability rather than a sacred bond—"replace one with another"—undermines its divine purpose and diminishes the reflection of God's love, faithfulness, and plan (Matt. 19:4-6; Heb. 13:4).

5. **Offering emotional shortcuts:** Certain cultural advice or perspectives can encourage quick remarriage or replacements as ways to deal with grief or rejection, leaving emotional and spiritual wounds unhealed. When loss or disappointment in marriage is seen as shameful, the erroneous belief is that quick remarriage restores honor, which can lead to repeated patterns or new unions enveloped in superficiality (Ps. 3:3; 84:11).

6. **Creating pressure on "rebounds" (substitutes or replacements):** For women, it risks reducing men to providers of validation, rather than partners in covenant under God. The pressure to commit to new relationships—often prematurely—intensifies when children, especially young ones, are involved, ostensibly to fill the parental void left behind. For men, societal pressure to prove their masculinity may lead to rushed remarriage or a display of options to save face, rather than pursuing genuine reconciliation and growth (Prov. 31:30; Phil. 2:3-5).

When we closely examine cultural norms, we begin to understand why people behave the way they do in relationships—often driven by false beliefs, insecurity, pride, or a misunderstanding of their God-given identity. Recognizing these cultural frameworks helps us look beneath the surface to the heart motives that fuel broken relationships and identity struggles—motives that only God's truth can rightly realign.

Cancel culture and certain *cultural philosophies* prioritize quick fixes, human solutions, and shortcuts—such as replacement, convenience, or survival—over covenantal faithfulness and spiritual growth. Instead of rushing into parallel relationships or remarriage, I encourage anyone facing marital challenges or separation first to seek inner healing and wholeness in Christ. Your worth is not defined by being a wife or husband, but by being God's beloved.[49]

Instead of rushing to end your marriage, entrust your plans and future to Him. You may reconcile if God restores your spouse, or you may meet someone new in His timing—not under the pressure of cultural expectations. Following God's original design helps avoid unnecessary complications from "entanglements" during cooling-off periods, allowing couples and individuals to move forward in a spiritually whole, emotionally healed, and God-honoring way.

Few enter marriage expecting a breakup, yet some cultural beliefs subtly weaken marital foundations by offering easy "exit strategies." In these systems, a husband may feel he cannot return to attempt reconciliation—*"to say good morning where he's said goodbye"*—and since he doesn't initiate or embrace such moves, the woman is encouraged to move on to the next available partner. Such perspectives are "cultural setups" where marriages are doomed to fail from the outset as they create an unspoken, yet persistent, pressure to resign oneself to loss at the slightest hint of a problem, rather than seek God's intervention. Scripture reminds us that God redeems pain, even rejection, and works all things together for good.[50] It's not over until God says so—let Him have the final word.

I hold deep love and respect for my husband. Yes, he made mistakes, and so did I. It may have taken him some time to retrace his steps, but I'm reminded—through the many stories we've encountered—that the *road back home* is often the least traveled by most *prodigal* spouses. Pride, ego, societal pressure, and the fear of rejection or humiliation are often barriers to their return. At the crossroads of decision-making, the cultural value placed on the *finality of farewells* often reemerges, discouraging even those who genuinely desire to do the right thing.

I'm grateful that Ségun and I chose to honor our marriage covenant despite these pressures. Over the past 27 years, I've witnessed, firsthand, the transformative power of surrendering our imperfect, raw lives to the Master Potter.[51] God initially worked on my rough edges, then gradually refined Ségun, turning the clay of our lives into vessels of His purpose.

After 16 years back together, I can boldly testify that God's hand continues to refine us both. I now enjoy the "super-deluxe" version of *Mr. Newman*, and I look forward to the continual transformation that God promises, knowing that His work in us is unfinished.[52] True *new beginnings* are not about perfection—they're about faithful, patient, covenantal love under God's guidance.

49. Isa. 62:4
50. Rom. 8:28
51. Isa. 64:8
52. Phil. 1:6

FAITH WITH A PRIDE PROBLEM—
THE "I KNOW BETTER" SPIRIT

I've seen many couples in situations like ours, but their outcomes differ—not because God failed, couldn't perform a miracle, or didn't want restoration for them, but because pride or spiritual arrogance blocked the way. Some act with a sense of superiority in Christ, believing they have a monopoly on all knowledge about God. They only listen to themselves or those who share their narrow perspectives. This has been the downfall of many Christian marriages.

When mistakes occur, one or both spouses often feel justified in their responses, rarely filtering their actions through Scripture or seeking the Holy Spirit for guidance. Instead of turning to God's direction, as David did,[53] they depend on their own understanding of what they believe to be the truth or solution[54]—excusing contradictions to God's will and sometimes misusing Scripture to defend their positions. This prolongs spiritual limbo, emotional distance, and wilderness experiences in relationships.

Sadly, we've seen the devastation this approach causes in families—brokenness that stems from pride, stubbornness, shame, and faulty perspectives. Yet God's mercies are new every morning, and He calls us daily to repentance and renewed understanding. God's Word is fresh! It is living and active;[55] it speaks to us differently as our experiences and comprehension deepen. Our grasp of this truth influences how we engage with God's Word. That's why some preachers revisit, revise, or even retract old sermons, and why authors update earlier editions of their books—because they've received fresh insight and revelation through deeper intimacy with the Holy Spirit, which has refueled and refocused their study of the Word. Scripture reminds us that the Spirit *"teaches us all things"* and guides us into truth.[56]

We understand only in part,[57] which is why nothing should be cast in stone until it is prayerfully examined through the lens of God's Word. We are to test every spirit[58] and correctly divide the Word of truth.[59] God confirms His Word through multiple witnesses and the inner witness of the Spirit.[60] Following Christ requires surrender—our will must yield to His. We are free to choose, but obedience offers the promise of life and blessing.

Jesus reminded His disciples that there was still much He wanted to say, but they couldn't bear it at the time. He sent the Holy Spirit as a Guide to all of us—into all truth.[61] What He

---

53. 1 Sam. 23:2
54. Prov. 3:5-6
55. Heb. 4:12
56. John 14:26; 16:13
57. 1 Cor. 13:9-12
58. 1 John 4:1
59. 2 Tim. 2:15
60. Deut. 19:15; John 16:13
61. John 16:12-15

taught during His earthly ministry was not the final word; He continues to speak through the Spirit, Scripture, and the counsel of godly witnesses today. Marriages and individuals who learn to listen, discern, and respond to God's ongoing instruction experience restoration and *new beginnings*, even in situations that once seemed impossible.

The entrance of God's Word brings light into our lives,[62] illuminating thought patterns and decision-making processes that may have been faulty for years without yielding fruit. Jesus taught us to pray, *"…give us this day our daily bread…"* (Matt. 6:11), underscoring the importance of daily spiritual nourishment. Just as God provided manna daily for the Israelites in the wilderness—enough for the day and no more[63]—we too must feed on His Word every day so we don't run on empty or rely on past knowledge, old unprofitable habits, and unreliable solutions.

To receive the "new" God has prepared, our spiritual senses must be transformed—eyes that see, ears that hear, pure hearts, renewed minds, and a receptive spirit.[64] Isaiah 43:19 challenges us: *"Do you not see or perceive it?"* It's a call to spiritual awareness that only the Holy Spirit can enable. Jesus emphasized this in Matthew 6:22-23 (AMP): If our spiritual eye is clear, our whole body is full of light; if it is dark, we are in darkness. True transformation begins with perception aligned with God.

HELD HOSTAGE BY YESTERDAY

Many claim to follow Christ yet remain unloving and unforgiving, indicating that they've not fully surrendered to God's refining work. Forgiveness, often the most difficult aspect of relationships and marriage, is the gateway to God's restoration, wholeness, and new beginnings. Our own experience was no different: Forgiving and letting go of resentment was tough, but when God's love replaces anger and bitterness, healing begins—and reconciliation finds room to grow. Colossians 3:12 (AMP) urges us to clothe ourselves as God's chosen—holy and beloved—showing tenderhearted mercy, humility, gentleness, and patience that never gives up. These qualities help us move toward relational renewal, marital bliss, and longevity.

You can't truly release the past without forgiveness, and you can't rebuild effectively with your spouse—or anyone—while holding on to bitterness.[65] Jesus calls us to be more like Him, to be more merciful, less judgmental, and reflective of His grace. Obedience to God is meant to be whole and complete; we can't pick and choose which commands matter. True believers

---

62. Ps. 119:105
63. Exod. 16:4-5
64. Isa. 6:9–10; 42:20; Jer. 5:21; Ezek. 36:26; Matt. 13:13–16; Mark 8:18; 1 Cor. 2:14; Eph. 4:13–15
65. Phil. 3:13

are both hearers and doers of God's Word.[66] God evaluates us not just by selective rule-keeping, but by how we live in light of His grace and love—His royal law.[67]

Since we depend on God's mercy, we are to extend mercy to others. Those who show mercy reflect God's heart and can expect His mercy in return. This echoes Jesus' teaching in Matthew 5:7: *"Blessed are the merciful, for they will be shown mercy."* Ecclesiastes 12:13-14 (NLT) reminds us to: *"Fear God and obey His commands, for this is everyone's duty. God will judge us for everything we do, including every secret thing, whether good or bad."* Likewise, James 2:10-13 (NLT) teaches that failing in one command is as serious as failing in all and that mercy shown to others ensures mercy from God. Selective obedience or a judgmental heart undermines true faith.

James 2:14-22 further explains that genuine faith is active—it reflects what we believe about God and how we live it out. Faith is demonstrated in our choices, actions, and the impact we have on others—whether family, community, or coworkers. Invisible faith that does nothing is ineffective; faith must produce visible fruit. As we practice our faith daily, relying on God's Word and guidance, it strengthens hope, which is not a feeling but a discipline lived out through obedience and trust. Faith pleases God when it aligns with His will and produces tangible results in our lives.

Paul warns Timothy—and all of us—in 2 Timothy 3:1-5 (AMP) that difficult times will come. The "last days" referenced in this scripture are already evident, as many professing believers drift from God's truth, adopting worldly trends instead of living counter-culturally like Jesus. Paul describes people in the church —not just the world —who are self-focused, greedy, arrogant, unloving, and devoted to outward religion while denying its power. He instructs us to avoid such people and keep our distance.

This growing culture of self-interest and compromise affects many Christian homes. Increasingly, believers reject or misinterpret God's Word because they depend on human reasoning, experience, or proof rather than faith. Some insist on *"seeing to believe,"* relying on their senses rather than approaching God with childlike trust.[68] Yet God's wisdom surpasses human understanding, and shortcuts or human constructs leave lives unproductive, stuck in cycles or empty patterns.

Challenges are inevitable, but even in those moments, God calls us to produce spiritual fruit—love, joy, peace, patience, kindness, goodness, faithfulness, gentleness, and self-control—through His grace.[69] He invites us to seek Him for wisdom and insight,[70] knowing that true

---

66. James 1:22
67. James 2:8
68. Luke 10:21
69. Gal. 5:22
70. Jer. 33:3

obedience is measured not by what we know, but by what we do with what we know.[71] Our reliance on ourselves, knowledge, experience, or culture can prevent us from receiving God's protection, power, and blessings.

To fulfill God's plan, we must think His thoughts, live by His love, and align our hearts with His ways. Jesus said, *"As the Father has loved Me, so I have loved you; continue in My love"* (John 15:9). God's love is constant, unchanging, and immeasurable. Our past does not have to dictate our future; in Christ, we can start fresh and experience *new beginnings*.[72]

LETTING GO TO GROW

A good marriage requires intentional, consistent effort. As Jim Rohn said, *"Your life does not get better by chance. It gets better by change."* Happiness isn't something we stumble upon—it's built through deliberate action. Winging it might allow coasting for a while, but eventually, neglect catches up. Wealth, looks, talent, or even marrying the "right" person cannot shield anyone from marital challenges. Following biblical principles provides a foundation for stability, but embracing God's presence transforms an ordinary marriage into one consistently infused with purpose, love, and grace.[73]

Our marriage isn't perfect—even on our fourth attempt (counting from our recent vow re-affirmation), we still face differences and have days when tensions arise. Yet, we're both committed to ensuring our happiness and love outweigh any unpleasantness. We've learned to adapt, accommodate, and compromise more graciously than we did when we first got married. Today, we're wiser, more deeply in love, and focused on pleasing God above all else. When challenges arise, we handle them more skillfully, and neither of us wants to return to old patterns of self-righteousness, resentment, or blame.[74]

Even with these strides, we faced initial hiccups as we adjusted to the fact that we were no longer the same people who had met, grown apart, and spent six and a half years building separate lives. Ségun wanted to pick up where we left off, while I needed answers and transparency to rebuild trust. Dwelling on the past, however, began to rob us of the future God had prepared for our family. Truth be told, forgetting while forgiving wasn't easy, and sometimes my focus on past hurts slowed my healing—and it showed!

Couples on this path should view past experiences as lessons and stepping stones into God's destiny and purpose. Clinging to old wounds, bitterness, or unrealistic expectations blinds

---

71. James 1:22
72. 2 Cor. 5:17
73. Eph. 5:21-33
74. Phil. 3:13

us to the "new" that God wants to reveal. If you're looking for this through the wrong lenses, you'll miss it! To fully embrace a fresh start, we must see through His eyes, let go of the past, and allow God to lead us into restoration, wholeness, and hope.[75]

Another challenge we faced was that I had become accustomed to handling things on my own, for myself and our children. This sometimes triggered a power struggle or a clash of wills—especially since I felt we were now operating on *my* turf. In some areas, we found ourselves competing rather than complementing each other, each trying to prove whose perspective or solution was better.

Watching Ségun grow in Christ was a meaningful learning experience. His determination, stubborn streak, and refusal to accept "no" for an answer—once aimed at worldly goals—were now being channeled toward trusting God and seeking His guidance. However, surrendering control wasn't easy for him. Learning to depend solely on God, rather than his own intellect, expertise, or past experiences, was a challenge that deeply affected our relationship for quite some time.

I had reservations about whether Ségun's changes were genuine during the early part of our reunion. I eventually relaxed my defenses as I saw that he was more receptive to my suggestions and, for the first time, willing to meet the cultural expectation of reaching out to my father—even though my father made it clear he wasn't interested in seeing Ségun. He felt deeply disrespected by how our separation was handled and, understandably, by the way his daughter had been treated.

However, I didn't give up on repairing strained relationships, trusting God for healing. Through perseverance and prayer, my father eventually agreed to accompany me on a visit to my in-laws, allowing us to reconnect and for them to meet their granddaughter for the first time. These traditional formalities helped break the ice and showed my in-laws that I still had strong family support, even after my mother's passing. My mother-in-law received us in my father-in-law's absence, and old issues were brought up again during our couple of hours together. As my dad and I parted ways after the visit, he asked once more if I was sure about my decision to stay in the marriage and if I was prepared to face the lingering, unresolved issues. I responded affirmatively, assuring him that everything would be fine as long as Ségun and I kept God at the center of our lives and marriage.

Not long after that meeting, my mother-in-law reached out, asking us to coordinate with our pastor to hold a small naming ceremony for our daughter at the family home. It was a brief prayer session and a blessing, but my father didn't attend the event. It was a long and hard road to recovery. While some relationships remained fragile, these steps created space for healing, re-bonding, and planning our future according to God's plan, not anyone else's.[76]

---

75. 2 Cor. 5:17
76. Rom. 12:18

Over time, Ségun and my father reconciled and maintained a good relationship until my dad's passing, demonstrating that patience, prayer, and God-centered commitment can restore even long-standing relational rifts.

Since that time, Ségun has been sincere and consistent in his pursuit of God, but my impatience with his spiritual growth often got the better of me. I had to learn to release control and resist the urge to criticize and intervene when things didn't go as planned.[77] Unintentionally, I was trying to play God in his life—and ours—slipping back into my old tendencies of caretaker, manager, rescuer, and fixer. Having once been let down by the people I trusted most—first by my father when my parents separated, then by my husband—I struggled with the need to hold everything and everyone tightly, demanding perfection and trying to protect my family's stability.

One of the recurring areas of tension was spiritual leadership. I encouraged church attendance, led prayers and family devotions, believing that if we had a spiritual foundation, everything else would fall into place. But only God can bring about true and lasting change from the inside out. Whenever I tried to force outcomes, resentment and frustration would build up. I was afraid that things might fall apart if I didn't hold everything together—but the truth was, it had been God all along who held us steady, not me.

I came to realize that my interference often stemmed from waning trust in God and a desire to control what only He could manage perfectly. I had to surrender fully, acknowledging that it was God—not me—who was protecting and guiding our family.[78] He also showed me that focusing on who Ségun *had been*, instead of who God was shaping him to *become*, was hindering progress.[79] I needed to step aside and allow God to elevate Ségun into his rightful role as the head and priest of our home.[80]

As I continued to nurture a life of prayer, worship, and fellowship within our home, my motivation began to change. I was no longer acting out of fear, frustration, or a sense of duty, but out of love and unity—living in the oneness God designed for marriage.[81] Standing in agreement with Ségun meant standing in the gap *for* him and *with* him—through prayer, grace, and honor.[82] I learned that true partnership in marriage doesn't compete for spiritual authority; it complements God's divine order (1 Cor. 11:11-12), strengthening both husband and wife under His covering.

In that process, God also reminded me of the beauty and uniqueness of our design. He

---

77. Luke 6:37-38, 41-42 (MSG)
78. Josh. 1:9; Prov. 16:9; John 10:28-29; Rom. 8:38-39
79. Col. 3:12-15
80. 1 Cor. 11:3; Eph. 5:22-24
81. Prov. 31:12; Eph. 5:33
82. Eccles. 4:9-12

has given a husband certain capacities and responsibilities that He didn't give to a wife, and vice versa. I wasn't created to be Ségun, nor was he made to be me. My role as his helpmeet is not about passivity or silence but about a purpose-driven union—supporting, covering, lifting, and encouraging him with respect. We both share this calling, for he, too, as my husband, is to love me as Christ loves the Church—selflessly, sacrificially, and steadfastly—so that together, our marriage reflects God's redemptive love as we walk in obedience to His plan for us.

Gradually, as my focus shifted from control to surrender, real change began to unfold. Ségun embraced his God-given role, growing into a faithful follower of Christ, a prayerful man, and the spiritual leader of our family. The headship I had longed for—marked not by dominance but by loving responsibility and protection—became evident.[83] As divine order was restored, peace and blessings flowed into our home, and every area of our lives began to flourish. In the end, it wasn't my persistence but God's perfect timing that produced lasting transformation—proof that surrendering to His plan always yields enduring fruit.[84]

LIVING ON PAUSE

Ségun has always been naturally sociable, and over time, God has transformed that trait into a quiet instrument for sharing His love. He often finds opportunities in everyday settings—airport lounges, airplane cabins, trains, malls, hotel lobbies, grocery stores, even barbershops—to speak of God's faithfulness and redemption in our story. He doesn't follow a script; he simply speaks from the Word hidden in his heart. His openness and sincerity draw others in, reminding us that ministry is not measured by how much Scripture we can quote but by how fully we embody God's Word through love, humility, and service. Each encounter becomes a seed of faith—echoing *"see what the Lord has done"* and *"taste and see that the Lord is good"*—as the Holy Spirit continues His work of drawing hearts to Jesus and shaping Ségun into the man God purposed him to be.[85]

Through one of these divine encounters, Ségun was invited to share his testimony at a men's breakfast. He returned home, moved, almost in tears, overwhelmed by God's presence and the response of the men who came forward during the altar call. This confirmed for him that God uses willing vessels, not just those deemed qualified by human standards.[86] Academic credentials are valuable, but God values surrender and a heart ready to obey.

Our testimony opened doors we never could have imagined—radio interviews, speaking engagements, seminars, church and marriage ministry panel discussions, and workshops. God

---

83. 1 Cor. 11:3, 7; Eph. 5:25-28; 1 Pet. 3:7

84. Gal. 6:9; Col. 3:16-17 (AMP)

85. Phil. 1:6

86. 1 Cor. 1:27-29

prepared every platform and opportunity; we didn't have to earn or strive for them. While I preferred the comfort of working behind the scenes, I had to step beyond my stage fright and embrace the opportunity to serve alongside my husband, trusting God to equip us both.[87]

That men's breakfast meeting connected Ségun to the host and senior pastor of the church, which developed into a cordial relationship. We were subsequently invited to share our testimony at a program for singles at his church, and Ségun's relationship with the pastor continued to flourish. These experiences restored Ségun's faith in the body of Christ after earlier disappointments, particularly at a time when he was earnestly seeking answers and spiritual guidance.

Prior to these moments of renewal, an earlier incident had shaken his confidence in the church. It happened during the height of our marital crisis when he felt like he was at a crossroads—what he later described to me as an epiphany. Desperate for answers and someone to pray with him, he thought about visiting his parents' Orthodox church, which he attended occasionally, but he didn't feel led to go that day. Instead, as he drove around looking for another option, he was drawn to a well-known Pentecostal church. After explaining his purpose and requesting to see the pastor for prayer and counsel, he was informed that, as he wasn't a member, he needed to complete a form and schedule an appointment for a later date. Despite sharing that he was in an extremely difficult emotional place, he was told that the pastor would not be available for several months.

This experience left a lasting impression of how inaccessible and unresponsive some churches can be when face-to-face with individuals in urgent need of compassionate pastoral care. Fortunately, it didn't stop Ségun from seeking God wholeheartedly. Soon after, the Lord guided him to a church conference, where he responded to an altar call—a pivotal moment in his spiritual journey. Unbeknownst to him, God was already at work—orchestrating relationships to restore his confidence and hope. He has a way of mending what man has bruised.

The aforementioned pastor with whom Ségun bonded was a kind and compassionate man. Although we could only attend a few church services because of the distance from our home, there were no conditions or pressures to join his church. Instead, he welcomed us as "friends of the house." Beyond the platforms he provided for us to share our testimony, there was a mutual fondness and respect between him and Ségun. He offered guidance and mentorship, engaging Ségun in meaningful discussions about faith, life, business, politics, and leadership. Sadly, he passed away at a time when Ségun was looking forward to their relationship becoming even closer. Ségun was deeply shaken upon learning of the pastor's passing. He had visited his home occasionally, and I later had the privilege of meeting his lovely wife, who has also gone to be with the Lord. This relationship provided exactly what Ségun needed at such a defining point in his journey, with its full significance revealed later as we continued on the path of restoration.[88]

---

87. Exod. 4:10-12
88. Prov. 27:17

God kept guiding us to the right people, and what started as simple acts of obedience in sharing our story led to platforms and opportunities beyond our expectations. Even with ongoing challenges at home, Ségun's vulnerability and honesty strengthened my resolve. He shared with me how Hebrews 11:6 inspired him to create a springboard for helping couples and marriages, which ultimately led to the formation of TRY HARD—*Trust and Revere Yahweh; He Always Rewards Diligence*. It was a tangible way to serve others, showing God's goodness and mercy in our own lives.

Seeing God's hand at work in Ségun about ten years ago felt like coming full circle—a beautiful reminder that nothing in God's plan is ever wasted. Around that time, I began teasing him, calling him *the "weeping prophet"* because of his deeply emotional storytelling, which is reminiscent of the compassion of Jeremiah in the books of Jeremiah and Lamentations. When Ségun shares our testimony, it's as though he channels God's heart for restoration—drawing many toward repentance, hope, and renewal.

Serving through TRY HARD has been both demanding and deeply fulfilling. Pouring our time, insights, and God's love into the lives of families helped shift the focus away from ourselves and promoted growth and healing in us as we walked alongside others on their journeys to restoration.[89] Yet, as small wins accumulated, complacency quietly crept in. We drifted from praying together and staying fully anchored in God, forgetting that prayer fuels faith; without it, doubt, fear, anxiety, and temptations find room to grow.[90]

This spiritual drift exposed the final "giant" that had to be defeated before we could truly settle in our Promised Land—a lingering strain that periodically surfaced, rooted in our differing perspectives on faith. The distance that formed between us and God gradually revealed what was still unresolved within us. It was as though God was shining a light on the very area He desired to refine, using that season to remind us that growth in ministry must never outpace intimacy with Him. Apostle Paul captured this truth in 1 Corinthians 9:24-27, where he compared the walk of faith to a disciplined race—urging believers to run with purpose and self-control, so that after sharing the Gospel with others, they themselves wouldn't be disqualified.

Ségun's approach to handling adversity or setbacks often contrasted sharply with mine. His cautious outlook and fluctuating moods sometimes weighed on me and the overall atmosphere in our home. Decisions and plans frequently had to wait until every detail was clear, finances were secured, and the timing seemed conducive. He may have viewed this as prudence, but I sensed that some opportunities were God's way of teaching us that faith doesn't wait for perfect conditions—it acts on trust in Him, even when the outcome is uncertain.[91]

I had learned early in life the importance of contentment and gratitude—finding joy in

---

89. Isa. 58:10-12; 2 Cor. 1:3-4
90. Matt. 13:25; 26:41
91. Eccles. 11:4; Heb. 11:1, 6

life's small blessings. We made the most of what we had, celebrating daily victories just as much as major breakthroughs, always hopeful and working toward more. My mother instilled in us the habit of seeing the sunny side of life and thanking God for being alive, for love, for family, for health, and for provision.[92] One of her favorite hymns, which we often sang along to, was "Count Your Blessings" by Johnson Oatman Jr. and Edwin O. Excell. Those early lessons became quiet anchors in my adult life, helping me steady my heart when gratitude felt harder to find.

Although we agreed on the foundation for rebuilding our marriage, our views on faith often differed. Ségun leaned toward a *"seeing-is-believing"* mindset, which, in practical terms, felt like holding his breath for the perfect moment before fully living—pausing in life and always waiting for the right time. I, on the other hand, embraced both *"seeing-is-believing"* and *"believing-is-seeing,"* choosing to act in faith while trusting God to fill in the gaps along the way.[93] I didn't need all the answers or evidence before taking a step or making a decision. I prayed, checked the essentials, and took bold steps forward in faith. Ségun, at the time, preferred intellectual assurance—tangible evidence before action. That isn't wrong, but it can lead to a dependence on visible outcomes or constant proof, and limit trust in God's unseen hand. Hebrews 11:6 reminds us that *"without faith it is impossible to please God."*

I sometimes assumed that my past experiences and reliance on God made me more spiritually mature than Ségun. Yet I, too, once leaned on evidential faith—like Thomas,[94] needing external facts, proofs, arguments, or logical reasoning to validate my belief and sustain my relationship with God. Over time, that shifted into experiential faith that grew deeper as I began to encounter God personally—through the Holy Spirit, relationships, and life experiences. Both expressions of faith are biblical, valid, and complementary, reflecting Hebrews 11:1: *"Now faith is the substance of things hoped for, the evidence of things not seen."*

Our faith must be anchored in the truth of God's Word—built on the evidence of His existence, the reliability of Scripture, and the record of His fulfilled promises.[95] However, it must also grow through a living relationship with Him—daily intimacy with the Holy Spirit, learning to recognize His voice, trusting His hand at work, and resting in the assurance that our Heavenly Father is faithful—no matter what comes our way![96]

These opposing perspectives sometimes caused friction. Ségun felt I "faith-shamed" him whenever we disagreed about decisions concerning our family's future, which only led to more arguments and less patience between us.[97] Old habits began to resurface, and my instinct was to

---

92. 1 Thess. 5:18
93. Exod. 4:2; 1 Kings 17:8-16; 2 Kings 4:1-7
94. John 20:24-29
95. Rom. 15:4
96. Ps. 37:5; John 15:4-5
97. Eph. 4:2-3

push back—something that rarely improved the situation. We both wanted to avoid falling into the pitfalls of the past, yet we hadn't quite figured out how. So, in moments when I had strong opinions and couldn't keep my "big mouth" shut, I'd just text or email them to him instead!

I truly felt for my husband as the pressure of providing for our family mounted—often relying mainly on his own efforts to turn our finances around. Watching him work tirelessly amid setbacks—in an environment where integrity seemed scarce, promises held little meaning, and contracts were merely ink on paper—was heartbreaking. The stress intensified when some of his business deals fell through, compounded by a major restructuring and downsizing at my previous job, where my position had been made redundant about two years earlier. When it rains, it pours!

After months of job hunting, I took advantage of a business opportunity that helped cover some bills and gave me more time with our children. I tried to maintain normalcy for their sake, but even small gestures—like birthday cakes or occasional treats—were often scrutinized or criticized by Ségun who felt that I had a tendency to go overboard when it came to our children. I struggled with his rigid approach, feeling frustrated that faith-driven "risks" were usually dismissed in favor of what felt "safe," familiar, or logical.

As results lagged, Ségun's frustration grew. Watching all of this unfold in front of me, it was hard to stay silent, knowing that what we urgently needed wasn't another plan but a shift in mindset—a spiritual realignment that could unlock the change we longed for. We didn't need a secret formula or a $1,000-an-hour business guru. The missing piece in our *puzzle* was faithful obedience to God. The first step was to align with godly principles rather than relying solely on human wisdom and effort.

I've personally witnessed remarkable turnarounds—clear evidence of what happens when people work wisely, align their efforts with faith, and apply God's Word in every area of life.[98] These biblical principles include seeking God first,[99] rejecting laziness,[100] trusting His provision,[101] giving generously,[102] staying diligent,[103] serving with love,[104] avoiding ungodly influences,[105] delighting in the Lord, and meditating on His Word daily.[106] When faith, obedience, and patience operate together, the timeless Word of God transforms ordinary effort into extraordinary results.[107]

---

98. Josh. 1:8; Matt. 7:24-25; John 13:17; Phil. 4:9; Heb. 4:12; James 1:22-25

99. Ps. 37:4-5; Jer. 29:13; Matt. 6:33

100. Prov. 6:6-11; Rom. 12:11

101. Phil. 4:19; Matt. 6:26

102. Luke 6:38; 2 Cor. 9:6-15

103. Prov. 10:4; Col. 3:23–24

104. Gal. 5:13; 1 Pet. 4:10

105. Ps. 1:1-3; Prov. 13:20

106. Ps. 1:2-3

107. Gal. 6:9; Heb. 6:9-12; James 1:22

But living by these principles isn't just about discipline—it's about devotion. Our actions and priorities always reveal where our allegiance lies. The truth is, everyone serves an altar—whether knowingly or not. An altar represents devotion, sacrifice, and worship. We all dedicate our time, energy, emotions, loyalty, and resources to something or someone we consider important or worthy. Jesus made this clear when He said, *"Seek first the kingdom of God and His righteousness, and all these things will be added to you"* (Matt. 6:33). So, we must ask ourselves: What altar are we truly serving—God, or something else—such as money, power, success, relationships, ideology, pleasure, or self?

For many, that altar is "self." Scripture warns that *"men will be lovers of themselves…"* (2 Tim. 3:2). When life revolves around our own desires, appetites, comfort, image, ambition, or achievements, we build altars of self-worship. Instead of honoring God, many "serve" self-interest, self-gratification, or self-promotion—subtle forms of idolatry where one's own wants and feelings become the "god" they serve. But Paul urges us in Romans 12:1 to *"present [our] bodies as a living sacrifice, holy and acceptable to God."* Every day, consciously or not, we're offering ourselves somewhere—either to God or to something else—because *"no one can serve two masters"* (Matt. 6:24).

For followers of Christ, the altar belongs to Him alone. To be Christian is to live out His example—love, humility, obedience, and service—not just in words, but in daily practice (Matt. 7:21; John 13:14-15; 1 John 2:6; 3:18). And it's not merely religious discipline or good behavior that transforms a life, but Christ Himself—His grace, His presence, and His power at work within the believer. While other faiths have their own practices that express devotion and pursuit of truth, for Christians, the difference lies in a living personal relationship with Jesus—the One who makes true transformation possible.

Throughout Scripture, God's people—Noah, Abraham, Jacob, Elijah, Gideon, and others—built altars to commemorate His mercy, covenant faithfulness, and deliverance (Gen. 8:20; 12:7-8; 35:1-3; Exod. 20:24; 1 Kings 18:30; Judg. 6:24). These altars marked moments of worship, repentance, renewed devotion, fulfilled promise, and revival. For believers today, the altar is no longer made of stone—but is spiritual. It's Christ Himself, the One who offered His life once for all, and who continues to intercede for us as our High Priest (Heb. 13:10; Rev. 8:3-4). Our hearts have become the place of worship, where our love and loyalty are revealed.

True transformation begins when we surrender our altars to God. His grace breathes new life into what once felt paused or stagnant, turning dead ends into fresh beginnings (2 Cor. 5:17; Phil. 1:6). That's exactly what God did for us when Ségun and I finally laid down our need for control and self-reliance—our "pause" became His preparation. Each act of surrender became a brick in the new foundation He was building for our marriage and ministry.

But it didn't happen immediately, and unfortunately, many things had to die on the altar of "self," which only heightened the tension between us. To me, the situation we faced seemed self-inflicted, and I couldn't understand why Ségun wouldn't fully trust God after exhausting every human option. One of our hardest decisions was withdrawing our children from private school at critical stages of their education.

It was a painful and humbling experience, not just for us but also for them, considering the potential shame and disappointment such steps could bring. Until that point, we had managed to keep them in school, shielding them from the embarrassment of being sent home over unpaid fees. But eventually, as we continued down this difficult path that Ségun strongly believed in, we had to make the tough choice. We homeschooled our children for about a year before transferring our boys to an excellent alternative school run by Ségun's in-laws, who magnanimously discounted their tuition fees.

I longed for us to get unstuck by stepping out in faith—beginning with uniting in prayer[108] and trusting God's unchanging nature and His faithfulness.[109] It was erroneous to expect something new while doing things the same way we always had. Real transformation requires a shift in thinking,[110] speech, associations, and sometimes even location. Immersing ourselves in God's Word had to become essential, because what we dwell on shapes the direction of our lives—our input determines our output, and what fills us ultimately forms us.

Tensions peaked as Ségun adopted the mindset, *"When I want your opinion, I'll ask for it."* Though an improvement from pre-separation conflicts—often marked by the attitude, *"If I want your opinion, I'll give it to you!"*—it still fell short of God's design for mutual respect and partnership in marriage.[111] I began to sense that he might be taking my dedication to our marriage and home for granted, assuming I could never leave. But I could—and I had to step back to examine my heart, our dynamic, and whether I was willing to continue under those conditions.

I needed some time alone to reflect. Living together had become increasingly difficult, even though we still shared moments of fun and laughter. I had run out of options for resolving the deadlock. Our prayer life—once our anchor—had nearly come to a standstill, a sobering reminder that neglecting God's guidance in marriage can cause spiritual stagnation.[112]

Things had reached a breaking point, and I made a bold decision one afternoon: I packed a small bag while Ségun was out for school runs and left home for what I intended to be at least a week. A recent argument had reopened old wounds, and the words exchanged cut deeply. I felt an urgent need to create space for clarity. I can't confidently say my decision was Spirit-led, but I genuinely believed such an intervention was necessary. Before leaving, I wrote a tearful

---

108. Matt. 18:20
109. Heb. 10:23
110. Phil. 4:8
111. Eph. 5:21-33
112. Matt. 18:19-20

note to our children, assuring them of my love and that my decision wasn't about them—it was about me needing time to rest, pray, and reset.

I didn't disclose my location or how long I planned to be away, and I switched off my phone. I called a ride-hailing service and checked into a hotel about 15 minutes away. *All that drama, just for a 15-minute drive? Girl!!* Well, yes, it felt like the safest distance from my five-and-a-half-year-old daughter, whom I'd never spent the night away from since her birth. Later that night, I confided in my best friend, insisting she not inform Ségun. My intention was to show that I, too, had a choice—and that staying in our marriage was a deliberate, conscious decision, and not a given.

I avoided responding to calls and messages. I knew Ségun would be concerned—after all, I hadn't given any warning, and it was a school night, so managing the three children alone and unprepared may have felt overwhelming at first. But I believed they'd be fine; Ségun loves his children immensely and has always been a hands-on dad. After two nights, he reached out to his pastor friend, who then called me to understand what was going on. I explained that I was not abandoning our marriage but rather hitting a "reset" button—to gain perspective, rest, and prayerfully seek God's guidance. The pastor graciously mediated, offering wisdom and support.[113]

He understood my position, and we agreed that I'd return within a week, although he suggested I do so immediately. I thought I had a few more nights of quiet—until a terrible stomach bug struck the next day, putting paid to any desire of staying longer! I had experienced God's sense of humor many times on this journey, but this?! With that big nudge—divine intervention—I cut my "trip" short and went back home, more reflective and ready to approach our marriage with renewed patience and purpose.

We remain profoundly grateful to our dear pastor-friend for his wisdom and generosity of spirit. His gentle nature and unwavering support during that season exemplified Christ's love, reminding us that God provides guidance through His servants.[114] May his soul and that of his darling wife continue to rest in peace, Amen.

I returned home unsure of what to expect, but Ségun and the children welcomed me warmly, immediately easing the tension. Even though it had only been a few days, I realized how much I'd missed them. That evening, Ségun and I had a long, heart-to-heart conversation. My unexpected departure had shaken him; he hadn't seen it coming. For months, I had quietly shared my dissatisfaction, but we had been in survival mode, and Ségun was more focused on maintaining stability rather than addressing my emotions.

I asked Ségun what he really wanted and if he still desired to be with me. His answer was an unequivocal "yes." But our marriage needed more—more than just a spouse; it required us

---

113. Prov. 16:13-15 (MSG)
114. Prov. 11:14; Heb. 13:7

to be partners and friends. Staying together out of pity, duty, guilt, desperation, or lingering sentiment would have been a disservice to both of us and our children. Our commitment had to be intentional, mutually nurturing, and, above all, God-honoring. I couldn't and wouldn't settle for anything less!

We agreed to give it our all—no half-measures. We wouldn't keep patching things up and hoping they'd improve further down the road. I was no longer willing to postpone my happiness or that of our children; it simply wasn't fair to any of us. We'd been fixated on salvaging the past, whereas God was doing something entirely new with our marriage. It was time to let old patterns, pride, and "self"—those seeds of the flesh—fall to the ground and die,[115] so that God could bring forth new fruit and we could walk in the abundance of His life. Transformation had to begin in our minds, renewing our thoughts, attitudes, and perspectives. Only by surrendering our old ways and trusting God could we embrace this season of restoration and experience a truly *new beginning*.

THE NEW BEGINS!

The answers to my prayers at the hotel didn't come through a fairy-tale wave of a wand over my husband's head, but through a deeper understanding on my part that every person has a unique walk with God that must be respected.[116] That shift in perspective changed everything. I had to accept that the transformation I longed to see in Ségun wouldn't happen overnight but would unfold supernaturally in God's timing—not through my arguing, nagging, or trying to control. Faith works hand in hand with patience,[117] and daily doses of grace provide the staying power needed to persevere until God's perfect will is accomplished.[118]

I realized that even "an old dog" can learn new tricks—it all depends on how hungry it is! And no, I'm not calling my husband a dog, but God used desperate circumstances to create in him a hunger and thirst, leading him to pause, reflect, and seek truth. In that stillness, God captured our full attention and began pruning and reshaping us—not just for ourselves but, as Joseph declared, *"for the saving of many lives."*[119]

Transformation accelerated when Ségun and I began to truly see ourselves as a unified team, seeking God's guidance in every decision. We prayed through challenges, dared to dream bigger, and worked strategically instead of merely toiling.[120] We persevered, rebuilding our family

---

115. John 12:24; Rom. 6:6-7; Gal. 2:20
116. Phil. 2:12-13
117. Heb. 6:12; James 1:3-4
118. 2 Cor. 12:9
119. Gen. 50:20
120. Luke 5:2-11

step by step according to God's blueprint, always leaving the final say to Him. The result: answered prayers, breakthroughs, and turnarounds that far exceeded our expectations. God proved faithful beyond measure.[121]

Our first bold test of faith came when I discovered a boarding school abroad that seemed perfect for our younger son. At that time, we had less than $100 across all our accounts, but I felt a strong conviction to attend a private presentation hosted by the school representative in our city. Ségun thought it was pointless, but I was determined to *faith it until we made it.* With barely enough fuel in the car, we showed up in our Sunday best as if we had abundant resources and enrolled our son. Not only did God open the door for him, but his older brother was able to begin his university education abroad at the same time. In His goodness, God gave us double for all our trouble.[122]

Not only did our two sons excel in their studies, but they also thrived, consistently earning spots on the Dean's and Provost's lists, with one graduating *summa cum laude.* Watching them pursue their dreams and carve out their paths fills us with immense pride and gratitude. As Ségun and I reflect on their journey, we are reminded that, even during our struggles, God was merciful—protecting and guiding them every step of the way. Truly, everything has worked together and continues to work together, for their good—and to God alone be all the glory!

The more Ségun and I grew intimate with the Holy Spirit—individually and prayerfully together—the closer we drew to each other. When your heart is aligned with God, thoughts of knowingly doing anything that will hurt or upset your spouse fade because you choose to follow and please God above all else.[123] Where there is forgiveness, love can blossom again, often in deeper and healthier ways. It may seem counterintuitive, but I've seen it repeatedly in our marriage and in others: Couples who persevere through trials often emerge stronger on the other side. As Paul wrote, *"suffering produces perseverance; perseverance, character; and character, hope"* (Rom. 5:3–4).

Over time, I noticed deliberate changes in Ségun. He began to reassure me of his commitment through concrete actions, and I no longer felt like an outsider in my own marriage. It was as if I was being wooed all over again. God expanded our capacity to love each other,[124] restored our trust, and reminded us that He must remain at the center of our union. Only His grace sustains us and gives us courage, perspective, and hope in every situation.[125]

From this renewed partnership, God brought something new to life. In the midst of a national health emergency, He prompted us to establish the CURE Initiative—*Communities*

---

121. Lam. 3:22-23; Eph. 3:20
122. Isa. 61:7; Zech. 9:12
123. Gal. 5:16
124. John 14:21; 2 John 1:6
125. Heb. 4:16

United to Remove Epidemics. I never imagined that Ségun and I would officially start working together professionally to serve others in the public health sector.

At first, I worried that working side by side might strain our marriage. But God used even this to strengthen us. Later in 2016, while we were still developing our operations, I came across an article about an old classmate from primary school and his wife. Their inspiring story of faith, vision, and perseverance reminded me that every God-given dream must be anchored in trust and obedience. They left successful careers to pursue a business that many dismissed as "impossible" to succeed in our environment. Yet, prayer and faith laid the foundation for their success, and they're still standing strong today. Their testimony reassured me that true success is built when two people fully trust God and the calling He has placed on their lives.[126]

Since then, I've not only been Ségun's partner in ministry and work, but also his protégé. He's helped me build confidence, broaden my perspective, and uncover gifts I didn't know I had. Walking in the same direction—blending our personalities, wisdom, and skills—has allowed us to complement each other and fulfill God's purpose together.[127] Recentering on God daily has been essential to sustaining our impact and preserving spiritual vitality in our hearts, home, ministry, and even business.[128]

We are deeply grateful for the "village" of supporters who have also prayed for us along the way, but we've had to make daily choices ourselves: to choose God, to choose each other, and to do the work of nurturing our love. In our leaner seasons, we started small—grabbing ice cream, *suya*, or sugar-coated popcorn (my favorite!), grocery shopping together, running school drop-offs and pick-ups, and fine-tuning proposals or presentations. These little shared moments became seeds of intimacy that blossomed into lasting memories. To this day, we remain intentional in creating experiences not only for ourselves but also with our children, weaving a tapestry of love, faith, and family legacy.

Looking back, I see how these *small beginnings*[129] were actually preparation for bigger steps of faith.[130] God was teaching us to trust Him not only for our marriage but also for the new assignments He was about to place in our hands. What began as a fragile new start at home soon became the launching pad for greater breakthroughs ahead. And just when it seemed like God had restored what was broken, He began to reveal that He wasn't finished with us yet. What we thought was the "end" of our struggle turned out to be only the beginning of something far greater—a new chapter that would stretch our faith, enlarge our vision, and position

---

126. Prov. 16:3
127. Eccles. 4:9–12
128. Jer. 29:12-14 (AMP)
129. Zech. 4:10
130. Job 8:5-7 (NLT); James 1:12 (MSG)

398 • Trilogy Refining Decisions

us for impact far beyond our marriage. *"For You, O God, have tested us; You have refined us as silver is refined… But You brought us out to rich fulfillment."* (Ps. 66:10, 12b)

WHEN YOUR "NEW" LOOKS DIFFERENT

We're not sharing our story as a cookie-cutter, one-size-fits-all solution for every marriage, but as an invitation to see fresh possibilities through the lens of God's Word. Every marriage journey is unique, yet many of us face similar struggles in different ways. What remains constant is God Himself—unchanging and faithful—who offers the same solution across all generations: Jesus Christ—the Way, the Truth, and the Life.[131] No one needs to feel stuck or walk their marital journey alone, whether their story feels near-perfect, strained by separation, or even marked by divorce.

The "new" may not always look like what we prayed for or imagined, but when our choices align with God's will, His grace carries us through.[132] Restoration takes many forms, and each of us must seek God's direction for our own path—*"continue to work out your salvation [that is, cultivate it, bring it to full effect, actively pursue spiritual maturity] with awe-inspired fear and trembling [using serious caution and critical self-evaluation to avoid anything that might offend God or discredit the name of Christ]"* (Phil. 2:12b AMP).

For some, that new path might include divorce—perhaps not by choice, but due to betrayal, abandonment, abuse, or other painful realities. Yet even then, God can redeem broken pieces and weave them into His greater good.[133] A *new beginning* doesn't erase the past; it transforms it if we allow God to heal instead of holding on to bitterness and regret.

When we embrace what God allows, we begin to see Him—and ourselves—in a new light. Your *new beginning* may not look the way you hoped or expected, but it always carries the potential to draw you closer to God's purpose. Remember, your identity and worth are never defined by your marital status but by who you are in Christ.[134]

Divorce is one of the most painful experiences the human heart can undergo, yet for some, it becomes an unexpected path to healing. You might have prayed fervently for your spouse to change or tried everything possible to help them turn around, but sometimes they choose a different route. Even then, God sees you, loves you, and can bring beauty out of ashes (Isa. 61:3).

Stand firm in Him and allow His Word to guide you. Divorce frequently stirs up intense emotions—guilt, shame, anger, loneliness, despair, and even the desire for revenge. However, these feelings don't have to keep you stuck in cycles of defeat. True freedom isn't found

---

131. John 14:6
132. Ps. 73:26; Isa. 41:10; Phil. 4:13
133. Rom. 8:28
134. Gal. 2:20; Eph. 1:4-5

in "liberating" ourselves from a spouse; it comes from Christ alone.[135] Without addressing the deeper issues of the heart, a person may repeat the same struggles in new relationships. Sometimes, instead of running, God calls us to face those broken places head-on and let Him heal what's beneath the surface.

The good news is that you will recover, rebuild, and not remain down forever. You may go through seasons of sadness, but God's grace will carry you into His joy. *"He heals the broken-hearted and binds up their wounds"* (Ps. 147:3). A *new beginning* after divorce flows best from a heart rooted in God, not in fear, regret, or anger. He is able to restore lost years,[136] redeem broken dreams, and make all things beautiful in His time.[137] Even in dark and lonely places, God deposits treasures—lessons and experiences that can enrich not only your journey but also the lives of others.[138] What was meant to harm you, He can turn around for good and for His glory. Your story isn't over. With God, every ending can become the doorway to a glorious fresh start.

The enemy's attack is rarely about your past—it's about your future. Don't let him steal God's good plans from you.[139] My prayer is that as you look around, you'll see signs of God rewriting your story. Bold steps of faith forward—such as choosing forgiveness, letting go of bitterness, overcoming fear, and opening channels of communication—can unlock blessings you never imagined. I could easily have missed the precious gift of our daughter if I had stayed stuck in past hurts. Too often, we let pain and disappointment blind us to what God is doing in the present and what He has prepared for our future.[140] Embrace your *new beginning* with hope, faith, and courage, believing that with God nothing is impossible.[141]

Perspective opens the door to a *new beginning*. Like Joseph, we must learn to say, *"You meant evil against me, but God meant it for good"* (Gen. 50:20). This requires faith-filled vision, intentionality, and the humility to align with God's will rather than our own.[142] It also involves applying His standards in our relationships—especially with spouses and children—not excusing sin, but addressing it in truth and love.[143] We are all a work in progress, and *new beginnings* demand both grace and accountability.

Sharing our struggles is not to spotlight weakness, but to help others recognize the enemy's schemes and be better prepared.[144] Knowing your adversary equips you to fight more effec-

---

135. John 8:36

136. Ps. 126:5-6; Isa. 61:3; Jer. 30:17

137. Eccles. 3:11

138. 2 Cor. 1:3-4

139. Rom. 8:28; Eph. 2:10; Phil. 1:6

140. James 5:11

141. Luke 1:37

142. Isa. 55:8-9

143. Eph. 4:15

144. 2 Cor. 2:11

tively. Just as a manual provides shortcuts and clarity, God's Word lights our path, guiding us toward His best.[145] Wise people don't wait to learn everything the hard way. As Scripture says, *"The prudent see danger and take refuge, but the simple keep going and pay the penalty"* (Prov. 22:3).

Fairy tales don't exist, but *God tales* do. Just as He has done for us, God can rewrite your story with a "happily ever after" if you let Him complete it. *"And after you have suffered a little while, the God of all grace, who called you to His eternal glory in Christ, will Himself restore, confirm, strengthen, and establish you."* (1 Pet. 5:10)

THROUGH SÉGUN'S LENSES

My altar call experience not only saved my life but also changed and reset it in a way that almost defies description. I often asked myself, *"Why me, why us, why now?"* in relation to the events of that night and how they resulted in an 11th-hour reconciliation between Funké and me. It is only with the benefit of hindsight that one knows that the God who knows the very end from the very beginning was perfecting His plan for us in His own time, in His own way, and in His own handpicked place.

I shudder whenever I think about the countless stories of people who lose their way due to marital crises and never manage to get back on track. I can relate to it because that could so easily have been my story. During one dark and chaotic period of my life, I traveled far down an incredibly torturous road that led to nowhere. At one point, the thought of ending my life appeared to be the easiest and most practical option.

During my separation, and before any such thought even entered my head, I had often tuned into a phone-in radio program in Nigeria hosted by Dr. Yolanda George-David (aka Aunty Landa). Callers would often discuss their personal struggles that frequently led to suicidal thoughts. Aunty Landa would compassionately counsel and encourage them and suggest avenues for seeking help. My feeling of incredulity continued until I realized that callers were simply voicing their unanswered cries for help.

I did not realize just how many people one meets, walks past daily, or pulls up next to in traffic are crying out for help. Unfortunately, most of the time, no one hears them, and when someone does, they often don't have an answer—or the right one. I know now what escaped me for forty-six years of my life. God, and God alone, is the answer.

The adjustment to living together again as husband and wife was tough. During our separation, Funké and I had unsurprisingly grown accustomed to controlling our

---

145. Ps. 119:105

own space and not having to incorporate a spouse into one's plans and thoughts. While freedom can be good, it can also be harmful in that it can promote a sense of self-sufficiency that breeds selfishness by way of the proverbial "me, myself, and I" mindset. It can move us away from a place where we enjoy communion with God and from where we bask in His presence.

Six and a half years apart changes the dynamics between two spouses, no matter how close they had been beforehand. We had to rediscover, and indeed reinvent, ourselves and make what seemed like unnatural allowances for each other. If only there were shoehorns that allowed individuals in such situations to simply slide back into their former positions and continue life as normal. Many of the tough patches that we initially faced after our reconciliation were probably a result of our inability to erase "territory" that we had subconsciously marked in our minds to ward off "intruders"— territory that we felt we had earned and were unwilling to relinquish without a fight!

The most difficult part of reconciliation was relearning how to communicate with one another without judgment and without inviting historical problems into our home. The latter was easier said than done, as it is only when conflict arises and one dips one's hands into what I call one's "response reservoirs" that one discovers its contents, a lot of which is negative and destructive. Malice. Hatred. Unforgiveness. Jealousy. Pride. Covetousness. Judgmentalism. The list goes on and on.

It took a while for us to settle into an ideal rhythm because we had to learn to trust one another again, to see one another the way that God sees us ... blameless, forgiven, restored. The process was slow, torturous, and painful at times, but there was a shared recognition of the fact that we had been given a second chance. We realized that, if for no other reason, we had to do right by our two delightful sons and ensure that our marriage worked on this third attempt. They were, and remain, our greatest blessing, as does our extraordinary daughter—the kindest and best-behaved children a parent could ever wish for—traits that, until today, even at the ages of twenty-six, twenty-three, and fifteen, set them apart.

Despite our best efforts, there were difficult moments that brought back memories of past crises during which there may previously have been an inclination to seek the intervention of third parties. However, this time was different. Funké and I had to decide to either rely on our own strength and/or third-party involvement or to entrust God with the entirety of the process. Fortunately for me, Funké was and remains a veteran prayer warrior and takes spiritual discipline to another level! It was through her fervent and consistent prayer for six and a half years, despite the severity of the storms we faced and the pushback she regularly received from me, that I came to fully appreciate the substance of Paul's words in 1 Corinthians 16:9. I learned that the Word of God truly opens great and effectual doors.

Our decision to place our reliance on God brought about a shift in us, in our marriage, and in our home. He rewarded us by ushering us into a season where we advertised Him as our Source, our Helper, and our Guide. Our separation had left its mark on various aspects of our marriage.

Some of our personal relationships came to an end, and new ones began. On the business front, things had taken a turn for the worse for me as, on several occasions, what appeared to be extremely promising opportunities inexplicably evaporated into thin air.

However, I remained optimistic and continued to believe that it was just a matter of time before things turned around. I refused to take a 9-to-5 job because, as a natural problem solver, I knew in my heart that that was not where my future or that of my family lay. In the interim, I went through phases when I was in disbelief at how I went from being one transaction away from buying investment properties in London and Paris simultaneously to being unsure of what would happen were we to face a significant, unexpected expense. I believe that God used that period to prune me and rid me of the spirit of self-reliance.

He also gave me a front row seat from which I was able to observe Funké at close quarters to appreciate, down to the minutest detail, the wife he had blessed me with. I saw and felt her love for me through thick and thin, and even today, 16 years after our reconciliation, I am truly blessed as I continue to discover new expressions of love, compassion, and selflessness that she exhibits on a daily basis as a wife and mother. The fasting, praying, immersing herself in the Word, filling our home with worship music, is a clear reflection to keep Christ at the center of our home—a quiet yet powerful testament to her faith in action and her commitment to nurturing an atmosphere where God's presence dwells richly.

During our period of restoration, we set up an informal marriage ministry, TRY HARD—*Trust and Revere Yahweh; He Always Rewards Diligence*, in recognition of God's role in not only preserving our marriage but also in guarding our lives when our marriage spiraled out of control and life did not appear to be worth living. TRY HARD gave us access to platforms where we were able to testify about God's faithfulness, His mercy, and His ability to turn seemingly hopeless marital situations around. The seeds we sowed at that time would later germinate in perfect alignment with His will, and it was apt that such a radical departure from the Ségun and Funké of old came about three years after the birth of our daughter, born on August 8, 2010. As the number eight symbolizes in the Bible new beginnings, resurrection, and spiritual generation, God showed us that He is also a God of perfect timing!

It is only just now, as I contribute to the penultimate chapter of this cathartic book, which Funké and I pray will give people hope, encouragement, and relatability that I grasp the fullness, breadth, and excitement of our new beginning. Speaking for myself, as undeserving of His mercy as I was, and still am, this is, of course, GOD's doing.

Our new beginnings took many forms. Newness of intimacy with GOD. Newness of reverential fear toward Him. Newness of understanding. Newness of answers. Newness of love for one another. Newness of appreciation for one another. Newness of attraction toward one another. Newness of patience toward one another.

While it is dawning on me that the foregoing looks and sounds like the Fruit of the Spirit, and I am not on a self-promotion tour, it makes perfect sense for that to be the case. By the time we yield to our Creator, be it by design or default, He is quick to show us that He truly rewards those who are all in, in terms of deciding to completely surrender to His will.

Rearview Mirror Lesson

After overcoming the initial difficulty in trying to live together post-reconciliation, we eventually found our feet by learning to trust God more, and our approach to marriage eventually became more Christ-centered. The more time we spent in obedience to Him, praying together for ourselves and our children, the more He showed Himself strong on our behalf. Our daughter's birth was the confirmation of God's promises for our lives and validation of Hebrews 11:6, which reads, *"But without faith, it is impossible to please Him, for he who comes to God must believe that He is, and that He is a rewarder of those who diligently seek Him."*

For the longest time, I did not know what that scripture meant until Funké and I made a conscious and intentional decision to place our trust in God. Funké did not back down even in the face of the most potentially faith-shaking adversity. With the help of the Holy Spirit, we prayed our way through and dug our way out of the proverbial pit. This was in keeping with the oft-quoted advice that we should "not let what we see change what we believe."

20

God's Proven System (GPS)

"Jesus looked at them intently and said, "Humanly speaking, it is impossible. But not with God. Everything is possible with God."

MARK 10:27

GOD'S PATH TO SUCCESS

"What a God! His road stretches straight and smooth. Every GOD-direction is road-tested. Everyone who runs toward Him makes it." (Ps. 18:30 MSG)

L ife can feel like a journey with winding roads, unexpected detours, and moments when the path ahead seems unclear. Yet, just as a Global Positioning System (GPS) helps us find our way and stay on course, God has given us His own "Proven System" to guide us through every season of life. His Word and His Spirit form a reliable and unchanging navigation system. Unlike human systems that crash or require constant updates, God's guidance never fails or needs a reboot.[1] When we follow His directions, even missteps become part of the route that leads us to purpose, fulfillment, fruitfulness, and peace.[2]

God never intended for His children to wander aimlessly. From creation, He established an order by which everything operates in harmony with His will. This "GPS" (God's Proven

---

1. Ps. 32:8; 119:105; Prov. 3:5-6; Isa. 40:8; John 16:13; James 1:17
2. Rom. 8:28

System) is built on His timeless Word. Just as a GPS guides travelers to their destination, God's Word and Spirit provide clear instructions for the believer's journey, helping us correct our course when we drift and keeping us aligned with His perfect plan. Operating outside this system can lead to confusion and frustration, but when we trust His process, we discover that His way is not only proven—it's perfect.

Each of us follows a different path to growth, restoration, and fulfillment. Your journey might be longer, shorter, easier, or more difficult than someone else's—but the GPS is the same. *"God works in different ways, but it is the same God who does the work in all of us."* (1 Cor. 12:6 NLT) By living according to God's Word, we stay aligned with His purpose, experience fruitfulness, and reach the finish line of our race.[3]

We have many satellite navigation systems today, each offering unique features—alternate routes, live traffic updates, or alerts about hidden hazards or cops lying in wait! Yet, no matter how advanced the app, our arrival depends on one crucial thing: connection to the source. If the link to the satellite fails, the guidance fails too. In the same way, no matter how capable or experienced we think we are, life's journey only stays on track when we remain connected to God—the ultimate Source of direction.[4]

Whether it's using GPS, stopping for directions, or following a paper map, we all need help to reach our destination. How much more when navigating life's more complex, emotionally demanding, and unpredictable roads and spaghetti highways—like marriage, parenting, or purpose! Some navigation apps even allow users to share real-time updates, helping others avoid pitfalls along the way. Similarly, God places people—who are plugged into His "Proven System" or "App"—in our paths to guide, support, and encourage us through their own "user experience."[5]

We all have a tendency to become attached to familiar routes and habits—doing things our own way, even when the Holy Spirit prompts us to change. Just because something has "worked" doesn't mean it's God's best, or even necessarily good for us. Pride, fear, or stubbornness can keep us stuck in cycles that delay progress and affect those who rely on us to make the right decisions for the family's overall good.[6] But humility allows God, our Good Shepherd, to lead us on His proven, *tried-and-true* path.[7]

Before the advent of the Global Positioning System (GPS), travelers had to stop and ask for directions or follow those who knew the way. It took humility and wisdom to admit, *"I don't know which way to go."* The same is true in life—especially in marriage or purpose. When

---

3. John 14:21, 23; 1 Cor. 9:24–25; Phil. 1:6; 2 Tim. 4:7
4. John 15:5
5. Ps. 68:6; 2 Cor. 1:3-5 (MSG)
6. Prov. 14:12
7. Ps. 23:1-3; Isa. 30:21

we're confused or at a crossroads, our safest option is to ask "The Navigator" (the Holy Spirit)[8] and to follow His "Map" (the Word of God).[9] *"He leads me beside the still waters; He restores my soul; He leads me in paths of righteousness for His name's sake."* (Ps. 23:2-3)

With God, we have a guaranteed navigation system—His integrity is tied to His Word. *"I will worship toward Your holy temple and praise Your name for Your lovingkindness and Your truth; for You have magnified Your Word above all Your name."* (Ps. 138:2) God places the highest honor on His Word—His promises, commands, and truth—even above His name, which represents His reputation and authority. If He has spoken it, He will fulfill it—because His Word reflects His very nature and character. *"God is not a man that He should lie."* (Num. 23:19) His Word is completely trustworthy and unshakable.[10]

This divine roadmap reveals a God who is not distant or abstract but relational, loving, and faithful … always. The Creator Himself became human, walked among us, and gave His life for us.[11] We don't have to second-guess His character or depend on outside proof of His truth. The Holy Spirit—God's indwelling presence—guides, teaches, and empowers us daily.[12] We're never disconnected from our Source. Salvation isn't earned by performance, rituals, or moral effort, but is received by grace through faith, in Christ's finished work.[13] In wisdom and moral guidance, the Bible is unparalleled for its prophetic depth,[14] historical accuracy,[15] spiritual authority,[16] and transformational impact across every culture and generation.[17] More than an ancient text, it remains living and relevant today, speaking truth to every age and circumstance.[18]

Because His Word is reliable and His promises infallible, we can trust His direction. Our outcomes depend on staying aligned with His plans and paying attention to His Spirit's promptings.[19] It's easy, and oftentimes tempting, to turn left when God says to go right, but obedience is what keeps us on course. Throughout Scripture, God's instructions have always led to breakthrough: Jesus told the centurion, *"Go; it will be done just as you believed"* (Matt. 8:13). The disciples waited in Jerusalem until they were *"endued with power from on high"* (Luke 24:49).

---

8. John 16:13
9. Isa. 58:11
10. Ps. 119:89; Isa. 55:11; Matt. 24:35
11. John 1:14; Rom. 5:8; 1 John 4:8
12. 1 Cor. 3:16
13. Eph. 2:8-9
14. Isa. 46:9-10; 2 Pet. 1:19-21
15. Ps. 119:160; Luke 1:1-4
16. 2 Tim. 3:16-17
17. Ps. 19:7-8; Isa. 55:11; Rom. 10:11-13
18. Isa. 40:8; Heb. 4:12
19. Ps. 5:8; 25:5; 27:11; 143:10

Their obedience positioned them for divine outcomes. Likewise, we too can stay connected to God's proven system through the following:

Read and meditate on the Word

> *"Do not let this Book of the Law depart from your mouth; meditate on it day and night, so that you may be careful to do everything written in it. Then you will be prosperous and successful."* (Josh. 1:8 NIV)

When our first child was born, one of the most meaningful gifts I received was an *e-Sword* CD-ROM—a digital Bible study tool that transformed my spiritual growth. Another was a CD album titled *Anybody Out There?* by Burlap to Cashmere. One of its tracks, "Basic Instructions," became our family's car anthem. We played it so often over the years that my sons eventually memorized the lyrics—before I even noticed it was built around the acronym BIBLE: *Basic Instructions Before Leaving Earth*. That moment reminded me how easy it is to read or listen to God's Word without real attention or reflection. The Bible isn't just a collection of "instructions"—it is alive, life-giving, and transformative.[20] We don't have to understand everything in the Bible to experience its power; we simply need to immerse ourselves in it and believe God.[21] The more we meditate on His Word, the clearer His voice becomes, and the more confidently we navigate life's roads—guided by the One who never loses signal.

Speak in agreement with God's Word

Interestingly, the first instruction God gave for success wasn't about doing something but about saying something. *"This Book of the Law shall not depart from your mouth…"* (Josh. 1:8) What we say matters. Our words are the fruit of our beliefs, and our beliefs shape our realities. *"Out of the abundance of the heart the mouth speaks."* (Matt. 12:34) In other words, what fills your heart essentially frames your world.

When our words align with God's Word, we activate His promises and declare His truth over our lives. *"Death and life are in the power of the tongue"* (Prov. 18:21), so every word spoken in faith carries creative power—just as God spoke creation into existence.[22] Consistently speaking God's Word trains our hearts to believe it and our minds to act on it.

In our marriage, Ségun and I have learned to practice this by inviting God into our conversations and decisions. We don't rush to agree just for the sake of agreement; rather, we pause to ask, "What does God's Word say about this?" Allowing Him to have the first and final say has often redirected us from conflict to clarity, from self-will to divine alignment. We don't

20. John 6:63; Heb. 4:12
21. Mark 11:23–24; John 3:16; Rom. 10:17; Heb. 11:6
22. Gen. 1:3

always get there on the first attempt—our interpretations of God's Word sometimes differ (and occasionally, in Ségun's case, quite conveniently!)—but we eventually align most times by leaning deeper into prayer.

Do what the Word of God says

Knowing God's Word is one thing; doing it is another. *"But be doers of the Word, and not hearers only, deceiving yourselves."* (James 1:22) It's easy to nod in agreement on Sunday and forget by Monday, but spiritual growth happens when obedience becomes our lifestyle. *God's Proven System* for success in life, particularly in marriage, isn't just about hearing instructions—it's about applying them in real life, even when it's hard or inconvenient.

Our choices often reveal who we truly are. Do we keep our word? Do we follow through on our promises? Integrity in daily life prepares us for faithfulness during bigger tests. During our marriage challenges, Ségun and I realized how our reactions exposed our character more than our intentions. But as we surrendered to God's Word, it began to shape and strengthen us from the inside out. Transformation requires humility, consistency, and a willingness to let Scripture confront our weaknesses. *"All Scripture is God-breathed and is useful for teaching, rebuking, correcting and training in righteousness."* (2 Tim. 3:16 NIV)

For example, respecting one's spouse isn't about whether they "deserve" it; it's about obedience to God. *"Wives, submit to your husbands as to the Lord ... Husbands, love your wives, just as Christ loved the church."* (Eph. 5:22, 25) We don't honor our spouse based on behavior but in reverence to Christ. When we choose obedience over emotion, we reflect His nature, not ours.

Ultimately, God's Word isn't just meant to inform—it's meant to transform. And when we live by it, we align ourselves with God's proven system—that leads us safely to His intended destination for our lives.

Apply the Word of God through faith

> *"Let every detail in your lives—words, actions, whatever—be done in the name of the Master, Jesus, thanking God the Father every step of the way."* (Col. 3:17 MSG)

Faith is the connection that activates God's proven system. We receive from God through faith.[23] Jesus said, *"According to your faith be it unto you"* (Matt. 9:29). The level of our faith often determines how deeply we experience God. That's why people in Scripture and across generations have called Him by different names—Jehovah Rapha, Shalom, El Shaddai, El Roi, Jireh—each revealing a personal encounter with His nature. Faith opens our eyes to see God move in ways that human reasoning cannot explain.

Unbelief, on the other hand, usually stems from a distorted view of who God is. As Jennie

---

23. Rom. 5:2; Gal. 3:14

Allen said, *"Every sin, at its root, is based in something we do not fully believe about God."*[24] When our faith is rightly placed, we stop trying to control everything and start trusting His will. Transformation always begins in the mind—the battlefield where thoughts are either surrendered to Christ or left unchecked.[25] When our thinking changes, so do our actions, attitudes, and outcomes.

None of us enters into new seasons or territories—whether marriage, parenting, or purpose—fully prepared. There will always be surprises along the way. That's why Jesus invites us to *"learn of Me"* (Matt. 11:29 KJV). In Nigerian Pidgin, there's a saying, *"Follow who sabi road!"*—meaning, "Follow the one who knows the way." Jesus doesn't just know the way—He *is* the Way (John 14:6). Yet sometimes, we take back control, switch to self-drive mode, and wonder why we're exhausted, keep getting lost, or constantly need rescuing from messy situations we could have avoided.

Faith requires endurance. It's not always easy, but it's crucial for growth. We can't afford to read the Word casually or treat it merely as a ritual. God's Word transforms when we engage with it intentionally—meditating, believing, and applying it daily through the power of the Holy Spirit (John 16:13). Ségun and I have learned the hard way that a performative approach to our relationship with God doesn't cut it. He calls for wholehearted commitment—serving and honoring Him, not just in our marriage, but in every area of life.

The key to victory in life isn't just knowing God's truth—it's about living it. The Bible becomes powerful when it's personal and ingrained, guiding our everyday steps. We can't depend solely on human wisdom or the "arm of flesh" (Jer. 17:5). True success comes from trusting and obeying God, not theories or trends. *"Follow those who through faith and patience inherit the promises."* (Heb. 6:12) When we apply the Word through faith, we align ourselves with Heaven's navigation system—God's proven system—that keeps us on the right path, no matter how unpredictable the journey gets.

GET PERSPECTIVE, SAINTS!

"So we have not stopped praying for you since we first heard about you. We ask God to give you complete knowledge of his will and to give you spiritual wisdom and understanding. Then the way you live will always honor and please the Lord, and your lives will produce every kind of good fruit. All the while, you will grow as you learn to know God better and better. We also pray that you will be strengthened with all his glorious power so you will have all the endurance and patience you need. May you be filled with joy." (Col. 1:9-11 NLT)

---

24. Jennie Allen, *Anything: The Prayer That Unlocked My God and My Soul* (Colorado Springs: David C. Cook, 2014).

25. Rom. 12:12; Cor. 10:4-5

Perspective is powerful—it's the lens through which we see life. The word itself comes from the Latin *perspicere*, meaning "to look through" or "to perceive." Our outlook influences our emotions, choices, and actions. Yet many live with distorted lenses—colored and sometimes broken by past experiences, upbringing, culture, or pain. Over time, this skewed perception becomes a cognitive bias that blinds us to truth and limits how we see God, ourselves, and others. That's why Jesus said, *"Your eyes are windows into your body. If you open your eyes wide in wonder and belief, your body fills up with light. If you live squinty-eyed in greed and distrust, your body is a dank cellar. If you pull the blinds on your windows, what a dark life you will have!"* (Matt. 6:22-23 MSG). Perspective isn't just about what you see—it's about how you see. The goal is to see life through God's Word, not our own "truth."

When Hagar was desperate and hopeless in the wilderness, God opened her eyes to see a well that had been there all along (Gen. 21:19). Likewise, Elisha prayed that his servant's eyes would be opened—and suddenly, the young man saw the mountain full of horses and chariots of fire surrounding them (2 Kings 6:17). What we see with our natural eyes is limited, but when God opens our spiritual eyes, everything changes!

Apostle Paul recognized this when he described his calling as *"to open their eyes and turn them from darkness to light"* (Acts 26:18). David prayed the same: *"Open my eyes that I may see wondrous things from Your law"* (Ps. 119:18). Until our eyes are opened by the Spirit, we remain blind to the treasures and solutions hidden in plain sight. The spiritual realm is always active around us, but we don't need to see into it to believe what God has said.[26] For instance, His Word assures us that His angels watch over us, guarding and protecting us wherever we go.[27] We don't normally see them, yet they surround us at all times, faithfully carrying out God's protection over His children.

Today, more than ever, believers need God's perspective. Spiritual blindness and arrogance have caused many to drift from truth, embracing watered-down teachings that misrepresent God's nature and design—including in marriage. Romans 1:18–32 vividly describes what happens when people lose sight of God: Truth becomes relative, passions rule, and wisdom turns to foolishness.

In God's "divine equation," He and His principles are the constants—unchanging, dependable, and absolute. We are the variables, shaped by His hand and refined by His Spirit. But the answer is always Jesus. Everything in life must align back to Him, because *"in Him all things hold together"* (Col. 1:17). Some say, "I've followed this 'divine formula,' but it hasn't worked—I prayed and fasted; still nothing changed." But what kind of prayer was it? Was it fervent and

---

26. 1 Cor. 2:14

27. Ps. 91:11-12

faith-filled,[28] or done "amiss?"[29] Others say, "I've tried talking to my spouse, but they won't listen." But how are you speaking? Is your tone gracious, your timing Spirit-led, your motive rooted in love?[30] God's ways always work—but only when applied His way.

We often forget that God is not obliged to act according to our wishes. Whether we understand Him or not, He remains God. Arguing or complaining doesn't accomplish anything. Instead, it's wiser to align ourselves with His plan. *"As for God, His way is perfect; the Lord's word is flawless"* (Ps. 18:30). Sometimes, our greatest need isn't for God to change our circumstances, but for Him to change our perspective. Once our view shifts, we start to see purpose in the process, peace in the waiting, and grace in the growth. When our eyes are fixed on Him, every detour and delay becomes part of His divine plan.

Perspective is everything, especially when life feels uncertain or unfair. It determines how we interpret God's actions, respond to challenges, and relate to others. However, not all perspectives are equal or given thoughtful consideration. Some are shaped by pain, pride, or impatience; others through faith, love, and obedience. That's why God calls us to see life through His eyes, not our own—because how we see determines how we stand or fall. Let's explore the four key perspectives that keep us aligned with God's proven system—starting with the foundation of all others:

1. Love perspective: the true lens

Before we can truly gain perspective, we must learn to see through the right lens—the lens of love. Jesus said, *"A new command I give you: Love one another. As I have loved you, so you must love one another"* (John 13:34 NIV). Love helps us view life from God's viewpoint, not our own. When you put on your love lenses, you begin to see people, problems, and even pain differently. Love is the true mark of maturity; it distinguishes God's children from the world.[31] It looks like grace that forgives easily, compassion that reaches out, empathy that listens, and kindness that chooses gentleness over judgment.[32]

Love also changes our beliefs. It reminds us that *"all have sinned and fall short of the glory of God"* (Rom. 3:23), and that God alone is the true Judge of human worth. The person you might have dismissed, excluded, or written off is still valuable enough for Christ to have died for (Rom. 5:8). When we forget this, our perspective narrows—and we lose sight of grace.

God's love is extravagant. Even when we walk through the *"valley of the shadow of death"* (Ps. 23:4)—whether through sin, suffering, or despair—His rod and staff comfort us. That

---

28. James 5:16
29. James 4:3
30. 1 Cor. 13:1-3
31. John 13:35
32. Gal. 5:22-23; Col. 3:12-14

same grace we've received is the grace we're called to extend, even to the spouse or loved one who seems beyond reach. Behind every destructive behavior is a spiritual battle,[33] and God has promised to fight for you.[34]

But this kind of love—love that keeps hoping, forgiving, and believing—isn't something humans can achieve on their own. Only through the Holy Spirit can we love as Christ loved.[35] Love hopes even when everything seems hopeless.[36] As C.S. Lewis once wrote, *"We can only hope for what we desire."* When you still desire your marriage, your healing, or your break-through, hope keeps you anchored.[37] *"The hope of the righteous will be gladness"* (Prov. 10:28), and *"the expectation of the righteous will not be cut off"* (Prov. 23:18 NIV).

So, before you try to "fix" what's broken, check your lens. Are you looking through love or through self? Love changes how you see—and once your vision shifts, your heart and actions follow. That's God's proven system at work: perspective shaped by love leads to transformation anchored in truth.

2. Soul perspective: the bigger picture

> *"Go and rescue the perishing! Be their savior! Why would you stand back and watch them stagger to their death? And why would you say, "But it's none of my business"? The one who knows you completely and judges your every motive is also the keeper of souls—and not just yours! He sees through your excuses and holds you responsible for failing to help those whose lives are threatened."* (Prov. 24:11-12 TPT)

When we talk about gaining perspective, it's not just about seeing differently—it's about seeing against a backdrop of eternity. God calls us to look beyond ourselves—beyond our pain, convenience, or comfort—and recognize that every soul matters to Him. Silence in the face of evil is itself evil. God sees through the excuses we make—our hurts, disappointments, or indifference—and holds us accountable when we fail to act in love. We are light bearers—hiding our light (truth, courage, or conviction) and refusing to share God's love is to deny our calling as children of God.[38]

James 4:17 reminds us, *"If anyone knows the good they ought to do and doesn't do it, it is sin."* Whether through prayer, truth spoken in love, or sharing the gospel, we are called to stand for righteousness—not lukewarm faith.[39] God's purpose extends far beyond personal happiness or even marriage—it's about redemption and His Kingdom agenda.

---

33. John 10:10
34. Exod. 14:14; Rom. 8:31; 1 Cor. 15:57
35. Phil. 2:1-4, 13; 1 Thess. 3:12
36. 1 Cor. 13:7
37. Rom. 5:5
38. Matt. 5:14-16; I Pet. 2:21
39. Heb. 10:38–39; Rev. 3:15–16

When my perspective shifted, I understood that the conflicts in my marriage weren't just about my husband and me—they involved our souls and the legacy we leave for our children.[40] Scripture states that marriage exists, in part, to *"produce godly offspring"* (Mal. 2:15). Once I embraced this truth, my prayers changed. I stopped praying out of frustration and started praying in alignment with God's will—according to His Word—which protects us from praying amiss. Like Hannah, when my desire aligned with God's purpose—when I sought not just a personal outcome but His greater plan—breakthrough arrived.[41]

God's proven system always begins with love and leads to compassion. He wants us to have both the courage and tenderness to reach out to those going astray—not with condemnation, but with truth and grace.[42] Not everyone will *"come to themselves"* like the prodigal son;[43] some need an Ananias—someone willing to step out in faith and obedience, despite fear or bias, to help others see the Light.[44]

Even Saul, once a persecutor of believers, was not beyond God's reach. When Ananias hesitated, God said, *"Go! This man is my chosen instrument."* (Acts 9:15 NIV). That's the power of divine perspective—it sees not just who someone is but who they can become in Christ. So don't write anyone off. *"For you were once darkness, but now you are light in the Lord. Live as children of light."* (Eph. 5:8)

God's proven system for saving souls is partnership. He uses people—ordinary, hesitant, and imperfect ones—to shine His light into dark places. So, whether it's your spouse, child, parent, colleague, or neighbor, remember: Your obedience could be the bridge that transforms someone from a Saul (persecutor of Christians) to a Paul (preacher of Christ's Gospel).[45] That's how we participate in God's GPS—God's Proven System—rescuing souls, one perspective shift at a time.

3. Generational perspective: the lasting impact

As parents, we need to remember that the choices we make today have lasting effects on our children, grandchildren, and future generations. In essence, our decisions—whether wise or foolish—set patterns that resonate through our lineage. I've met many adults in their twenties to their forties who still carry wounds from their parents' decisions—such as broken marriages, emotional neglect, misplaced priorities, or lack of spiritual guidance. Some were raised by adults who were so focused on pursuing their own happiness, purpose, or healing that

---

40. Ps. 78:4-7; 2 Tim. 1:5

41. 1 Sam. 1:10-20

42. Gal. 6:1

43. Luke 15:17

44. Acts 9:10-18

45. 2 Cor. 5:17

they didn't take enough time to nurture the precious souls God entrusted to them. Many of these individuals are now struggling with identity issues, trauma, or bitterness that began long before they were born.

In God's proven system, His principles for holiness, family order, and covenant love aren't meant to restrict us but to protect us—and those who come after us.[46] When we align with His truth, we become conduits of blessing instead of carriers of brokenness. But when we rebel against His design, we risk transferring confusion and chaos to our descendants.

This is why perspective matters. Every choice either sows into a godly legacy or creates a painful inheritance. God's "GPS" doesn't just guide us for our own sake—it safeguards future generations. Let's start living with legacy in mind. Our children will remember the paths we walked—whether they were marked by mess or mercy.

4. An eternal perspective: the ultimate reality

We live in a world that thrives on instant gratification. Everything is "now"—fast food, quick answers, immediate success. Yet God's Word reminds us that life on earth is only a small part of a much longer journey. The New Testament consistently points us forward—to the restoration of all creation, the return of Jesus Christ, and the promise of *"a new heaven and a new earth"* (Rev. 21:1). This life is not the destination; it's a waiting room of sorts—preparation for eternity. That's why Jesus urged us not to store up treasures on earth but to *"store up treasures in heaven"* (Matt. 6:19-21). The believer's "GPS" must always be set on eternal coordinates. When our hearts are fixed on what is unseen and everlasting,[47] we begin to live with purpose, patience, and peace—even when the route feels long or uncertain.

The writer of Hebrews encourages us to run life's race with endurance, keeping our eyes on Jesus, *"the pioneer and perfecter of our faith"* (Heb. 12:1-2 NIV). The path has already been marked out; we're simply called to follow faithfully. Like a divine marathon, the goal isn't speed—it's consistency and steadfastness.

Of course, unexpected events sometimes knock us off course. We stumble, we struggle, and occasionally feel like giving up entirely. But those who walk with eternity in mind know how to get back up. They refuse to see or accept defeat as the final word. Instead, they echo Paul's conviction: *"We are hard pressed on every side, but not crushed … struck down, but not destroyed"* (2 Cor. 4:8-9). Every setback becomes a lesson, every detour an opportunity to deepen trust. And so, we keep moving forward—eyes lifted, hearts anchored, steps guided by God. For those who stay on the course, the finish line is not the end but the beginning of forever with Him.

---

46. Deut. 7:9; Ps. 103:17-18

47. 2 Cor. 4:18

FAITH COORDINATES: WHEN LOGIC AND FEELINGS LOSE SIGNAL

I'm going to piggyback off an internet trend—"Girl Math"—that describes the *creative excuses* some people (mainly women, in the meme's context) use to justify their spending habits or financial decisions. It has since evolved into a self-aware humor that playfully exaggerates gender-coded reasoning in everyday life—to illustrate how we often justify illogical choices or rationalize certain behavior. It's not meant to be taken literally or as a universal truth, but rather as a lighthearted way to highlight how differently we sometimes think—and how much we all need God's perspective to realign our reasoning.

We all navigate life using some kind of internal "math." For some, it's "Girl Math"—the emotional rationalization that says, *"If it feels right, it must be right."* For example: *"I'm frustrated with him, but if I ignore the issue, maybe he'll realize his mistake—this counts as teaching him a lesson."* The only problem is that feelings change like the wind. When we let emotions lead, we risk mistaking temporary feelings for lasting direction. *"The heart is deceitful above all things…"* (Jer. 17:9)

Then there's "Boy Math"— pseudo-logical rationalization. Human reasoning, although useful, often lacks insight because it's usually self-referential—*it depends on itself rather than on God.* It insists, *"If it makes sense to me, it must be true."* And it justifies all sorts of shortcuts and half-measures in relationships—*"I didn't talk through the problem, but I brought home pizza—problem solved."* But logic alone can't explain grace, miracles, or the mystery of God's timing. *"There is a way that seems right to a man, but its end is the way to death."* (Prov. 14:12)

"God Math," however, operates differently. It runs on faith coordinates, not emotional impulses or intellectual equations. It may not always make sense on paper, but it never fails to align with God's promises. It says, *"Even when I don't understand, I trust the One who does."* That's why we're called to *"walk by faith, not by sight"* (2 Cor. 5:7). It puts aside self-interest, pride, or convenience. For example: *"Even if I feel hurt or frustrated, I choose to love and forgive because God's Word instructs me to, trusting Him to work in both of us"* (1 Cor. 13:4-7; Col. 3:12-14). When logic says, "Walk away," or emotions scream, "I can't," I pray and ask for wisdom, letting the Spirit guide my actions (James 1:5; Prov. 3:5-6).

When we navigate using God's Proven System (GPS)—His Word and His Spirit—our journey coordinates are divinely calibrated. He aligns our hearts and minds so we no longer wander aimlessly or react emotionally, but we move intentionally toward His will. *"Trust in the Lord with all your heart and lean not on your own understanding; in all your ways acknowledge Him, and He will make your paths straight."* (Prov. 3:5-6)

So, don't wait until your feelings and logic lose signal—or steer you off course—before checking your coordinates. Plug into God's "GPS" now. Is your route guided by self-confidence, emotional comfort, or divine conviction? Only "God Math"—faith anchored in His

Word—can lead you to the right destination. God's Proven System (GPS) operates by revelation, not calculation. It doesn't just give directions; it imparts discernment and provides accurate coordinates for every step. It recalibrates our emotions, refines our reasoning, and aligns both under the power of faith.[48] When God's truth sets our course, we stop wandering in circles. We move with clarity, peace, and purpose—trusting the "Divine Math" that never miscalculates.

On our faith journey, God offers spiritual reference points—unmissable and unmistakable markers through His Word, the Holy Spirit, and life experiences—to help us find our place spiritually, stay on track, and navigate life's twists without losing sight of the goal. These markers remind us that faith isn't guesswork; it's guided travel under divine direction. Some of these journey coordinates include:

- The Word of God → our *map*: *"Your word is a lamp to my feet and a light to my path."* (Ps. 119:105)

- The Holy Spirit → our internal Navigator and real-time compass: *"He will guide you into all truth."* (John 16:13)

- Faith → our *engine* (Heb. 11:6)

- Obedience → our *steering wheel* (James 1:22)

- Love → our *fuel* (1 Cor. 16:14)

- Godly counsel and community → *checkpoints* to keep us aligned (Prov. 11:14)

- Purpose (earthly and eternal) → our *destination* (Eph. 2:10; Matt. 5:14-16; 28:18-20; Jer. 29:11; Phil. 3:20-21; 1 Pet. 1:3-4; John 14:2-3)

THE ROAD FROM VALUES TO VIRTUE

Many people today lament the erosion of "strong values" in families, cultures, and societies. Yet, those same values are often beautifully displayed on our walls or etched on plaques in schools and churches—more admired than applied. The truth is, values alone cannot transform lives. They must move from mere decoration to genuine demonstration, which happens only when God's Word is inscribed on our hearts and minds,[49] and we live it out daily through godly character and consistent action.

Virtues are values in action—visible, tangible, and shown through how we treat others.[50] For example, honesty becomes a virtue when we tell the truth, even if it costs us something.

48. Matt. 17:20
49. Ps. 119:11; Jer. 31:33; 2 Cor. 3:3; Heb. 10:16
50. Matt. 5:13-16; Rom. 12:9-18 (AMP); James 2:14-17

Compassion turns into a virtue when we go beyond sympathy to act in service. Faith becomes a virtue when we trust God even in uncertain times. Forgiveness is a virtue when we let go of resentment and choose peace. Essentially, values are what we believe; virtues are how we live out those beliefs.

Since God *is* Love, our connection to Him should cause that love to flow naturally into our relationships, families, and communities[51]—but that's not always the case. On this road from values to virtue, the Holy Spirit recalibrates us each time we drift off course. He guides us from simply *knowing* what is right to *becoming* right in heart and deed. This sacred progression—from information to transformation—marks the evidence of a life truly guided by God's hand.

God's Proven System (GPS) doesn't just guide us; it develops in us the strength, humility, and discipline needed to stay committed. Throughout this journey, belief must turn into action, conviction into consistency, and inspiration into integrity. God is not looking for people who only *profess* good values but for those whose hearts are being transformed to *embody* them.[52]

While values can be taught and admired, virtue is painstakingly formed through testing, prayer, and daily yielding to the Holy Spirit's refining work.[53] Values give us direction, but virtue keeps us steady when the road gets rough. That's the difference between *knowing* the way and *walking* in it.[54] The path from values to virtue is often slow and refining, but it's along this sacred road that Christ's likeness is formed in us—one choice, one test, one surrender at a time.

I started reading *The Road to Character* by David Brooks—a book my husband once suggested we read as a family—but I haven't finished it yet, despite how compelling it is. In it, Brooks explores the deeper moral and spiritual dimensions of life, encouraging readers to move beyond society's obsession with achievement and self-promotion and rather focus on developing inner virtue and humility. He distinguishes between what he calls "résumé virtues"—the skills and accomplishments that build careers and reputations—and "eulogy virtues"—the qualities that truly define us and how we'll be remembered: kindness, integrity, courage, and faithfulness.

Brooks argues that our modern culture glorifies visibility and success at the expense of moral depth and inner strength—qualities often cultivated during hidden seasons rather than through outward accomplishments. Though philosophical, his insights resonate with a timeless biblical truth: Character is not built in comfort but in the furnace of trial and testing, where God refines us for His purposes. Through hardships, we develop endurance, humility,

---

51. 1 John 4:7-12
52. Phil. 2:13
53. Eph. 6:13-18 (MSG)
54. John 13:17; James 1:22–25

and reliance on Him.[55] While the world applauds outward manifestations of what we achieve, God delights in who we're becoming—with a heart that is broken, contrite, and teachable.[56]

God's Proven System (GPS) guides us from the shallow waters of self-sufficiency into the deeper flow of divine transformation. It's not just about doing good but about becoming good—moving from holding values in theory to living them out through the Holy Spirit's work within us. This is the road every believer must travel—the narrow path where values mature into virtues, and the fruit of the Spirit[57] becomes our daily evidence of Christ's life in us. As He molds us through His Word and Spirit, our character begins to reflect not our résumé, but our Redeemer.

Ignorance is definitely not bliss! No one deliberately sets out on a journey to nowhere, yet many do, simply because they've ignored the divine map already provided. God's Word is a single, comprehensive resource for navigating life's challenges with wisdom and grace. Some people choose to remain on the familiar but futile path, while others become so accustomed to struggle that they find it hard to believe a better, proven route exists. A life filled only with confusion, frustration, and missed turns is not what God intended for any of His children.[58] Sadly, not everyone will embark on the journey of change or spiritual growth that leads to the abundant life God planned. Not everyone will take the right routes, make divine connections, or stay plugged into Heaven's navigation system—the Holy Spirit. As a result, not everyone will reach the right destination.

The good news is that some will—and you can be among them. God's Proven System (GPS) is available to everyone who seeks God's truth and follows Christ as their Navigator.[59] Those who refuse to drift through life on autopilot or adopt a *"que sera, sera"* mindset—but instead travel with purpose, allowing Scripture and the Holy Spirit to guide each turn—are the ones who ultimately arrive at their God-designated destination. So, what journey are you on? What destination are you heading toward? Who's navigating your path? Are you blindly tailgating others down the road of popular opinion, or are you consistently using God's Word to steer your life? And who are your fellow travelers? Are they connected to the same divine signal—encouraging and sharpening you along the way[60]—or are they draining your focus, leading you on detours, or acting as "jeer-leaders" rather than cheerleaders of faith?

As you read this book, you might notice that Ségun and I still perceive some past details differently. That's part of the reality of human relationships and the complexity of perspective—perhaps

---

55. Rom. 5:3–4; Heb. 12:10–11; James 1:2–4; 1 Pet. 1:6–7
56. Ps. 51:17; Isa. 66:2
57. Gal. 5:22-23
58. Jer. 29:11
59. John 14:6
60. Prov. 27:17

even a bit of self-preservation! After many conversations, reflections, and moments of grace, we've learned to accept our differences and embrace the growth they bring. Unity doesn't require uniformity, and it doesn't mean everyone is the same. God made us beautifully diverse in His own image so we can enjoy the fullness and richness of life, relationships, and the unique gifts He has placed within each of us.

What matters most is that we both keep pursuing Christ, allowing His truth to shape our responses and refine our hearts. When we view our past, present, and future through God's lens—His unbiased truth—we find clarity, peace, and direction.[61] The destination isn't perfection but pleasing our Father and becoming more like Christ as we walk this journey together, growing in love every day until we see Him face to face... and He will tell Ségun that I was right on all of those issues where our opinions differed!

Our meeting point is always in God's presence, and our foundation of agreement is His Word. For some marriages, unity is based on shared hobbies, wealth, travel, or even physical attraction—but what happens when beauty fades, success diminishes, hormones change, or emotions fluctuate? God is the only constant on this journey. Pleasing Him must remain our top priority, because as Jesus said, *"Whoever wants to save their life will lose it, but whoever loses their life for My sake will find it"* (Matt. 16:25 NIV). At the end of our long and fruitful lives, what truly matters is hearing Him say, *"Well done, good and faithful servant"* (Matt. 25:23). That hope propels us to live not for self-preservation, but for the preservation of truth—God's truth.

Our story is not an exception; it's simply an example of what God still delights to do. *"God does not show favoritism."* (Acts 10:34) I've witnessed marriages restored after decades apart—like an aunt and uncle who reconciled in their seventies—and heard inspiring comeback stories, such as a Nigerian couple who reunited after ten years apart. Their beautiful love story, shared on Instagram, is a powerful reminder that nothing is ever too far gone for God to redeem. Whether through quiet prayer, tears, or obedience, those who sought Him found Him faithful. *"All things are possible to those who believe."* (Mark 9:23; Eph. 3:20; Luke 1:37) What He did for us, He can do for you too.

Each of us is writing a story, but only God's authorship guarantees a divine ending. Paul wrote, *"Your lives are a letter... known and read by everyone"* (2 Cor. 3:2 NLT). Every page—the pain, the pause, the progress—reveals what's written on your heart. The question is: Who's holding the pen? You or God?

It doesn't matter where you've been—single, married, separated, divorced, or remarried— what matters is what happens from now on. Life offers many paths, but only one leads to true purpose. You can keep circling the same mountain or choose to course-correct by letting God

---

61. Phil. 3:13-14; Col. 3:15

recalibrate your heart through His GPS—Grace, Purpose, and Scripture. The journey from values to virtue begins with one decision: to let Him lead.

So, wherever you are today, pause, pray, and plug into God's proven system. Because when Jesus is your Navigator, you'll not only reach the right destination—you'll become the right person along the way.

THROUGH SÉGUN'S LENSES

This book project has proven to be even more demanding and potentially consequential than I thought when I wrote my Author's Foreword earlier in the year. I knew the process would be as involved as it would be emotive at times. It has forced me to interrogate, and re-interrogate, facts that I have long held to be true and to look at myself with an unfamiliar, and occasionally uncomfortable, degree of introspection.

Revisiting past events and trying to insert myself into them, in an attempt to rediscover proper context in my thought process at particular points in time—being determinants of my actions and inactions—was particularly challenging. However, it was only when I realized that God had been by my side even when things appeared to be at their most shambolic, and I was at my wits' end, that I understood the real significance of Psalm 46:1, which assures us that *"God is our refuge and strength, an ever-present help in trouble."* He is truly our Helper—at all times and in all places—and an exceedingly perfect one at that! Scripture after scripture speaks to God's perfect nature by pointing to His indescribable greatness, unimpeachable character, and unchangeable promises.

This chapter is deliberately entitled God's Proven System (GPS) because, like the navigational aid that shares the same acronym, Christ-facing praying husbands, especially those experiencing marital turmoil, possess considerable power. We husbands can daily enter coordinates into our spirits—our built-in navigational compass—through supplication to God to direct our marriages toward their intended destination. However, the correct coordinates must be entered, and these are available in the Word of God, which we, as husbands and priests of our homes, are expected to diligently study. Such diligence pleases God because it promotes greater reverence for and intimacy with Him. Psalm 119:105 tells us that *"Your word is a lamp to my feet and a light to my path."* What closer approximation to the purpose of a conventional GPS can one have than that?!

When men who are overwhelmed by marital struggles reach out to God in Bible study, prayer, and supplication, He will gladly intervene. That is because He wants to play His role (ideally, alongside those of two spouses committed to seeing their marriages as a sacred honor and a form of reverence to God) in steering their marriages away from storm clouds and protruding or hidden rocks, and instead toward safe harbors. However, the correct coordinates must be inputted, especially as storm clouds in marriage do not go by their meteorological names. Instead, they appear in many variants and combinations that add to their intensity and potential destructiveness that can equal those typically associated with Category 5 hurricanes.

In marriage, storm clouds assume names such as "unforgiveness," "vindictiveness," "jealousy," "pride," "infidelity," or "bitterness." Moreover, husbands must be crystal clear about their desired destinations when storm clouds gather and marriages begin to take on water. If panic or anger sets in, or trading blame replaces the better alternative of allowing a calm head to prevail, there is little to no chance of being able to successfully navigate the marriage toward calm waters. Nowadays, abandoning ship is often the easy route for either spouse. However, like on a cloudy day when visibility is reduced to zero feet, already challenging journeys become even more hazardous. This is where our trust in God and His proven system becomes indispensable.

In Psalm 18:30, we read that *"The Lord's word is flawless, He shields all who take refuge in Him."* In Deuteronomy 32:4, we are told that *"He is the Rock, His works are perfect, and all His ways are just. A faithful God who does no wrong, upright and just is He."* I cannot think of words that are more confidence-inspiring than these, especially when one has no idea where to turn when a severe marital crisis strikes! Only God knows what effect my getting out of the way a lot sooner and letting God be God in my life would have had on the length and nature of my separation from Funké. However, He who knew the final outcome of my journey with Funké before we were even conceived never took, and has never taken, His eyes off us throughout our marriage ... not for a second.

I pray that Funké and I never lose sight of that powerful thought, and that husbands and other men who may have reached breaking point in their marriages or may be questioning their will to live or whether God truly exists or cares about them, will derive tremendous encouragement from what I know to be an incontrovertible truth based on my lived experience. As a husband, one just needs to reach out to God in bold expression of his faith in Him and His power to do all things, including the seemingly impossible.

While collaborating on *Trilogy Refining Decisions*, Funké and I have had to draw strength from reservoirs that I certainly did not know held such copious amounts of grace. Difficult subjects and painful memories at times elicited individual and collective responses and discussions that took us back in time, turning us into relational archaeologists with only our memories (in my case) and forensic notes (in Funké's case) as excavating tools. In some instances, we discovered that our interpretations of certain historical events were very different, resulting in wrong conclusions being reached at the time. Sadly, these were then carried forward like figures in a balance sheet, sometimes for years, typically due to wrong assumptions, where our divergent conclusions often festered and became more entrenched.

It may seem like an obvious point to make, but Funké and I are two very different people today than we were when we first met and at the time of our separation. Our progression from when we were separated until the present time has been especially spectacular, not in a vainglorious way but expressed in humility because the transformation was entirely God's doing. A perfect example is our ongoing propensity to pray our way through challenges as opposed to relying on our own strength, which was my default setting for many years. I am still working on the vestiges of that tendency and intend to continue doing so until they are reduced to imperceptible levels.

Rearview Mirror Lesson

One factor that has remained constant and transformative throughout the improbable journey presented in this book is God's faithfulness. Over the years, His faithfulness has found expression in many different forms. This is one of the reasons for the choice of title for the closing chapter of this book, coupled with the fact that He completes everything He begins.

God's mercy suffices for us in all situations and for all time. He has remained, and will always remain, faithful to His Word and to His promises. The typical human instinct to look inward, as opposed to Heavenward, when trouble arises, almost invariably lands us in deep or deeper water. That was the pattern that characterized my life almost throughout my separation from Funké. It was only as our seemingly improbable reconciliation approached and I had a personal and powerful encounter with God during an altar call that I realized how foolish I had been and how much time that had been wasted.

The blessing from which anyone in a similar situation can seek encouragement and look forward to is that our Heavenly Father is a God of restitution who allows His children to make up for lost time—in no time at all. Joel 2:25 (KJV) says, *"And I will restore to you the years that the locust hath eaten, the cankerworm, and the caterpillar, and the palmerworm, my great army which I sent among you."*

Through every season Funké and I endured for six and a half years, no matter how dark or traumatic, God was present. Always accessible. Always available. Always reliable. The tragedy is that many of us do not know this or do not believe it. This is usually because of our perception of the magnitude of whatever situation in which we find ourselves, which makes us take our eyes off God, usually due to fear.

It is in the arena of perception that the enemy is at his most destructive, as the mind determines how we react to trouble, danger, or even opportunity. By the time our focus is consumed by problems that beset us, we lose sight of the God who created us and who is bigger than all of the problems in the world—past, present, and future.

Marital problems are no different. Beyond looking at details of our own journey and learning lessons from them, we have also seen through our marriage ministry, TRY HARD—*Trust and Revere Yahweh; He Always Rewards Diligence*, that battles to restore marriages are usually lost when one or both spouses perceive their problem(s) as being too hard to resolve.

There is no such thing for God, and all that is required to turn such situations around is for a change in perspective and an invitation to allow God to do that which only He can do. As Romans 12:2 says, *"Do not conform to the pattern of this world, but be transformed by the renewing of your mind. Then you will be able to test and approve what God's will is—His good, pleasing, and perfect will."*

God will position Himself where and when we invite Him in. We must make room for Him in places and spaces that were previously occupied by pride, unforgiveness, and other unhelpful mindsets. His GPS is accurate and, unlike manmade technology, the connection to Him is never shaky due to poor connectivity.

I am beyond grateful to God for His many mercies and to Funké for her courage, faith, and determination in embarking on this book project. We hope and pray that *Trilogy Refining Decisions* will bless others just as the process of writing it has blessed us and our family beyond description.

The Trilogy Celebration

Reaffirmation of our vows

Ségun

As I reminisce on the last 26 years
I pause as my eyes well up with tears;
Periods of joy and, yes, periods of pain,
But through it all GOD remained the same.

At one point it seemed we wouldn't make it through,
But our Heavenly FATHER had plans for me and you.
A miraculous reconciliation I just didn't foresee,
After six-and-a-half years and a divorce nisi.

For six-and-a-half years you sent scriptures to me,
You didn't miss a day because you could see.
The Word of GOD doing what the Word of GOD does,
As you released your prayers to Heaven above.

One day I woke up and I could see clearly,
What our LORD had built the Enemy nearly
Destroyed, but now I knew without a shadow of a doubt,
That a miracle had happened and so with a shout,

I proclaim before GOD and before all of you
"Funke my Darling, I will always be true.
I will honour and protect you, I will give you my all,
My love for you will always, always stand tall."

Funké

Twenty-six and a half years, a journey long and true,
A path of highs and lows we've walked, just me and you.
Through seasons bright with joy, and those with bitter rain,
We faced the storms, endured the loss, and weathered all the pain.

Six and a half years we drifted far, apart in mind and heart,
Yet, through the silence and the tears, love never fully did depart.
With each step away, God's hands were there, guiding us unseen,
Turning brokenness into hope, into all that could have been.

One breath from letting go, from closing every door,
But grace swept in, and we found love—stronger than before.
Fifteen years now, since we chose to heal, to fight, to stand,
And I am still in awe of how we found new life hand in hand.

So here we stand, as one once more, with vows to now renew,
For every joy, for every trial, I choose again, I choose you.
Not perfect love, but love refined, by fire, time, and grace,
Together, we've rebuilt our dreams, found beauty in this place.

Today we celebrate not just the years that passed us by,
But the love that rose from ashes, the tears that made us try.
Forevermore, my heart is yours, no matter what life sends,
We'll face it all, we'll keep rising, together till the end.

From our vow reaffirmation ceremony keepsake booklet, October 19, 2024.

ACKNOWLEDGEMENTS

THANK YOU TO:

🤍 **Dear Holy Spirit**, my Divine "Ghostwriter," I couldn't have written a single page without You! Through countless distractions, setbacks, and moments of doubt, You provided me with words, wisdom, and perseverance. You helped me navigate challenges and granted me the grace to push through every wall of opposition. Thank You, Heavenly Father, for turning our story around—for Your glory!

🤍 **My Segstar!** You're an outstanding husband, father, and partner—and yes, I'm now officially a thoroughly over-pampered wife! I'm grateful we didn't give up on our marriage, which is now better and sweeter than before. Thank you for saying "yes" to writing this book with me, for trusting God with us, and for loving me through every draft and detail included. You truly are the best!

🤍 **My terrific trio**—'Seyi, 'Sayo, and 'Sopé, my greatest earthly treasures and my arrows of light—each shining in their own beautiful way, all for God's glory. Seyi, thank you for lending me your laptop with "few" complaints after mine crashed; Sayo, for your solid advice; and Sope, for letting me turn your room into my makeshift writing studio and giving me the space and quiet I needed for nearly a year. You've all been patient, loving, and endlessly supportive—thank you!

🤍 **Akinkunmi, my darling big brother**, for your faith and for speaking life over my marriage from the very first sign of trouble. It was just the two of us for a long time, and even as our branches have spread, I'm grateful that God has kept our roots grounded in His love.

🤍 **My mother-in-law**, for your love. Though our start was rocky, I'm grateful to God that you're alive to witness His goodness in our marriage and share our joy today. I appreciate you and Dad for raising Ségun with the values and faith that made our turnaround from the brink of divorce possible. Those truths "planted" in him took root and helped his heart return to God—and our home. Thank you for giving me a second chance and for your quiet support during our "lean" season. I look forward to building more beautiful memories with you and our entire family.

🩶 **Sis Yemisi and Bruv Femi**, for being atypical Nigerian in-laws—embracing me as part of your family, for not complicating matters, and giving Ségun and me the space to rediscover each other amid the chaos. Your quiet love and support spoke volumes and made a huge impact.

🩶 **Sister-friends—Yinka Okubena** (my bestie of blessed memory), **Nneka Egbuwoku, Efe Ogbe, Kehinde Aluko, Kaltume Mshelia, 'Biola Dania,** and **'Keji Odeyemi**— you've all been my Aarons and Hurs at different points during my journey. For some, our treasured friendship has lasted over forty years, evolving through laughter and tears. I'm immensely grateful for your support and all the beautiful memories we've shared. **Nneka**, thank you especially for embodying and showing what grace and true forgiveness really are. Thank you for all your warm "teddy bear" hugs when I needed them most, for opening your home to me and my boys in the middle of the storm, and for sticking with me through everything. My life is richer because of all of you. May God, who multiplies every seed of love, enrich your lives with joy, peace, and lasting fulfillment.

🩶 **Casmir and Blossom Maduafokwa**, for believing in this project the moment you heard about it. We deeply appreciate your love and encouragement. God bless you!

🩶 **Pastors**, who have nurtured, prayed for, and guided us through the years:

- **Pastors Fred and Nandir Williams**, my pastors during my time at university, thank you for making Christ Academy a safe space for many of us, especially freshmen. Both of you and **Pastor Chucks Ugoihe** were like big brothers, a sister, and surrogate parents all in one! Thank you for laying a strong foundation of truth and faith. May the Lord richly reward your labor of love and bless your homes and the work of your hands.

- **Pastor Mazino and Nneka Egbuwoku**, for loving our family so deeply and walking beside us on our path to restoration. Your *"mission to revive"* God's people goes far beyond church walls—it breathes life into the ordinary, transforms relationships, and turns everyday living into worship. May the fragrance of your surrender continue to renew hearts and draw many to behold God's beauty in the rhythm of real life.

- **Pastor Emmanuel and 'Biola Dania**, for your friendship and all the ways you've stood by us. Your warmth, laughter, scrumptious meals, and honest conversations are just some of the ways you've poured love into our lives. May God continue to bless your home with joy, strength, and the grace to refresh others as you refreshed us.

- The late **Pastors Taiwo and Nomthi Odukoya**, for your kindness and spirit of generosity when we needed it the most. May your gentle souls rest in peace, and may your legacy continue to inspire.

- **Pastors Bunmi and Kunle Salami,** for your prayers, love, and steady encouragement. May God abundantly reward your kindness and uphold you always.

- **Sis Nike Fambegbe,** for your time, your availability, and the blessing you've been to our family. May God surround you with His favor and continually strengthen you.

- **Pastor Brian Jones of Sensational Ceremonies**—thank you for making our vow-reaffirmation ceremony truly memorable. Our guests were surprised to learn that we met you for the very first time on the day of the ceremony, given the warmth between us! Your ministry is a blessing, and you reflect God's love so graciously. May your life continue to overflow with God's spectacular goodness.

💜 **My adopted mothers**—**Aunty Damilola Akinwale, Aunty Bimbo Rotifa, Aunty Gbemi Tejuoso, Aunty Bimbo Adeoba** (of blessed memory), **Aunty Tinu Oyediran ("Grandma T")**, and **Aunty Joke Rosanwo**—thank you for stepping up and stepping in to mother me after my mom's passing. Your nurturing love, wise counsel, and faith have filled countless gaps and guided me through many valleys. May God return to you a hundredfold every measure of love and support you've sown into my life.

💜 **My "MiP" sisters**, praying with all of you has been a wonderful gift. I'm grateful for our sisterhood, your encouragement, and your intercession once I shared my vision for this book. Knowing I was covered in prayer strengthened me through every chapter. Special thanks to **Christie**, who connected us to **Lezli**, our editor extraordinaire and now dear friend.

💜 **Dr. Patrick and Sherese Ijewere**, for making my physical and emotional bounce-back journey easier. Your wellness center marked a divine turning point. I've stumbled a few times since, but your tools and insights continue to serve as guardrails toward holistic wholeness.

💚 **Our fantastic team of support behind the book:**

- **Kristina Houser Wikle**, the gifted lens behind our 2024 Trilogy celebration memories—thank you for capturing our joy so beautifully.

- **Lezli Urlacher**, our exceptional editor and gift from God—your patience, insight, and graciousness guided us through every "divine delay." Thank you for being part referee, part cheerleader, and part encourager when I almost gave up.

- **Jennifer Stimson**, our talented cover designer—for your professionalism, patience, and flexibility through multiple revisions and extensions.

- **Steve Kuhn**, our brilliant interior designer/typesetter—thank you for taking us to the finish line on short notice and under a tight timeline. We're deeply grateful for your skill and your willingness to make the impossible timeline possible.

💚 **Advanced copy reviewers: Dr. Chris E. Stout, Pastor Ituah Ighodalo, Natasha Mahtani, Prof. Konyin Ajayi, SAN, Dr. Blossom Maduafokwa, Remi Okunola, Adenike Oyetunde-Lawal, Ayodeji Megbope, Kaltume Mshelia, Ayo Mairo-Ese, Ian P., and Fauzi Fahm**—we sincerely appreciate the time and attention you devoted to reviewing portions of the manuscript, as well as the thoughtful feedback and insights you provided. **Remi** and **Kaltume**, thank you for selflessly setting aside time to share your thoughts on the first drafts; your perspectives were invaluable in strengthening and elevating this project.

💚 **My network of friends, colleagues, and alumni,** thank you for indulging my endless research and for your honest survey responses regarding relationships and marriage. Your perspectives confirmed that, deep down, most women everywhere share the same desire—to love and be loved, to be seen and valued, and to flourish in relationships that reflect wholeness and partnership.

💚 **My extraordinary parents, Ms. Margaret Taiwo Vaughan and Chief Edward Akindele Leigh**—last but not least—although you're no longer here, I believe you're smiling down on me. Thank you for demonstrating through your lives and relationship that love is still possible even after a breakup. Being your daughter is one of my greatest blessings, and I miss you both more than words can express.

- **Mom**, I have a little confession: The only reason I paid attention in Shorthand class in junior secondary school was so I could finally decode your journals! That sparked my own journaling habit, which eventually birthed this book. Thank you for preserving the letters, telexes, and the many beautiful cards and post-cards you exchanged with Dad—they tell your story so vividly. You were both expressive and gifted writers, and each keepsake is a timeless reminder of the love you shared.

- **Daddy**, I'll forever cherish the bond God restored before you left this earth. Your emails, long phone calls, and heartfelt words made up for lost time. I felt your love more deeply in that season than ever before.

*Our deepest gratitude goes **to all who have touched our lives** along this journey with your love, encouragement, and wisdom. May God bless each of you, in ways only He can, and continue to use your lives to bring hope, joy, and light to those around you.* ♥ *Amen.*

Printed in Dunstable, United Kingdom